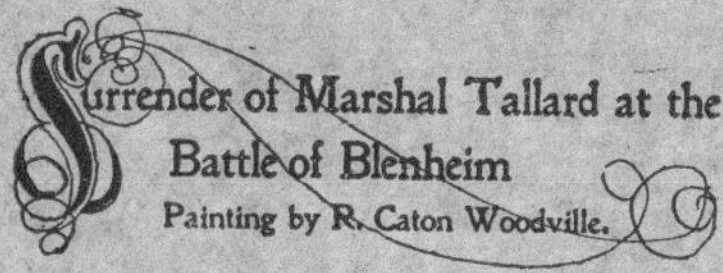

Surrender of Marshal Tallard at the Battle of Blenheim

Painting by R. Caton Woodville.

THE GREAT EVENTS

BY

FAMOUS HISTORIANS

A COMPREHENSIVE AND READABLE ACCOUNT OF THE WORLD'S HISTORY, EMPHASIZING THE MORE IMPORTANT EVENTS, AND PRESENTING THESE AS COMPLETE NARRATIVES IN THE MASTER-WORDS OF THE MOST EMINENT HISTORIANS

NON-SECTARIAN NON-PARTISAN NON-SECTIONAL

ON THE PLAN EVOLVED FROM A CONSENSUS OF OPINIONS GATHERED FROM THE MOST DISTINGUISHED SCHOLARS OF AMERICA AND EUROPE, INCLUDING BRIEF INTRODUCTIONS BY SPECIALISTS TO CONNECT AND EXPLAIN THE CELEBRATED NARRATIVES, ARRANGED CHRONOLOGICALLY, WITH THOROUGH INDICES, BIBLIOGRAPHIES, CHRONOLOGIES, AND COURSES OF READING

EDITOR-IN-CHIEF

ROSSITER JOHNSON, LL.D.

ASSOCIATE EDITORS

CHARLES F. HORNE, Ph.D.
JOHN RUDD, LL.D.

With a staff of specialists

VOLUME XII

The National Alumni

CONTENTS

VOLUME XII

LIST OF ILLUSTRATIONS

VOLUME XII

AN OUTLINE NARRATIVE

TRACING BRIEFLY THE CAUSES, CONNECTIONS, AND CONSEQUENCES OF

THE GREAT EVENTS

(AGE OF LOUIS XIV)

CHARLES F. HORNE

T is related that in 1661, on the day following the death of the great Cardinal Mazarin, the various officials of the State approached their young King, Louis XIV. "To whom shall we go now for orders, Your Majesty?" "To me," answered Louis, and from that date until his death in 1715 they had no other master. Whether we accept the tale as literal fact or only as the vivid French way of visualizing a truth, we find here the central point of over fifty years of European history. The two celebrated cardinals, Richelieu and Mazarin, had, by their strength and wisdom, made France by far the most powerful state in Europe. Moreover, they had so reduced the authority of the French nobility, the clergy, and the courts of law as to have become practically absolute and untrammelled in their control of the entire government. Now, all this enormous power, both at home and abroad, over France and over Europe, was assumed by a young man of twenty-three. "I am the state," said Louis at a later period of his career. He might almost have said, "I am Europe," looking as he did only to the Europe that dominated, and took pleasure in itself, and made life one continued glittering revel of splendor. Independent Europe, that claimed the right of thinking for itself, the suffering Europe of the peasants, who starved and shed their blood in helpless agony—these were against Louis almost from the beginning, and ever increasingly against him.

At first the young monarch found life very bright around him. His courtiers called him "the rising sun," and his ambition was to justify the title, to be what with his enormous wealth and authority was scarcely difficult, the Grand Monarch. He rushed into causeless war and snatched provinces from his feeble neighbors, exhausted Germany and decaying Spain. He built huge fortresses along his frontiers, and military roads from end to end of his domains. His court was one continuous round of splendid entertainments. He encouraged literature, or at least pensioned authors and had them clustered around him in what Frenchmen call the Augustan Age of their development.[1]

The little German princes of the Rhine, each of them practically independent ruler of a tiny state, could not of course compete with Louis or defy him. Nor for a time did they attempt it. His splendor dazzled them. They were content to imitate, and each little prince became a patron of literature, or giver of entertainments, or builder of huge fortresses absurdly disproportioned to his territory and his revenues. Germany, it has been aptly said, became a mere tail to the French kite, its leaders feebly dragging after where Louis soared. Never had the common people of Europe or even the nobility had less voice in their own affairs. It was an age of absolute kingly power, an age of despotism.

England, which under Cromwell had bid fair to take a foremost place in Europe, sank under Charles II into unimportance. Its people wearied with tumult, desired peace more than aught else; its King, experienced in adversity, and long a homeless wanderer in France and Holland, seemed to have but one firm principle in life. Whatever happened he did not intend, as he himself phrased it, to go on his "travels" again. He dreaded and hated the English Parliament as all the Stuarts had; and, like his father, he avoided calling it together. To obtain money without its aid, he accepted a pension from the French King. Thus England also became a servitor of Louis. Its policy, so far as Charles could mould it, was France's policy. If we look

[1] See *Louis XIV Establishes Absolute Monarchy*, page 1.

for events in the English history of the time we must find them in internal incidents, the terrible plague that devastated London in 1665,[1] the fire of the following year, that checked the plague but almost swept the city out of existence.[2] We must note the founding of the Royal Society in 1660 for the advancement of science, or look to Newton, its most celebrated member, beginning to puzzle out his theory of gravitation in his Woolsthorpe garden.[3]

CONTINENTAL WARS

Louis's first real opponent he found in sturdy Holland. Her fleets and those of England had learned to fight each other in Cromwell's time, and they continued to struggle for the mastery of the seas. There were many desperate naval battles. In 1664 an English fleet crossed the ocean to seize the Dutch colony of New Amsterdam, and it became New York.[4] In 1667 a Dutch fleet sailed up the Thames and burned the shipping, almost reaching London itself

Yet full as her hands might seem with strife like this, Holland did not hesitate to stand forth against the aggression of Louis's "rising sun." When in his first burst of kingship, he seized the Spanish provinces of the Netherlands and so extended his authority to the border of Holland, its people, frightened at his advance, made peace with England and joined an alliance again him Louis drew back; and the Dutch authorized a medal which depicted Holland checking the rising sun Louis never forgave them, and in 1672, having secured German neutrality and an English alliance, he suddenly attacked Holland with all his forces.[5]

For a moment the little republic seemed helpless. Her navy indeed withstood ably the combined assaults of the French and English ships, but the French armies overran almost her entire territory. It was then that her people talked of entering their ships and sailing away together, transporting their nation bodily

[1] See *Great Plague in London*, page 29.

[2] See *Great Fire in London*, page 45.

[3] See *Discovery of Gravitation*, page 51.

[4] See *New York Taken by the English*, page 19.

[5] See *Struggle of the Dutch against France and England*, page 86.

to some colony beyond Louis's reach. It was then that Amsterdam set the example which other districts heroically followed, of opening her dykes and letting the ocean flood the land to drive out the French. The leaders of the republic were murdered in a factional strife, and the young Prince William III of Orange, descended from that William the Silent who had led the Dutch against Philip II, was made practically dictator of the land. This young Prince William, afterward King William III of England, was the antagonist who sprang up against Louis, and in the end united all Europe against him and annihilated his power.

Seeing the wonderful resistance that little Holland made against her apparently overwhelming antagonists, the rest of Germany took heart; allies came to the Dutch. Brandenburg and Austria and Spain forced Louis to fall back upon his own frontier, though with much resolute battling by his great general, Turenne.

Next to young William, Louis found his most persistent opponent in Frederick William, the "Great Elector" of Brandenburg and Prussia, undoubtedly the ablest German sovereign of the age, and the founder of Prussia's modern importance. He had succeeded to his hereditary domains in 1640, when they lay utterly waste and exhausted in the Thirty Years' War; and he reigned until 1688, nearly half a century, during which he was ever and vigorously the champion of Germany against all outside enemies. He alone, in the feeble Germany of the day, resisted French influence, French manners, and French aggression.

In this first general war of the Germans and their allies against Louis, Frederick William proved the only one of their leaders seriously to be feared. Louis made an alliance with Sweden and persuaded the Swedes to overrun Brandenburg during its ruler's absence with his forces on the Rhine. But so firmly had the Great Elector established himself at home, so was he loved, that the very peasantry rose to his assistance. "We are only peasants," said their banners, "but we can die for our lord." Pitiful cry! Pitiful proof of how unused the commons were to even a little kindness, how eagerly responsive! Frederick William came riding like a whirlwind from the Rhine, his army straggling along behind in a vain effort to keep up. He hurled himself with his foremost troops upon the Swedes, and won the celebrated battle of Fehrbellin. He swept his astonished foes back into their northern peninsula. Brandenburg became the chief power of northern Germany.[1]

In 1679 the Peace of Ryswick ended the general war, and left Holland unconquered, but with the French frontier extended to the Rhine, and Louis at the height of his power, the acknowledged head of European affairs. Austria was under the rule of Leopold I, Emperor of Germany from 1657 to 1705, whose pride and incompetence wholly prevented him from being what his position as chief of the Hapsburgs would naturally have made him, the leader of the opposition, the centre around whom all Europe could rally to withstand Louis's territorial greed. Leopold hated Louis, but he hated also the rising Protestant "Brandenburger," he hated the "merchant" Dutch, hated everybody in short who dared intrude upon the ancient order of his superiority, who refused to recognize his impotent authority. So he would gladly have seen Louis crush every opponent except himself, would have found it a pleasant vengeance indeed to see all these upstart powers destroying one another.

Moreover, Austria was again engaged in desperate strife with the Turks. These were in the last burst of their effort at European conquest. No longer content with Hungary, twice in Leopold's reign did they advance to attack Vienna. Twice were they repulsed by Hungarian and Austrian valor. The final siege was in 1683. A vast horde estimated as high as two hundred thousand men marched against the devoted city. Leopold and most of the aristocracy fled, in despair of its defence. Only the common people who could not flee, remained, and with the resolution of despair beat off the repeated assaults of the Mahometans.[2]

They were saved by John Sobieski, a king who had raised Poland to one of her rare outflashing periods of splendor. With his small but gallant Polish army he came to the rescue of Chris-

[1] See *Growth of Prussia under the Great Elector: His Victory at Fehrbellin*, page 138.

[2] See *Last Turkish Invasion of Europe: Sobieski Saves Vienna*, page 164.

tendom, charged furiously upon the huge Turkish horde, and swept it from the field in utter flight. The tide of Turkish power receded forever; that was its last great wave which broke before the walls of Vienna. All Hungary was regained, mainly through the efforts of Austria's greatest general, Prince Eugene of Savoy. The centre of the centuries of strife shifted back where it had been in Hunyady's time, from Vienna to the mighty frontier fortress of Belgrad, which was taken and retaken by opposing forces.

LATER EFFORTS OF LOUIS XIV

The earlier career of Louis XIV seems to have been mainly influenced by his passion for personal renown; but he had always been a serious Catholic, and in his later life his interest in religion became a most important factor in his world. The Protestants of France had for wellnigh a century held their faith unmolested, safeguarded by that Edict of Nantes, which had been granted by Henry IV, a Catholic at least in name, and confirmed by Cardinal Richelieu, a Catholic by profession. Persuasive measures had indeed been frequently employed to win the deserters back to the ancient Church; but now under Louis's direction, a harsher course was attempted. The celebrated "dragonades" quartered a wild and licentious soldiery in Protestant localities, in the homes of Protestant house-owners, with special orders to make themselves offensive to their hosts. Under this grim discouragement Protestantism seemed dying out of France, and at last, in 1685, Louis, encouraged by success, took the final step and revoked the Edict of Nantes, commanding all his subjects to accept Catholicism, while at the same time forbidding any to leave the country. Huguenots who attempted flight were seized; many were slain. Externally at least, the reformed religion disappeared from France.[1]

Of course, despite the edict restraining them, many Huguenots, the most earnest and vigorous of the sect, did escape by flight; and some hundred thousands of France's ablest citizens were thus lost to her forever. Large numbers found a welcome in neighboring Holland; the Great Elector stood forward and gave homes to a wandering host of the exiles. England received

[1] See *Revocation of the Edict of Nantes*, page 180.

colonies of them; and even distant America was benefited by the numbers who sought her freer shores. No enemy to France in all the world but received a welcome accession to its strength against her.

In the same year that Protestant Europe was thus assailed and terrified by the reviving spectre of religious persecution, Charles II of England died and his brother James II succeeded him. Charles may have been Catholic at heart, but in name at least he had retained the English religion. James was openly Catholic. A hasty rebellion raised against him by his nephew, Monmouth, fell to pieces;[1] and James, having executed Monmouth and approved a cruel persecution of his followers, began to take serious steps toward forcing the whole land back to the ancient faith.

So here was kingly absolutism coming to the aid of the old religious intolerance. The English people, however, had already killed one king in defence of their liberties; and their resolute opposition to James began to suggest that they might kill another. Many of the leading nobles appealed secretly to William of Orange for help. William was, as we have said, the centre of opposition to Louis, and that began to mean to Catholicism as well. Also, William had married a daughter of King James and had thus some claim to interfere in the family domains. And, most important of all, as chief ruler of Holland, William had an army at command. With a portion of that army he set sail late in 1688 and landed in England. Englishmen of all ranks flocked to join him. King James fled to France, and a Parliament, hastily assembled in 1689, declared him no longer king and placed William and his wife Mary on the throne as joint rulers.[2] Thus William had two countries instead of one to aid him in his life-long effort against Louis.

Louis, indeed, accepted the accession of his enemy as a threat of war and, taking up the cause of the fugitive James, despatched him with French troops to Ireland, where his Catholic faith made the mass of the people his devoted adherents. There were, however, Protestant Irish as well, and these defied James and held his troops at bay in the siege of Londonderry, while King

[1] See *Monmouth's Rebellion*, page 172.

[2] See *The English Revolution: Flight of James II*, page 200.

William hurried over to Ireland with an army. Father-in-law and son-in-law met in the battle of the Boyne, and James was defeated in war as he had been in diplomacy. He fled back to France, leaving his Catholic adherents to withstand William as best they might. Limerick, the Catholic stronghold, was twice besieged and only yielded when full religious freedom had been guaranteed. Irishmen to this day call it with bitterness "the city of the violated treaty."[1]

Meanwhile the strife between Louis and William had spread into another general European war. William had difficulties to encounter in his new kingdom. Its people cared little for his Continental aims and gave him little loyalty of service. In fact, peculation among public officials was so widespread that, despite large expenditures of money, England had only a most feeble, inefficient army in the field, and William was in black disgust against his new subjects. It was partly to aid the Government in its financial straits that the Bank of England was formed in 1694.[2]

Yet Louis's troubles were greater and of deeper root. Catholic Austria and even the Pope himself, unable to submit to the arrogance of the "Grand Monarch," took part against him in this war. It can therefore no longer be regarded as a religious struggle. It marks the turning-point in Louis's fortunes. His boundless extravagance had exhausted France at last. Both in wealth and population she began to feel the drain. The French generals won repeated victories, yet they had to give slowly back before their more numerous foes; and in 1697 Louis purchased peace by making concessions of territory as well as courtesy.

This peace proved little more than a truce. For almost half a century the European sovereigns had been waiting for Charles II of Spain to die. He was the last of his race, last of the Spanish Hapsburgs descended from the Emperor Charles V, and so infirm and feeble was he that it seemed the flickering candle of his life must puff out with each passing wind. Who should succeed him? In Mazarin's time, that crafty minister had schemed that the prize should go to France, and had wedded young Louis XIV to a Spanish princess. The Austrian Hapsburgs

[1] See *Siege of Londonderry and the Battle of the Boyne*, page 258.

[2] See *Establishment of the Bank of England*, page 286.

of course wanted the place for themselves, though to establish a common ancestry with their Spanish kin they must turn back over a century and a half to Ferdinand and Isabella.

But strong men grew old and died, while the invalid Charles II still clung to his tottering throne. Louis ceased hoping to occupy it himself and claimed it for his son, then for his grandson, Philip. Not until 1700, after a reign of nearly forty years, did Charles give up the worthless game and expire. He declared Philip his heir, and the aged Louis sent the youth to Spain with an eager boast, "Go; there are no longer any Pyrenees." That is, France and Spain were to be one, a mighty Bourbon empire.

That was just what Europe, experienced in Louis's unscrupulous aggression, dared not allow. So another general alliance was formed, with William of Holland and England at its head, to drive Philip from his new throne in favor of a Hapsburg. William died before the war was well under way, but the British people understood his purposes now and upheld them. Once more they felt themselves the champions of Protestantism in Europe. Anne, the second daughter of the deposed King James, was chosen as queen; and under her the two realms of England and Scotland were finally joined in one by the Act of Union (1707), with but a single Parliament.[1]

Meanwhile Marlborough was sent to the Rhine with a strong British army. Prince Eugene paused in fighting the Turks and joined him with Austrian and German troops. Together they defeated the French in the celebrated battle of Blenheim (1704),[2] and followed it in later years with Oudenarde and Malplaquet. Louis was beaten. France was exhausted. The Grand Monarch pleaded for peace on almost any terms.

Yet his grandson remained on the Spanish throne. For one reason, the Spaniards themselves upheld him and fought for him. For another, the allies' Austrian candidate became Emperor of Germany, and to make him ruler of Spain as well would only have been to consolidate the Hapsburg power instead of that of the Bourbons. Made dubious by this balance between evils,

[1] See *Union of England and Scotland*, page 341.
[2] See *Battle of Blenheim: Curbing of Louis XIV*, page 327.

Europe abandoned the war. So there were two Bourbon kingdoms after all—but both too exhausted to be dangerous.

Louis had indeed outlived his fame. He had roused the opposition of all his neighbors, and ruined France in the effort to extend her greatness. The praises and flattery of his earlier years reached him now only from the lips of a few determined courtiers. His people hated him, and in 1715 celebrated his death as a release. Frenchmen high and low had begun the career which ended in their terrific Revolution. Lying on his dreary death-bed, the Grand Monarch apologized that he should "take so long in dying." Perhaps he, also, felt that he delayed the coming of the new age. What his career had done was to spread over all Europe a new culture and refinement, to rouse a new splendor and recklessness among the upper classes, and to widen almost irretrievably the gap between rich and poor, between kings and commons. In the very years that parliamentary government was becoming supreme in England, absolutism established itself upon the Continent.

CHANGES IN NORTHERN EUROPE

Toward the close of this age the balance of power in Northern Europe shifted quite as markedly as it had farther south. Three of the German electoral princes became kings. The Elector of Saxony was chosen King of Poland, thereby adding greatly to his power. George, Elector of Hanover, became King of England on the death of Queen Anne. And the Elector of Brandenburg, son of the Great Elector, when the war of 1701 against France and Spain broke out, only lent his aid to the European coalition on condition that the German Emperor should authorize him also to assume the title of king, not of Brandenburg but of his other and smaller domain of Prussia, which lay outside the empire. Most of the European sovereigns smiled at this empty change of title without a change of dominions; but Brandenburg or Prussia was thus made more united, more consolidated, and it soon rose to be the leader of Northern Germany. A new family, the Hohenzollerns, contested European supremacy with the Hapsburgs and the Bourbons.[1]

More important still was the strife between Sweden and

[1] See *Prussia Proclaimed a Kingdom*, page 310.

Russia. Sweden had been raised by Gustavus Adolphus to be the chief power of the North, the chosen ally of Richelieu and Mazarin. Her soldiers were esteemed the best of the time. The prestige of the Swedes had, to be sure, suffered somewhat in the days when the Great Elector defeated them so completely at Fehrbellin and elsewhere. But Louis XIV had stood by them as his allies, and saved them from any loss of territory, so that in 1700 Sweden still held not only the Scandinavian peninsula but all the lands east of the Baltic as far as where St. Petersburg now stands, and much of the German coast to southward. The Baltic was thus almost a Swedish lake, when in 1697 a new warrior king, Charles XII, rose to reassert the warlike supremacy of his race. He was but fifteen when he reached the throne; and Denmark, Poland, and Russia all sought to snatch away his territories. He fought the Danes and defeated them. He fought the Saxon Elector who had become king of Poland. Soon both Poland and Saxony lay crushed at the feet of the "Lion of the North," as they called him then—"Madman of the North," after his great designs had failed. Only Russia remained to oppose him—Russia, as yet almost unknown to Europe, a semi-barbaric frontier land, supposedly helpless against the strength and resources of civilization.

Russia was in the pangs of a most sudden revolution. Against her will she was being suddenly and sharply modernized by Peter the Great, most famous of her czars. He had overthrown the turbulent militia who really ruled the land, and had waded through a sea of bloody executions to establish his own absolute power.[1] He had travelled abroad in disguise, studied shipbuilding in Holland, the art of government in England, and fortification and war wheresoever he could find a teacher. Removing from the ancient, conservative capital of Moscow, he planted his government, in defiance of Sweden, upon her very frontier, causing the city of St. Petersburg to arise as if by magic from a desolate, icy swamp in the far north.[2]

Charles of Sweden scorned and defied him. At Narva in 1700, Charles with a small force of his famous troops drove

[1] See *Peter the Great Modernizes Russia: Suppression of the Streltsi*, page 223.

[2] See *Founding of St. Petersburg*, page 319.

Peter with a huge horde of his Russians to shameful flight. "They will teach us to beat them," said Peter philosophically; and so in truth he gathered knowledge from defeat after defeat, until at length at Poltava in 1709 he completely turned the tables upon Charles, overthrew him and so crushed his power that Russia succeeded Sweden as ruler of the extreme North, a rank she has ever since retained.[1]

GROWTH OF AMERICA

The vast political and social changes of Europe in this age found their echo in the New World. The decay of Spain left her American colonies to feebleness and decay. The islands of the Caribbean Sea became the haunt of the buccaneers, pirates, desperadoes of all nations who preyed upon Spanish ships, and, as their power grew, extended their depredations northward along the American coast. So important did these buccaneers become that they formed regular governments among themselves. The most famed of their leaders was knighted by England as Sir Henry Morgan; and the most renowned of his achievements was the storm and capture of the Spanish treasure city, Panama.[2]

As Spain grew weak in America, France grew strong. From her Canadian colonies she sent out daring missionaries and traders, who explored the great lakes and the Mississippi valley.[3] They made friends with the Indians; they founded Louisiana.[4] All the north and west of the continent fell into their hands.

Never, however, did their numbers approach those of the English colonists along the Atlantic coast. Both Massachusetts and Virginia were grown into important commonwealths, almost independent of England, and well able to support the weaker settlements rising around them. After the great Puritan exodus to New England to escape the oppression of Charles I, there had come a Royalist exodus to Virginia to escape the Puri-

[1] See *Downfall of Charles XII at Poltava: Triumph of Russia*, page 352.

[2] See *Morgan, the Buccaneer, Sacks Panama*, page 66.

[3] See *Discovery of the Mississippi*, page 108.

[4] See *Colonization of Louisiana*, page 297.

tanic tyranny of Cromwell's time. Large numbers of Catholics fled to Maryland. Huguenots established themselves in the Carolinas and elsewhere. Then came Penn to build a great Quaker state among the scattered Dutch settlements along the Delaware.[1] The American seaboard became the refuge of each man who refused to bow his neck to despotism of whatever type.

Under such settlers English America soon ceased to be a mere offshoot of Europe. It became a world of its own; its people developed into a new race. They had their own springs of action, their own ways of thought, different from those of Europe, more simple and intense as was shown in the Salem witchcraft excitement, or more resolute and advanced as was revealed in Bacon's Virginia rebellion.[2]

The aboriginal inhabitants, the Indians, found themselves pressed ever backward from the coast. They resisted, and in 1675 there arose in New England, King Philip's war, which for that section at least settled the Indian question forever. The red men of New England were practically exterminated.[3] Those of New York, the Iroquois, were more fortunate or more crafty. They dwelt deeper in the wilderness, and formed a buffer state between the French in Canada and the English to the south, drawing aid now from one, now from the other.

Each war between England and Louis XIV was echoed by strife between their rival colonies. When King William supplanted James in 1688 there followed in America also a "bloodless revolution."[4] Governor Andros, whom James had sent to imitate his own harsh tyranny in the colonies, was seized and shipped back to England. William was proclaimed king. The ensuing strife with France was marked by the most bloody of all America's Indian massacres. The Iroquois descended suddenly on Canada; the very suburbs of its capital, Montreal, were burned, and more than a thousand of the unsuspecting settlers were tortured, or more mercifully slain outright.[5]

[1] See *William Penn Receives the Grant of Pennsylvania: Founding of Philadelphia*, page 153.

[2] See *Salem Witchcraft Trials*, page 268.

[3] See *King Philip's War*, page 125.

[4] See *Tyranny of Andros in New England: The Bloodless Revolution*, page 241.

[5] See *Massacre of Lachine*, page 248.

In the later war about the Spanish throne, England captured Nova Scotia, the southern extremity of the French Canadian seaboard; and part of the price Louis XIV paid for peace was to leave this colony in England's hands.[1] The scale of American power began to swing markedly in her favor. Everywhere over the world, as the eighteenth century progressed, England with her parliamentary government was rising into power at the expense of France and absolutism.

[1] See *Capture of Port Royal: France Surrenders Nova Scotia to England*, page 373.

[FOR THE NEXT SECTION OF THIS GENERAL SURVEY SEE VOLUME XIII.]

LOUIS XIV ESTABLISHES ABSOLUTE MONARCHY

A.D. 1661

JAMES COTTER MORISON

Not only was the reign of Louis XIV one of the longest in the world's history, but it also marked among Western nations the highest development of the purely monarchical principle. Including the time that Louis ruled under the guardianship of his mother and the control of his minister, Cardinal Mazarin, the reign covered more than seventy years (1643–1715).

The sovereign who could say, " I am the state " (" *l'État c'est moi* "), and see his subjects acquiesce with almost Asiatic humility, while Europe looked on in admiration and fear, may be said to have embodied for modern times the essence of absolutism.

That all things, domestic and foreign, seemed to be in concurrence for giving practical effect to the Grand Monarque's assumption of supremacy is shown by the fact that his name dominates the whole history of his time. His reign was not only " the Augustan Age of France "; it marked the ascendency of France in Europe.

Of such a reign no adequate impression is to be derived from reading even the most faithful narrative of its thronging events. But the reign as well as the personality of Louis is set in clear perspective for us by Morison's picturesque and discriminating treatment.

THE reign of Louis XIV was the culminating epoch in the history of the French monarchy. What the age of Pericles was in the history of the Athenian democracy, what the age of the Scipios was in the history of the Roman Republic, that was the reign of Louis XIV in the history of the old monarchy of France. The type of polity which that monarchy embodied, the principles of government on which it reposed or brought into play, in this reign attain their supreme expression and development. Before Louis XIV the French monarchy has evidently not attained its full stature; it is thwarted and limited by other forces in the state. After him, though unresisted from without, it manifests symptoms of decay from within. It rapidly declines, and totally disappears seventy-seven years after his death.

But it is not only the most conspicuous reign in the history of France—it is the most conspicuous reign in the history of monarchy in general. Of the very many kings whom history mentions, who have striven to exalt the monarchical principle, none of them achieved a success remotely comparable to his. His two great predecessors in kingly ambition, Charles V and Philip II, remained far behind him in this respect. They may have ruled over wider dominions, but they never attained the exceptional position of power and prestige which he enjoyed for more than half a century. They never were obeyed so submissively at home nor so dreaded and even respected abroad. For Louis XIV carried off that last reward of complete success, that he for a time silenced even envy, and turned it into admiration. We who can examine with cold scrutiny the make and composition of this colossus of a French monarchy; who can perceive how much the brass and clay in it exceeded the gold; who know how it afterward fell with a resounding ruin, the last echoes of which have scarcely died away, have difficulty in realizing the fascination it exercised upon contemporaries who witnessed its first setting up.

Louis XIV's reign was the very triumph of commonplace greatness, of external magnificence and success, such as the vulgar among mankind can best and most sincerely appreciate. Had he been a great and profound ruler, had he considered with unselfish meditation the real interests of France, had he with wise insight discerned and followed the remote lines of progress along which the future of Europe was destined to move, it is lamentably probable that he would have been misunderstood in his lifetime and calumniated after his death.

Louis XIV was exposed to no such misconception. His qualities were on the surface, visible and comprehensible to all; and although none of them was brilliant, he had several which have a peculiarly impressive effect when displayed in an exalted station. He was indefatigably industrious; worked on an average eight hours a day for fifty-four years; had great tenacity of will; that kind of solid judgment which comes of slowness of brain, and withal a most majestic port and great dignity of manners. He had also as much kindliness of nature as the very great can be expected to have; his temper was under severe control; and, in his earlier years at least, he had a moral apprehensiveness greater than the limitations of his intellect would have led one to expect.

His conduct toward Molière was throughout truly noble, and the more so that he never intellectually appreciated Molière's real greatness. But he must have had great original fineness of tact, though it was in the end nearly extinguished by adulation and incense. His court was an extraordinary creation, and the greatest thing he achieved. He made it the microcosm of all that was the most brilliant and prominent in France. Every order of merit was invited there and received courteous welcome. To no circumstance did he so much owe his enduring popularity. By its means he impressed into his service that galaxy of great writers, the first and the last classic authors of France, whose calm and serene lustre will forever illumine the epoch of his existence. It may even be admitted that his share in that lustre was not so accidental and undeserved as certain king-haters have supposed.

That subtle critic, M. Sainte-Beuve, thinks he can trace a marked rise even in Bossuet's style from the moment he became a courtier of Louis XIV. The King brought men together, placed them in a position where they were induced and urged to bring their talents to a focus. His court was alternately a high-bred gala and a stately university. If we contrast his life with those of his predecessor and successor, with the dreary existence of Louis XIII and the crapulous lifelong debauch of Louis XV, we become sensible that Louis XIV was distinguished in no common degree; and when we further reflect that much of his home and all of his foreign policy was precisely adapted to flatter, in its deepest self-love, the national spirit of France, it will not be quite impossible to understand the long-continued reverberation of his fame.

But Louis XIV's reign has better titles than the adulations of courtiers and the eulogies of wits and poets to the attention of posterity. It marks one of the most memorable epochs in the annals of mankind. It stretches across history like a great mountain range, separating ancient France from the France of modern times. On the further slope are Catholicism and feudalism in their various stages of splendor and decay—the France of crusade and chivalry, of St. Louis and Bayard. On the hither side are freethought, industry, and centralization — the France of Voltaire, Turgot, and Condorcet.

When Louis came to the throne the Thirty Years' War still wanted six years of its end, and the heat of theological strife was at its intensest glow. When he died the religious temperature had cooled nearly to freezing-point, and a new vegetation of science and positive inquiry was overspreading the world. This amounts to saying that his reign covers the greatest epoch of mental transition through which the human mind has hitherto passed, excepting the transition we are witnessing in the day which now is. We need but recall the names of the writers and thinkers who arose during Louis XIV's reign, and shed their seminal ideas broadcast upon the air, to realize how full a period it was, both of birth and decay; of the passing away of the old and the uprising of the new forms of thought.

To mention only the greatest; the following are among the chiefs who helped to transform the mental fabric of Europe in the age of Louis XIV: Descartes, Newton, Leibnitz, Locke, Boyle. Under these leaders the first firm irreversible advance was made out of the dim twilight of theology into the clear dawn of positive and demonstrative science.

Inferior to these founders of modern knowledge, but holding a high rank as contributors to the mental activity of the age, were Pascal, Malebranche, Spinoza, and Bayle. The result of their efforts was such a stride forward as has no parallel in the history of the human mind. One of the most curious and significant proofs of it was the spontaneous extinction of the belief in witchcraft among the cultivated classes of Europe, as the English historian of rationalism has so judiciously pointed out. The superstition was not much attacked, and it was vigorously defended, yet it died a natural and quiet death from the changed moral climate of the world.

But the chief interest which the reign of Louis XIV offers to the student of history has yet to be mentioned. It was the great turning-point in the history of the French people. The triumph of the monarchical principle was so complete under him, independence and self-reliance were so effectually crushed, both in localities and individuals, that a permanent bent was given to the national mind—a habit of looking to the government for all action and initiative permanently established.

Before the reign of Louis XIV it was a question which might fairly be considered undecided: whether the country would be able or not, willing or not, to coöperate with its rulers in the work of the government and the reform of abuses. On more than one occasion such coöperation did not seem entirely impossible or improbable. The admirable wisdom and moderation shown by the Tiers-État in the States-General of 1614, the divers efforts of the Parliament of Paris to check extravagant expenditure, the vigorous struggles of the provincial assemblies to preserve some relic of their local liberties, seemed to promise that France would continue to advance under the leadership indeed of the monarchy, yet still retaining in large measure the bright, free, independent spirit of old Gaul, the Gaul of Rabelais, Montaigne, and Joinville.

After the reign of Louis XIV such coöperation of the ruler and the ruled became impossible. The government of France had become a machine depending upon the action of a single spring. Spontaneity in the population at large was extinct, and whatever there was to do must be done by the central authority. As long as the government could correct abuses it was well; if it ceased to be equal to this task, they must go uncorrected. When at last the reform of secular and gigantic abuses presented itself with imperious urgency, the alternative before the monarchy was either to carry the reform with a high hand or perish in the failure to do so. We know how signal the failure was, and could not help being, under the circumstances; and through having placed the monarchy between these alternatives, it is no paradox to say that Louis XIV was one of the most direct ancestors of the "Great Revolution."

Nothing but special conditions in the politics both of Europe and of France can explain this singular importance and prominence of Louis XIV's reign. And we find that both France and Europe were indeed in an exceptional position when he ascended the throne. The Continent of Europe, from one end to the other, was still bleeding and prostrate from the effect of the Thirty Years' War when the young Louis, in the sixteenth year of his age, was anointed king at Rheims. Although France had suffered terribly in that awful struggle, she had probably suffered less than any of the combatants, unless it be Sweden.

It happened by a remarkable coincidence that precisely at this moment, when the condition of Europe was such that an aggressive policy on the part of France could be only with difficulty resisted by her neighbors, the power and prerogatives of the French crown attained an expansion and preëminence which they had never enjoyed in the previous history of the country. The schemes and hopes of Philip the Fair, of Louis XI, of Henry IV, and of Richelieu had been realized at last; and their efforts to throw off the insolent coercion of the great feudal lords had been crowned with complete success. The monarchy could hardly have conjectured how strong it had become but for the abortive resistance and hostility it met with in the Fronde.

The flames of insurrection which had shot up, forked and menacing, fell back underground, where they smouldered for four generations yet to come. The kingly power soared, single and supreme, over its prostrate foes. Long before Louis XIV had shown any aptitude or disposition for authority, he was the object of adulation as cringing as was ever offered to a Roman emperor. When he returned from his consecration at Rheims, the rector of the University of Paris, at the head of his professorial staff, addressed the young King in these words: "We are so dazzled by the new splendor which surrounds your majesty that we are not ashamed to appear dumfounded at the aspect of a light so brilliant and so extraordinary"; and at the foot of an engraving at the same date he is in so many words called a demigod.

It is evident that ample materials had been prepared for what the vulgar consider a great reign. Abundant opportunity for an insolent and aggressive foreign policy, owing to the condition of Europe. Security from remonstrance or check at home, owing to the condition of France. The temple is prepared for the deity; the priests stand by, ready to offer victims on the smoking altar; the incense is burning in anticipation of his advent. On the death of Mazarin, in 1661, he entered into his own.

Louis XIV never forgot the trials and humiliations to which he and his mother had been subjected during the troubles of the Fronde. It has often been remarked that rulers born in the purple have seldom shown much efficiency unless they have been exposed to exceptional and, as it were, artificial probations during their youth. During the first eleven years of Louis' reign—incomparably the most creditable to him—we can trace unmistakably the influence of the wisdom and experience acquired in that period of anxiety and defeat. He then learned the value of money and the supreme benefits of a full exchequer. He also acquired a thorough dread of subjection to ministers and favorites—a dread so deep that it implied a consciousness of probable weakness on that side. As he went on in life he to a great extent forgot both these valuable lessons, but their influence was never entirely effaced. To the astonishment of the courtiers and even of his mother he announced his intention of governing independently, and of looking after everything himself. They openly doubted his perseverance. "You do not know him," said Mazarin. "He will begin rather late, but he will go further than most. There is enough stuff in him to make four kings and an honest man besides."

His first measures were dictated less by great energy of initiative than by absolute necessity. The finances had fallen into such a chaos of jobbery and confusion that the very existence of the government depended upon a prompt and trenchant reform. It was Louis' rare good-fortune to find beside him one of the most able and vigorous administrators who have ever lived—Colbert. He had the merit—not a small one in that age—of letting this great minister invent and carry out the most daring and beneficial measures of reform, of which he assumed all the credit to himself. The first step was a vigorous attack on the gang of financial plunderers, who, with Fouquet at their head, simply embezzled the bulk of the state revenues. The money-lenders not only obtained the most usurious interest for their loans, but actually held in mortgage the most productive sources of the national taxation: and, not content with that, they bought up, at 10 per cent. of their nominal value, an enormous amount of discredited bills, issued by the government in the time of the Fronde, which they forced the treasury to pay off at par; and this was done with the very money they had just before advanced to the government.

Such barefaced plunder could not be endured, and Colbert

was the last man to endure it. He not only repressed peculation, but introduced a number of practical improvements in the distribution, and especially in the mode of levying the taxes. So imperfect were the arrangements connected with the latter that it was estimated that of eighty-four millions paid by the people, only thirty-two millions entered into the coffers of the state. The almost instantaneous effects of Colbert's measures—the yawning deficit was changed into a surplus of forty-five millions in less than two years—showed how gross and flagrant had been the malversation preceding.

Far more difficult, and far nobler in the order of constructive statesmanship, were his vast schemes to endow France with manufactures, with a commercial and belligerent navy, with colonies, besides his manifold reforms in the internal administration—tariffs and customs between neighboring provinces of France; the great work of the Languedoc canal; in fact, in every part and province of government. His success was various, but in some cases really stupendous. His creation of a navy almost surpasses belief. In 1661, when he first became free to act, France possessed only thirty vessels-of-war of all sizes. At the peace of Nimwegen, in 1678, she had acquired a fleet of one hundred twenty ships, and in 1683 she had got a fleet of one hundred seventy-six vessels; and the increase was quite as great in the size and armament of the individual ships as in their number.

A perfect giant of administration, Colbert found no labor too great for his energies, and worked with unflagging energy sixteen hours a day for twenty-two years. It is melancholy to be forced to add that all this toil was as good as thrown away, and that the strong man went broken-hearted to the grave, through seeing too clearly that he had labored in vain for an ungrateful egotist. His great visions of a prosperous France, increasing in wealth and contentment, were blighted; and he closed his eyes upon scenes of improvidence and waste more injurious to the country than the financial robbery which he had combated in his early days. The government was not plundered as it had been, but itself was exhausting the very springs of wealth by its impoverishment of the people.

Boisguillebert, writing in 1698, only fifteen years after Colbert's death, estimated the productive powers of France to have diminished by one-half in the previous thirty years. It seems, indeed, probable that the almost magical rapidity and effect of Colbert's early reforms turned Louis XIV's head, and that he was convinced that it only depended on his good pleasure to renew them to obtain the same result. He never found, as he never deserved to find, another Colbert; and he stumbled onward in ever deeper ruin to his disastrous end.

His first breach of public faith was his attack on the Spanish Netherlands, under color of certain pretended rights of the Queen, his wife—the Infanta Marie Thérèse; although he had renounced all claims in her name at his marriage. This aggression was followed by his famous campaign in the Low Countries, when Franche-Comté was overrun and conquered in fifteen days. He was stopped by the celebrated triple alliance in mid-career. He had not yet been intoxicated by success and vanity; Colbert's influence, always exerted on the side of peace, was at its height, the menacing attitude of Holland, England, and Sweden awed him, and he drew back. His pride was deeply wounded, and he revolved deep and savage schemes of revenge. Not on England, whose abject sovereign he knew could be had whenever he chose to buy him, but on the heroic little republic which had dared to cross his victorious path. His mingled contempt and rage against Holland were indeed instinctive, spontaneous, and in the nature of things. Holland was the living, triumphant incarnation of the two things he hated most—the principle of liberty in politics and the principle of free inquiry in religion.

With a passion too deep for hurry or carelessness he made his preparations. The army was submitted to a complete reorganization. A change in the weapons of the infantry was effected, which was as momentous in its day as the introduction of the breech-loading rifle in ours. The old inefficient firelock was replaced by the flint musket, and the rapidity and certainty of fire vastly increased. The undisciplined independence of the officers commanding regiments and companies was suppressed by the rigorous and methodical Colonel Martinet, whose name has remained in other armies besides that of France as a synonyme of punctilious exactitude.

The means of offence being thus secured, the next step was

to remove the political difficulties which stood in the way of Louis' schemes; that is, to dissolve Sir W. Temple's diplomatic masterpiece, the triple alliance. The effeminate Charles II was bought over by a large sum of money and the present of a pretty French mistress. Sweden also received a subsidy, and her schemes of aggrandizement on continental Germany were encouraged. Meanwhile the illustrious man who ruled Holland showed that kind of weakness which good men often do in the presence of the unscrupulous and wicked. John de Witt could not be convinced of the reality of Louis' nefarious designs. France had ever been Holland's best friend, and he could not believe that the policy of Henry IV, of Richelieu and Mazarin, would be suddenly reversed by the young King of France. He tried negotiations in which he was amused by Louis so long as it suited the latter's purpose. At last, when the King's preparations were complete, he threw off the mask, and insultingly told the Dutch that it was not for hucksters like them, and usurpers of authority not theirs, to meddle with such high matters.

Then commenced one of the brightest pages in the history of national heroism. At first the Dutch were overwhelmed; town after town capitulated without a blow. It seemed as if the United Provinces were going to be subdued, as Franche-Comté had been five years before. But Louis XIV had been too much intoxicated by that pride which goes before a fall to retain any clearness of head, if indeed he ever had any, in military matters. The great Condé, with his keen eye for attack, at once suggested one of those tiger-springs for which he was unequalled among commanders. Seeing the dismay of the Dutch, he advised a rapid dash with six thousand horse on Amsterdam. It is nearly certain, if this advice had been followed, that the little commonwealth, so precious to Europe, would have been extinguished; and that that scheme, born of heroic despair, of transferring to Batavia, "under new stars and amid a strange vegetation," the treasure of freedom and valor ruined in its old home by the Sardanapalus of Versailles, might have been put in execution. But it was not to be.

Vigilant as Louis had been in preparation, he now seemed to be as careless or incompetent in execution. Not only he neglected the advice of his best general, and wasted time, but he did his best to drive his adversaries to despair and the resistance which comes of despair. They were told by proclamation that "the towns which should try to resist the forces of his majesty by opening the dikes or by any other means would be punished with the utmost rigor; and when the frost should have opened roads in all directions, his majesty would give no sort of quarter to the inhabitants of the said towns, but would give orders that their goods should be plundered and their houses burned."

The Dutch envoys, headed by De Groot, son of the illustrious Grotius, came to the King's camp to know on what terms he would make peace. They were refused audience by the theatrical warrior, and told not to return except armed with full powers to make any concessions he might dictate. Then the "hucksters" of Amsterdam resolved on a deed of daring which is one of the most exalted among "the high traditions of the world." They opened the sluices and submerged the whole country under water. Still, their position was almost desperate, as the winter frosts were nearly certain to restore a firm foothold to the invader.

They came again suing for peace, offering Maestricht, the Rhine fortresses, the whole of Brabant, the whole of Dutch Flanders, and an indemnity of ten millions. This was proffering more than Henry IV, Richelieu, or Mazarin had ever hoped for. These terms were refused, and the refusal carried with it practically the rejection of Belgium, which could not fail to be soon absorbed when thus surrounded by French possessions. But Louis met these offers with the spirit of an Attila. He insisted on the concession of Southern Gueldres and the island of Bommel, twenty-four millions of indemnity, the endowment of the Catholic religion, and an extraordinary annual embassy charged to present his majesty with a gold medal, which should set forth how the Dutch owed to him the conservation of their liberties. Such vindictive cruelty makes the mind run forward and dwell with a glow of satisfied justice on the bitter days of retaliation and revenge which in a future, still thirty years off, will humble the proud and pitiless oppressor in the dust; when he shall be a suppliant, and a suppliant in vain, at the feet of the haughty victors of Blenheim, Ramillies, and Oudenarde.

But Louis' mad career of triumph was gradually being

brought to a close. He had before him not only the waste of waters, but the iron will and unconquerable tenacity of the young Prince of Orange, "who needed neither hope to made him dare nor success to make him persevere." Gradually, the threatened neighbors of France gathered together and against her King. Charles II was forced to recede from the French alliance by his Parliament in 1674. The military massacre went on, indeed, for some years longer in Germany and the Netherlands; but the Dutch Republic was saved, and peace ratified by the treaty of Nimwegen.

After the conclusion of the Dutch War the reign of Louis XIV enters on a period of manifest decline. The cost of the war had been tremendous. In 1677 the expenditure had been one hundred ten millions, and Colbert had to meet this with a net revenue of eighty-one millions. The trade and commerce of the country had also suffered much during the war. With bitter grief the great minister saw himself compelled to reverse the beneficent policy of his earlier days, to add to the tax on salt, to increase the ever-crushing burden of the *taille*, to create new offices—hereditary employments in the government—to the extent of three hundred millions, augmenting the already monstrous army of superfluous officials, and, finally, simply to borrow money at high interest. The new exactions had produced widespread misery in the provinces before the war came to an end. In 1675 the Governor of Dauphiné had written to Colbert, saying that commerce had entirely ceased in his district, and that the larger part of the people had lived during the winter on bread made from acorns and roots, and that at the time of his writing they were seen to be eating the grass of the fields and the bark of trees. The long-continued anguish produced at last despair and rebellion.

In Bordeaux great excesses were committed by the mob, which were punished with severity. Six thousand soldiers were quartered in the town, and were guilty of such disorders that the best families emigrated, and trade was ruined for a long period. But Brittany witnessed still worse evils. There also riots and disturbances had been produced by the excessive pressure of the imposts. An army of five thousand men was poured into the province, and inflicted such terror on the population that the wretched peasants, at the mere sight of the soldiers, threw themselves on their knees in an attitude of supplication and exclaimed, "*Mea culpa.*" The lively Madame de Sévigné gives us some interesting details concerning these events in the intervals when court scandal ran low and the brave doings of Madame de Montespan suffered a temporary interruption. "Would you like," says the tender-hearted lady to her daughter, "would you like to have news of Rennes? There are still five thousand soldiers here, as more have come from Nantes. A tax of one hundred thousand crowns has been laid upon the citizens, and if the money is not forthcoming in twenty-four hours the tax will be doubled and levied by the soldiers. All the inhabitants of a large street have already been driven out and banished, and no one may receive them under pain of death; so that all these poor wretches, old men, women recently delivered, and children, were seen wandering in tears as they left the town, not knowing whither to go or where to sleep or what to eat. The day before yesterday one of the leaders of the riot was broken alive on the wheel. Sixty citizens have been seized, and to-morrow the hanging will begin." In other letters she writes that the tenth man had been broken on the wheel, and she thinks he will be the last, and that by dint of hanging it will soon be left off.

Such was the emaciated France which Louis the Great picked systematically to the bone for the next thirty-five years. He had long ceased to be guided by the patriotic wisdom of the great Colbert. His evil genius now was the haughty and reckless Louvois, who carefully abstained from imitating the noble and daring remonstrances against excessive expenditure which Colbert addressed to his master, and through which he lost his influence at court. Still, with a self-abnegation really heroic, Colbert begged, urged, supplicated the King to reduce his outlay. He represented the misery of the people. "All letters that come from the provinces, whether from the intendants, the receivers-general, and even the bishops, speak of it," he wrote to the King. He insisted on a reduction of the taille by five or six millions; and surely it was time, when its collection gave rise to such scenes as have just been described. It was in vain. The King shut his eyes to mercy and reason. His gigantic war expenditure, when peace came, was only partially reduced. For, indeed, he was still at war, but with nature and self-created difficulties of his own making.

He was building Versailles: transplanting to its arid sands whole groves of full-grown trees from the depths of distant forests, and erecting the costly and fantastic marvel of Marli to afford a supply of water. Louis' buildings cost, first and last, a sum which would be represented by about twenty million pounds. The amount squandered on pensions was also very great. The great Colbert's days were drawing to a close, and he was very sad. It is related that a friend on one occasion surprised him looking out of a window in his château of Sceau, lost in thought and apparently gazing on the well-tilled fields of his own manor. When he came out of his reverie his friend asked him his thoughts. "As I look," he said, "on these fertile fields, I cannot help remembering what I have seen elsewhere. What a rich country is France! If the King's enemies would let him enjoy peace it would be possible to procure the people that relief and comfort which the great Henry promised them. I could wish that my projects had a happy issue, that abundance reigned in the kingdom, that everyone were content in it, and that without employment or dignities, far from the court and business, I saw the grass grow in my home farm."

The faithful, indefatigable worker was breaking down, losing strength, losing heart, but still struggling on manfully to the last. It was noticed that he sat down to his work with a sorrowful, despondent look, and not, as had been his wont, rubbing his hands with the prospect of toil, and exulting in his almost superhuman capacity for labor. The ingratitude of the King, whom he had served only too well, gave him the final blow. Louis, with truculent insolence, reproached him with the "frightful expenses" of Versailles. As if they were Colbert's fault. Colbert, who had always urged the completion of the Louvre and the suppression of Versailles.

At last the foregone giant lay down to die. A tardy touch of feeling induced Louis to write him a letter. He would not read it. "I will hear no more about the King," he said; "let him at least allow me to die in peace. My business now is with the King of kings. If," he continued, unconsciously, we may be sure, plagiarizing Wolsey, "if I had done for God what I have done for that man, my salvation would be secure ten times over; and now I know not what will become of me."

Surely a tender and touching evidence of sweetness in the strong man who had been so readily accused of harshness by grasping courtiers. The ignorant ingratitude of the people was even perhaps more melancholy than the wilful ingratitude of the King. The great Colbert had to be buried by night, lest his remains should be insulted by the mob. He, whose heart had bled for the people's sore anguish, was rashly supposed to be the cause of that anguish. It was a sad conclusion to a great life. But he would have seen still sadder days if he had lived.

The health of the luxurious, self-indulgent Louis sensibly declined after he had passed his fortieth year. In spite of his robust appearance he had never been really strong. His loose, lymphatic constitution required much support and management. But he habitually over-ate himself. He was indeed a gross and greedy glutton. "I have often seen the King," says the Duchess of Orleans, "eat four platefuls of various soups, a whole pheasant, a partridge, a large dish of salad, stewed mutton with garlic, two good slices of ham, a plate of pastry, and then fruit and sweetmeats." A most unwholesome habit of body was the result.

An abscess formed in his upper jaw, and caused a perforation of the palate, which obliged him to be very careful in drinking, as the liquid was apt to pass through the aperture and come out by the nostrils. He felt weak and depressed, and began to think seriously about "making his salvation." His courtly priests and confessors had never inculcated any duties but two—that of chastity and that of religious intolerance—and he had been very remiss in both. He now resolved to make hasty reparation. The ample charms of the haughty Montespan fascinated him no more. He tried a new mistress, but she did not turn out well. Madame de Fontanges was young and exquisitely pretty, but a giddy, presuming fool. She moreover died shortly. He was more than ever disposed to make his salvation—that is, to renounce the sins of the flesh, and to persecute his God-fearing subjects, the Protestants.

The Revocation of the Edict of Nantes, one of the greatest crimes and follies which history records, was too colossal a misdeed for the guilt of its perpetration to be charged upon one man, however wicked or however powerful he may have been. In this case, as in so many others, Louis was the exponent of conditions, the visible representative of circumstances which he had done nothing to create. Just as he was the strongest king France ever had, without having contributed himself to the predominance of the monarchy, so, in the blind and cruel policy of intolerance which led to the Revocation of the Edict of Nantes, he was the delegate and instrument of forces which existed independently of him. A willing instrument, no doubt; a representative of sinister forces; a chooser of the evil part when mere inaction would have been equivalent to a choice of the good. Still, it is due to historic accuracy to point out that, had he not been seconded by the existing condition of France, he would not have been able to effect the evil he ultimately brought about.

Louis' reign continued thirty years after the Revocation of the Edict of Nantes, years crowded with events, particularly for the military historian, but over the details of which we shall not linger on this occasion. The brilliant reign becomes unbearably wearisome in its final period. The monotonous repetition of the same faults and the same crimes—profligate extravagance, revolting cruelty, and tottering incapacity—is as fatiguing as it is uninstructive. Louis became a mere mummy embalmed in etiquette, the puppet of his women and shavelings. The misery in the provinces grew apace, but there was no disturbance: France was too prostrate even to groan.

In 1712 the expenditure amounted to two hundred forty millions, and the revenue to one hundred thirteen millions; but from this no less than seventy-six millions had to be deducted for various liabilities the government had incurred, leaving only a net income of thirty-seven millions—that is to say, the outlay was more than six times the income.

The armies were neither paid nor fed, the officers received "food-tickets" (*billets de subsistance*), which they got cashed at a discount of 80 per cent. The government had anticipated by ten years its revenues from the towns. Still, this pale corpse of France must needs be bled anew to gratify the inexorable Jesuits, who had again made themselves complete masters of Louis XIV's mind. He had lost his confessor, Père la Chaise (who died in 1709), and had replaced him by the hideous Letellier, a blind and fierce fanatic, with a horrible squint and a countenance fit for the gallows. He would have frightened anyone, says Saint-Simon, who met him at the corner of a wood. This repulsive personage revived the persecution of the Protestants into a fiercer heat than ever, and obtained from the moribund King the edict of March 8, 1715, considered by competent judges the clear masterpiece of clerical injustice and cruelty. Five months later Louis XIV died, forsaken by his intriguing wife, his beloved bastard (the Duc de Maine), and his dreaded priest.

The French monarchy never recovered from the strain to which it had been subjected during the long and exhausting reign of Louis XIV. Whether it could have recovered in the hands of a great statesman summoned in time is a curious question. Could Frederick the Great have saved it had he been *par impossible* Louis XIV's successor? We can hardly doubt that he would have adjourned, if not have averted, the great catastrophe of 1789. But it is one of the inseparable accidents of such a despotism as France had fallen under, that nothing but consummate genius can save it from ruin; and the accession of genius to the throne in such circumstances is a physiological impossibility.

The house of Bourbon had become as effete as the house of Valois in the sixteenth century; as effete as the Merovingians and Carlovingians had become in a previous age; but the strong chain of hereditary right bound up the fortunes of a great empire with the feeble brain and bestial instincts of a Louis XV. This was the result of concentrating all the active force of the state in one predestined irremovable human being. This was the logical and necessary outcome of the labors of Philip Augustus, Philip the Fair, of Louis XI, of Henry IV, and Richelieu. They had reared the monarchy like a solitary obelisk in the midst of a desert; but it had to stand or fall alone; no one was there to help it, as no one was there to pull it down. This consideration enables us to pass into a higher and more reposing order of reflection, to leave the sterile impeachment of individual incapacity, and rise to the broader question, and ask why and how that incapacity was endowed with such fatal potency for evil. As it has been well remarked, the loss of a battle may lead to the loss of a state; but then, what are the deeper reasons which explain why the loss of a battle should lead to the loss of a state? It is not enough to say that Louis XIV was an improvident and passionate ruler, that Louis XV was a dreary and revolting voluptuary. The problem is rather this: Why were improvidence, passion, and debauchery in two men able to bring down in utter ruin one of the greatest monarchies the world has ever seen? In other words, what was the cause of the consummate failure, the unexampled collapse, of the French monarchy?

No personal insufficiency of individual rulers will explain it; and, besides, the French monarchy repeatedly disposed of the services of admirable rulers. History has recorded few more able kings than Louis le Gros, Philip Augustus, Philip le Bel, Louis XI, and Henry IV; few abler ministers than Sully, Richelieu, Colbert, and Turgot. Yet the efforts of all these distinguished men resulted in leading the nation straight into the most astounding catastrophe in human annals. Whatever view we take of the Revolution, whether we regard it as a blessing or as a curse, we must needs admit it was a reaction of the most violent kind—a reaction contrary to the preceding action.

The old monarchy can only claim to have produced the Revolution in the sense of having provoked it; as intemperance has been known to produce sobriety, and extravagance parsimony. If the *ancien régime* led in the result to an abrupt transition to the modern era, it was only because it had rendered the old era so utterly execrable to mankind that escape in any direction seemed a relief, were it over a precipice.

NEW YORK TAKEN BY THE ENGLISH

A.D. 1664

JOHN R. BRODHEAD

For half a century the Dutch colony in New York, then called New Netherlands, had developed under various administrations, when British conquest brought it under another dominion. This transfer of the government affected the whole future of the colony and of the great State into which it grew, although the original Dutch influence has never disappeared from its character and history.

Under Peter Stuyvesant, the last Dutch Governor (1647–1664), the colony made great progress. He conciliated the Indians, agreed upon a boundary line with the English colonists at Hartford, Connecticut, and took possession of the colony of New Sweden, in Delaware.

Meanwhile the English colonists in different parts of North America were carrying on illicit trade with the Dutch at New Amsterdam (New York city). The English government, already jealous of the growing commerce of Holland, was irritated by the loss of revenue, and resolved in 1663 upon the conquest of New Netherlands. Brodhead, the historian of New York, recounts the steps of this conquest in a manner which brings the rival powers and their agents distinctly before us.

ENGLAND now determined boldly to rob Holland of her American province. King Charles II accordingly sealed a patent granting to the Duke of York and Albany a large territory in America, comprehending Long Island and the islands in its neighborhood—his title to which Lord Stirling had released—and all the lands and rivers from the west side of the Connecticut River to the east side of Delaware Bay. This sweeping grant included the whole of New Netherlands and a part of the territory of Connecticut, which, two years before, Charles had confirmed to Winthrop and his associates.

The Duke of York lost no time in giving effect to his patent. As lord high admiral he directed the fleet. Four ships, the Guinea, of thirty-six guns; the Elias, of thirty; the Martin, of sixteen; and the William and Nicholas, of ten, were detached for service against New Netherlands, and about four hundred fifty regular soldiers, with their officers, were embarked. The command of the expedition was intrusted to Colonel Richard Nicolls, a faithful Royalist, who had served under Turenne with James, and had been made one of the gentlemen of his bedchamber. Nicolls was also appointed to be the Duke's deputy-governor, after the Dutch possessions should have been reduced.

With Nicolls were associated Sir Robert Carr, Colonel George Cartwright, and Samuel Maverick, as royal commissioners to visit the several colonies in New England. These commissioners were furnished with detailed instructions; and the New England governments were required by royal letters to "join and assist them vigorously" in reducing the Dutch to subjection. A month after the departure of the squadron the Duke of York conveyed to Lord Berkeley and Sir George Carteret all the territory between the Hudson and Delaware rivers, from Cape May north to 41° 40′ latitude, and thence to the Hudson, in 41° latitude, "hereafter to be called by the name or names of Nova Cæsarea or New Jersey."

Intelligence from Boston that an English expedition against New Netherlands had sailed from Portsmouth was soon communicated to Stuyvesant by Captain Thomas Willett; and the burgomasters and *schepens* of New Amsterdam were summoned to assist the council with their advice. The capital was ordered to be put in a state of defence, guards to be maintained, and *schippers* to be warned. As there was very little powder at Fort Amsterdam a supply was demanded from New Amstel, and a loan of five or six thousand guilders was asked from Rensselaerswyck. The ships about to sail for Curaçao were stopped; agents were sent to purchase provisions at New Haven; and as the enemy was expected to approach through Long Island Sound, spies were sent to obtain intelligence at West Chester and Milford.

But at the moment when no precaution should have been relaxed, a despatch from the West India directors, who appear to have been misled by advices from London, announced that no danger need be apprehended from the English expedition, as it was sent out by the King only to settle the affairs of his colonies and establish episcopacy, which would rather benefit the company's interests in New Netherlands. Willett now retracting his previous statements, a perilous confidence returned. The Curaçao ships were allowed to sail; and Stuyvesant, yielded to the solicitation of his council, went up the river to look after affairs at Fort Orange.

The English squadron had been ordered to assemble at Gardiner's Island. But, parting company in a fog, the Guinea, with Nicolls and Cartwright on board, made Cape Cod, and went on to Boston, while the other ships put in at Piscataway. The commissioners immediately demanded the assistance of Massachusetts, but the people of the Bay, who feared, perhaps, that the King's success in reducing the Dutch would enable him the better to put down his enemies in New England, were full of excuses. Connecticut, however, showed sufficient alacrity; and Winthrop was desired to meet the squadron at the west end of Long Island, whither it would sail with the first fair wind.

When the truth of Willett's intelligence became confirmed, the council sent an express to recall Stuyvesant from Fort Orange. Hurrying back to the capital, the anxious director endeavored to redeem the time which had been lost. The municipal authorities ordered one-third of inhabitants, without exception, to labor every third day at the fortifications; organized a permanent guard; forbade the brewers to malt any grain; and called on the provincial government for artillery and ammunition. Six pieces, besides the fourteen previously allotted, and a thousand pounds of powder were accordingly granted to the city. The colonists around Fort Orange, pleading their own danger from the savages, could afford no help; but the soldiers of Esopus were ordered to come down, after leaving a small garrison at Ronduit.

In the mean time the English squadron had anchored just below the Narrows, in Nyack Bay, between New Utrecht and Coney Island. The mouth of the river was shut up; communication between Long Island and Manhattan, Bergen and Achter Cul, interrupted; several yachts on their way to the South River captured; and the blockhouse on the opposite shore of Staten Island seized. Stuyvesant now despatched Counsellor de Decker, Burgomaster Van der Grist, and the two domines Megapolensis with a letter to the English commanders inquiring why they had come, and why they continued at Nyack without giving notice. The next morning, which was Saturday, Nicolls sent Colonel Cartwright, Captain Needham, Captain Groves, and Mr. Thomas Delavall up to Fort Amsterdam with a summons for the surrender of "the town situate on the island and commonly known by the name of Manhatoes, with all the forts thereunto belonging."

This summons was accompanied by a proclamation declaring that all who would submit to his majesty's government should be protected "in his majesty's laws and justice," and peaceably enjoy their property. Stuyvesant immediately called together the council and the burgomasters, but would not allow the terms offered by Nicolls to be communicated to the people, lest they might insist on capitulating. In a short time several of the burghers and city officers assembled at the Stadt-Huys. It was determined to prevent the enemy from surprising the town; but, as opinion was generally against protracted resistance, a copy of the English communication was asked from the director. On the following Monday the burgomasters explained to a meeting of the citizens the terms offered by Nicolls. But this would not suffice; a copy of the paper itself must be exhibited. Stuyvesant then went in person to the meeting. "Such a course," said he, "would be disapproved of in the Fatherland—it would discourage the people." All his efforts, however, were in vain; and the director, protesting that he should not be held answerable for the "calamitous consequences," was obliged to yield to the popular will.

Nicolls now addressed a letter to Winthrop, who with other commissioners from New England had joined the squadron, authorizing him to assure Stuyvesant that, if Manhattan should be delivered up to the King, "any people from the Netherlands may freely come and plant there or thereabouts; and such vessels of their own country may freely come thither, and any of them may as freely return home in vessels of their own country." Visiting the city under a flag of truce Winthrop delivered this to Stuyvesant outside the fort and urged him to surrender. The director declined; and, returning to the fort, he opened Nicolls' letter before the council and the burgomasters, who desired that it should be communicated, as "all which regarded the public welfare ought to be made public." Against this Stuyvesant earnestly remonstrated, and, finding that the burgomasters continued firm, in a fit of passion he "tore the letter in pieces." The citizens, suddenly ceasing their work at the palisades, hurried to the Stadt-Huys, and sent three of their numbers to the fort to demand the letter.

In vain the director hastened to pacify the burghers and urge them to go on with the fortifications. "Complaints and curses" were uttered on all sides against the company's misgovernment; resistance was declared to be idle; "The letter! the letter!" was the general cry. To avoid a mutiny Stuyvesant yielded, and a copy, made out from the collected fragments, was handed to the burgomasters. In answer, however, to Nicolls' summons he submitted a long justification of the Dutch title; yet while protesting against any breach of the peace between the King and the States-General, "for the hinderance and prevention of all differences and the spilling of innocent blood, not only in these parts, but also in Europe," he offered to treat. "Long Island is gone and lost;" the capital "cannot hold out long," was the last despatch to the "Lord Majors" of New Netherlands, which its director sent off that night "in silence through Hell Gate."

Observing Stuyvesant's reluctance to surrender, Nicolls directed Captain Hyde, who commanded the squadron, to reduce the fort. Two of the ships accordingly landed their troops just below Breuckelen (Brooklyn), where volunteers from New England and the Long Island villages had already encamped. The other two, coming up with full sail, passed in front of Fort Amsterdam and anchored between it and Nutten Island. Standing on one of the angles of the fortress—an artilleryman with a lighted match at his side—the director watched their approach. At this moment the two domines Megapolensis, imploring him not to begin hostilities, led Stuyvesant from the rampart, who then, with a hundred of the garrison, went into the city to resist the landing of the English. Hoping on against hope, the director now sent Counsellor de Decker, Secretary Van Ruyven, Burgomaster Steenwyck, and "Schepen" Cousseau with a letter to Nicolls stating that, as he felt bound "to stand the storm," he desired if possible to arrange on accommodation. But the English commander merely declared, "To-morrow I will speak with you at Manhattan."

"Friends," was the answer, "will be welcome if they come in a friendly manner."

"I shall come with ships and soldiers," replied Nicolls; "raise the white flag of peace at the fort, and then something may be considered."

When this imperious message became known, men, women, and children flocked to the director, beseeching him to submit. His only answer was, "I would rather be carried out dead." The next day the city authorities, the clergymen, and the officers of the burgher guard, assembling at the Stadt-Huys, at the suggestion of Domine Megapolensis adopted a remonstrance to the director, exhibiting the hopeless situation of New Amsterdam, on all sides "encompassed and hemmed in by enemies," and protesting against any further opposition to the will of God. Besides the *schout*, burgomasters, and schepens, the remonstrance was signed by Wilmerdonck and eighty-five of the principal inhabitants, among whom was Stuyvesant's own son, Balthazar.

At last the director was obliged to yield. Although there were now fifteen hundred souls in New Amsterdam, there were not more than two hundred fifty men able to bear arms, besides the one hundred fifty regular soldiers. The people had at length refused to be called out, and the regular troops were already heard talking of "where booty is to be found, and where the young women live who wear gold chains." The city, entirely open along both rivers, was shut on the northern side by a breastwork and palisades, which, though sufficient to keep out the savages, afforded no defence against a military siege. There were scarcely six hundred pounds of serviceable powder in store.

A council of war had reported Fort Amsterdam untenable; for though it mounted twenty-four guns, its single wall of earth, not more than ten feet high and four thick, was almost touched by the private dwellings clustered around, and was commanded, within a pistol-shot, by hills on the north, over which ran the "Heereweg" or Broadway.

Upon the faith of Nicolls' promise to deliver back the city and fort "in case the difference of the limits of this province be agreed upon betwixt his majesty of England and the high and mighty States-General," Stuyvesant now commissioned Counsellor John de Decker, Captain Nicholas Varlett, Dr. Samuel Megapolensis, Burgomaster Cornelius Steenwyck, old Burgomaster Oloff Stevenson van Cortlandt, and old Schepen Jacques Cousseau to agree upon articles with the English commander or his representatives. Nicolls, on his part, appointed Sir Robert Carr and Colonel George Cartwright, John Winthrop, and Samuel Willys, of Connecticut, and Thomas Clarke and John Pynchon, of Massachusetts. "The reason why those of Boston and Connecticut were joined," afterward explained the royal commander, "was because those two colonies should hold themselves the more engaged with us if the Dutch had been overconfident of their strength."

At eight o'clock the next morning, which was Saturday, the commissioners on both sides met at Stuyvesant's "bouwery" and arranged the terms of capitulation. The only difference which arose was respecting the Dutch soldiers, whom the English refused to convey back to Holland. The articles of capitulation promised the Dutch security in their property, customs of inheritance, liberty of conscience and church discipline. The municipal officers of Manhattan were to continue for the present unchanged, and the town was to be allowed to choose deputies, with "free voices in all public affairs." Owners of property in Fort Orange might, if they pleased, "slight the fortifications there," and enjoy their houses "as people do where there is no fort."

For six months there was to be free intercourse with Holland. Public records were to be respected. The articles, consented to by Nicolls, were to be ratified by Stuyvesant the next Monday morning at eight o'clock, and within two hours afterward, the "fort and town called New Amsterdam, upon the Isle of Manhatoes," were to be delivered up, and the military officers and soldiers were to "march out with their arms, drums beating, and colors flying, and lighted matches."

On the following Monday morning at eight o'clock Stuyvesant, at the head of the garrison, marched out of Fort Amsterdam with all the honors of war, and led his soldiers down the Beaver Lane to the water-side, whence they were embarked for Holland. An English corporal's guard at the same time took possession of the fort; and Nicolls and Carr, with their two companies, about a hundred seventy strong, entered the city, while Cartwright took possession of the gates and the Stadt-Huys. The New England and Long Island volunteers, however, were prudently kept at the Breuckelen ferry, as the citizens dreaded most being plundered by them. The English flag was hoisted on Fort Amsterdam, the name of which was immediately changed to "Fort James." Nicolls was now proclaimed by the burgomasters deputy-governor for the Duke of York, in compliment to whom he directed that the city of New Amsterdam should thenceforth be known as "New York."

To Nicolls' European eye the Dutch metropolis, with its earthen fort enclosing a windmill and high flag-staff, a prison and a governor's house, and a double-roofed church, above which loomed a square tower, its gallows and whipping-post at the river's side, and its rows of houses which hugged the citadel, presented but a mean appearance. Yet before long he described it to the Duke as "the best of all his majesty's towns in America," and assured his royal highness that, with proper management, "within five years the staple of America will be drawn hither, of which the brethren of Boston are very sensible."

The Dutch frontier posts were thought of next. Colonel Cartwright, with Captains Thomas Willett, John Manning, Thomas Breedon, and Daniel Brodhead, were sent to Fort Orange, as soon as possible, with a letter from Nicolls requiring La Montagne and the magistrates and inhabitants to aid in prosecuting his majesty's interest against all who should oppose a peaceable surrender. At the same time Van Rensselaer was desired to bring down his patent and papers to the new governor and likewise to observe Cartwright's directions.

Counsellor de Decker, however, travelling up to Fort George ahead of the English commissioners, endeavored, without avail, to excite the inhabitants to opposition; and his conduct being judged contrary to the spirit of the capitulation which he had signed, he was soon afterward ordered out of Nicolls' government. The garrison quietly surrendered, and the name of Fort Orange was changed to that of "Fort Albany," after the second title of the Duke of York. A treaty was immediately signed between Cartwright and the sachems of the Iroquois, who were promised the same advantages "as heretofore they had from the Dutch"; and the alliance which was thus renewed continued unbroken until the beginning of the American Revolution.

It only remained to reduce the South River; whither Sir Robert Carr was sent with the Guinea, the William and Nicholas, and "all the soldiers which are not in the fort." To the Dutch he was instructed to promise all their privileges, "only that they change their masters." To the Swedes he was to "remonstrate their happy return under a monarchical government." To Lord Baltimore's officers in Maryland he was to say that, their pretended rights being a doubtful case, "possession would be kept until his majesty is informed and satisfied otherwise."

A tedious voyage brought the expedition before New Amstel. The burghers and planters, "after almost three days' parley," agreed to Carr's demands, and Ffob Oothout with five others signed articles of capitulation which promised large privileges. But the Governor and soldiery refusing the English propositions, the fort was stormed and plundered, three of the Dutch being killed and ten wounded. In violation of his promises, Carr now exhibited the most disgraceful rapacity; appropriated farms to himself, his brother, and Captains Hyde and Morely, stripped bare the inhabitants, and sent the Dutch soldiers to be sold as slaves in Virginia. To complete the work, a boat was despatched to the city's colony at the Horekill, which was seized and plundered of all its effects, and the marauding party even took "what belonged to the Quacking Society of Plockhoy, to a very naile."

The reduction of New Netherlands was now accomplished. All that could be further done was to change its name; and, to glorify one of the most bigoted princes in English history, the royal province was ordered to be called "New York." Ignorant of James' grant of New Jersey to Berkeley and Carteret, Nicolls gave to the region west of the Hudson the name of "Albania," and to Long Island that of "Yorkshire," so as to comprehend all the titles of the Duke of York. The flag of England was at length triumphantly displayed, where, for half a century, that of Holland had rightfully waved; and from Virginia to Canada, the King of Great Britain was acknowledged as sovereign.

Viewed in all its aspects, the event which gave to the whole of that country a unity in allegiance, and to which a misgoverned people complacently submitted, was as inevitable as it was momentous. But whatever may have been its ultimate consequences, this treacherous and violent seizure of the territory and possessions of an unsuspecting ally was no less a breach of private justice than of public faith.

It may, indeed, be affirmed that, among all the acts of selfish perfidy which royal ingratitude conceived and executed, there have been few more characteristic and none more base.

GREAT PLAGUE IN LONDON

A.D. 1665

DANIEL DEFOE

None of the great visitations of disease that have afflicted Europe within historic times has wholly spared England. But from the time of the "Black Death" (1349) the country experienced no such suffering from any epidemic as that which fell upon London in 1665. That year the "Great Plague" is said to have destroyed the lives of nearly one hundred thousand people in England's capital. The plague had previously cropped up there every few years, from lack of proper sanitation. At the time of this outbreak the water-supply of the city was notoriously impure. In 1665 the heat was uncommonly severe. Pepys said that June 7th of that year was the hottest day that he had ever known.

The plague of 1665 is said, however, to have been brought in merchandise directly from Holland, where it had been smouldering for several years. Its ravages in London have often been described, and Defoe found in the calamity a subject for a special story on history. Probably he was not more than six years old when the plague appeared; but he assumes throughout the pose of a respectable and religious householder of the period. All his own recollections, all the legends of the time, and the parish records are grouped in masterly fashion to form a single picture. The account has been described as a "masterpiece of verisimilitude."

IN the first place a blazing star or comet appeared for several months before the plague, as there did the year after, a little before the great fire; the old women and the weak-minded portion of the other sex, whom I could almost call old women too, remarked—especially afterward, though not till both those judgments were over—that those two comets passed directly over the city, and that so very near the houses that it was plain they imported something peculiar to the city alone; that the comet before the pestilence was of a faint, dull, languid color, and its motion very heavy, solemn, and slow; but that the comet before the fire was bright and sparkling, or, as others said, flaming, and its motion swift and furious; and that, accordingly, one foretold a heavy judgment, slow, but severe, terrible, and frightful, as the plague was; but the other foretold a stroke, sudden, swift, and fiery, like the conflagration. Nay, so particular some people were that, as they looked upon that comet preceding the fire, they fancied that they not only saw it pass swiftly and fiercely, and could perceive the motion with the eye, but they even heard it; that it made a rushing, mighty noise, fierce and terrible, though at a distance and but just perceivable.

I saw both these stars, and I must confess, had so much of the common notion of such things in my head that I was apt to look upon them as the forerunners and warnings of God's judgments; and especially, when after the plague had followed the first, I yet saw another of the like kind, I could not but say, God had not yet sufficiently scourged the city.

But I could not at the same time carry these things to the height that others did, knowing, too, that natural causes are assigned by the astronomers for such things; and that their motions, and even their evolutions, are calculated, or pretended to be calculated; so that they cannot be so perfectly called the forerunners or foretellers, much less the procurers of such events as pestilence, war, fire, and the like.

But let my thoughts, and the thoughts of the philosophers, be or have been what they will, these things had a more than ordinary influence upon the minds of the common people, and they had, almost universally, melancholy apprehensions of some dreadful calamity and judgment coming upon the city; and this principally from the sight of this comet, and the little alarm that was given in December by two people dying in St. Giles.

The apprehensions of the people were likewise strangely increased by the error of the times; in which, I think the people, from what principles I cannot imagine, were more addicted to prophecies, and astrological conjurations, dreams, and old wives' tales, than ever they were before or since. Whether this unhappy temper was originally raised by the follies of some people who got money by it—that is to say, by printing predictions and prognostications—I know not; but certain it is books frightened them terribly; such as *Lilly's Almanack, Gadbury's Allogical Predictions, Poor Robin's Almanack,* and the like; also several pretended religious books—one entitled *Come out of her, my people, lest you be partaker of her plagues;* another, called *Fair Warn-*

ing; another, *Britain's Remembrancer;* and many such, all or most part of which foretold directly or covertly the ruin of the city: nay, some were so enthusiastically bold as to run about the streets with their oral predictions, pretending they were sent to preach to the city; and one in particular, who like Jonah to Nineveh, cried in the streets, "Yet forty days, and London shall be destroyed." I will not be positive whether he said "yet forty days" or "yet a few days."

Another ran about naked, except a pair of drawers about his waist, crying day and night. As a man that Josephus mentions, who cried, "Woe to Jerusalem!" a little before the destruction of that city, so this poor naked creature cried, "O the great and the dreadful God!" and said no more, but repeated these words continually, with a voice and countenance full of horror, a swift pace; and nobody could ever find him to stop or rest or take any sustenance, at least that ever I could hear of. I met this poor creature several times in the streets, and would have spoken to him, but he would not enter into conversation with me, or any-one else, but held on his dismal cries continually. These things terrified the people to the last degree; and especially when two or three times, as I have mentioned already, they found one or two in the bills dead of the plague at St. Giles.

The justices of peace for Middlesex, by direction of the secretary of state, had begun to shut up houses in the parishes of St. Giles-in-the-Fields, St. Martin's, St. Clement Danes, etc., and it was with good success; for in several streets where the plague broke out, after strictly guarding the houses that were infected, and taking care to bury those that died immediately after they were known to be dead, the plague ceased in those streets. It was also observed that the plague decreased sooner in those parishes, after they had been visited in detail, than it did in the parishes of Bishopsgate, Shoreditch, Aldgate, Whitechapel, Stepney, and others; the early care taken in that manner being a great check to it.

This shutting up of houses was a method first taken, as I understand, in the plague which happened in 1603, on the accession of King James I to the crown; and the power of shutting people up in their own houses was granted by an act of Parliament entitled "An act for the charitable relief and ordering of persons infected with the plague." On which act of Parliament the lord mayor and aldermen of the city of London founded the order they made at this time, viz., June, 1665; when the numbers infected within the city were but few, the last bill for the ninety-two parishes being but four. By these means, when there died about one thousand a week in the whole, the number in the city was but twenty-eight; and the city was more healthy in proportion than any other place all the time of the infection.

These orders of my lord mayor were published, as I have said, toward the end of June. They came into operation from July 1st, and were as follows:

"*Orders conceived and published by the lord mayor and aldermen of the city of London, concerning the infection of the plague,* 1665.

"Whereas, in the reign of our late sovereign, King James, of happy memory, an act was made for the charitable relief and ordering of persons infected with the plague; whereby authority was given to justices of the peace, mayors, bailiffs, and other head officers, to appoint within their several limits, examiners, searchers, watchmen, surgeons, and nurse-keepers, and buriers, for the persons and places infected, and to minister unto them oaths for the performance of their offices. And the same statute did also authorize the giving of other directions, as unto them for the present necessity should seem good in their discretions. It is now upon special consideration thought very expedient for preventing and avoiding of infection of sickness (if it shall so please Almighty God) that these officers be appointed, and these orders hereafter duly observed."

Then follow the orders giving these officers instructions in detail and prescribing the extent and limits of their several duties. Next, "*Orders concerning infected houses and persons sick of the plague.*" These had reference to the "notice to be given of the sickness," "sequestration of the sick," "airing the stuff," "shutting up of the house," "burial of the dead," "forbidding infected stuff to be sold, and of persons leaving infected houses," "marking of infected houses," and "regulating hackney coaches that have been used to convey infected persons."

Lastly there followed "*Orders for cleansing and keeping the streets and houses sweet*" and "*Orders concerning loose persons and idle assemblies,*" such as "beggars," "plays," "feasts," and "tippling-houses."

"(Signed) SIR JOHN LAWRENCE, *Lord Mayor.*
"SIR GEORGE WATERMAN, } *Sheriffs.*"
"SIR CHARLES DOE, }

I need not say that these orders extended only to such places as were within the lord mayor's jurisdiction; so it is requisite to observe that the justices of the peace, within those parishes, and those places called the hamlets and out-parts, took the same method: as I remember, the orders for shutting up of houses did not take place so soon on our side, because, as I said before, the plague did not reach the eastern parts of the town, at least not begin to be very violent, till the beginning of August.

Now, indeed, it was coming on amain; for the burials that same week were in the next adjoining parishes thus:

		The next week prodigiously increased, as	To the 1st of Aug. thus
St. Leonard's, Shoreditch...	64	84	110
St. Botolph, Bishopsgate...	65	105	116
St. Giles, Cripplegate......	213	421	554
	342	610	780

The shutting up of houses was at first considered a very cruel and unchristian thing, and the poor people so confined made bitter lamentations; complaints were also daily brought to my lord mayor, of houses causelessly—and some maliciously—shut up. I cannot say, but, upon inquiry, many that complained so loudly were found in a condition to be continued; and others again, inspection being made upon the sick person, on his being content to be carried to the pesthouse, were released.

Indeed, many people perished in these miserable confinements, which it is reasonable to believe would not have been distempered if they had had liberty, though the plague was in the house; at which the people were at first very clamorous and uneasy, and several acts of violence were committed on the men who were set to watch the houses so shut up; also several people broke out by force, in many places, as I shall observe by and by; still it was a public good that justified the private mischief; and there was no obtaining the least mitigation by any application to magistrates. This put the people upon all manner of stratagems, in order, if possible, to get out; and it would fill a little volume to set down the arts used by the people of such houses to shut the eyes of the watchmen who were employed, to deceive them, and to escape or break out from them. A few incidents on this head may prove not uninteresting.

As I went along Houndsditch one morning, about eight o'clock, there was a great noise; it is true, indeed, there was not much crowd, because people were not very free to gather or to stay long together; but the outcry was loud enough to prompt my curiosity, and I called to one that looked out of a window, and asked what was the matter.

A watchman, it seems, had been employed to keep his post at the door of a house which was infected, or said to be infected, and was shut up; he had been there all night for two nights together, as he told his story, and the day watchman had been there one day, and had now come to relieve him; all this while no noise had been heard in the house, no light had been seen; they called for nothing, sent him no errands, which was the chief business of the watchman; neither had they given him any disturbance, as he said, from the Monday afternoon, when he heard great crying and screaming in the house, which, as he supposed, was occasioned by some of the family dying just at that time. It seems the night before, the dead-cart, as it was called, had been stopped there, and a servant-maid had been brought down to the door dead, and the buriers or bearers, as they were called, put her into the cart, wrapped only in a green rug, and carried her away.

The watchman had knocked at the door, it seems, when he heard that noise and crying, as above, and nobody answered a great while; but at last one looked out, and said, with an angry, quick tone, "What do ye want, that ye make such a knocking?" He answered: "I am the watchman! how do you do? what is the matter?" The person answered: "What is that to you? Stop the dead-cart." This, it seems, was about one o'clock; soon after, as the fellow said, he stopped the dead-cart, and then knocked again, but nobody answered: he continued knocking, and the bellman called out several times, "Bring out your dead!" but nobody answered, till the man that drove the cart, being called to other houses, would stay no longer, and drove away.

The watchman knew not what to make of all this, so he let them alone till the day watchman came to relieve him, giving him an account of the particulars. They knocked at the door a great while, but nobody answered; and they observed that the window or casement at which the person had looked out continued open, being up two pair of stairs. Upon this the two men, to satisfy their curiosity, got a long ladder, and one of them went up to the window and looked into the room, where he saw a woman lying dead upon the floor in a dismal manner, having no clothes on her but her shift. Although he called aloud, and knocked hard on the floor with his long staff, yet nobody stirred or answered; neither could he hear any noise in the house.

Upon this he came down again and acquainted his fellow, who went up also, and, finding the case as above, they resolved either to acquaint the lord mayor or some other magistrate with it. The magistrate, it seems, upon the information of the two men, ordered the house to be broken open, a constable and other persons being appointed to be present, that nothing might be plundered; and accordingly it was so done, when nobody was found in the house but that young woman, who, having been infected, and past recovery, the rest had left her to die by herself. Everyone was gone, having found some way to delude the watchman and to get open the door or get out at some back door or over the tops of the houses, so that he knew nothing of it; and as to those cries and shrieks which the watchman had heard, it was supposed they were the passionate cries of the family at the bitter parting, which, to be sure, it was to them all, this being the sister to the mistress of the house.

Many such escapes were made out of infected houses, as particularly when the watchman was sent some errand, that is to say, for necessaries, such as food and physic, to fetch physicians if they would come, or surgeons, or nurses, or to order the dead-cart, and the like. Now, when he went it was his duty to lock up the outer door of the house and take the key away with him; but to evade this and cheat the watchman, people got two or three keys made to their locks, or they found means to unscrew the locks, open the door, and go out as they pleased. This way of escape being found out, the officers afterward had orders to padlock up the doors on the outside and place bolts on them, as they thought fit.

At another house, as I was informed, in the street near Aldgate, a whole family was shut up and locked in because the maid-servant was ill: the master of the house had complained, by his friends, to the next alderman and to the lord mayor, and had consented to have the maid carried to the pesthouse, but was refused, so the door was marked with a red cross, a padlock on the outside, as above, and a watchman set to keep the door according to public order.

After the master of the house found there was no remedy, but that he, his wife, and his children were to be locked up with this poor distempered servant, he called to the watchman and told him he must go then and fetch a nurse for them to attend this poor girl, for that it would be certain death to them all to oblige them to nurse her; and that if he would not do this the maid must perish, either of the distemper, or be starved for want of food, for he was resolved none of his family should go near her, and she lay in the garret, four-story high, where she could not cry out or call to anybody for help.

The watchman went and fetched a nurse as he was appointed, and brought her to them the same evening; during this interval the master of the house took the opportunity of breaking a large hole through his shop into a stall where formerly a cobbler had sat, before or under his shop window, but the tenant, as may be supposed, at such a dismal time as that, was dead or removed, and so he had the key in his own keeping. Having made his way into this stall, which he could not have done if the man had been at the door—the noise he was obliged to make being such as would have alarmed the watchman—I say, having made his way into this stall, he sat still till the watchman returned with the nurse, and all the next day also. But the night following, having contrived to send the watchman another trifling errand, he conveyed himself and all his family out of the house, and left the nurse and the watchman to bury the poor woman, that is, to throw her into the cart and take care of the house.

I could give a great many such stories as these which in the long course of that dismal year I met with, that is, heard of, and which are very certain to be true or very near the truth; that is to say, true in general, for no man could at such a time learn all the particulars. There was, likewise, violence used with the watchmen, as was reported, in abundance of places; and I believe that, from the beginning of the visitation to the end, not less than eighteen or twenty of them were killed or so severely wounded as to be taken up for dead; which was supposed to have been done by the people in the infected houses which were shut up, and where they attempted to come out and were opposed.

For example, not far from Coleman Street they blowed up a watchman with gunpowder, and burned the poor fellow dreadfully; and while he made hideous cries, and nobody would venture to come near to help him, the whole family that were able to stir got out at the windows one story high, two that were left sick calling out for help. Care was taken to give the latter nurses to look after them, but the fugitives were not found till after the plague abated, when they returned; but as nothing could be proved, so nothing could be done to them.

It is to be considered, too, that as these were prisons without bars or bolts, which our common prisons are furnished with, so the people let themselves down out of their windows, even in the face of the watchman, bringing swords or pistols in their hands, and threatening to shoot the poor wretch if he stirred or called for help.

In other cases some had gardens and walls or palings between them and their neighbors; or yards and back houses; and these, by friendship and entreaties, would get leave to get over those walls or palings, and so go out at their neighbors' doors, or, by giving money to their servants, get them to let them through in the night; so that, in short, the shutting up of houses was in no wise to be depended upon. Neither did it answer the end at all; serving more to make the people desperate and drive them to violent extremities in their attempts to break out.

But what was still worse, those that did thus break out spread the infection by wandering about with the distemper upon them; and many that did so were driven to dreadful exigencies and extremities and perished in the streets or fields or dropped down with the raging violence of the fever upon them. Others wandered into the country and went forward any way as their desperation guided them, not knowing whither they went or would go, till faint and tired; the houses and villages on the road refusing to admit them to lodge, whether infected or no, they perished by the roadside.

On the other hand, when the plague at first seized a family, that is to say, when any one of the family had gone out and unwarily or otherwise caught the distemper and brought it home, it was certainly known by the family before it was known to the officers who were appointed to examine into the circumstances of all sick persons when they heard of their being sick.

I remember—and while I am writing this story I think I hear the very shrieks—a certain lady had an only daughter, a young maiden about nineteen years old and who was possessed of a very considerable fortune. The young woman, her mother, and the maid had been out for some purpose, for the house was not shut up; but about two hours after they came home the young lady complained she was not well; in a quarter of an hour more she vomited and had a violent pain in her head. "Pray God," says her mother, in a terrible fright, "my child has not the distemper!" The pain in her head increasing, her mother ordered the bed to be warmed, and resolved to put her to bed, and prepared to give her things to sweat, which was the ordinary remedy to be taken when the first apprehensions of the distemper began.

While the bed was being aired, the mother undressed the young woman, and, on looking over her body with a candle, immediately discovered the fatal tokens. Her mother, not being able to contain herself, threw down her candle and screeched out in such a frightful manner that it was enough to bring horror upon the stoutest heart in the world. Overcome by fright, she first fainted, then recovered, then ran all over the house, up the stairs and down the stairs, like one distracted. Thus she continued screeching and crying out for several hours, void of all sense, or at least government of her senses, and, as I was told, never came thoroughly to herself again. As to the young maiden, she was dead from that moment; for the gangrene which occasions the spots had spread over her whole body, and she died in less than two hours: but still the mother continued crying out, not knowing anything more of her child, several hours after she was dead.

I went all the first part of the time freely about the streets, though not so freely as to run myself into apparent danger, except when they dug the great pit in the church-yard of our parish of Aldgate. A terrible pit it was, and I could not resist the curiosity to go and see it. So far as I could judge, it was about forty feet in length and about fifteen or sixteen feet broad, and, at the time I first looked at it, about nine feet deep; but it was said they dug it nearly twenty feet deep afterward, when they could go no deeper, for the water.

They had dug several pits in another ground when the distemper began to spread in our parish, and especially when the dead-carts began to go about, which in our parish was not till the beginning of August. Into these pits they had put perhaps fifty or sixty bodies each; then they made larger holes, wherein they buried all that the cart brought in a week, which, by the middle to the end of August, came to from two hundred to four hundred a week. They could not dig them larger, because of the order of the magistrates confining them to leave no bodies within six feet of the surface. Besides, the water coming on at about seventeen or eighteen feet, they could not well put more in one pit. But now at the beginning of September, the plague being at its height, and the number of burials in our parish increasing to more than were ever buried in any parish about London of no larger extent, they ordered this dreadful gulf to be dug, for such it was, rather than a pit.

They had supposed this pit would have supplied them for a month or more when they dug it, and some blamed the church-wardens for suffering such a frightful thing, telling them they were making preparations to bury the whole parish, and the like; but time made it appear the church-wardens knew the condition of the parish better than they did; for the pit being finished September 4th, I think they began to bury in it on the 6th, and by the 20th, which was just two weeks, they had thrown into it one thousand one hundred fourteen bodies, when they were obliged to fill it up, the bodies being within six feet of the surface.

It was about September 10th that my curiosity led or rather

drove me to go and see this pit again, when there had been about four hundred people buried in it; and I was not content to see it in the daytime, as I had done before, for then there would have been nothing to see but the loose earth; for all the bodies that were thrown in were immediately covered with earth by those they called the buriers, but I resolved to go in the night and see some of the bodies thrown in.

There was a strict order against people coming to those pits, and that was only to prevent infection; but after some time that order was more necessary, for people that were infected and near their end, and delirious also, would run to those pits, wrapped in blankets or rags, and throw themselves in and bury themselves.

I got admittance into the church-yard by being acquainted with the sexton, who, though he did not refuse me at all, yet earnestly persuaded me not to go, telling me very seriously—for he was a good and sensible man—that it was indeed their business and duty to run all hazards, and that in so doing they might hope to be preserved; but that I had no apparent call except my own curiosity, which he said he believed I would not pretend was sufficient to justify my exposing myself to infection. I told him "I had been pressed in my mind to go, and that perhaps it might be an instructing sight that might not be without its uses." "Nay," says the good man, "if you will venture on that score, i' name of God go in; for depend upon it, 'twill be a sermon to you; it may be the best that you ever heard in your life. It is a speaking sight," says he, "and has a voice with it, and a loud one, to call us to repentance;" and with that he opened the door and said, "Go, if you will."

His words had shocked my resolution a little and I stood wavering for a good while; but just at that interval I saw two links come over from the end of the Minories, and heard the bellman, and then appeared a dead-cart, so I could no longer resist my desire, and went in. There was nobody that I could perceive at first in the church-yard or going into it but the buriers and the fellow that drove the cart or rather led the horse and cart; but when they came up to the pit they saw a man going to and fro muffled up in a brown cloak and making motions with his hands under his cloak, as if he was in a great agony, and the buriers immediately gathered about him, supposing he was one of those poor delirious or desperate creatures that used to bury themselves. He said nothing as he walked about, but two or three times groaned very deeply and loud, and sighed as he would break his heart.

When the buriers came up to him they soon found he was neither a person infected and desperate, as I have observed above, nor a person distempered in mind, but one oppressed with a dreadful weight of grief, indeed, having his wife and several of his children in the cart that had just come in, and he followed it in an agony and excess of sorrow. He mourned heartily, as it was easy to see, but with a kind of masculine grief that could not give itself vent in tears, and, calmly desiring the buriers to let him alone, said he would only see the bodies thrown in and go away; so they left importuning him. But no sooner was the cart turned round and the bodies shot into the pit promiscuously, which was a surprise to him, for he at least expected they would have been decently laid in, though indeed he was afterward convinced that was impracticable—I say, no sooner did he see the sight but he cried out aloud, unable to contain himself.

I could not hear what he said, but he went backward and forward two or three times and fell down in a swoon. The buriers ran to him and took him up, and in a little while he came to himself, and they led him away to the Pye tavern, over against the end of Houndsditch, where it seems the man was known and where they took care of him. He looked into the pit again as he went away, but the buriers had covered the bodies so immediately with throwing in the earth that, though there was light enough, for there were lanterns and candles placed all night round the sides of the pit, yet nothing could be seen.

This was a mournful scene, indeed, and affected me almost as much as the rest, but the other was awful and full of terror. The cart had in it sixteen or seventeen bodies; some were wrapped up in linen sheets, some in rugs, some all but naked or so loose that what covering they had fell from them in being shot out of the cart, for coffins were not to be had for the prodigious numbers that fell in such a calamity as his.

It was reported, by way of scandal upon the buriers, that if any corpse was delivered to them decently wrapped in a winding-sheet, the buriers were so wicked as to strip them in the cart and carry them quite naked to the ground; but as I cannot easily credit anything so vile among Christians, and at a time so filled with terrors as that was, I can only relate it and leave it undetermined.

I was indeed shocked at the whole sight; it almost overwhelmed me, and I went away with my heart full of the most afflicting thoughts, such as I cannot describe. Just at my going out at the church-yard and turning up the street toward my own house I saw another cart with links and a bellman going before, coming out of Harrow Alley, in the Butcher Row, on the other side of the way, and being, as I perceived, very full of dead bodies, it went directly toward the church; I stood awhile, but I had no desire to go back again to see the same dismal scene over again, so I went directly home, where I could not but consider, with thankfulness, the risk I had run.

Here the poor unhappy gentleman's grief came into my head again, and, indeed, I could not but shed tears in reflecting upon it, perhaps more than he did himself; but his case lay so heavy upon my mind that I could not constrain myself from going again to the Pye tavern, resolving to inquire what became of him. It was by this time one o'clock in the morning and the poor gentleman was still there; the truth was the people of the house, knowing him, had kept him there all the night, notwithstanding the danger of being infected by him, though it appeared the man was perfectly sound himself.

It is with regret that I take notice of this tavern: the people were civil, mannerly, and obliging enough, and had till this time kept their house open and their trade going on, though not so very publicly as formerly; but a dreadful set of fellows frequented their house, who, in the midst of all this horror, met there every night, behaved with all the revelling and roaring extravagances as are usual for such people to do at other times, and, indeed, to such an offensive degree that the very master and mistress of the house grew first ashamed and then terrified at them.

They sat generally in a room next the street, and, as they always kept late hours, so when the dead-cart came across the street end to go into Houndsditch, which was in view of the tavern windows, they would frequently open the windows as soon as they heard the bell, and look out at them; and as they might often hear sad lamentations of people in the streets or at their windows as the carts went along, they would make their impudent mocks and jeers at them, especially if they heard the poor people call upon God to have mercy upon them, as many would do at those times in passing along the streets.

These gentlemen, being something disturbed with the clatter of bringing the poor gentleman into the house, as above, were first angry and very high with the master of the house for suffering such a fellow, as they called him, to be brought out of the grave into their house; but being answered that the man was a neighbor, and that he was sound, but overwhelmed with the calamity of his family, and the like, they turned their anger into ridiculing the man and his sorrow for his wife and children; taunting him with want of courage to leap into the great pit and go to heaven, as they jeeringly expressed it, along with them; adding some profane and blasphemous expressions.

They were at this vile work when I came back to the house, and as far as I could see, though the man sat still, mute and disconsolate, and their affronts could not divert his sorrow, yet he was both grieved and offended at their words: upon this, I gently reproved them, being well enough acquainted with their characters, and not unknown in person to two of them. They immediately fell upon me with ill language and oaths: asked me what I did out of my grave at such a time when so many honester men were carried into the church-yard? and why I was not at home saying my prayers till the dead-cart came for me?

I was indeed astonished at the impudence of the men, though not at all discomposed at their treatment of me. However, I kept my temper. I told them that though I defied them or any man in the world to tax me with any dishonesty, yet I acknowledged that in this terrible judgment of God many a better than I was swept away and carried to his grave. But to answer their question directly, it was true that I was mercifully preserved by that great God whose name they had blasphemed and taken in vain by cursing and swearing in a dreadful manner; and that I believed I was preserved in particular, among other ends of his goodness, that I might reprove them for their audacious boldness in behaving in such a manner and in such an awful time as this was; especially for their jeering and mocking at an honest gentleman and a neighbor who they saw was overwhelmed with sorrow for the sufferings with which it had pleased God to afflict his family.

They received all reproof with the utmost contempt and made the greatest mockery that was possible for them to do at me, giving me all the opprobrious, insolent scoffs that they could think of for preaching to them, as they called it, which, indeed, grieved me rather than angered me. I went away, however, blessing God in my mind that I had not spared them though they had insulted me so much.

They continued this wretched course three or four days after this, continually mocking and jeering at all that showed themselves religious or serious, or that were any way touched with a sense of the terrible judgment of God upon us; and I was informed they flouted in the same manner at the good people who, notwithstanding the contagion, met at the church, fasted, and prayed God to remove his hand from them.

I say, they continued this dreadful course three or four days —I think it was no more—when one of them, particularly he who asked the poor gentleman what he did out of his grave, was struck with the plague and died in a most deplorable manner; and in a word, they were every one of them carried into the great pit which I have mentioned above, before it was quite filled up, which was not above a fortnight or thereabout.

GREAT FIRE IN LONDON

A.D. 1666

JOHN EVELYN

In the reign of Charles II—the "Merry Monarch," of whom one of his ministers observed that "he never said a foolish thing and never did a wise one"—the calamities which happened eclipsed the merriment of his people, if not that of the sovereign himself.

In 1666 England had not fully recovered from the civil wars of 1642-1651. She was now at war with the allied Dutch and French, and was suffering from the terrible effects of the "Great Plague" which ravaged London in 1665. During September 2-5, 1666, occurred a catastrophe of almost equal horror. A fire, which broke out in a baker's house near the bridge, spread on all sides so rapidly that the people were unable to extinguish it until two-thirds of the city had been destroyed.

Evelyn's account, from his famous *Diary*, is that of an eye-witness who took a prominent part in dealing with the conflagration, during which the inhabitants of London—like those of some of our cities in recent times—"were reduced to be spectators of their own ruin." Besides suspecting the French and Dutch of having landed and, as Evelyn records, of "firing the town," people assigned various other possible origins for the disaster, charging it upon the republicans, the Catholics, etc. It was obviously due, as Hume thought it worth while to note, to the narrow streets, the houses built entirely of wood, the dry season, and a strong east wind.

"But the fire," says a later writer, "though destroying so much, was most beneficial in thoroughly eradicating the plague. The fever dens in which it continually lurked were burned, and the new houses which were erected were far more healthy and better arranged."

IN the year of our Lord 1666. 2d Sept. This fatal night, about ten, began that deplorable fire near Fish Street, in London.

3. The fire continuing, after dinner I took coach with my wife and son, and went to the Bankside in Southwark, where we beheld that dismal spectacle, the whole city in dreadful flames near the water-side; all the houses from the bridge, all Thames Street, and upward toward Cheapside, down to the Three Cranes, were now consumed.

The fire having continued all this night—if I may call that

night which was as light as day for ten miles round about, after a dreadful manner—when conspiring with a fierce eastern wind in a very dry season; I went on foot to the same place, and saw the whole south part of the city burning from Cheapside to the Thames, and all along Cornhill—for it kindled back against the wind as well as forward—Tower Street, Fenchurch Street, Gracechurch Street, and so along to Bainard's castle, and was now taking hold of St. Paul's Church, to which the scaffolds contributed exceedingly. The conflagration was so universal, and the people so astonished, that from the beginning, I know not by what despondency or fate, they hardly stirred to quench it; so that there was nothing heard or seen but crying out and lamentation, running about like distracted creatures, without at all attempting to save even their goods; such a strange consternation there was upon them, so as it burned both in breadth and length, the churches, public halls, exchange, hospitals, monuments, and ornaments, leaping after a prodigious manner from house to house, and street to street, at great distances one from the other; for the heat, with a long set of fair and warm weather, had even ignited the air and prepared the materials to conceive the fire, which devoured, after an incredible manner, houses, furniture, and everything.

Here we saw the Thames covered with goods floating, all the barges and boats laden with what some had time and courage to save, as, on the other, the carts, etc., carrying out to the fields, which for many miles were strewed with movables of all sorts, and tents erecting to shelter both people and what goods they could get away. Oh, the miserable and calamitous spectacle! such as haply the world had not seen the like since the foundation of it, nor be outdone till the universal conflagration. All the sky was of a fiery aspect, like the top of a burning oven, the light seen above forty miles round about for many nights.

God grant my eyes may never behold the like, now seeing above ten thousand houses all in one flame; the noise, and cracking, and thunder of the impetuous flames, the shrieking of women and children, the hurry of people, the fall of towers, houses, and churches was like a hideous storm, and the air all about so hot and inflamed that at last one was not able to approach it; so that they were forced to stand still and let the flames burn on, which they did for near two miles in length and one in breadth. The clouds of smoke were dismal, and reached, upon computation, near fifty miles in length. Thus I left it this afternoon burning, a resemblance of Sodom or the last day. London was, but is no more!

4. The burning still rages, and it has now gotten as far as the Inner Temple, all Fleet Street, the Old Bailey, Ludgate Hill, Warwick Lane, Newgate, Paul's Chain, Watling Street, now flaming, and most of it reduced to ashes; the stones of St. Paul's flew like granados, the melting lead running down the streets in a stream, and the very pavements glowing with fiery redness, so as no horse nor man was able to tread on them, and the demolition had stopped all the passages, so that no help could be applied. The eastern wind still more impetuously drove the flames forward. Nothing but the almighty power of God was able to stop them, for vain was the help of man.

5. It crossed toward Whitehall; oh, the confusion there was then at that court! It pleased his majesty to command me among the rest to look after the quenching of Fetter Lane, and to preserve, if possible, that part of Holborn, while the rest of the gentlemen took their several posts—for now they began to bestir themselves, and not till now, who hitherto had stood as men intoxicated, with their hands across—and began to consider that nothing was likely to put a stop, but the blowing up of so many houses might make a wider gap than any had yet been made by the ordinary method of pulling them down with engines; this some stout seamen proposed early enough to have saved nearly the whole city, but this some tenacious and avaricious men, aldermen, etc., would not permit, because their houses must have been of the first.

It was therefore now commanded to be practised, and my concern being particularly for the hospital of St. Bartholomew, near Smithfield, where I had many wounded and sick men, made me the more diligent to promote it, nor was my care for the Savoy less. It now pleased God, by abating the wind, and by the industry of the people, infusing a new spirit into them, and the fury of it began sensibly to abate about noon, so as it came no further than the Temple westward, nor than the entrance of Smithfield north; but continued all this day and night so impetuous toward Cripplegate and the Tower, as made us all despair. It also broke out again in the Temple, but the courage of the multitude persisting, and many houses being blown up, such gaps and desolations were soon made, as with the former three-days' consumption, the back fire did not so vehemently urge upon the rest as formerly. There was yet no standing near the burning and glowing ruins by near a furlong's space.

The coal and wood wharfs, and magazines of oil, resin, etc., did infinite mischief, so as the invective which a little before I had dedicated to his majesty and published, giving warning what might probably be the issue of suffering those shops to be in the city, was looked on as a prophecy.

The poor inhabitants were dispersed about St. George's Fields and Moorfields, as far as Highgate, and several miles in circle, some under tents, some under miserable huts and hovels, many without a rag, or any necessary utensils, bed, or board; who, from delicateness, riches, and easy accommodations in stately and well-furnished houses, were now reduced to extremest misery and poverty.

In this calamitous condition I returned with a sad heart to my house, blessing and adoring the mercy of God to me and mine, who in the midst of all this ruin was like Lot, in my little Zoar, safe and sound.

7. I went this morning on foot from Whitehall as far as London bridge, through the late Fleet Street, Ludgate Hill, by St. Paul's, Cheapside, Exchange, Bishopsgate, Aldersgate, and out to Moorfields, thence through Cornhill, etc., with extraordinary difficulty clambering over heaps of yet smoking rubbish, and frequently mistaking where I was. The ground under my feet was so hot that it even burned the soles of my shoes.

In the mean time his majesty got to the Tower by water, to demolish the houses about the graff, which, being built entirely about it, had they taken fire, and attacked the White Tower, where the magazine of powder lay, would undoubtedly not only have beaten down and destroyed all the bridge, but sunk and torn the vessels in the river, and rendered the demolition beyond all expression for several miles about the country.

At my return I was infinitely concerned to find that goodly church, St. Paul's, now a sad ruin, and that beautiful portico—

or structure comparable to any in Europe, as not long before repaired by the King—now rent in pieces, flakes of vast stones split asunder, and nothing remaining entire but the inscription in the architrave, showing by whom it was built, which had not one letter of it defaced. It was astonishing to see what immense stones the heat had in a manner calcined, so that all the ornaments, columns, friezes, and projectures of massy Portland stone flew off, even to the very roof, where a sheet of lead covering a great space was totally melted; the ruins of the vaulted roof falling broke into St. Faith's, which being filled with the magazines of books belonging to the stationers, and carried thither for safety, they were all consumed, burning for a week following.

It is also observable that the lead over the altar at the east end was untouched, and among the divers monuments the body of one bishop remained entire. Thus lay in ashes that most venerable church, one of the most ancient pieces of early piety in the Christian world, besides near one hundred more. The lead, ironwork, bells, plate, etc., melted; the exquisitely wrought Mercer's Chapel, the sumptuous Exchange, the august fabric of Christ Church, all the rest of the Companies' Halls, sumptuous buildings, arches, all in dust; the fountains dried up and ruined, while the very waters remained boiling; the *voragoes* of subterranean cellars, wells, and dungeons, formerly warehouses, still burning in stench and dark clouds of smoke, so that in five or six miles traversing about I did not see one load of timber unconsumed, nor many stones but what were calcined white as snow.

The people who now walked about the ruins appeared like men in a dismal desert, or rather in some great city laid waste by a cruel enemy: to which was added the stench that came from some poor creatures' bodies, beds, etc. Sir Thomas Gresham's statue, though fallen from its niche in the Royal Exchange, remained entire, when all those of the kings since the Conquest were broken to pieces; also the standard in Cornhill, and Queen Elizabeth's effigies, with some arms on Ludgate, continued with but little detriment, while the vast iron chains of the city streets, hinges, bars, and gates of prisons, were many of them melted and reduced to cinders by the vehement heat.

I was not able to pass through any of the narrow streets, but kept the widest; the ground and air, smoke and fiery vapor, continued so intense that my hair was almost singed and my feet insufferably surheated. The by-lanes and narrower streets were quite filled up with rubbish, nor could one have known where he was but by the ruins of some church or hall that had some remarkable tower or pinnacle remaining. I then went toward Islington and Highgate, where one might have seen two hundred thousand people of all ranks and degrees, dispersed and lying along by their heaps of what they could save from the fire, deploring their loss, and, though ready to perish for hunger and destitution, yet not asking one penny for relief, which to me appeared a stranger sight than any I had yet beheld.

His majesty and council, indeed, took all imaginable care for their relief, by proclamation for the country to come in and refresh them with provisions. In the midst of all this calamity and confusion there was, I know not how, an alarm begun that the French and Dutch, with whom we are now in hostility, were not only landed, but even entering the city. There was in truth some days before great suspicion of these two nations joining; and now, that they had been the occasion of firing the town. This report did so terrify that on a sudden there was such an uproar and tumult that they ran from their goods, and, taking what weapons they could come at, they could not be stopped from falling on some of those nations whom they casually met, without sense or reason.

The clamor and peril grew so excessive that it made the whole court amazed, and they did with infinite pains and great difficulty reduce and appease the people, sending troops of soldiers and guards to cause them to retire into the fields again, where they were watched all this night. I left them pretty quiet, and came home sufficiently weary and broken. Their spirits thus a little calmed, and the affright abated, they now began to repair into the suburbs about the city, where such as had friends or opportunity got shelter for the present, to which his majesty's proclamation also invited them.

DISCOVERY OF GRAVITATION

A.D. 1666

SIR DAVID BREWSTER

Many admirers of Sir Isaac Newton have asserted that his was the most gigantic intellect ever bestowed on man. He discovered the law of gravitation, and by it explained all the broader phenomena of nature, such as the movements of the planets, the shape and revolution of the earth, the succession of the tides. Copernicus had asserted that the planets moved, Newton demonstrated it mathematically.

His discoveries in optics were in his own time almost equally famous, while in his later life he shared with Leibnitz the honor of inventing the infinitesimal calculus, a method which lies at the root of all the intricate marvels of modern mathematical science.

Newton should not, however, be regarded as an isolated phenomenon, a genius but for whom the world would have remained in darkness. His first flashing idea of gravitation deserves perhaps to be called an inspiration. But in all his other labors, experimental as well as mathematical, he was but following the spirit of the times. The love of science was abroad, and its infinite curiosity. Each of Newton's discoveries was claimed also by other men who had been working along similar lines. Of the dispute over the gravitation theory Sir David Brewster, the great authority for the career of Newton, gives some account. The controversy over the calculus was even more bitter and prolonged.

It were well, however, to disabuse one's mind of the idea that Newton's work was a finality, that it settled anything. As to why the law of gravitation exists, why bodies tend to come together, the philosopher had little suggestion to offer, and the present generation knows no more than he. Before Copernicus and Newton men looked only with their eyes, and accepted the apparent movements of sun and stars as real. Now, going one step deeper, we look with our brains and see their real movements which underlie appearances. Newton supplied us with the law and rate of the movement—but not its cause. It is toward that cause, that great "Why?" that science has ever since been dimly groping.

IN the year 1666, when the plague had driven Newton from Cambridge, he was sitting alone in the garden at Woolsthrope, and reflecting on the nature of gravity, that remarkable power which causes all bodies to descend toward the centre of the earth. As this power is not found to suffer any sensible diminution at the greatest distance from the earth's centre to which we can reach—being as powerful at the tops of the highest mountains as at the bottom of the deepest mines—he conceived it highly probable that it must extend much further than was usually supposed. No sooner had this happy conjecture occurred to his mind than he considered what would be the effect of its extending as far as the moon. That her motion must be influenced by such a power he did not for a moment doubt; and a little reflection convinced him that it might be sufficient for retaining that luminary in her orbit round the earth.

Though the force of gravity suffers no sensible diminution at those small distances from the earth's centre at which we can place ourselves, yet he thought it very possible that, at the distance of the moon, it might differ much in strength from what it is on the earth. In order to form some estimate of the degree of its diminution, he considered that, if the moon be retained in her orbit by the force of gravity, the primary planets must also be carried round the sun by the same power; and by comparing the periods of the different planets with their distances from the sun he found that, if they were retained in their orbits by any power like gravity, its force must decrease in the duplicate proportion, or as the squares of their distances from the sun. In drawing this conclusion, he supposed the planets to move in orbits perfectly circular, and having the sun in their centre. Having thus obtained the law of the force by which the planets were drawn to the sun, his next object was to ascertain if such a force emanating from the earth, and directed to the moon, was sufficient, when diminished in the duplicate ratio of the distance, to retain her in her orbit.

In performing this calculation it was necessary to compare the space through which heavy bodies fall in a second at a given distance from the centre of the earth, viz., at its surface, with the space through which the moon, as it were, falls to the earth in a second of time while revolving in a circular orbit. Being at a distance from books when he made this computation, he adopted the common estimate of the earth's diameter then in use among geographers and navigators, and supposed that each degree of latitude contained sixty English miles.

In this way he found that the force which retains the moon in her orbit, as deduced from the force which occasions the fall of heavy bodies to the earth's surface, was one-sixth greater than that which is actually observed in her circular orbit. This difference threw a doubt upon all his speculations; but, unwilling to abandon what seemed to be otherwise so plausible, he endeavored to account for the difference of the two forces by supposing that some other cause must have been united with the force of gravity in producing so great velocity of the moon in her circular orbit. As this new cause, however, was beyond the reach of observation, he discontinued all further inquiries into the subject, and concealed from his friends the speculations in which he had been employed.

After his return to Cambridge in 1666 his attention was occupied with optical discoveries; but he had no sooner brought them to a close than his mind reverted to the great subject of the planetary motions. Upon the death of Oldenburg in August, 1678, Dr. Hooke was appointed secretary to the Royal Society; and as this learned body had requested the opinion of Newton about a system of physical astronomy, he addressed a letter to Dr. Hooke on November 28, 1679. In this letter he proposed a direct experiment for verifying the motion of the earth, viz., by observing whether or not bodies that fall from a considerable height descend in a vertical direction; for if the earth were at rest the body would describe exactly a vertical line; whereas if it revolved round its axis, the falling body must deviate from the vertical line toward the east.

The Royal Society attached great value to the idea thus casually suggested, and Dr. Hooke was appointed to put it to the test of experiment. Being thus led to consider the subject more attentively, he wrote to Newton that wherever the direction of gravity was oblique to the axis on which the earth revolved, that is, in every part of the earth except the equator, falling bodies should approach to the equator, and the deviation from the vertical, in place of being exactly to the east, as Newton maintained, should be to the southeast of the point from which the body began to move.

Newton acknowledged that this conclusion was correct in theory, and Dr. Hooke is said to have given an experimental demonstration of it before the Royal Society in December, 1679.

Newton had erroneously concluded that the path of the falling body would be a spiral; but Dr. Hooke, on the same occasion on which he made the preceding experiment, read a paper to the society in which he proved that the path of the body would be an eccentric ellipse *in vacuo*, and an ellipti-spiral if the body moved in a resisting medium.

This correction of Newton's error, and the discovery that a projectile would move in an elliptical orbit when under the influence of a force varying in the inverse ratio of the square of the distance, led Newton, as he himself informs us in his letter to Halley, to discover "the theorem by which he afterward examined the ellipsis," and to demonstrate the celebrated proposition that a planet acted upon by an attractive force varying inversely as the squares of the distances, will describe an elliptical orbit in one of whose *foci* the attractive force resides.

But though Newton had thus discovered the true cause of all the celestial motions, he did not yet possess any evidence that such a force actually resided in the sun and planets. The failure of his former attempt to identify the law of falling bodies at the earth's surface with that which guided the moon in her orbit, threw a doubt over all his speculations, and prevented him from giving any account of them to the public.

An accident, however, of a very interesting nature induced him to resume his former inquiries, and enabled him to bring them to a close. In June, 1682, when he was attending a meeting of the Royal Society of London, the measurement of a degree of the meridian, executed by M. Picard in 1679, became the subject of conversation. Newton took a memorandum of the result obtained by the French astronomer, and having deduced from it the diameter of the earth, he immediately resumed his calculation of 1665, and began to repeat it with these new data. In the progress of the calculation he saw that the result which he had formerly expected was likely to be produced, and he was thrown into such a state of nervous irritability that he was unable to carry on the calculation. In this state of mind he intrusted it to one of his friends, and he had the high satisfaction of finding his former views amply realized. The force of gravity which regulated the fall of bodies at the earth's surface, when diminished as the square of the moon's distance from the earth, was found to be almost exactly equal to the centrifugal force of the moon as deduced from her observed distance and velocity.

The influence of such a result upon such a mind may be more easily conceived than described. The whole material universe was spread out before him; the sun with all his attending planets; the planets with all their satellites; the comets wheeling in every direction in their eccentric orbits; and the systems of the fixed stars stretching to the remotest limits of space. All the varied and complicated movements of the heavens, in short, must have been at once presented to his mind as the necessary result of that law which he had established in reference to the earth and the moon.

After extending this law to the other bodies of the system, he composed a series of propositions on the motion of the primary planets about the sun, which were sent to London about the end of 1683, and were soon afterward communicated to the Royal Society.

About this period other philosophers had been occupied with the same subject. Sir Christopher Wren had many years before endeavored to explain the planetary motions "by the composition of a descent toward the sun, and an impressed motion; but he at length gave it over, not finding the means of doing it." In January, 1683–1684, Dr. Halley had concluded from Kepler's law of the periods and distances, that the centripetal force decreased in the reciprocal proportion of the squares of the distances, and having one day met Sir Christopher Wren and Dr. Hooke, the latter affirmed that he had demonstrated upon that principle all the laws of the celestial motions. Dr. Halley confessed that his attempts were unsuccessful, and Sir Christopher, in order to encourage the inquiry, offered to present a book of forty shillings value to either of the two philosophers who should, in the space of two months, bring him a convincing demonstration of it. Hooke persisted in the declaration that he possessed the method, but avowed it to be his intention to conceal it for time. He promised, however, to show it to Sir Christopher; but there is every reason to believe that this promise was never fulfilled.

In August, 1684, Dr. Halley went to Cambridge for the express purpose of consulting Newton on this interesting subject. Newton assured him that he had brought this demonstration to perfection, and promised him a copy of it. This copy was received in November by the doctor, who made a second visit to Cambridge, in order to induce its author to have it inserted in the register book of the society. On December 10th Dr. Halley announced to the society that he had seen at Cambridge Newton's treatise *De Motu Corporum*, which he had promised to send to the society to be entered upon their register, and Dr. Halley was desired to unite with Mr. Paget, master of the mathematical school in Christ's Hospital, in reminding Newton of his promise, "for securing the invention to himself till such time as he can be at leisure to publish it."

On February 25th Mr. Aston, the secretary, communicated a letter from Newton in which he expressed his willingness "to enter in the register his notions about motion, and his intentions to fit them suddenly for the press." The progress of his work was, however, interrupted by a visit of five or six weeks which he made in Lincolnshire; but he proceeded with such diligence on his return that he was able to transmit the manuscript to London before the end of April. This manuscript, entitled *Philosophiæ Naturalis Principia Mathematica*, and dedicated to the society, was presented by Dr. Vincent on April 28, 1686, when Sir John Hoskins, the vice-president and the particular friend of Dr. Hooke, was in the chair.

Dr. Vincent passed a just encomium on the novelty and dignity of the subject; and another member added that "Mr. Newton had carried the thing so far that there was no more to be added." To these remarks the vice-president replied that the method "was so much the more to be prized as it was both invented and perfected at the same time." Dr. Hooke took offence at these remarks, and blamed Sir John for not having mentioned "what he had discovered to him"; but the vice-president did not seem to recollect any such communication, and the consequence of this discussion was that "these two, who till then were the most inseparable cronies, have since scarcely seen one another, and are utterly fallen out." After the breaking up of the meeting, the society adjourned to the coffee-house, where Dr. Hooke stated that he not only had made the same discovery, but had given the first hint of it to Newton.

An account of these proceedings was communicated to Newton through two different channels. In a letter dated May 22d Dr. Halley wrote to him "that Mr. Hooke has some pretensions upon the invention of the rule of the decrease of gravity being reciprocally as the squares of the distances from the centre. He says you had the notion from him, though he owns the demonstration of the curves generated thereby to be wholly your own. How much of this is so you know best, as likewise what you have to do in this matter; only Mr. Hooke seems to expect you would make some mention of him in the preface, which it is possible you may see reason to prefix."

This communication from Dr. Halley induced the author, on June 20th, to address a long letter to him, in which he gives a minute and able refutation of Hooke's claims; but before this letter was despatched another correspondent, who had received his information from one of the members that were present, informed Newton "that Hooke made a great stir, pretending that he had all from him, and desiring they would see that he had justice done him." This fresh charge seems to have ruffled the tranquillity of Newton; and he accordingly added an angry and satirical postscript, in which he treats Hooke with little ceremony, and goes so far as to conjecture that Hooke might have acquired his knowledge of the law from a letter of his own to Huygens, directed to Oldenburg, and dated January 14, 1672–1673. "My letter to Hugenius was directed to Mr. Oldenburg, who used to keep the originals. His papers came into Mr. Hooke's possession. Mr. Hooke, knowing my hand, might have the curiosity to look into that letter, and there take the notion of comparing the forces of the planets arising from their circular motion; and so what he wrote to me afterward about the rate of gravity might be nothing but the fruit of my own garden."

In replying to this letter Dr. Halley assured him that Hooke's "manner of claiming the discovery had been represented to him in worse colors than it ought, and that he neither made public application to the society for justice nor pretended that you had all from him." The effect of this assurance was to make Newton regret that he had written the angry postscript to his letter; and in replying to Halley on July 14, 1686, he not only expresses his regret, but recounts the different new ideas which he had acquired from Hooke's correspondence, and suggests it as the best method "of compromising the present dispute" to add a *scholium* in which Wren, Hooke, and Halley are acknowledged to have independently deduced the law of gravity from the second law of Kepler.

At the meeting of April 28th, at which the manuscript of the *Principia* was presented to the Royal Society, it was agreed that the printing of it should be referred to the council: that a letter of thanks should be written to its author; and at a meeting of the council on May 19th it was resolved that the manuscript should be printed at the society's expense, and that Dr. Halley should superintend it while going through the press. These resolutions were communicated by Dr. Halley in a letter dated May 22d; and in Newton's reply on June 20th, already mentioned, he makes the following observations:

"The proof you sent me I like very well. I designed the whole to consist of three books; the second was finished last summer, being short, and only wants transcribing and drawing the cuts fairly. Some new propositions I have since thought on which I can as well let alone. The third wants the theory of comets. In autumn last I spent two months in calculation to no purpose, for want of a good method, which made me afterward return to the first book and enlarge it with diverse propositions, some relating to comets, others to other things found out last winter. The third I now design to suppress. Philosophy is such an impertinently litigious lady that a man had as good be engaged in lawsuits as have to do with her. I found it so formerly, and now I can no sooner come near her again but she gives me warning. The first two books, without the third, will not so well bear the title of *Philosophiæ Naturalis Principia Mathematica;* and therefore I had altered it to this: *de Moti Corporum, Libri duo.* But after second thoughts I retain the former title. 'Twill help the sale of the book, which I ought not to diminish now 'tis yours."

In replying to this letter on June 29th Dr. Halley regrets that our author's tranquillity should have been thus disturbed by envious rivals, and implores him in the name of the society not to suppress the third book. "I must again beg you," says he, "not to let your resentments run so high as to deprive us of your third book, wherein your applications of your mathematical doctrine to the theory of comets, and several curious experiments which, as I guess by what you write ought to compose it, will undoubtedly render it acceptable to those who will call themselves philosophers without mathematics, which are much the greater number."

To these solicitations Newton seems to have readily yielded. His second book was sent to the society, and presented on March 2, 1687. The third book was also transmitted, and presented on April 6th, and the whole work was completed and published in the month of May, 1687.

Such is the brief account of the publication of a work which is memorable not only in the annals of one science or of one country, but which will form an epoch in the history of the world, and will ever be regarded as the brightest page in the records of human reason. We shall endeavor to convey to the reader some idea of its contents, and of the brilliant discoveries which it disseminated over Europe.

The *Principia* consists of three books. The first and second, which occupy three-fourths of the work, are entitled *On the Motion of Bodies*, and the third bears the title *On the System of the World.* The two first books contain the mathematical principles of philosophy, namely, the laws and conditions of motions and forces; and they are illustrated with several philosophical *scholia* which treat of some of the most general and best-established points in philosophy, such as the density and resistance of bodies, spaces void of matter, and the motion of sound and light. The object of the third book is to deduce from these principles the constitution of the system of the world; and this book has been drawn up in as popular a style as possible, in order that it may be generally read.

The great discovery which characterizes the *Principia* is that of the principle of universal gravitation, as deduced from the motion of the moon, and from the three great facts or laws discovered by Kepler. This principle is: *That every particle of matter is attracted by or gravitates to every other particle of matter, with a force inversely proportional to the squares of their distances.* From the first law of Kepler, namely, the proportionality of the areas to the times of their revolution, Newton inferred that the force which kept the planet in its orbit was always directed to the sun; and from the second law of Kepler, that every planet moves in an ellipse with the sun in one of its foci, he drew the still more general inference that the force by which the planet moves round that focus varies inversely as the square of its distance from the focus. As this law was true in the motion of satellites round their primary planets Newton deduced the equality of gravity in all the heavenly bodies toward the sun, upon the supposition that they are equally distant from its centre; and in the case of terrestrial bodies he succeeded in verifying this truth by numerous and accurate experiments.

By taking a more general view of the subject Newton demonstrated that a conic section was the only curve in which a body could move when acted upon by a force varying inversely as the square of the distance; and he established the conditions depending on the velocity and the primitive position of the body, which were requisite to make it describe a circular, an elliptical, a parabolic, or a hyberbolic orbit.

Notwithstanding the generality and importance of these results, it still remained to be determined whether the forces resided in the centres of the planets or belonged to each individual particle of which they were composed. Newton removed this uncertainty by demonstrating that if a spherical body acts upon a distant body with a force varying as the distance of this body from the centre of the sphere, the same effect will be produced as if each of its particles acted upon the distant body according to the same law. And hence it follows that the spheres, whether they are of uniform density or consist of concentric layers, with densities varying according to any law whatever, will act upon each other in the same manner as if their force resided in their centres alone.

But as the bodies of the solar system are very nearly spherical they will all act upon one another, and upon bodies placed on their surfaces, as if they were so many centres of attraction; and therefore we obtain the law of gravity which subsists between spherical bodies, namely, that one sphere will act upon another with a force directly proportional to the quantity of matter, and inversely as the square of the distance between the centres of the spheres. From the equality of action and reaction, to which no exception can be found, Newton concluded that the sun gravitated to the planets, and the planets to their satellites; and the earth itself to the stone which falls upon its surface, and, consequently, that the two mutually gravitating bodies approached to one another with velocities inversely proportional to their quantities of matter.

Having established this universal law, Newton was enabled not only to determine the weight which the same body would have at the surface of the sun and the planets, but even to calculate the quantity of matter in the sun, and in all the planets that had satellites, and even to determine the density or specific gravity of the matter of which they were composed. In this way he found that the weight of the same body would be twenty-three times greater at the surface of the sun than at the surface of the earth, and that the density of the earth was four times greater than that of the sun, the planets increasing in density as they receded from the centre of the system.

If the peculiar genius of Newton has been displayed in his investigation of the law of universal gravitation, it shines with no less lustre in the patience and sagacity with which he traced the consequences of this fertile principle. The discovery of the spheroidal form of Jupiter by Cassini had probably directed the attention of Newton to the determination of its cause, and consequently to the investigation of the true figure of the earth. The next subject to which Newton applied the principle of gravity was the tides of the ocean.

The philosophers of all ages had recognized the connection between the phenomena of the tides and the position of the moon. The College of Jesuits at Coimbra, and subsequently Antonio de Dominis and Kepler, distinctly referred the tides to the attraction of the waters of the earth by the moon; but so imperfect was the explanation which was thus given of the phenomena that Galileo ridiculed the idea of lunar attraction, and substituted for it a fallacious explanation of his own. That the moon is the principal cause of the tides is obvious from the well-known fact that it is high water at any given place about the time when she is in the meridian of that place; and that the sun performs a secondary part in their production may be proved from the circumstance that the highest tides take place when the sun, the moon, and the earth are in the same straight line; that is, when the force of the sun conspires with that of the moon; and that the lowest tides take place when the lines drawn from the sun and moon to the earth are at right angles to each other; that is, when the force of the sun acts in opposition to that of the moon.

By comparing the spring and neap tides Newton found that the force with which the moon acted upon the waters of the earth was to that with which the sun acted upon them as 4.48 to 1; that the force of the moon produced a tide of 8.63 feet; that of the sun, one of 1.93 feet; and both of them combined, one of 10½ French feet, a result which in the open sea does not deviate much from observation. Having thus ascertained the force of the moon on the waters of our globe, he found that the quantity of matter in the moon was to that in the earth as 1 to 40, and the density of the moon to that of the earth as 11 to 9.

The motions of the moon, so much within the reach of our own observation, presented a fine field for the application of the theory of universal gravitation. The irregularities exhibited in the lunar motions had been known in the time of Hipparchus and Ptolemy. Tycho had discovered the great inequality, called the "variation," amounting to 37′, and depending on the alternate acceleration and retardation of the moon in every quarter of a revolution, and he had also ascertained the existence of the annual equation. Of these two inequalities Newton gave a most satisfactory explanation.

Although there could be little doubt that the comets were retained in their orbits by the same laws which regulated the motions of the planets, yet it was difficult to put this opinion to the test of observation. The visibility of comets only in a small part of their orbits rendered it difficult to ascertain their distance and periodic times; and as their periods were probably of great length, it was impossible to correct approximate results by repeated observations. Newton, however, removed this difficulty by showing how to determine the orbit of a comet, namely, the form and position of the orbit, and the periodic time, by three observations. By applying this method to the comet of 1680 he calculated the elements of its orbit, and, from the agreement of the computed places with those which were observed, he justly inferred that the motions of comets were regulated by the same laws as those of the planetary bodies. This result was one of great importance; for as the comets enter our system in every possible direction, and at all angles with the ecliptic, and as a great part of their orbits extends far beyond the limits of the solar system, it demonstrated the existence of gravity in spaces far removed beyond the planet, and proved that the law of the inverse ratio of the squares of the distance was true in every possible direction, and at very remote distances from the centre of our system.

Such is a brief view of the leading discoveries which the *Principia* first announced to the world. The grandeur of the subjects of which it treats, the beautiful simplicity of the system which it unfolds, the clear and concise reasoning by which that system is explained, and the irresistible evidence by which it is supported might have insured it the warmest admiration of contemporary mathematicians and the most welcome reception in all the schools of philosophy throughout Europe. This, however, is not the way in which great truths are generally received. Though the astronomical discoveries of Newton were not assailed by the class of ignorant pretenders who attacked his optical writings, yet they were everywhere resisted by the errors and prejudices which had taken a deep hold even of the strongest minds.

The philosophy of Descartes was predominant throughout Europe. Appealing to the imagination, and not to the reason, of mankind it was quickly received into popular favor, and the same causes which facilitated its introduction, extended its influence and completed its dominion over the human mind. In explaining all the movements of the heavenly bodies by a system of vortices in a fluid medium diffused through the universe Descartes had seized upon an analogy of the most alluring and deceitful kind. Those who had seen heavy bodies revolving in the eddies of a whirlpool or in the gyrations of a vessel of water thrown into a circular motion had no difficulty in conceiving how the planets might revolve round the sun by an analogous movement. The mind instantly grasped at an explanation of so palpable a character and which required for its development neither the exercise of patient thought nor the aid of mathematical skill. The talent and perspicuity with which the Cartesian system was expounded, and the show by which it was sustained, contributed powerfully to its adoption, while it derived a still higher sanction from the excellent character and the unaffected piety of its author.

Thus intrenched, as the Cartesian system was, in the strongholds of the human mind, and fortified by its most obstinate prejudices, it was not to be wondered at that the pure and sublime doctrines of the *Principia* were distrustfully received and perseveringly resisted. The uninstructed mind could not readily admit the idea that the great masses of the planets were suspended in empty space and retained in their orbits by an invisible influence residing in the sun; and even those philosophers who had been accustomed to the rigor of true scientific research, and who possessed sufficient mathematical skill for the examination of the Newtonian doctrines, viewed them at first as reviving the occult qualities of the ancient physics, and resisted their introduction with a pertinacity which it is not easy to explain.

Prejudiced, no doubt, in favor of his own metaphysical views, Leibnitz himself misapprehended the principles of the Newtonian philosophy, and endeavored to demonstrate the truths in the *Principia* by the application of different principles. Huygens, who above all other men was qualified to appreciate the new philosophy, rejected the doctrine of gravitation as existing between the individual particles of matter and received it only as an attribute of the planetary masses. John Bernouilli, one of the first mathematicians of his age, opposed the philosophy of Newton. Mairan, in the early part of his life, was a strenuous defender of the system of vortices. Cassini and Maraldi were quite ignorant of the *Principia*, and occupied themselves with the most absurd methods of calculating the orbits of comets long after the Newtonian method had been established on the most impregnable foundation; and even Fontenelle, a man of liberal views and extensive information, continued, throughout the whole of his life, to maintain the doctrines of Descartes.

The chevalier Louville of Paris had adopted the Newtonian philosophy before 1720; Gravesande had introduced it into the Dutch universities at a somewhat earlier period; and Maupertuis, in consequence of a visit which he paid to England in 1728, became a zealous defender of it; but notwithstanding these and some other examples that might be quoted, we must admit the truth of the remark of Voltaire, that though Newton survived the publication of the *Principia* more than forty years, yet at the time of his death he had not above twenty followers out of England.

MORGAN, THE BUCCANEER, SACKS PANAMA

A.D. 1671

JOHANN W. VON ARCHENHOLZ

In the seventeenth century appeared "a class of rovers wholly distinct from any of their predecessors in the annals of the world, differing as widely in their plans, organizations, and exploits as in the principles that governed their actions." These adventurers were a piratical gang called buccaneers, or sometimes, as in the following narrative, freebooters, who became noted for their exploits in the West Indies and on South American coasts.

The nucleus of this association of pirates is traced to bands of smugglers—English, French, and Dutch—who carried on a secret trade with the island of Santo Domingo. Later they settled there and on other islands, and after a while began to prey upon Spanish commerce. In 1630 they made their chief head-quarters on the island of Tortuga; in 1655 they aided in the English conquest of Jamaica, and ten years later settled the Bahamas. All these islands became centres of their activities.

Most renowned among the leaders of the buccaneers was Sir Henry Morgan, a Welshman, who died in Jamaica in 1688. For years he carried stolen riches to England, and Charles II rewarded him with knighthood. Having pillaged parts of Cuba, he took and ransomed Puerto Bello, in Colombia (1668), and Maracaibo, in Venezuela (1669). In 1670 Morgan gathered a fleet of nearly forty vessels, and a force of over two thousand men, for the greatest of the exploits of the buccaneers, the capture and plunder of the wealthy city of Panama.

By the end of the century the buccaneers had become dispersed among contending European armies, and little more was heard of them.

MORGAN'S plan of capturing Panama was apparently attended with innumerable difficulties. The chief obstacle was the position of that city on the Pacific coast at such a great distance from the Caribbean Sea; and not an individual on board the fleet was acquainted with the road that led to the goal. To remedy this inconvenience, Morgan determined, in the first instance, to go to the island of St. Catharine, where the Spaniards confined their criminals, and thence to supply himself with guides.

The passage was rapid. Morgan landed in that island one thousand men, who, by threatening to put to death everyone that hesitated for a moment to surrender, so terrified the Spaniards that they speedily capitulated. It was stipulated that, to save at least the honor of the garrison, there should be a sham fight. In consequence of this, a very sharp fire ensued, from the forts on one side, and on the other from the ships; but on both sides the cannons discharged only powder. Further, to give a serious appearance to this military comedy, the governor suffered himself to be taken, while attempting to pass from Fort Jerome to another fort. At the beginning the crafty Morgan did not rely too implicitly on this feint; and to provide for every event, he secretly ordered his soldiers to load their fusees with bullets, but to discharge them in the air, unless they perceived some treachery on the part of the Spaniards. But his enemies adhered most faithfully to their capitulation; and this mock engagement, in which neither party was sparing of powder, was followed for some time with all the circumstances which could give it the semblance of reality. Ten forts surrendered, one after another, after sustaining a kind of siege or assault; and this series of successes did not cost the life of a single man, nor even a scratch, on the part either of the victors or of the conquered.

All the inhabitants of the island were shut up in the great fort of Santa Teresa, which was built on a steep rock; and the conquerors, who had not taken any sustenance for twenty-four hours, declared a most serious war against the horned cattle and game of the district.

In the isle of St. Constantine Morgan found four hundred fifty-nine persons of both sexes; one hundred ninety of whom were soldiers, forty-two criminals, eighty-five children, and sixty-six negroes. There were ten forts, containing sixty-eight cannons, which were so defended in other respects by nature that very small garrisons were deemed amply sufficient to protect them. Besides an immense quantity of fusees and grenades—which were at that time much used—upward of three hundred quintals of gunpowder were found in the arsenal. The whole of this ammunition was carried on board the pirate's ships; the cannon, which could be of no service to them, were spiked; their carriages were burned, and all the forts demolished excepting one, which the freebooters themselves garrisoned. Morgan selected three of the criminals to serve him as guides to Panama. These he afterward, on his return to Jamaica, set at liberty, even giving them a share in the booty.

The plan, conceived by this intrepid chieftain, inspired all his companions in arms with genuine enthusiasm; it had a character of grandeur and audacity that inflamed their courage; how capable they were of executing it the subsequent pages will demonstrate.

Panama, which stood on the shore of the Pacific Ocean, in the ninth degree of northern latitude, was at that time one of the greatest, as well as most opulent cities in America. It contained two thousand large houses, the greater number of which were very fine piles of building, and five thousand smaller dwellings, each mostly three stories in height. Of these, a pretty considerable number were erected of stone, all the rest of cedar-wood, very elegantly constructed and magnificently furnished. That city was defended by a rampart and was surrounded with walls. It was the emporium for the silver of Mexico and the gold of Peru, whence those valuable metals were brought on the backs of mules—two thousand of which animals were kept for this purpose only—across the isthmus toward the northern coast of the Pacific. A great commerce was also carried on at Panama in negroes; which trade was at that time almost exclusively confined to the English, Dutch, French, and Danes. With this branch of commerce the Italians were intimately acquainted. They gave lessons in it to all the rest of Europe; and, as two things were necessary, in which the Genoese were by no means deficient—money and address—they were chiefly occupied in the slave trade, and supplied the provinces of Peru and Chile with negroes.

At the period now referred to, the President of Panama was the principal intendant or overseer of the civil department, and captain-general of all the troops in the viceroyalty of Peru. He had in his dependency Puerto Bello and Nata, two cities inhabited by the Spaniards, together with the towns of Cruces, Panama, Capira, and Veragua. The city of Panama had also a bishop, who was a suffragan of the Archbishop of Lima.

The merchants lived in great opulence; and their churches

were decorated with uncommon magnificence. The cathedral was erected in the Italian style, surmounted with a large cupola, and enriched with gold and silver ornaments; as also were the eight convents which this city comprised. At a small distance from its walls there were some small islands, alike embellished by art and by nature, where the richest inhabitants had their country houses; from which circumstance they were called the "gardens of Panama." In short, everything concurred to render this place important and agreeable. Here several of the European nations had palaces for carrying on their commerce; and among these were the Genoese, who were held in great credit, and who had vast warehouses for receiving the articles of their immense trade, as also a most magnificent edifice. The principal houses were filled with beautiful paintings and the masterpieces of the arts, which had here been accumulated—more from an intense desire of being surrounded with all the splendor of luxury—since they possessed the means of procuring it—than from a refined taste. Their superabundance of gold and silver had been employed in obtaining these splendid superfluities, which were of no value but to gratify the vanity of their possessors.

Such was Panama in 1670, when the freebooters selected it as the object of their bold attempt, and as the victim of their extravagancies, and immortalized their name by reducing it to a heap of ruins.

In the execution of this design, which stupefied the New World, they displayed equal prudence and cruelty. Previous to the adoption of any other measure, it was necessary that the pirates should get possession of Fort St. Laurent, which was situated on the banks of the river Chagres. With this view, Morgan detached four ships, with four hundred men, under the command of the intrepid Brodely, who had happily succeeded in victualling the fleet, and who was intimately acquainted with the country. Morgan continued at the island of St. Catharine with the rest of his forces.

His plan was to dissemble his vast projects against Panama as long as it was possible, and to cause the pillage of Fort St. Laurent to be regarded as a common expedition to which he would confine himself. Brodely discharged his commission with equal courage and success. That castle was situated on a lofty mountain, at the mouth of the river, and was inaccessible on almost every side. The first attempts were fruitless; and the freebooters, who advanced openly, without any other arms than their fusees and sabres, at first lost many of their comrades; for the Spaniards not only made use of all their artillery and musketry against them, but were also seconded by the Indians that were with them in the fort and whose arrows were far more fatal than the bullets.

The assailants saw their companions-in-arms fall by their side without being able to avenge them. The danger of their present situation and the nature of their arms seemed to render the enterprise altogether impracticable. Their courage began to waver, their ranks were thrown into disorder, and they already thought of retiring, when the provocations of the Spaniards inspired them with new vigor. "You heretic dogs," cried they in a triumphant tone; "you cursed English, possessed by the devil! Ah, you will go to Panama, will you? No, no; that you shall not; you shall all bite the dust here, and all your comrades shall share the same fate."

From these insulting speeches the pirates learned that the design of their expedition was discovered; and from that moment they determined to carry the fort or die to a man upon the spot. They immediately commenced the assault in defiance of the shower of arrows that were discharged against them, and undismayed by the loss of their commander, both of whose legs had been carried away by a cannon-ball. One of the pirates, in whose shoulder an arrow was deeply fixed, tore it out himself, exclaiming: "Patience, comrades, an idea strikes me; all the Spaniards are lost!" He tore some cotton out of his pocket, with which he covered his ramrod, set the cotton on fire, and shot this burning material, in lieu of bullets, at the houses of the fort, which were covered with light wood and the leaves of palm trees. His companions collected together the arrows which were strewed around them upon the ground, and employed them in a similar manner. The effect of this novel mode of attack was most rapid; many of the houses caught fire; a powder-wagon blew up. The besieged, being thus diverted from their means of defence, thought only of stopping the progress of the fire.

Night came on; under cover of the darkness the freebooters attempted also to set on fire the palisades, which were made of a kind of wood that was easily kindled. In this attempt likewise they were crowned with success. The soil, which the palisades supported, fell down for want of support, and filled up the ditch. The Spaniards nevertheless continued to defend themselves with much courage, being animated by the example of their commander, who fought till the very moment he received a mortal blow. The garrison had, throughout, the use of their cannon, which kept up a most violent fire; but the enemy had already made too much progress to be disconcerted with it; they persevered in their attack, until they at length became masters of the fort.

A great number of Spaniards, finding themselves deprived of all resource, precipitated themselves from the top of the walls into the river, that they might not fall alive into the hands of the freebooters, who made only twenty-four prisoners, and ten of these were wounded men, who had concealed themselves among the dead, in the hope of escaping their ferocious conquerors. These twenty-four men were all that remained of three hundred forty who had composed the garrison, which had shortly before been reënforced, for the President of Panama, having been apprised from Carthagena of the real object of the pirates' expedition, came to encamp, with thirty-six hundred men, in the vicinity of the threatened city. This information was confirmed to the freebooters after the capture of the fort. At the same time they learned that among this body of troops there were four hundred horsemen, six hundred Indians, and two hundred mulattoes; the last of whom, being very expert in hunting bulls, were intended, in case of necessity, to send two thousand of those animals among the freebooters.

It is scarcely credible that Brodely continued to command, notwithstanding the severity of his wounds; but he would not, by retiring, compromise the advantages which he had so dearly purchased; for out of four hundred men who had composed his little army, one hundred sixty had been killed, eighty wounded; and of these eighty, sixty were altogether out of the battle.

The bodies of the French and English were interred; but those of the Spaniards were thrown down from the top of the fort and remained in a heap at the foot of its walls. Brodely found much ammunition and abundance of provisions, with which he was the more satisfied, as he knew that the grand fleet was greatly in want of both those articles. He caused the fort to be rebuilt, as far as was practicable, in order that he might defend himself there in case the Spaniards should make a speedy attempt to retake it. In this situation he waited for Morgan, who in a short time appeared with his fleet.

As the pirates approached, they beheld the English flag flying on the fort, and abandoned themselves to the most tumultuous joy and excessive drinking, without dreaming of the dangers occurring at the mouth of the river Chagres, beneath whose waters there was a sunken rock. The coasting pilots of those latitudes came to their assistance, but their intoxication and their impatience would not permit them to attend to the latter. This negligence was attended with most fatal consequences and cost them four ships, one of which was the admiral's vessel. The crews, however, together with their ladings, were saved. This loss greatly affected Morgan, who was wholly intent upon his vast designs, but who, nevertheless, made his entrance into St. Laurent, where he left a garrison of five hundred men. He also detached from his body of troops one hundred fifty men for the purpose of seizing several Spanish vessels that were in the river.

The remainder of his forces Morgan directed to follow himself. They carried but a small supply of provisions, not only that his march might not be impeded, but also because the means of conveyance were very limited. Besides, he was apprehensive lest he should expose to famine the garrison he had left in the fort, which did not abound with provisions, and was cut off on every side from receiving supplies; and it was likewise necessary that he should leave sufficient for the support of all the prisoners and slaves, whose number amounted very nearly to one thousand.

After all these steps had been taken, Morgan briefly addressed his comrades, whom he exhorted to arm themselves with courage calculated to subdue every obstacle, that they might return to Jamaica with an increase of glory, and riches sufficient to supply all their wants for the rest of their lives. At length, on January 18th, he commenced his march toward Panama, with a chosen body of freebooters, who were thirteen hundred strong.

The greatest part of their journey was performed by water, following the course of the river. Five vessels were laden with the artillery; and the troops were placed in a very narrow compass on board thirty-two boats. One reason why they had brought only a small quantity of provisions was because they hoped to meet with a supply on their route; but on the very day of their arrival at Rio de los Bravos the expectations of the pirates were frustrated. At the place where they landed they literally found nothing: the terror which they everywhere inspired had preceded them; the Spaniards had betaken themselves to flight, and had carried with them all their cattle and even the very last article of their movables. They had cut the grain and pulse without waiting for their maturity, the roots of which were even torn out of the ground: the houses and stables were empty.

The first day of their voyage was spent in abstinence, tobacco affording them the only gratification that was not refused them. The second day was not more prosperous. In addition to the various impediments by which their passage was obstructed, want of rain had rendered the waters of the river very shallow, and a great number of trees had fallen into it, presenting almost insurmountable obstacles. On their arrival at the Cruz de Juan Gallego, they had no other alternative left but to abandon their boats and pursue their route by land; otherwise, they must have resigned themselves to the confusion necessarily consequent on retracing their steps.

Animated, however, by their chieftains, they determined to try the adventure. On the third day their way led them to a forest, where there was no beaten path, and the soil of which was marshy. But it was indispensably necessary that they should leave this wretched passage, in order that they might reach—with incredible difficulties, indeed—the town of Cedro Bueno. For all these excessive fatigues they found no indemnification whatever; there were no provisions, not even a single head of game.

These luckless adventurers at length saw themselves surrounded by all the horrors of famine. Many of them were reduced to devour the leaves of trees; the majority were altogether destitute of sustenance. In this state of severe privations, and with very light clothing, they passed the nights lying on the shore, benumbed with cold, incapable of enjoying, even in the smallest degree, the solace of sleep, and expecting with anxiety the return of day. Their courage was supported only with the hope of meeting some bodies of Spaniards, or some groups of fugitive inhabitants, and consequently of finding provisions, with an abundance of which the latter never failed to supply themselves when they abandoned their dwellings. Further, the pirates were obliged to continue their route at a small distance only from the river, as they had contrived to drag their canoes along with them, and, whenever the water was of sufficient depth, part of the men embarked on board them, while the remainder prosecuted their journey by land. They were preceded a few hundred paces by an advanced guard of thirty men under the direction of a guide who was intimately acquainted with the country; and the strictest silence was observed, in order that they might discover the ambuscades of the Spaniards, and, if it were possible, make some of them prisoners.

On the fourth day the freebooters reached Torna Cavellos, a kind of fortified place which also had been evacuated, the Spaniards having carried away with them everything that was portable and consumed the rest by fire. Their design was to leave the pirates neither movables nor utensils; in fact, this was the only resource left them by which they could reduce those formidable guests to such a state of privation as to compel them to retire. The only things which had not been burned or carried off were some large sacks of hides, which were to these freebooters objects of avidity, and which had almost occasioned a bloody dispute. Previously to devouring them, it was necessary to cut them into pieces with all possible equity. Thus divided, the leather was cut into small bits, these were scraped and violently beaten between two stones. It was then soaked in water, in order to become soft, after which it was roasted; nor, thus prepared, could it have been swallowed if they had not taken most copious draughts of water.

After this repast the freebooters resumed their route, and arrived at Torna-Munni, where also they found an abandoned fortress. On the fifth day they reached Barbacoas; but still no place presented to their view either man, animal, or any kind of provisions whatever. Here likewise the Spaniards had taken the precaution of carrying away or destroying everything that could serve for food. Fortunately, however, they discovered in the hollow of a rock two sacks of flour, some fruit, and two large vessels filled with wine. This discovery would have transported with joy a less numerous troop; but, to so many famished men it presented only very feeble resource. Morgan, who did not suffer less from hunger than the rest, generously appropriated none of it to his own use, but caused this scanty supply to be distributed among those who were just ready to faint. Many, indeed, were almost dying. These were conveyed on board the boats, the charge of which was committed to them; while those who had hitherto had the care of the vessels, were reunited to the body that was travelling by land. Their march was very slow, both on account of the extreme weakness of these men, even after the very moderate refreshment they had just taken, as well as from the roughness and difficulties of the way; and during the fifth day the pirates had no other sustenance but the leaves of trees and the grass of the meadows.

On the following day the freebooters made still less progress; want of food had totally exhausted them, and they were frequently obliged to rest. At length they reached a plantation, where they found a vast quantity of maize in a granary that had just been abandoned. What a discovery was this to men whose appetites were sharpened by such long protractions! A great many of them devoured the grains in a raw state; the rest covered their shares with the leaves of the banana-tree, and thus cooked or roasted the maize. Reinvigorated by this food, they pursued their route; and, on the same day, they discovered a troop of Indians on the other side of the river, but those savages betook themselves to flight, so that it was impossible to reach them. The cruel freebooters fired on them and killed some of them; the rest escaped, exclaiming: "Come, you English dogs, come into the meadow; we will there wait for you."

To this challenge the pirates were little tempted to answer. Their supply of maize was exhausted; and they were further obliged to lie down in the open air without eating anything.

Hitherto, in the midst of privations the most severely painful, as well as of the most difficult labors, they had evinced an inexhaustible patience, but at length violent murmurs arose. Morgan and his rash enterprise became the object of their execrations: a great number of the freebooters were desirous of returning; but the rest, although discontented, declared that they would rather perish than not terminate an expedition so far advanced and which had cost them so much trouble.

On the following day they crossed the river and directed their march toward a place which they took for a town or, at all events, for a village, where, to their great satisfaction, they thought they perceived at a distance the smoke issuing from several chimneys. "There, at last," said they, "we shall surely find both men and provisions." Their expectations were completely frustrated; not a single individual appeared throughout the place. They found no other articles of sustenance but a leather sack full of bread, together with a few cats and dogs, which were instantly killed and devoured. The place where they had now arrived was the town of Cruces, at which were usually landed those commodities which were conveyed up the river Chagres, in order to be carried by land to Panama, which was eight French leagues distant. Here were some fine warehouses built of stone, and likewise some stables belonging to the King of Spain, which, at the moment of the pirates' arrival, were the only buildings that remained untouched, all the inhabitants having betaken themselves to flight after they had set their houses on fire.

Every corner of these royal buildings was ransacked by the freebooters, who at length discovered seventeen large vessels full of Peruvian wine, which were immediately emptied. Scarcely, however, had they drunk this liquor, which was to recruit their exhausted strength, than they all fell ill. At first they thought the wine was poisoned; they were overwhelmed with consternation, and were fully persuaded that their last hour was come. Their terrors were unfounded; as their sudden indisposition was easily accounted for by the nature of the unwholesome food they had so recently taken, by the extreme diminution of their strength, and the avidity with which they had swallowed the wine; in fact, they found themselves much better on the following day.

As Morgan had been reduced to the necessity of removing, at this place, to a distance from all his ships, he was obliged to land all his men, not even excepting those who were most exhausted by weakness. The shallops alone, with sixty men, were sent to the spot where his vessels and largest ships had been left. A single shallop only was reserved to carry news, if occasion offered, to the flotilla. Morgan prohibited every man from going alone to any distance; and even required that they should not make excursions in troops amounting to less than a hundred men. Famine, however, compelled the freebooters to infringe this prohibition. Six of them went out to some distance in quest of food; the event justified the foresight of their chieftain. They were attacked by a large body of Spaniards, and could not without very great difficulty regain the village: they had also the mortification to see one of their comrades taken prisoner.

Morgan now determined to prosecute his march. After reviewing his companions-in-arms he found that they amounted to eleven hundred men. As he foresaw that they were apprehensive lest their lost comrade should betray the secret of their enterprise and the state of their forces, Morgan made them believe that he had not been taken; that he had only lost his way in the woods, but had now returned to the main body.

The freebooters were on the eighth day of their painful journey, and nothing but the hope of speedily terminating their labors could support them much longer, for they had now ascertained that they were on the way to Panama. An advanced guard of two hundred men was therefore formed, which was to watch the movements of the enemy. They marched onward for a whole day without perceiving any living object whatever, when suddenly a shower of three or four thousand arrows was discharged upon them from the top of a rock. For some minutes they were struck with astonishment; no enemy presented himself to their view. They beheld around them, at their feet, above their heads, nothing but steep rocks, trees, and abysses; and, without striking a single blow, they reckoned twenty of their comrades killed or wounded. This unexpected attack not being continued, they pursued their march across a forest, where, in a hollow way, they fell upon a large body of Indians who opposed their progress with much valor. In this engagement the freebooters were victorious, though they lost eight killed and ten wounded.

They made every possible effort to catch some of the fugitives, but these fled away with the velocity of stags across the rocks, with all the turnings and windings of which they were intimately acquainted. Not a single man fell into their hands; the Indian chieftain was wounded; and, notwithstanding he lay on the ground, he continued to fight most obstinately until he received a mortal blow. He wore a crown of party-colored feathers. His death made a great impression on the Indians and was the principal cause of their defeat. The ground on which they had attacked the pirates was so favorable that one hundred men would have been fully sufficient to have destroyed the whole troop of freebooters. The latter availed themselves of the inconceivable negligence of the Spaniards in not taking more effectual measures for the defence of such an important pass. They exerted all possible diligence to make their way out of this labyrinth of rocks, where a second attack of a similar kind would have been attended with consequences of the most fatal tendency to them, and to get into an open and level country.

On the ninth day they found themselves in a plain or spacious meadow, entirely divested of trees, so that nothing could shelter them against the ardor of the solar rays. It rained, however, most copiously at the moment of their arrival; and this circumstance added yet more to their difficulties. In a short time they were wetted to their skins. In case of a sudden attack their arms and ammunition would have afforded them but little assistance; while the Spaniards would be able most effectively to use their spears, which could not be damaged by the rain.

No human means could remedy this inconvenience. The pirates had only to abandon themselves to their fate. Morgan most ardently desired that some prisoner might fall into his hands, from whose confessions, either voluntary or involuntary, he might obtain some information by which to direct his march. With this intention, fifty men were detached in different directions, with a promised reward of three hundred piasters, out of the society's stock, to the man who should bring in either a Spaniard or an Indian, exclusive of the share of booty to which he should be entitled.

About noon they ascended a steep hill, from whose summit they began to discover the Pacific. At this sight, which announced the speedy termination of their miseries, they were transported with joy. From the top of this eminence they also perceived six ships departing from Panama, and sailing toward the islands of Taroga and Tarogiela, which were situated in the vicinity of that city. Panama itself for the present escaped their observation; but how was their satisfaction increased on beholding, in a valley, a vast number of bulls, cows, horses, and particularly of asses, which were under the care of some Spaniards, who betook themselves to flight the moment they saw the formidable pirates approaching? To the latter no *rencontre* could be more desirable. They were ready to faint with famine and fatigue; the sustenance which they immediately devoured would contribute to give them that strength which every moment would become so necessary to them, and it is altogether inconceivable how the Spaniards could abandon such a prey to their famished enemies. This want of foresight can only be accounted for by the panic with which the Spaniards were seized.

The spot which had just been deserted was occupied for some hours by the freebooters; they stood in great need of rest, and were in much greater want of provisions. They rushed therefore on the animals that had been left behind, of which they killed a great number, and devoured their half-raw flesh with such avidity that the blood streamed in torrents from their lips over the whole of their bodies. What could not be consumed on the spot they carried away with them, for Morgan, apprehensive of an attack by the flower of the Spaniards' troops, allowed them only a small space of time for repose. They resumed their march, but the uncertainty in which they had so long been involved was not yet at an end.

Notwithstanding all that chieftain's experience, his spies could not succeed in taking a single prisoner—a circumstance which seems almost incredible in a populous country—and after nine days' march Morgan was deprived of every hint that was so essentially necessary to him. Further, the freebooters were utterly ignorant how near they were to Panama, when, from the summit of a hill, they discovered the towers of that city. They could not refrain from shouting for joy. The air reëchoed with the sound of trumpets and cymbals; they threw up their caps in the air, vociferating, "Victory! victory!" In this place they halted and pitched their camp, with the firm determination of attacking Panama on the following day.

At this time the Spaniards were in the utmost confusion. The first defensive step which they deemed it advisable to take was to despatch fifty horsemen for the purpose of reconnoitring the enemy. The detachment approached the camp within musket-shot and offered some insults to the freebooters, but speedily returned toward the city, exclaiming, "*Perros, nos veromos!*" ("You dogs, we will see you again!") Shortly after a second detachment of two hundred men appeared, who occupied every pass, in order that, after the victory—which they considered as infallible—not one single pirate might escape. The freebooters, however, beheld with the utmost concern the measures which were adopted in order to block them up, and, previously to every other consideration, turned their attention toward their abundant supply of provision. As they were prohibited from kindling any fire, they devoured the meat they had brought with them *entirely in a raw state*. They could not conceive how the Spaniards could carry their neglect or their fancied security to such a length as not to disturb that repose of which they stood so greatly in need; nor how they could allow them the necessary leisure for recruiting their exhausted strength and thus become the more fit for battle. They availed themselves of this oversight and were perfectly at ease; after they had glutted themselves with animal food they lay down upon the grass and slept quietly. Throughout the night the Spaniards made their artillery roar without intermission, in order to display their vigilance.

On the ensuing day, which was the tenth of their march, January 27, 1671, the pirates advanced at a very early hour, with their military music, and took the road leading to Panama. By the advice, however, of one of their guides, they quitted the main road and went out of the way across a thick wood through which there was no footpath. For this the Spaniards were unprepared, having confined themselves to the erection of batteries and construction of redoubts on the highway. They soon perceived the inutility of this measure and were obliged to relinquish their guns in order to oppose their enemies on the contrary side; but not being able to take their cannons away from their batteries, they were, consequently, incapacitated from making use of one part of their defensive means.

After two hours' march the freebooters discovered the hostile army, which was a very fine one, well equipped, and was advancing in battle array. The soldiers were clad in party-colored silk stuffs, and the horsemen were seated upon their mettlesome steeds as if they were going to a bull-fight. The President in person took the command of this body of troops, which was of considerable importance, both for the country and likewise for the forces supported there by Spain. He marched against the pirates with four regiments of the line consisting of infantry, besides twenty-four hundred foot-soldiers of another description, four hundred horsemen, and twenty-four hundred wild bulls under the conduct of several hundred Indians and negroes.

This army, which extended over the whole plain, was discovered by the pirates from the summit of a small eminence, and presented to them a most imposing appearance, insomuch that they were struck with a kind of terror. They now began to feel some anxiety as to the event of an engagement with forces so greatly superior to them in point of numbers, but they were soon convinced that they must actually conquer or die, and encouraged each other to fight till the very last drop of their blood was shed; a determination this, which, on the part of these intrepid men, was by no means a vain resolution.

They divided themselves into three bodies, placed two hundred of their best marksmen in the front, and marched boldly against the Spaniards, who were drawn up in order of battle on a very spacious plain. The Governor immediately ordered the cavalry to charge the enemy, and the wild bulls to be at the same time let loose upon them. But the ground was unfavorable for this purpose; the horsemen encountered nothing but marshes, behind which were posted the two hundred marksmen, who kept up such a continual and well-directed fire that horses and men fell in heaps beneath their shots before it was possible to effect a retreat. Fifty horsemen only escaped this formidable discharge of musketry.

The bulls, on whose services they had calculated so highly, it became impracticable to drive among the pirates. Hence such a confusion arose as to completely reverse the whole plan of the battle. The freebooters, in consequence, attacked the Spanish infantry with so much the greater vigor. They successively knelt on the ground, fired, and rose up again. While those who were on one knee directed their fire against the hostile army, which began to waver; the pirates, who continued standing, rapidly charged their fire-arms. Every man, on this occasion, evinced a dexterity and presence of mind which decided the fate of the battle. Almost every shot was fatal. The Spaniards, nevertheless, continued to defend themselves with much valor, which proved of little service against an exasperated enemy whose courage, inflamed by despair, derived additional strength from their successes. At length the Spaniards had recourse to their last expedient: the wild cattle were let loose upon the rear of the freebooters.

The buccaneers were in their element: by their shouts they intimidated the bulls, at the same time waving party-colored flags before them; fired on the animals and laid them all upon the ground, without exception. The engagement lasted two hours; and notwithstanding the Spaniards were so greatly superior, both in numbers and in arms, it terminated entirely in favor of the freebooters. The Spaniards lost the chief part of their cavalry, on which they had built their expectations of victory; the remainder returned to the charge repeatedly, but their efforts only tended to render their defeat the more complete. A very few horsemen only escaped, together with some few of the infantry who threw down their arms to facilitate the rapidity of their flight. Six hundred Spaniards lay dead on the field of battle; besides these, they sustained a very considerable loss in such as were wounded and taken prisoner.

Among the latter were some Franciscans who had exposed themselves to the greatest dangers in order that they might animate the combatants and afford the last consolations of religion to the dying. They were conducted into Morgan's presence, who instantly pronounced sentence of death upon them. In vain did these hapless priests implore that pity which they might have expected from a less ferocious enemy. They were all killed by pistol-shots. Many Spaniards who were apprehensive lest they should be overtaken in their flight had concealed themselves in the flags and rushes along the banks of the river. They were mostly discovered and hacked to pieces by the merciless pirates.

The freebooters' task, however, was by no means completed. They had yet to take Panama, a large and populous city, which was defended by forts and batteries, and into which the Governor had retired, together with the fugitives. The conquest of this place was the more difficult, as the pirates had dearly purchased their victory, and their remaining forces were in no respect adequate to encounter the difficulties attending such an enterprise. It was, however, determined to make an attempt. Morgan had just procured from a wounded captive Spanish officer the necessary information; but he had not a moment to lose. It would not do to allow the Spaniards time to adopt new measures of defence; the city was therefore assaulted on the same day, in defiance of a formidable artillery which wrought great havoc among the freebooters; and at the end of three hours they were in possession of Panama.

The capture of that city was followed by a general pillage. Morgan, who dreaded the consequence of excessive intoxication—especially after his men had suffered such a long abstinence—prohibited them from drinking any wine under the severest penalties. He foresaw that such a prohibition would infallibly be infringed, unless it were sanctioned by an argument far more powerful than the fear of punishment. He therefore caused it to be announced that he had received information that the Spaniards had poisoned all their wine. This dexterous falsehood produced the desired effect, and for the first time the freebooters were temperate.

The majority of the inhabitants of Panama had betaken themselves to flight. They had embarked their women, their riches, all their movables that were of any value and small in bulk, and had sent this valuable cargo to the island of Taroga. The men were dispersed over the country, but in sufficiently great numbers to appear formidable to the pirates, whose forces were much diminished, and who could not expect any assistance from abroad. They therefore continued constantly together, and for their greater security, most of them encamped without the walls.

We have now reached the time when Morgan committed a barbarous and incomprehensible action, concerning which his comrades—some of whom were his historians—have given only a very ambiguous explanation.

Notwithstanding that all the precious articles had been carried away from Panama, there still remained—as in every great European trading city—a vast number of shops, warehouses, and magazines filled with every kind of merchandise. Besides a very great quantity of wrought and manufactured articles, the productions of luxury and industry, that city contained immense stores of flour, wine, and spices; vast magazines of that metal which is justly deemed the most valuable of all because it is the most useful: extensive buildings, in which were accumulated prodigious stores of iron tools and implements, anvils and ploughs which had been received from Europe and were destined to revive the Spanish colonies. Some judgment may be formed respecting the value of the last-mentioned articles only when it is considered that a quintal (one hundredweight) of iron was sold at Panama for thirty-two piasters (about thirty-three dollars).

All these multifarious articles, so essentially necessary for furnishing colonists with the means of subsistence, were, it should seem, of no value in the estimation of the ferocious Morgan because he could not carry them away; although, by preserving them, he might have made use of them by demanding a specific ransom for them. Circumstances might also enable him to derive some further advantages from them, but, in fact, whatever was distant or uncertain presented no attraction to this barbarian, who was eager to enjoy, but more ardent to destroy.

He was struck by one consideration only. All these bulky productions of art and industry were for the moment of no use to the freebooters. Of what importance to him was the ruin of many thousand innocent families? He consulted only the ferocity of his character, and without communicating his design to any individual he secretly caused the city to be set on fire in several places. In a few hours it was almost entirely consumed. The Spaniards that had remained in Panama—as well as the pirates themselves, who were at first ignorant whence the conflagration proceeded—ran together and united their efforts in order to extinguish the flames. They brought water, and pulled down houses, with a view to prevent the further progress of that destructive element. All their exertions were fruitless. A violent wind was blowing, and, in addition to this circumstance, the principal part of the buildings in that city were constructed of wood. Its finest houses, together with their valuable furniture, among which was the magnificent palace belonging to the Genoese, the churches, convents, courthouse, shops, hospitals, pious foundations, warehouses loaded with sacks of flour, nearly two hundred other warehouses filled with merchandise—all were reduced to ashes! The fire also consumed a great number of animals, horses, mules, and many slaves who had concealed themselves and who were burned alive. A very few houses only escaped the fire, which continued burning upward of four weeks. Amid the havoc produced in every quarter by the conflagration, the freebooters did not neglect to pillage as much as they possibly could, by which means they collected a considerable booty.

Morgan seemed ashamed of his atrocious act; he carefully concealed that he had ever executed it, and gave out that the Spaniards themselves had set their city on fire.

STRUGGLE OF THE DUTCH AGAINST FRANCE AND ENGLAND

A.D. 1672

C. M. DAVIES

Seldom has any people held out so heroically against overwhelming numbers as did the Dutch in 1672. Of the various wars during the reign of Louis XIV, that which he carried on against Holland was one of the most important. By its settlement, at the Peace of Nimwegen (1678-1679), the long hostilities between France and Holland and their allies were brought to a close, and Holland was once more saved from threatened destruction.

Louis, having invaded the Spanish Netherlands, had reluctantly consented to the Treaty of Aix-la-Chapelle (1668), by which he retained a small part of the Low Countries. By insisting on this treaty Holland gave deep offence to the French monarch, who in 1672 began a war of revenge against the Netherlands, where his schemes of large acquisition had been thwarted. His first attempt was to isolate Holland, and having purchased the King of Sweden, he bribed Charles II of England, uncle of William of Orange, to enter into a secret treaty against the Netherlands.

The principal events of the war are narrated by Davies, who shows how the old spirit of the Dutch returned to them in this supreme hour of new peril to their liberties.

THE Dutch, though, in defence of their religion and liberties, they had beaten the first soldiers in the world, were never essentially a military nation; and in 1672 a long interval of peace, and devotion to the pursuits of commerce, had rendered them quite unfit for warlike enterprises. The army was entirely disorganized; the officers, appointed by the magistrates of the towns on the score of relationship or party adherence, without the slightest regard to their efficiency, were suffered, without fear of punishment, to keep the numbers of their regiments incomplete, in order that they might appropriate the pay of the vacancies; while the men, independent and undisciplined, were allowed to spend their time in the pursuit of some gainful trade or peaceful occupation, instead of practising military exercises. The disputes concerning the appointment of a captain-general had impeded any fresh levies, the recruits refusing to take the oath to the States except in conjunction with the Prince of Orange, and had induced many of the best and most experienced officers to take service in the French army; the fortifications of the towns were in a dilapidated condition, and no measures had been adopted for the security of the frontier.

Such was the state to which party spirit had reduced a nation filled with brave, intelligent, and virtuous inhabitants, and governed by statesmen as able and wise as the world ever saw, when the two most powerful sovereigns of Europe declared war against her. The manifests were both issued on the same day. That of the King of England is strongly marked by the duplicity which was the distinguishing characteristic both of himself and of his court as then constituted. From the style of the document one might be led to suppose that he was forced into the war with extreme reluctance and regret, and only in consequence of the impossibility of obtaining redress by any other means for the deep injuries he had sustained. He declared that, so far back as the year 1664, his Parliament had complained of the wrongs and oppressions exercised by the Dutch on his subjects in the East Indies, and for which they had refused to make reparation by amicable means.

They had openly refused him the honor of the flag, one of the most ancient prerogatives of his crown; had sought to invite the King of France to hostilities against him; and had insulted his person and dignity by the abusive pictures and medals exposed in all their towns. This expression was understood to allude to a medal complained of three years before, and to a portrait of Cornelius de Witt, in the perspective of which was a representation of the burning of Chatham. Cornelius de Witt being an ex-burgomaster of Dordrecht, the council of that town had, with a natural pride, caused this picture to be painted and hung up in the council-chamber. The extreme sensitiveness manifested by Charles on this point appeared to the States rather superfluous in a monarch whose own kingdom teemed with the most offensive truths relative to himself and his government.

As if determined that the mode of commencing hostilities

should be as lawless and unjust as the war itself, the court of England, several days before the declaration was issued, had commanded Sir Robert Holmes to attack the Dutch Smyrna fleet on its return. While cruising near the Isle of Wight, Holmes met the admiral, Sprague, by whom he was informed of the near approach of the vessels; but, anxious to secure to himself the whole of the booty, estimated at near a million and a half of guilders, he suffered Sprague to sail away in ignorance of his instructions, and leaving him with no more than nine frigates and three yachts. His covetousness, happily, proved the salvation of the fleet. After a short encounter of two days' duration, Holmes was forced to retire, having captured no more than three or four of the more inconsiderable ships, while the remainder gained their harbors in safety.

The King of France appeared, by the tenor of his declaration of war, to imagine that his power and dignity entitled him to set at naught alike the natural rights of mankind and the law of nations; it resembled, indeed, rather the threat of a predatory incursion on the part of a barbarian chief than the justification of the taking up of arms by a civilized government. Without adducing a single cause of complaint, he satisfied himself with declaring that the conduct of the States had been such as it was not consistent with his glory to endure any longer.

If anything, indeed, could justify the arrogant tone assumed by Louis, the circumstances in which he found himself would have done so. An army of one hundred twenty thousand, able and well-equipped troops, commanded by Condé and Turenne, and numbering in its ranks volunteers of the noblest families in France eager to distinguish themselves under the eye of their sovereign; funds lavishly supplied by the able minister of finance, Colbert; with vast magazines of ammunition and every other necessary collected, and winter quarters secured in the neighboring and friendly territories of Cologne and Muenster, seemed means almost absurdly disproportioned in magnitude to the end to be attained. At the same time he was but too well informed of the defenceless condition of the enemy. Jan de Witt and the States conceived that his first attempt would be upon Maestricht, the possession of which he was known to have long coveted, and that the difficulties of its conquest would be sufficient to deter from further enterprise a monarch of whose military prowess no very high idea was entertained, and who was supposed to be far more enamoured of the pomp and circumstance of war than of its toils and dangers. They accordingly fortified and provided Maestricht with the utmost care, leaving the frontier towns on the Rhine in an utterly inefficient state of defence. Aware of this fact, Louis commenced his operations on the side of Cleves, and, separating his army into four divisions, laid siege simultaneously to as many places. He himself summoned the town of Rhynberg, the Duke of Orléans sat down before Orsay, Condé was commanded to reduce Wesel, and Turenne, Burick. All surrendered within a week. To give an account of the capture of the towns which followed, would be but to heap example upon example of cowardice or treachery, or—as they are generally found together—both.

Nothing less than entire unanimity and the most undaunted resolution could have enabled the Dutch to resist the overwhelming force employed against them; whereas, the miserable effect of the internal dissensions of the republic had been to destroy for the time all mutual confidence. In some places the garrisons, despising their incapable commanders, refused to act; or the governors, mistrustful of their undisciplined troops, lost all hope of prolonging a defence; in others, the detestation entertained by the magistrates toward the Orange party was so great that, preferring to submit to France rather than to a native stadtholder, they hastened to deliver up their towns to the invader; on the other hand, the friends of the house of Orange looked not without some complacency on the misfortunes which threatened the state, and which they hoped would reduce it to the necessity of raising the Prince to the dignities of his family; while in those places where the Catholics were numerous, the populace, under the guidance of the priests, forced both garrisons and governments to open their gates to the sovereign whom they hailed as the restorer of their religion. With scarcely a show of opposition, therefore, Louis advanced to the Rhine.

The drought of the summer was so excessive that this river had become fordable in three places, which, being pointed out to the French by some peasants of Guelderland, the King determined on attempting the passage between Schenkenschans and

Arnhem, near the Tollhuys, a village and tower about two miles distant from the separation of the branch of the river called the Wahal. The Prince of Orange, who was stationed with about twenty-two thousand men at Arnhem, and along the banks of the Yssel, instead of concentrating his forces to oppose the passage of the enemy, contented himself with detaching De Montbas to guard the Betuwe, and to throw succors if requisite into Nimwegen. But this general, deeming the troops placed under his command insufficient for the purpose required, abandoned his post. He was arrested and sent to Utrecht, but afterward allowed to escape. Immediately on the retreat of Montbas the Prince despatched General Wurtz, but still with a vastly inadequate force, to occupy the post at the Tollhuys. The French cuirassiers, led on by the Counts de Guiche and Revel, first waded into the ford under the fire of the artillery from the tower, which, however, as there were no more than seventeen men stationed in it, was not very formidable. They were followed by a number of volunteers, and in a short time the whole of the cavalry passed over with trifling loss. The Dutch troops, discouraged as well by the unexpectedness of the attempt as by their own inferiority in number, were driven back after a short skirmish. A bridge was then thrown across the river for the infantry, and thus this famous passage was accomplished with comparative ease and safety.

As the position of the Prince of Orange on the Yssel, which in consequence of the drought was fordable throughout nearly the whole of its course, was now no longer tenable, he retired to Utrecht, abandoning Arnhem to the enemy, who soon after received the submission of Nimwegen and the whole of Guelderland, Thiel, and the Bommel. In order to put Utrecht into a state of defence, the Prince considered it necessary to burn down all the suburbs; a measure which, when he proposed to the States of the Province, he found them reluctant to comply with. He therefore immediately quitted that city, and with the whole of his forces made a further retreat into Holland. Thus left wholly unprotected, the States of Utrecht conceived that the only resource which remained to them was to mollify the conqueror by a speedy submission; and accordingly, while Louis was yet at Doesburg, they sent deputies to tender to him the keys of the city and the submission of the whole province. The King shortly after entered Utrecht in triumph.

While the good-fortune, rather than the arms, of Louis subdued Guelderland and Utrecht, his allies, the Bishops of Cologne and Muenster, found no more vigorous resistance in Overyssel. Oldenzeel, Entschede, and other small towns yielded at once to their summons; Deventer, though well garrisoned and amply provided, was surrendered at once by the municipal government, who, by their exhortations and example, induced that of Zwol to adopt a like disgraceful course of conduct. The easily acquired spoil was divided among the captors; the King of France, who had furnished a subsidy of troops, placed garrisons in Campen and Elburg; the Archbishop of Cologne retained Deventer; Groll and Breevoort being allotted to the Bishop of Muenster, while Zwol was held in common. The troops of these warlike prelates exercised everywhere unbounded license and cruelties. Numbers of unhappy families were driven from their homes, and, taking refuge in Holland, added to the consternation which prevailed there.

This province was now in imminent danger. No barrier remained, as it appeared, to oppose the progress of the enemy; the army of the Prince had dwindled to about thirteen thousand men; two of the frontier towns, Woerden and Oudewater, had solicited safeguards from the invaders; and Naarden was surprised by the Count of Rochefort. Had he marched on at once to Muyden he might have occupied that town also, a post of immense importance from its situation, as ships going to Amsterdam must come within reach of its cannon; and by means of a sluice there, the surrounding country may at any time be inundated. It had been left destitute of a garrison; but, the French commander remaining two or three days inactive at Naarden, time was afforded to John Maurice of Nassau to enter Muyden with a strong body of troops, and the chance thus lost was gone forever.

Amazed at the rapid advances of the invader, and dispirited by the symptoms of daily increasing aversion which the great body of the people manifested to his government, the courage of Jan de Witt at this crisis so entirely forsook him that he took upon himself the disgrace of being the first to propose to the

States of Holland that they should implore mercy from the conqueror. The resolution was immediately adopted, and by them proposed to the States-General, where it was passed with the dissentient voice only of Zealand, who was of opinion that they should treat simultaneously with England, from whence that province had to apprehend the principal danger. A deputation was accordingly sent to Louis, at Keppel, near Doesburg, headed by De Groot, and commissioned to inquire upon what terms his majesty was inclined to grant peace to the republic. They were answered by Louvois, that the King was not disposed to restore any of the conquests he had made or to enter into any negotiation unless the deputies were furnished with full powers and instructions as to what the States intended to offer. Returning to The Hague, De Groot made his report to the States of Holland, and, representing the desperate condition of their affairs, recommended that Louis should be gratified with Maestricht and all the other towns of the generality; and that a sum should be offered him to defray the expenses of the war, provided the King would leave them in possession of their liberty and sovereignty. Leyden, Haarlem, and most of the other towns followed the example of the nobles in receiving these pusillanimous counsels with approbation.

Amsterdam, however, proved that the spirit of the "Gueux" was not yet utterly extinct in Holland. Prevailing with four towns of North Holland to follow their example, the Council of Amsterdam refused to send deputies to debate upon the question of granting full powers to the ambassadors, and made vigorous preparations for the defence of their city. They repaired the fortifications, and strengthened them with considerable outworks, the magistrates themselves being the first to sacrifice their magnificent country houses in the suburbs for this purpose; they assigned to each of the regiments of burgher guards, who were ten thousand in number, a portion of the city to watch; took into their pay as soldiers all those inhabitants whom the cessation of trade would throw out of employment; stationed outlyers in the Y, Amstel, Zuyder Zee, and Pampus, and, cutting the dikes, laid the country to a great distance round under water. They likewise passed a resolution that, though all the rest of Holland should make terms with the conqueror, they would sustain the siege single-handed till some friendly power should afford them assistance.

The causes which combined to expose the United Provinces to these terrible disasters by land had, happily, no influence on their affairs by sea. The fleet, commanded by De Ruyter, an officer surpassed by none of any age or nation in ability and courage, and of devoted fidelity to the present government, had been increased to ninety-one ships and frigates of war, fifty-four fire-ships, and twenty-three yachts. That of the allies, commanded by the Duke of York, comprised after the junction of the French squadron under the Count d'Etrées, one hundred forty-nine ships-of-war, besides the smaller vessels. Sailing in quest of the enemy, De Ruyter discovered them lying in Solebay, evidently unprepared for his approach. On this occasion was felt the disadvantage of intrusting an officer with the chief command without at the same time giving him sufficient authority to insure its beneficial exercise. In consequence of the presence on board of Cornelius de Witt, the deputy of the States, De Ruyter, instead of ordering an immediate attack, was obliged to call a council of war, and thus gave the English time to arrange themselves in order of battle, which they did with astonishing celerity.

The Dutch advanced in three squadrons, nearly in a line with each other; the Admiral Bankert on the left to the attack of the French; Van Gend on the right, with the purpose of engaging the blue squadron commanded by Montague, Earl of Sandwich; while De Ruyter in the middle directed his course toward the red flag of the English, and, pointing with his finger to the Duke of York's vessel, said to his pilot, "There is our man." The pilot instantly steered the ship right down upon that of the Duke, and a terrific broadside was returned with equal fury. After two hours' incessant firing, the English admiral retreated, his ship being so damaged that he was obliged to transfer his flag on board the London. At the same time Braakel, a captain who had signalized himself in the burning of Chatham, with a vessel of sixty-two guns, attacked the Royal James, of one hundred four guns, the ship of the Earl of Sandwich, which he boarded and fired. Montague, refusing to surrender, was drowned in the attempt to escape in a boat. On the other hand, Van Gend, the admiral of the squadron engaged with the Earl's, was killed in the beginning of the action. The contest was maintained with the daring and steady valor characteristic of both nations, from seven in the morning until nightfall. The French had received instructions to keep aloof from the fight, and allow the two fleets to destroy each other; and these they took care to carry out to the full. Thus, the only assistance they afforded to the English was to prevent the Dutch squadron engaged in watching their movements from acting, an advantage more than counterbalanced by the discouragement their behavior occasioned among their allies.

Though both parties claimed the victory, it undoubtedly inclined in favor of the Dutch, who sustained a loss somewhat inferior to that of their antagonists, and had the satisfaction, moreover, of preventing a descent upon Zealand by the combined fleets, which was to have been the immediate consequence of a defeat. This was, however, attempted about a month after, when the disasters attending the arms of the States by land, having induced them to diminish the number of their ships, De Ruyter received commands to remain in the ports and avoid an engagement. The whole of the English fleet appeared in the Texel provided with small craft for the purpose of landing. But, by a singular coincidence, it happened that, on the very day fixed for the attempt, the water continued, from some unknown cause, so low as to render it impossible for the vessels to approach the shore, and to impress the people with the idea that the ebb of the tide lasted for the space of twelve hours. Immediately after, a violent storm arose, which drove the enemy entirely away from the coasts.

The internal condition of the United Provinces was at this time such as to incite the combined monarchs, no less than their own successes, to treat them with insolence and oppression. They beheld the inhabitants, instead of uniting with one generous sentiment of patriotism in a firm and strenuous defence of their fatherland, torn by dissensions, and turning against each other the rage which should have been directed against their enemies. The divisions in every province and town were daily becoming wider and more embittered. Though both parties had merited an equal share of blame for the present miscarriages, the people imputed them exclusively to the government of Jan de Witt and his adherents; who, they said, had betrayed and sold the country to France; and this accusation to which their late pusillanimous counsels gave but too strong a color of plausibility, the heads of the Orange party, though well aware of its untruth, diligently sustained and propagated. The ministers of the Church, always influential and always on the alert, made the pulpits resound with declamations against the treachery and incapacity of the present government as the cause of all the evils under which they groaned; and emphatically pointed to the elevation of the Prince of Orange to the dignities of his ancestors as the sole remedy now left them. To this measure De Witt and his brother were now regarded as the only obstacles; and, so perverted had the state of public feeling become that the most atrocious crimes began to be looked upon as meritorious actions, provided only they tended to the desired object of removing these obnoxious ministers.

On one occasion, Jan de Witt, having been employed at the Chamber of the States to a late hour of the night, was returning home attended by a single servant, according to his custom, when he was attacked by four assassins. He defended himself for a considerable time, till having received some severe wounds he fell, and his assailants decamped, leaving him for dead. One only, James van der Graaf, was arrested; the other three took refuge in the camp, where, though the States of Holland earnestly enjoined the Prince of Orange and the other generals to use diligent means for their discovery, they remained unmolested till the danger was passed. Van der Graaf was tried and condemned to death. The pensionary was strongly solicited by his friends to gratify the people by interceding for the pardon of the criminals; but he resolutely refused to adopt any such mode of gaining popularity. Impunity, he said, would but increase the number and boldness of such miscreants; nor would he attempt to appease the causeless hatred of the people against him by an act which he considered would tend to endanger the life of every member of the Government. The determination, however just, was imprudent. The criminal, an account of whose last moments was published by the minister who attended him, was regarded by the populace as a victim to the vengeance of Jan de Witt, and a martyr to the good of his country. On the same day a similar attempt was made on the life of his brother, Cornelius de Witt, at Dordrecht, by a like number of assassins, who endeavored to force their way into his house, but were prevented by the interference of a detachment of the burgher guard.

Cornelius had already, on his return from the fleet in consequence of impaired health, been greeted with the spectacle of his picture, which had given such umbrage to the King of England, cut into strips and stuck about the town, with the head hanging upon the gallows. These symptoms of tumult rapidly increased in violence. A mob assembling, with loud cries of "*Oranje boven! de Witten onder!*" ("Long live the Prince of Orange! down with the De Witts!") surrounded the houses of the members of the council, whom they forced to send for the Prince, and to pass an act, repealing the "Perpetual Edict," declaring him stadtholder, and releasing him from the oath he had taken not to accept that office while he was captain-general. Having been signed by all the other members of the council, this act was carried to the house of Cornelius de Witt, who was confined to his bed by sickness, the populace at the same time surrounding the house and threatening him with death in case of refusal. He long resisted, observing that he had too many balls falling around him lately to fear death, which he would rather suffer than sign that paper; but the prayers and tears of his wife and her threats, that if he delayed compliance she would throw herself and her children among the infuriated populace, in the end overcame his resolution. He added to his signature the letters V. C. (*vi coactus*), but the people, informed by a minister of their purport, obliged him to erase them.

Similar commotions broke out at Rotterdam, Haarlem, Leyden, Amsterdam, and in other towns, both of Holland and Zealand, where the populace constrained the magistrates by menace and violence to the repeal of the edict. Reluctant to have such a measure forced upon them by tumult and sedition, the States of Holland and Zealand now unanimously passed an act revoking the Perpetual Edict, and conferring on the Prince of Orange the dignity of stadtholder, captain, and admiral-general of these provinces.

Soon afterward Cornelius de Witt was thrown into prison and put to the torture on a false charge of planning the assassination of the Prince of Orange. Jan de Witt visited his brother in his agony, and a mob, bursting into the jail, seized upon both brothers as traitors and murdered them with horrid brutality.

From this time the authority of William became almost uncontrolled in the United Provinces. Most of the leaders of the Louvestein party, either convinced of the necessity of his elevation to power in the present emergency or unwilling to encounter the vexation of a fruitless opposition, acquiesced in the present state of things; many were afterward employed by him, and distinguished themselves by fidelity and zeal in his service. The constant coöperation and participation in his views also of the pensionary, Fagel, gave him an advantage which none of his predecessors had ever enjoyed; the influence of the pensionaries of Holland having hitherto been always opposed, and forming a counterpoise, to that of the stadtholder.

Unquestionably the Dutch, while thus parting with their liberties, reaped in some degree the benefits usually attendant on such a sacrifice, in the increased firmness and activity of a government conducted by a sole responsible head. At the time of the embassy of Peter de Groot to solicit peace from the King of France, the Prince had so far partaken of the general dejection as to ask permission of the States to nominate a deputy to treat of his particular interests; but no sooner was he created stadtholder than he began to adopt bolder and more spirited resolutions for the safety of a country to which he felt himself attached by new and stronger ties. Being invited by the Assembly of the States to give his opinion on the terms offered by the allied monarchs, he declared that their acceptance would entail upon them certain ruin, and that the very listening to such was pernicious in the highest degree to affairs, as tending to disunite and dispirit the people.

He encouraged them to hope for speedy assistance from his allies; pointed out the resources which yet existed for the support of the war; and persuaded them rather to resolve, if they were driven to extremity, to embark on board their vessels and found a new nation in the East Indies, than accept the conditions. At the same time he spurned with indignation the flattering proposals made him both by the Kings of France and England; for—so singularly are men appointed to work out their own destiny—these monarchs now vied with each other, and were in fact principally instrumental, in exalting the power and dignity of a prince who ere long was to hurl the brother of the one from the throne of his ancestors, and prepare for the other an old age of vexation and disgrace, if not to lay the first foundation of the ruin of his kingdom in the next century.

Louis, upon the appointment of the Prince to the office of stadtholder, was liberal in offers of honor and advantages to his person and family, and among the rest was one which he considered could scarcely fail of its effect; that, namely, of making him sovereign of the provinces under the protection of France and England. William, however, was found wholly immovable on this point, declaring that he would rather retire to his lands in Germany, and spend his life in hunting, than sell his country and liberty to France. Nor were the dispiriting representations made by the English ambassadors, that Holland was utterly lost unless he consented to the terms proposed, at all more influential; "I have thought of a means," he replied, "to avoid beholding the ruin of my country—to die in the last ditch."

Neither, indeed, was the state of the country, though sufficiently deplorable, such as to leave him no choice but to become the vassal of her haughty enemies. The progress of the invader in Holland was effectually arrested by the state of defence into which that province had been put. Imitating the noble example set them by Amsterdam, the other towns readily opened the sluices of the Lek, Meuse, Yssel, and Vecht, inundating by that means the whole of the intervening tracts of land.

The Dutch army was stationed at the five principal posts of the provinces; Prince Maurice John being placed at Muyden and Weesp; Field Marshal Wurtz at Gorcum; the Count of Horn at the Goejanverwellen Sluys; another detachment occupied Woerden; and the Prince himself took up his head-quarters at Bodergrave and Nieuwerburg.

At length, finding his army increased by the addition of subsidies from Spain to twenty-four thousand men, William determined to infuse new vigor into the public mind by the commencement of offensive hostilities. He first formed the design of surprising Naarden and Woerden, both of which attempts, however, proved unsuccessful. He then marched toward Maestricht, captured and demolished the fort of Valckenburg, by which that town was straitened, and, with the view of diverting the force of the enemy by carrying the war into his own territory, advanced to the siege of Charleroi. But the middle of winter having already arrived before he commenced the enterprise, he was soon after compelled, by the severity of the weather, to abandon it and retire to Holland, which, during his absence, had, from the same cause, been exposed to imminent danger.

The Duke of Luxemburg, who had been left in command of the forces in Utrecht on the departure of the King of France, for Paris, finding that the ice with which the land-water was covered, was sufficiently strong to bear the passage of cavalry, marched with a strong body of troops to Zwammerdam, and thence to Bodergrave, both of which were abandoned. The purpose of the French commander was to advance directly upon The Hague, and to force the States to acknowledge the sovereignty of the King of France; a measure which would, he conceived, involve the immediate submission of the whole of the provinces. But, happily, his project was defeated by a sudden thaw, which obliged him to return to Utrecht; and had it not been that the fort of Nieuwerburg, situated on the dike, which afforded the only passage thither, was deserted by the commander, *Pain-et-Vin*, his retreat must have been cut off, and his army exposed to almost certain destruction. Before his departure, Luxemburg revenged himself on the luckless villages he had captured, which he pillaged and burned to the ground.[1] Pain-et-Vin was afterward tried for breach of duty and executed.

Though it might well have been feared that the failure of all the enterprises of the Prince of Orange would have renewed the discontents lately prevalent in the United Provinces, such an

[1] The accounts given by the Dutch historians of the revolting outrages and barbarities exercised by the invaders on this expedition are strenuously denied by the writers on the French side; their conduct in Utrecht, however, which we shall have occasion hereafter to notice, affords but too ample evidence that there was some truth in the accusations. On the other hand, that the Dutch authors are guilty of exaggeration may be easily believed, since one of them gravely puts into the mouth of the Duke of Luxemburg the following address to his soldiers: "Go, my children, plunder, murder, destroy, and if it be possible to commit yet greater cruelties, be not negligent therein, that I may see I am not deceived in my choice of the flower of the king's troops."

effect was in no degree produced. The very boldness of the designs, it seemed, had been the cause of their ill-success, and argued a zeal and activity for the public good which inspired unbounded confidence in his future measures. The appearance of renovated vigor in the United Provinces, moreover, encouraged surrounding states to make some demonstrations in their favor. They had wished to see them humbled, but not destroyed. The Emperor and princes of Germany, in especial, contemplated with dread the prospect of exchanging the neighborhood of the inoffensive and industrious people, who rarely appeared to them in any other light than as the dispensers of abundance, wealth, and luxury, for that of an ambitious and unscrupulous monarch, whose glory was in destruction, and from whose encroachments their boundaries would be for not one moment safe.

Though deeply imbued with these sentiments, the Elector of Brandenburg had hitherto been deterred from lending them any assistance, lest, should they be forced to make a peace with the King of France, the whole power and vengeance of that monarch might be directed against himself. He now induced the Emperor Leopold to enter into an alliance with him, by virtue of which he levied a force of twenty-four thousand men, to be joined with an equal number furnished by himself, for the purpose of opposing the advances of Louis. Though the secret treaty which the Emperor had made with France, binding himself not to afford aid to any member of the Triple Alliance, and of which the Elector was in ignorance, limited the employment of the imperial army strictly to the protection of the empire, and consequently prevented it from marching at once to the support of the provinces, its movement was of considerable advantage to their affairs, in calling off Turenne from Bois-le-Duc, to which he had laid siege, to the defence of the places on the Rhine. The Bishops of Muenster and Cologne, also, whom the brave defence of the garrison of Groningen had forced to raise the siege, were under the necessity of abandoning both that province and Guelderland, and hastening to the protection of their own territories.

Among the benefits which the Dutch anticipated with the utmost confidence as the consequence of the elevation of the Prince of Orange to his paternal dignities was the appeasing the hostility of his uncle, the King of England. In this, however, they were wholly deceived. On the meeting of Parliament in this year, the chancellor, Shaftesbury, addressed the two Houses in a strain of hostile feeling to the Dutch nation, more bitter than the court as yet ventured to express. He represented that, "besides the personal indignities in the way of pictures, medals, and other public affronts which the King received from the States, they came at last to such a height of insolence as to deny him the honor of the flag, though an undoubted jewel of the crown, and disputed the King's title to it in all the courts of Europe, making great offers to the French King if he would stand by them in this particular.

"But both kings, knowing their own interest, resolved to join against them, who were the common enemies of all monarchies, but especially the English, their only competitor in commerce and naval power, and the chief obstacle to their attainment of the dominion they aimed at, a dominion as universal as that of Rome; and so intoxicated were they with that vast ambition that under all their present distress and danger they haughtily rejected every overture for a treaty or a cessation of arms; that the war was a just and necessary measure, advised by the Parliament itself from the conviction that, at any rate, *Delenda est Carthago*—such a government must be destroyed; and that therefore the King may well say it was their war; which had never been begun, but that the States refused him satisfaction because they believed him to be in so great want of money that they must sit down under any affronts."

But the Parliament, always disinclined to the war, had now begun to view it with absolute aversion; and though moved, by the King's representations of the embarrassed condition he should be reduced to if the supply were refused, to yield a subsidy of seventy thousand pounds a month for eighteen months, they forced him to pay a high price for their complaisance by extorting his consent to the "Test Act." By the operation of this act, the Duke of York, the inveterate enemy of the Dutch, and Sir Thomas Clifford, the minister who had the most zealously pushed forward the business of the war, were forced to resign their offices. With the funds granted him by Parliament, Charles was enabled to complete the equipment of a fleet, which, when joined to a squadron of French ships under D'Estrées, numbered one hundred fifty sail.

The Prince of Orange had wisely continued De Ruyter in the command of the fleet as lieutenant-admiral of the provinces, with almost unlimited instructions, and suffered himself to be wholly guided by him in naval affairs, interfering only so far as to reinstate Tromp in the office of admiral under the College of Amsterdam, and to effect a perfect reconciliation between him and De Ruyter—a matter which the placable and magnanimous temper of the latter rendered of easy accomplishment. Having failed in a scheme of blocking up the Thames by means of sinking vessels in the bed of that river, De Ruyter stationed himself at Schooneveldt, with the purpose of protecting the coast of Zealand against a meditated descent of the enemy. While at anchor he descried the hostile fleet approaching; but a calm, succeeded by rough weather, prevented them for some days from coming to an engagement.

The Dutch were considerably inferior in strength to the allies, the number of their vessels being no more than fifty-two men-of-war and twelve frigates, of which, moreover, the equipages were, owing to the scarcity of seamen, by no means complete. But this deficiency was more than compensated by the spirit and conduct of their great commander. "The weaker our fleet is," observed De Ruyter, in answer to some remark made to him on the subject, "the more confidently I expect a victory, not from our own strength, but from the arm of the Almighty." Under a favorable breeze, the French and English ships bore down upon their unequal antagonists, in the full expectation that they would avoid the encounter, by retiring behind the sand-banks of Flushing. The Dutch, however, firmly awaited the shock, commenced by the squadron of French ships, which on this occasion had been placed in the van to avoid the imputation cast upon them in the last battle. They engaged with that of Tromp, whose impetuous firing compelled the French admiral to retire for a time; but quickly rallying, he returned to the charge with such vigor that Tromp was obliged to remove his flag on four different vessels successively.

De Ruyter, meanwhile, had engaged the red squadron, commanded by Prince Rupert, which after a sharp contest he threw into some disorder, and succeeded in cutting off a considerable number of ships from the remainder. Instead, however, of pursuing his advantage, De Ruyter, becoming aware of the danger of his rival, who was now entirely surrounded by the enemy, hastened to his rescue. On seeing him approach, Tromp exclaimed: "Comrades, here is our grandsire [a pet name given to De Ruyter among the sailors] coming to help us; so long as I live I will never forsake him!" The generous aid was no less effectual than well timed, since the enemy, astonished at his unexpected appearance, fell back. "I am pleased to see," he said, "that our enemies still fear the Seven Provinces," the name of the vessel which carried his flag. The fight was continued with unremitting obstinacy till darkness separated the combatants, when the Dutch found that they had gained about three miles upon their antagonists.

That the issue of such a contest should be doubtful was in itself equivalent to a victory on the side of the Dutch; a victory of which they reaped all the advantages, as well as the glory, since, besides delivering their coasts from the intended invasion, their loss was so inconsiderable that within a week the fleet was able to put to sea in its original numbers and strength. Another engagement, fought with less of energy and resolution on the side of the English than usually distinguished them, terminated in their retreat toward the Thames, which, De Ruyter conceiving to be a feint to draw the Dutch fleet off their coasts, he declined the pursuit. The movement, however, had its origin in a far different cause. The English sailors fully participated in the feelings entertained by the great body of the nation, who viewed the aggrandizement of their ally with jealousy, and the undeserved misfortunes of their enemy with pity, and considered every advantage gained over the Dutch as a step toward the completion of the sinister designs they suspected their own sovereign of harboring against their religion and liberties. They accordingly made no concealment of their reluctance to fight longer in such a quarrel.

It was now become evident to the Government that the only mode of reconciling the people in any degree to the present state of things was the execution of some brilliant achievement which should flatter their national vanity and kindle their ambition or lead to the acquisition of spoil sufficiently considerable to afford some sensible assistance in supporting the war. A descent on Holland was therefore resolved on, or, if that were found impracticable, it was proposed to intercept the Indian fleet, whose arrival was hourly expected. With this view a formidable fleet of one hundred fifty sail made its appearance in the Texel, and was met by De Ruyter about five miles from the village of the Helder. The Dutch, though far inferior in number, having only seventy-five vessels, convinced that this struggle was to be the most desperate and the last, prepared themselves for it as men who had everything at stake. After a short but inspiring harangue, De Ruyter gave the signal for attack. As if with a presentiment that long years would elapse before they should again try the strength of each other's arm, the English and Dutch seemed mutually determined to leave upon the minds of their foes an ineffaceable impression of their skill and prowess.

All the resources which ability could suggest or valor execute were now employed. Each admiral engaged with the antagonist against whom it had before been his fortune to contend. De Ruyter attached himself to the squadron of Prince Rupert; Tromp attacked Sprague, who commanded the blue flag; while Bankert was opposed to the French; the latter, however, after a short skirmish on the part of Rear Admiral Martel, who was unacquainted with the secret orders given to the commander, D'Estrées, dropped off to a distance; nor could all the signals made by Prince Rupert induce them to take any further share in the fight. Bankert, therefore, joined De Ruyter, who was engaged in a terrific contest with the squadron of Prince Rupert. The firing was kept up for several hours without cessation; the discharges from the cannon of the Dutch vessels being, it was said, as rapid as those of musketry, and in proportion of three to one to those of the enemy. Tromp, whose actions always reflected more honor on his courage than conduct, separated himself, as was his custom, from the remainder of the fleet, and pressed forward into the midst of the enemy.

He had sustained a continued cannonading from the vessel of Sprague for upward of three hours, without a single one of his crew being wounded, when De Ruyter, who had forced Prince Rupert to retire, came to his assistance. The Prince, on the other side, joined Admiral Sprague, and the fight was renewed with increased ardor. The vessel of Tromp was so damaged that he was obliged to remove his flag on board of another; Sprague was reduced to a similar necessity of quitting his ship, the Royal Prince, for the St. George, which, ere long, was so much disabled that he was obliged to proceed to a third; but the boat in which he was passing being struck by a cannon-ball, sank, and himself and several others were drowned. Toward the close of evening one English man-of-war was on fire, and two foundered. Not a single ship-of-war was lost on the side of the Dutch, but both fleets were so much damaged as to be unable to renew the engagement on the next morning. Each side, as usual, returned thanks for the victory, to which, however, the English failed to establish their claim, neither by accomplishing the projected invasion or intercepting the East India fleet, the whole of which, except one vessel, reached the ports in safety.

In the more distant quarters of the world the war was carried on with various success. The French captured the ports of Trincomalee, in Ceylon, and St. Thomas, on the coast of Coromandel—which were, however, recovered in the next year—and made an unsuccessful attempt on Curaçao. The English possessed themselves of the island of Tobago and seized four merchantmen returning from India. But, on the other hand, the States' admiral, Evertson, made himself master of New York, and, attacking the Newfoundland ships, took or destroyed no less than sixty-five, and returned to Holland laden with booty.

The King of France, meanwhile, well satisfied to have secured at so easy a rate a powerful diversion of the forces of Holland, and the mutual enfeebling of the two most formidable maritime powers of Europe, cared little how the affairs of his ally prospered, so that he had been enabled to pursue the career of his conquests on land. Marching in person at the head of his troops he laid siege to Maestricht, a town famous for its gallant defence against the Duke of Parma in 1579, but which now, notwithstanding several brisk and murderous sallies, capitulated in less than a month. With this achievement the campaign of Louis ended. The progress of his arms, and the development of his schemes of ambition had now raised him up a phalanx of enemies, such as not even his presumption could venture to despise.

He had planned and executed his conquests in full reliance on the coöperation or neutrality of the neighboring powers, and found himself in no condition to retain them in defiance of their actual hostility. He had, from the first, been strongly advised by Condé and Turenne to destroy the fortifications of the less important towns, retaining so many only of the larger as to insure the subjection of the provinces. He had, however, deemed it more consonant to his "glory" to follow the advice of Louvois in preserving all his conquests entire, and had thus been obliged to disperse a large portion of his army into garrisons, leaving the remainder, thinned, moreover, by sickness and desertion, wholly insufficient to make head against the increasing number of his opponents. He therefore came to the mortifying resolution of abandoning the United Provinces, the possession of which he had anticipated with so much pride.

This auspicious dawn of better fortunes to the provinces was followed by the long and ardently desired peace with England. The circumstances of the last battle, in which, as the English declared, "themselves, and the Dutch had been made the gladiators for the French spectators," had more than ever disgusted that nation with the alliance of an ambitious and selfish monarch, who, they perceived, was but gratifying his own rapacity at the expense of their blood and treasure. Spain had threatened a rupture with England unless she would consent to a reasonable peace; and even Sweden herself had declared, during the conferences at Cologne, that she should be constrained to adopt a similar course if the King of France persisted in extending his conquests. Should a war with these nations occur, the English saw themselves deprived of the valuable commerce they carried on in their ports, to be transferred, most probably, to the United Provinces; in addition to which consideration, their navigation had already sustained excessive injury from the privateering of the Zealanders, who had captured, it is said, no less than twenty-seven hundred English merchant-ships. These, and various other causes, had provoked the Parliament to use expressions of the highest indignation at the measures of the court, and to a peremptory refusal of further supplies for the war unless the Dutch, by their obstinacy in rejecting terms of peace, should render its continuance unavoidable.

Aware of this disposition, the States had addressed a letter to the King, which, with sufficient adroitness, they had contrived should arrive precisely at the meeting of Parliament, offering the King restitution of all the places they had gained during the war, and satisfaction with respect to the flag, or "any other matter they had not already ordered according to his wishes." This communication, received with feelings of extreme irritation by the court, had all the effect intended on the House of Commons. It was in vain that the King complained of the personal insults offered him by the Dutch; in vain that the chancellor expatiated on their obstinacy, arrogance, and enmity to the English; and that the court party remonstrated against the imprudence of exposing England defenceless to the power of her haughty enemy. The Parliament persisted in refusing the solicited supply; voted the standing army a grievance; bitterly complained of the French alliance, and resolved that his majesty should be advised to proceed in a treaty with the States-General, in order to a speedy peace.

A few days sufficed to accomplish a treaty; the Dutch obviating the principal difficulty by yielding the honor of the flag in the most ample manner. They now agreed that all their ships should lower their topsails and strike the flag upon meeting one or more English vessels bearing the royal standard, within the compass of the four seas, from Cape Finisterre to Staaten in Norway, and engaged to pay the King two million guilders for the expenses of the war.

Shortly after, the Bishops of Muenster and Cologne, alarmed at the probability of being abandoned by the French to the anger of the Emperor, who had threatened them with the ban of the empire, consented to a treaty with the United Provinces, in virtue of which they restored all the places they had conquered.

DISCOVERY OF THE MISSISSIPPI

LA SALLE NAMES LOUISIANA

A.D. 1673-1682

FRANÇOIS XAVIER GARNEAU[1]

During the early colonization of New France, in the era of Count Frontenac, a remarkable spirit of adventure and discovery manifested itself in Canada among both clerics and laymen. This enterprise, in seeking to open up and colonize the country, indeed, showed itself under each successive governor, from the first settlement of Quebec, in 1608, down to the fall, in 1759, of the renowned capital on the St. Lawrence. In the entailed arduous labor, full as it was of hazard and peril, the pathfinders of empire in the New World, besides laymen, were largely the Jesuit missionaries.

This spirit of adventure specially began to show itself in the colony at the period when M. Talon became intendant, when the government of New France, at the time of Louis XIV's minister, Colbert, became vested directly in the French crown. Through Talon's instrumentality the colony revived, and by his large-minded policy its commerce, which had fallen into the hands of a company of monopolists, was in time set free from many of its restrictions.

Before Talon quitted the country, he took steps to extend the dominion of France in the New World toward Hudson's Bay, and westward, in the direction of the Great Lakes. In 1671 he despatched a royal commissioner to Sault Ste. Marie, at the foot of Lake Superior, to assemble the Indians of the region and induce them to place themselves under the protection, and aid the commerce, of the French King.

While thus engaged, the commissioner heard of the Mississippi River from the Indians; and Talon intrusted the task of tracking its waters to Father Marquette and to M. Joliet, a merchant of Quebec. With infinite toil these two adventurous spirits reached the great river they were in search of, and explored it as far south as the Arkansas. Here unfriendly Indian tribes compelled them to return, without being permitted to trace the mighty stream to its outlet. This, however, is supposed to have been accomplished, in 1682, by Robert Cavalier, Sieur de la Salle, a daring young Frenchman, who descended the Mississippi, it is currently believed, to the Gulf of Mexico, naming the whole region Louisiana, in honor of Louis XIV.

[1] Translated by Andrew Bell.

Whether La Salle actually explored the great river to its mouth is, among historians, still a moot point. It is supposed that early in his adventures he retraced his steps and returned to Canada, where, as well as in France, he had numerous detractors, among whom was De la Barre, the then Governor of New France. It is known that he was soon again in Quebec, to meet his enemies, which he did successfully, after which he proceeded to France. Here he was royally received by the King, and, as a proof of the monarch's confidence in him, La Salle was intrusted with the command of a colonizing expedition which was sent to Louisiana by sea.

This expedition never reached its destination, for differences with the commander of the vessels (Beaujeu) interfered with the direction of the expedition. The mouths of the Mississippi, it seems, were passed, and the ships reached the coast of Texas. Disaster now dogged the leader's footsteps, for Beaujeu ran one of the ships on the rocks, and then deserted with another. La Salle and some of his more trusty followers were left to their fate, which was a cruel one, for disease broke out in the ranks, and famine and savage foes made havoc among the survivors. His colony being reduced to forty persons, La Salle set out overland with sixteen men for Canada to procure recruits. On the way his companions mutinied, put La Salle to death, and but a handful of the party reached Canada, the remainder perishing in the wilderness.

WERE we to express in the briefest of terms the motives which induced the leading European races of the fifteenth and sixteenth centuries who came to the Americas, we should say that the Spaniards went thither in quest of gold, the English for the sake of enjoying civil and religious freedom, the French in view of propagating the Gospel among the aborigines. Accordingly, we find, from the beginning, in the annals of New France, religious interests overlying all others. The members of the Society of Jesus, becoming discredited among the nations of Europe for their subserviency to power—usually exalting the rights of kings, but at all times inculcating submission, both by kings and their subjects, to the Roman pontiffs—individual Jesuits, we say, whatever may have been their demerits as members of the confraternity in Europe or in South America, did much to redeem these by their apostolic labors in the wilderness of the northern continent; cheerfully encountering, as they did, every form of suffering, braving the cruelest tortures, and even welcoming death as the expected seal of their martyrdom for the cause of Christ and for the advancement of civilization among barbarous nations.

From Quebec as a centre-point the missionary lines of the Jesuit fathers radiated in all directions through every region inhabited by our savages, from the Laurentian Valley to the Hudson's Bay territory, along the great-lake countries, and down the valley of the Mississippi. Scantily equipped, as it seemed to the worldly eye, with a breviary around the neck and a crucifix in hand, the missionary set forth, and became a pioneer for the most adventurous secular explorers of the desert. To such our forefathers owed their best earliest knowledge of vast regions, to whose savage inhabitants they imparted the glad tidings of the Gospel, and smoothed the way for native alliances with their compatriots of the laity, of the greatest after-import to the colony.

Such devotedness, at once heroic and humble, could not but confound worldly philosophy, while it has gained for the members of the order the admiration of many Protestants. Thus we have the candid testimony of Bancroft, the able historian of the English plantations in this continent, that "The annals of missionary labors are inseparably connected with the origin of all the establishments of French America. Not a cape was doubled nor a stream discovered that a Jesuit did not show the way."

On the other hand, there were instances where secular explorers, seeking to illustrate their names by great discoveries or to enrich themselves by traffic, opened a way for the after-labors of the missionary. The most celebrated of such were Champlain, Nicolet, Perrot, Joliet, La Salle, and La Verendrye.

In regions south of the St. Lawrence, Père Druillettes was the first European who passed overland from that river to the eastern Atlantic seaboard, ascending the Chaudière and descending the Kennebec in 1646. He did good service to the colony by preserving for it the amity of that brave nation, the only one which the Iroquois were slow to attack.

In another direction, the traffickers and missionaries, constantly moving onward toward the sources of the St. Lawrence, had reached the upper extremity of Lake Huron. Pères Brébeuf, Daniel, Lalemant, Jogues, and Raimbault founded in the regions around its waters the Christianized settlements (*villages*) of St. Joseph, St. Michel, St. Ignace, and Ste. Marie. The last-named, seated at the point where Lake Huron communicates with Lake Erie, was long the central point of the northwestern missions.

In 1639 Jean Nicholet, following the course of a river flowing out of Lake Michigan at Green Bay, was led within three days' navigation of "the Great Water," such was the distinctive name the aborigines gave to the Mississippi. In 1671 the relics of the Huron tribes, tired of wandering from forest to forest, settled down in Michilimackinac, at the end of Lake Superior, under the care of Père Marquette, who thus became the earliest founder of a European settlement in Michigan. The natives of the vicinity were of the Algonquin race; but the French called them *Sauteurs*, from their being near to Sault Ste. Marie.

Between the years 1635 and 1647 communication with the region was little attempted, the hostile feeling of the Iroquois making the navigation of Lake Ontario perilous to adventurers, and obliging them to pass to and from the western mission field by the valley of the Ottawa. The Neuters' territory, visited by Champlain, and the southern lakeboard of Erie beyond Buffalo, were as yet almost unknown.

The new impulse which had been given to Canada by Colbert and Talon began to bear fruit. Commerce revived, immigration increased, and the aborigines, dominated by the genius of civilization, feared and respected everywhere the power of France. Perrot, a famous explorer, was the first European who reached the end of Lake Michigan and the Miâmis country, where deputies from all the native tribes of the regions irrigated by the head waters of the Mississippi, the sources of the Red River and the St. Lawrence, responded to his call to meet him at the Sault Ste. Marie. From one discovery to another, as so many successive stages in a journey, the French attained a certainty that "the Great Water" did exist, and they could, in advance, trace its probable course. It appeared certain, from the recent search made for it in northerly and eastern directions, that its waters, so voluminous as the natives asserted, must at last find their sea-vent either in the Bay of Mexico or in the Pacific Ocean. Talon, who took a strong interest in the subject, during his intendancy recommended Captain Poulet, a skilful mariner of Dieppe, to verify the passage from sea to sea, through the Straits of Magellan.

He induced M. de Frontenac to send M. Joliet into the region where the great stream, yet unseen, must take its rise; and follow its course, if found, till its waters reached the sea. The person thus employed on a mission which interested everyone at the time was a man of talent, educated in the Jesuits' College of Quebec, probably in view of entering the Church, but who had gone into the peltry trade. He had travelled much in the countries around Lake Superior and gained great experience of the natives, especially those of the Ottawa tribes. M. Joliet and Père Marquette set out together in the year 1673. The latter, who had lived among the Potowatami Indians as a missionary, and gained their affections, was forewarned by them of the perils, they alleged, which would beset his steps in so daring an enterprise, admonishing him and his companion that the people of the farther countries would allow no stranger to pass through them; that travellers were always pillaged at the least; that the great river swarmed with monsters who devoured men,[1] and that the climate was so hot that human flesh could not endure it.

Having progressed to the farthest horde, over the Fox River, where Père Allouez was known, and the extremest point yet touched by any European, the adventurers found the people of the divers tribes living together in harmony; viz., the Kikapoos, Mascoutins, and Miâmis. They accorded the strangers a kind reception and furnished guides to direct the party, which was composed of nine persons in all—Joliet, Marquette, with five other whites, and two natives. On June 10th they set out, bearing two light canoes on their shoulders for crossing the narrow portage which separates the Fox River from that of Wisconsin, where the latter, after following a southerly, takes a western, course. Here their Indian guides left them, fearing to go farther.

Arrived at the Lower Wisconsin they embarked and glided down the stream, which led the travellers through a solitude; they remarking that the levels around them presented an unbroken expanse of luxuriant herbage or forests of lofty trees. Their progress was slow, for it was not till the tenth day that they attained the confluence of the Wisconsin and Mississippi. But

[1] There was some foundation for this report, as alligators abounded, at that time, in the lower waters of the river.

the goal was surely, if tardily, attained. They were now floating on the bosom of the "Father of Waters," a fact they at once felt assured of, and fairly committed themselves to the course of the doubled current. This event constituted an epoch in American annals.

"The two canoes," says Bancroft, "with sails outspread under a new sky, sped their way, impelled by favoring breezes, along the surface of the calm and majestic ocean tributary. At one time the French adventurers glided along sand-banks, the resting-places of innumerable aquatic birds; at others they passed around wooded islands in midflood; and otherwhiles, again, their course lay through the vast plains of Illinois and Iowa, covered with magnificent woods or dotted with clumps of bush scattered about limitless prairie lands."

It was not till the voyagers had descended sixty leagues of the great stream that they discovered any signs of the presence of man; but at length, observing on the right bank of the river a foot-track, they followed it for six miles, and arrived at a horde (*bourgade*), situated on a river called by the natives Moingona, an appellation afterward corrupted into "Rivière des Moines." Seeing no one, the visitors hollowed lustily, and four old men answered the call, bearing in hand the calumet of peace. "We are Illinois," said the Indians: "you are our fellow-men; we bid you welcome." They had never before seen any whites, but had heard mention of the French, and long wished to form an alliance with them against the Iroquois, whose hostile excursions extended even to their country. They were glad to hear from Joliet that the colonists had lately chastised those whom no others could vanquish, and feasted the visitors, to manifest their gratitude as well as respect. The chief of the tribe, with some hundreds of his warriors, escorted the party to their canoes; and, as a mark of parting esteem, he presented a calumet, ornamented with feathers of various colors; a safe-conduct this, held inviolable among the aborigines.

The voyagers, again on their way, were forewarned of the confluence of the Missouri with the main stream, by the noise of its discharging waters. Forty leagues lower, they reached the influx of the Ohio, in the territory of the Chouanows. By degrees the region they traversed changed its aspect. Instead of vast prairies, the voyagers only saw thick forests around them, inhabited by savages whose language was to them unknown. In quitting the southern line of the Ohio, they left the Algonquin family of aborigines behind, and had come upon a region of nomads, the Chickasaw nation being here denizens of the forest. The Dacotas, or Sioux, frequented the riverain lands, in the southern region watered by the great flood. Thus interpreters were needed by the natives, who wished to parley from either bank of the Mississippi, each speaking one of two mother-tongues, both distinct from those of the Hurons and Algonquins, much of the latter being familiar to Joliet and others of the party.

Continuing their descent, the confluence of the Arkansas with the Mississippi was attained. The voyagers were now under the thirty-third parallel of north latitude, at a point of the river-course reported to have been previously reached, from the opposite direction, by the celebrated Spanish mariner De Soto. Here the Illinois chief's present stood the party in good stead, for on exhibiting his ornate calumet they were treated with profuse kindness. Bread, made of maize, was offered by the chief of the horde located at the mouth of the Arkansas River. Hatchet-heads of steel, in use by the natives, gave intimation that they traded with Europeans, and that the Spanish settlements on the Bay of Mexico were probably not far off. The waxing summer heats, too, gave natural corroboration to the same inferences. The party had now, in fact, attained to a region without a winter, unless as such be reckoned that part of its year known as "the rainy season."

It now became expedient to call a halt, for the stored provisions were beginning to fail, and chance supplies could not be depended upon in such a wilderness as the bold adventurers had already traversed; and they were still more uncertain as to what treatment they might receive from savage populations if they proceeded farther. One thing was made plain to their perceptions: the Mississippi afforded no passage to the East Indian seas. They rightly concluded, also, that it found its sea outlet in the Bay of Mexico, not the Pacific Ocean. They had therefore now done enough to entitle them to the grateful thanks of their compatriots, and for the names of their two leaders to take a permanent place in the annals of geographical discovery.

The task of ascending the great river must have been arduous, and the return voyage protracted. Arrived at the point where it is joined by the Illinois, they left it for that stream, which, ascending for a part of its lower course, Père Marquette elected to remain with the natives of tribes located near to its banks; while M. Joliet, with the rest of the party, passed overland to Chicago. Thence he proceeded to Quebec, and reported his proceedings to the Governor, M. Talon at that time being in France. This duty he had to perform orally, having lost all his papers when shooting the rapids of the St. Lawrence, above Montreal. He afterward drew up a written report, with a tracing of his route, from memory.

The encouragement the intendant procured for the enterprise fairly entitles him to share its glory with those who so ably carried it out; for we cannot attach too much honor to the memory of statesmen who turn to account their opportunities of patronizing useful adventure. M. Joliet received in property the island of Anticosti as a reward for his Western discoveries and for an exploratory voyage he made to Hudson's Bay. He was also nominated hydrographer-royal, and got enfeoffed in a seigniory near Montreal. Expecting to reap great advantage from Anticosti as a fishing and fur-trading station, he built a fort thereon; but after living some time on the island with his family, he was obliged to abandon it. His patronymic was adopted as the name of a mountain situated near the Rivière des Plaines, a tributary of the Illinois; and Joliet is also the appellation, given in his honor, of a town near Chicago.

Père Marquette proceeded to Green Bay by Lake Michigan, in 1673; but he returned soon afterward and resumed his missionary labors among the Illinois Indians. Being then at war with the Miâmis, they came to him asking for gunpowder. "I have come among you," said the apostolic priest, "not to aid you to destroy your enemies' bodies, but to help you to save your own souls. Gunpowder I cannot give you, but my prayers you can have for your conversion to that religion which gives glory to God in the highest and on earth peace to all men." Upon one occasion he preached before two thousand warriors of their nation, besides the women and children present. His bodily powers, however, were now wellnigh exhausted. He decided to return to Mackinac; but while coasting the lower shores of Lake Michigan, feeling that his supreme hour was nigh, he caused the people in his canoe to set him ashore. Having obtained for him the shelter of a hut formed of branches, he there died the death of the righteous. His companions interred his remains near the river which yet bears his name, and set up a crucifix to mark the spot. Thus ended, amid the solitudes of the Western wilderness, the valuable existence of one whose name, too little known to his own age, will be remembered when hundreds of those which, however loudly sounded in the present, shall have passed into utter oblivion.[1]

The news of the discovery of the Mississippi made a great sensation in Canada, and eclipsed for a time the interest attaching to other explorations of the age, which were becoming more and more rife every year. Every speculative mind was set to work, as was usual on such occasions, to calculate the material advantages which might result, first to the colonists, and next to their mother-country, from access being obtained to a second gigantic waterway through the territories of New France; serving, as it virtually might in times to come, as a complement, or completing moiety for the former, enabling the colonists to have the command of two seas. Still, as the Gulf of Mexico had not been reached by the adventurers upon the present occasion, some persons had their doubts about the real course of the lower flood. There was therefore still in store credit for those who should succeed in clearing up whatever uncertainty there might be about a matter so important.

"New France," says Raynal, "had among its people a Norman named Robert Cavalier de la Salle, a man inspired with the double passion of amassing a large fortune and gaining an illustrious name. This person had acquired, under the training of the Jesuits, among whom his youth was passed, activity, enthusiasm, firmness of character, and high-heartedness—qualities

[1] Guérin observes that, according to some authorities, La Salle, some time between the years 1669 and 1671, descended the Mississipi, as far as the Arkansas, by the river Ohio. There can be no doubt that the story is a mere figment.

which that celebrated confraternity knew so well to discern and cultivate in promising natures committed to their care. Their most audacious and enterprising pupil, La Salle, was especially impatient to seize every occasion that chance presented for distinguishing himself, and ready to create such opportunities if none occurred." He had been resident some years in Canada when Joliet returned from his expedition to the Mississippi. The effect of so promising a discovery, upon such a mind as La Salle's, was of the most awakening kind. Joliet's report of what he experienced, and his shrewd conjectures as to what he did not see but which doubtless existed, well meditated upon by his fellow-genius, inspired the latter to form a vast design of exploration and traffic conjoined, in realizing which he determined to hazard both his fortunes and reputation.

Cavalier Sieur de la Salle was born in Rouen, and the son of respectable parents. While yet a young man he came to Canada full of a project he had conceived of seeking a road to Japan and China by a northern or western passage, but did not bring with him the pecuniary means needful even to make the attempt. He set about making friends for himself in the colony, and succeeded in finding favor with the Count de Frontenac, who discerned in him qualities somewhat akin to his own. With the aid of M. de Courcelles and Talon he opened a factory for the fur traffic at Lachine, near Montreal, a name which (*China*) he gave to the place in allusion to the oriental goal toward which his hopes tended as an explorer.

In the way of trade he visited Lakes Ontario and Erie. While the Canadians were yet excited about the discovery of the Mississippi, he imparted his aspirations regarding it to the Governor-general. He said that, by ascending, instead of descending, that great stream, a means might be found for reaching the Pacific Ocean; but that the outlay attending the enterprise could only be defrayed by combining with it an extended traffic with the nations of the West; that he would gladly make the attempt himself if a trading-post were erected for his use at the foot of Lake Ontario, as a basis for his operations, with an exclusive license to traffic in the Western countries. The Governor gave him the command of Fort Frontenac, to begin with. Obtaining, also, his recommendations to the Court, La Salle sailed for

France in 1675, and gained all he wanted from the Marquis de Seignelai, son and successor of the great Colbert as minister of marine. The King bestowed on La Salle the seigniory of Cataraqui (Kingston) and ennobled him. This seigniory included Fort Frontenac, of which he was made the proprietor, as well as of Lake Ontario; conditioned, however, that he was to reconstruct the fort in stone. His majesty also invested him with all needful credentials for beginning and continuing his discoveries.

La Salle, on his return to Canada, actively set about aggrandizing his new possession. Several colonists and some of the natives repaired to the locality, and settled under protection of his fort. He built in its vicinity three decked vessels—the first ever seen upon Lake Ontario. In 1677 he visited France again, in quest of aid to carry out his plans. Colbert and Seignelai got him a royal commission as recognized explorer of Northwest America, with permission to erect fortified posts therein at his discretion. He found a potent protector, also, in the Prince de Conti.

La Salle, full of hope, sailed from La Rochelle in summer, 1678, with thirty seamen and artisans, his vessel freighted with equipments for his lake craft, and merchandise for barter with the aborigines. A brave officer, Chevalier de Tonti, went with him, proposing to share his fortunes. Arrived at Cataraqui, his energy put all his workpeople in activity. On November 18th he set sail from Fort Frontenac in one of his barks, loaded with goods and materials for constructing a second fort and a brigantine at Niagara. When he reached the head of Lake Ontario, his vessel excited the admiration of the savages; while the Falls of Niagara no less raised the wonder of the French. Neither had before seen the former so great a triumph of human art; nor the latter, so overpowering a spectacle of nature.

La Salle set about founding his proposed stronghold at Niagara; but the natives, as soon as the defensive works began to take shape, demurred to their being continued. Not caring to dispute the matter with them, he gave his erections the form of a palisaded storehouse merely. During winter following, he laid the keel of a vessel on the stocks, at a place some six miles above the Falls.

His activity redoubled as his operations progressed. He sent on his friend Tonti with the famous Récollet, Père Hennepin, to seek out several men whom he had despatched as forerunners, in autumn preceding, to open up a traffic he intended to carry on with the aborigines of the West. In person he visited the Iroquois and several other nations, with whom he wished to form trading relations. He has the honor of founding the town of Niagara. The vessel he there built he called the Griffin, because, said he, "the griffin has right of mastery over the ravens": an allusion, as was said, to his hope of overcoming all his ill-willers, who were numerous.[1] Be this as it may, the Griffin was launched in midsummer, 1679, under a salute of cannon, with a chanting of *Te Deum* and shouts from the colonists; the natives present setting up yells of wonder, hailing the French as so many *Otkou* (or "men of a contriving mind").

On August 7th the Griffin, equipped with seven guns and loaded with small arms and goods, entered Lake Erie; when La Salle started for Detroit, which he reached in safety after a few days' sail. He gave to the expansion of the channel between Lakes Erie and Huron the name of Lake Ste. Claire, traversing which, on August 23d he entered Lake Huron. Five days later he reached Michilimackinac, after having encountered a violent storm, such as are not unfrequent in that locality. The aborigines of the country were not less moved than those of Niagara had been, at the appearance of the Griffin; an apparition rendered terrible as well as puzzling when the sound of her cannon boomed along the lake and reverberated from its shores.

On attaining to the chapel of the Ottawa tribe, at the mission station, he landed and attended mass. Continuing his voyage, some time in September he reached the Baie des Puants, on the western lake board of Michigan, where he cast anchor. So far the first ship navigation of the great Canadian lakes had been a triumph; but the end was not yet, and it proved to be disastrous,

[1] Some authors say that he named his vessel the Griffin in honor of the Frontenacs, the supporters in whose family coat-of-arms were two Griffins. Where all is so uncertain in an important matter, a third suggestion may be as near the mark as the first two. As the Norse or Norman sea-kings bore the raven for a standard, perhaps La Salle adopted the raven's master-symbol, in right of a hoped-for sovereignty over the American lakes.

for La Salle, hearing that his creditors had in his absence confiscated his possessions, despatched the Griffin, loaded with peltry, to Niagara, probably in view of redeeming them; but his vessel and goods were totally lost on the way.

Meanwhile he started, with a trading-party of thirty men of different callings, bearing arms and merchandise. Passing to St. Joseph's, at the lower end of Lake Michigan, whither he had ordered that the Griffin should proceed on her proposed second voyage from Niagara, he laid the foundations of a fort on the crest of a steep height, washed on two sides by the river of the Miâmis, and defended on another side by a deep ravine. He set buoys at the entrance of the stream for the direction of the crew of the anxiously expected vessel, upon whose safety depended in part the continuation of his enterprises; sending on some skilful hands to Michilimackinac to pilot her on the lake. The vessel not appearing, and winter being near, he set out for the country of the Illinois Indians, leaving a few men in charge of the fort, and taking with him the missionaries Gabriel, Hennepin, and Zénobe, also some private men; Tonti, who was likewise of the party, having rejoined his principal, but without the men he was sent to seek, as he could not find them.

The expedition, thus constituted, arrived toward the close of December at a deserted native village situated near the source of the Illinois River, in the canton which still bears La Salle's name. Without stopping here he descended that stream as far as Lake Peoria—called by Hennepin, "Pimiteoui"—on the margin of which he found encamped a numerous body of the Illinois. These Indians, though naturally gentle, yet turned unfriendly regards at first on the party, but, soon recovering from surprise at the appearance of the French, treated them with great hospitality; one of their attentions to the supposed wants of the visitors being to rub their wearied legs with bear's-grease and buffalo fat. These friendly people were glad to learn that La Salle meant to form establishments in their country. Like the Huron savages of Champlain's time, the Illinois, harassed as they were by the Iroquois, trusted that the French would protect them in future. The visitors remarked that the Illinois formed the sides of their huts with mats of flat reeds, lined and sewed together. All those the party saw were tall, robust in body, and dexterous with the bow. But the nation has been stigmatized by some early reporters as cowardly, lazy, debauched, and without respect for their chiefs.

La Salle's people, hearing no mention of his ship all this while, began first to murmur, and then to leave him: six of them deserted in one night. In other respects events occurred ominous of evil for the termination of the enterprise. To occupy the attention of his companions, and prevent them from brooding on apprehended ills, as well as to guard them against a surprise by any hostile natives, he set them on erecting a fort upon an eminence, at a place four days' journey distant from Lake Peoria; which, when finished, he named Breakheart (*Crèvecœur*), in allusion to the mental sufferings he then endured. To put an end to an intolerable state of suspense, in his own case he resolved to set out on foot for Frontenac, four hundred or five hundred leagues distant—hoping there to obtain good news about the Griffin; also in order to obtain equipments for a new bark, then in course of construction at Crèvecœur, in which he meant to embark upon his return thither, intending to descend the Mississippi to its embouchure. He charged Père Hennepin to trace the downward course of the Illinois to its junction with the Mississippi, then to ascend the former as high as possible and examine the territories through which its upper waters flow. After making Tonti captain of the fort in his absence, he set out, March 2, 1680, armed with a musket, and accompanied by three or four whites and one Indian.[1]

Père Hennepin, who left two days before, descended the Illinois to the Mississippi, made several excursions in the region around their confluence; then ascended the latter to a point beyond the Sault St. Antony, where he was detained for some months by Sioux Indians, who only let him go on his promise to return to them next year. One of the chiefs traced on a scrap of paper the route he desired to follow; and this rude but correct chart, says Hennepin, "served us truly as a compass." By fol-

[1] Charlevoix, by following the relation attributed to Tonti, has fallen into some obvious errors respecting La Salle's expedition to the Illinois River. Hennepin, an ocular witness, is assuredly the best authority, corroborated, as his narration is, by the relation and letters of Père Zénobe Mambré.

lowing the Wisconsin, which falls into the Mississippi, and Fox River, when running in the opposite direction, he reached Lake Michigan mission station, passing through, intermediately, vast and interesting countries. Such was the famous expedition of Hennepin; who, on his return, was not a little surprised to find a company of fur-traders near the Wisconsin River, led by one De Luth, who had probably preceded him in visiting that remote region.

While Hennepin was exploring the upper valley of the Mississippi, La Salle's interests were getting from bad to worse at Crèvecœur. But, for rightly understanding the events which at last obliged him to abandon that post, it is necessary to explain the state of his affairs in Canada, and to advert to the jealousies which other traffickers cherished regarding his monopolizing projects in the western regions of the continent. He came to the colony, as we have seen, a fortuneless adventurer—highly recommended, indeed; while the special protection he obtained from the Governor, with the titular and more solid favors he obtained at court, made him a competitor to all other commercialists, whom it was impossible to contend with directly. Underhand means of opposition, therefore—and these not always the fairest—were put in play to damage his interests and, if possible, effect his ruin.

For instance, feuds were stirred up against him among the savage tribes, and inducements held out to his own people to desert him. They even induced the Iroquois and the Miâmis to take up arms against the Illinois, his allies. Besides this hostility to him within New France, he had to face the opposition of the Anglo-American colonists, who resisted the realization of his projects, for nationally selfish reasons. Thus they encouraged the Iroquois to attack La Salle's Indian allied connections of the Mississippi Valley; a measure which greatly increased the difficulties of a position already almost untenable. In a word, the odds against him became too great; and he was constrained to retire from the high game he wished to play out, which, indeed, was certainly to the disadvantage of individuals, if tending to enhance the importance of the colony as a possession of France.

La Salle's ever-trusty lieutenant, the Chevalier de Tonti, meanwhile did all he could, at Crèvecœur, to engage the Illinois to stand firm to their engagements with his principal. Having learned that the Miâmis intended to join the Iroquois in opposition to them, he hastened to teach the use of fire-arms to those who remained faithful, to put the latter on a footing of equality with these two nations, who were now furnished with the like implements of war. He also showed them how to fortify their hordes with palisades. But while in the act of erecting Fort Louis, near the sources of the river Illinois, most of the garrison at Crèvecœur mutinied and deserted, after pillaging the stores of provision and ammunition there laid up.

At this crisis of La Salle's affairs (1680) armed bands of the Iroquois suddenly appeared in the Illinois territory and produced a panic among its timid inhabitants. Tonti, acting with spirit and decision as their ally, now intervened, and enforced upon the Iroquois a truce for the Illinois; but the former, on ascertaining the paucity of his means, recommenced hostilities. Attacking the fort, they murdered Père Gabriel, disinterred the dead, and wasted the cultivated land of the French residents. The Illinois dispersed in all directions, leaving the latter isolated among their enemies. Tonti, who had at last but five men under his orders, also fled the country.

While the Chevalier, in his passage from Crèvecœur, was descending the north side of Lake Michigan, La Salle was moving along its southern side with a reënforcement of men, and rigging for the bark he left in course of construction at the above-named post, where, having arrived, he had the mortification to find it devastated and deserted. He made no attempt to refound it, but passed the rest of the year in excursions over the neighboring territories, in which he visited a great number of tribes; among them the Outagamis and Miâmis, whom he persuaded to renounce an alliance they had formed with the Iroquois. Soon afterward he returned to Montreal, taking Frontenac on his way. Although his pecuniary losses had been great, he was still able to compound with his creditors, to whom he conceded his own sole rights of trade in the Western countries, they in return advancing moneys to enable him to prosecute his future explorations.

Having got all things ready for the crowning expedition he had long meditated, he set out with Tonti, Père Mambré, also some French and native followers, and directed his course toward the Mississippi, which river he reached February 6, 1682. The mildness of the climate in that latitude, and the beauties of the country, which increased as he proceeded, seemed to give new life to his hopes of finally obtaining profit and glory.[1] In descending the majestic stream, he recognized the Arkansas and other riverain tribes visited by Marquette; he traversed the territories of many other native nations, including the Chickasaws, the Taensas, the Chactas, and the Natchez—the last of these rendered so celebrated, in times near our own, by the genius of Châteaubriand.

Halting often in his descent to note the outlets of the many streams tributary to the all-absorbing Mississippi, among others the Missouri and the Ohio—at the embouchure of the latter erecting a fort—he did not reach the ocean mouths of the "Father of Waters" till April 5th, that brightest day of his eventful life. With elated heart, he took formal possession of the country—eminently in the name of the reigning sovereign of France; as he gave to it, at the same time, the distinctive appellation of Louisiana. Thus was completed the discovery and exploration of the Mississippi, from the Sault St. Antony to the sea; a line more than six hundred leagues in length.

[1] "A vessel loaded with merchandise belonging to La Salle, valued at 22,000 livres, had just been lost in the Gulf of St. Lawrence; several canoes, also loaded with his goods, were lost in the rapids of the same river. On learning these new misfortunes [in addition to others, of his enemies' procuring], he said it seemed to him that all Canada had risen up against his enterprises, with the single individual exception of the Governor-general. He asserted that the subordinates, whom he had brought from France, had been tempted to quit his service by rival traders, and that they had gone to the New Netherlands with the goods he had intrusted to their care; and as for the Canadians in his hire, his enemies had found means to detach them, also, from his interests."—Yet, "under the pressure of all his misfortunes," says a missionary, "I have never remarked the least change in him; no ill news seemed to disturb his usual equanimity: they seemed rather to spur him on to fresh efforts to retrieve his fortunes, and to make greater discoveries than he had yet effected."

KING PHILIP'S WAR

A.D. 1675

RICHARD HILDRETH

This was the most extensive and most important of the Indian wars of the early European settlers in North America. It led to the practical extermination of the red men in New England.

Various policies toward the natives were pursued by different colonists in different parts of the country. In New England the first white settlers found themselves in contact with several powerful tribes, chief among which were the Mohegans, the Narragansetts, and the Pequots.

Some attempt was made to convert and civilize these savages, but it was not long before the English colonists were at war with the Pequots, the most dreaded of the tribes in southern New England. This contest (1636–1638) was mainly carried on for the colonists by the settlers of Connecticut. It resulted in the almost complete extermination of the Pequot tribe.

After the union of the New England colonies (1643), formed principally for common defence against the natives, there was no considerable conflict between whites and Indians until the outbreak of King Philip's War, here described by Hildreth.

EXCEPT in the destruction of the Pequots, the native tribes of New England had as yet undergone no very material diminution. The Pokanokets or Wampanoags, though somewhat curtailed in their limits, still occupied the eastern shore of Narragansett Bay. The Narragansetts still possessed the western shore. There were several scattered tribes in various parts of Connecticut; though, with the exception of some small reservations, they had already ceded all their lands. Uncas, the Mohegan chief, was now an old man. The Pawtucket or Pennacook confederacy continued to occupy the falls of the Merrimac and the heads of the Piscataqua. Their old sachem, Passaconaway, regarded the colonists with awe and veneration. In the interior of Massachusetts and along the Connecticut were several other less noted tribes. The Indians of Maine and the region eastward possessed their ancient haunts undisturbed; but their intercourse was principally with the French, to whom, since the late peace with France, Acadia had been again yielded up. The New England Indians were occasionally annoyed by war parties of Mohawks; but, by the intervention of Massachusetts, a peace had recently been concluded.

Efforts for the conversion and civilization of the Indians were still continued by Eliot and his coadjutors, supported by the funds of the English society. In Massachusetts there were fourteen feeble villages of these praying Indians, and a few more in Plymouth colony. The whole number in New England was about thirty-six hundred, but of these near one-half inhabited the islands of Nantucket and Martha's Vineyard.

A strict hand was held by Massachusetts over the Narragansetts and other subject tribes, contracting their limits by repeated cessions, not always entirely voluntary. The Wampanoags, within the jurisdiction of Plymouth, experienced similar treatment. By successive sales of parts of their territory, they were now shut up, as it were, in the necks or peninsulas formed by the northern and eastern branches of Narragansett Bay, the same territory now constituting the continental eastern portion of Rhode Island. Though always at peace with the colonists, the Wampanoags had not always escaped suspicion. The increase of the settlements around them, and the progressive curtailment of their limits, aroused their jealousy. They were galled, also, by the feudal superiority, similar to that of Massachusetts over her dependent tribes, claimed by Plymouth on the strength of certain alleged former submissions. None felt this assumption more keenly than Pometacom, head chief of the Wampanoags, better known among the colonists as King Philip of Mount Hope, nephew and successor of that Massasoit, who had welcomed the Pilgrims to Plymouth. Suspected of hostile designs, he had been compelled to deliver up his fire-arms and to enter into certain stipulations. These stipulations he was accused of not fulfilling; and nothing but the interposition of the Massachusetts magistrates, to whom Philip appealed, prevented Plymouth from making war upon him. He was sentenced instead to pay a heavy fine and to acknowledge the unconditional supremacy of that colony.

A praying Indian, who had been educated at Cambridge and

employed as a teacher, upon some misdemeanor had fled to Philip, who took him into service as a sort of secretary. Being persuaded to return again to his former employment, this Indian accused Philip anew of being engaged in a secret hostile plot. In accordance with Indian ideas, the treacherous informer was waylaid and killed. Three of Philip's men, suspected of having killed him, were arrested by the Plymouth authorities, and, in accordance with English ideas, were tried for murder by a jury half English, half Indians, convicted upon very slender evidence, and hanged. Philip retaliated by plundering the houses nearest Mount Hope. Presently he attacked Swanzey, and killed several of the inhabitants. Plymouth took measures for raising a military force. The neighboring colonies were sent to for assistance. Thus, by the impulse of suspicion on the one side and passion on the other, New England became suddenly engaged in a war very disastrous to the colonists and utterly ruinous to the native tribes. The lust of gain, in spite of all laws to prevent it, had partially furnished the Indians with fire-arms, and they were now far more formidable enemies than they had been in the days of the Pequots. Of this the colonists hardly seem to have thought. Now, as then, confident of their superiority, and comparing themselves to the Lord's chosen people driving the heathen out of the land, they rushed eagerly into the contest, without a single effort at the preservation of peace. Indeed, their pretensions hardly admitted of it. Philip was denounced as a rebel in arms against his lawful superiors, with whom it would be folly and weakness to treat on any terms short of absolute submission.

A body of volunteers, horse and foot, raised in Massachusetts, marched under Major Savage, four days after the attack on Swanzey, to join the Plymouth forces. After one or two slight skirmishes, they penetrated to the Wampanoag villages at Mount Hope, but found them empty and deserted. Philip and his warriors, conscious of their inferiority, had abandoned their homes. If the Narragansetts, on the opposite side of the bay, did not openly join the Wampanoags, they would, at least, be likely to afford shelter to their women and children. The troops were therefore ordered into the Narragansett country, accompanied by commissioners to demand assurances of peaceful intentions, and a promise to deliver up all fugitive enemies of the colonists—pledges which the Narragansetts felt themselves constrained to give.

Arrived at Taunton on their return from the Narragansett country, news came that Philip and his warriors had been discovered by Church, of Plymouth colony, collected in a great swamp at Pocasset, now Tiverton, the southern district of the Wampanoag country, whence small parties sallied forth to burn and plunder the neighboring settlements. After a march of eighteen miles, having reached the designated spot, the soldiers found there a hundred wigwams lately built, but empty and deserted, the Indians having retired deep into the swamp. The colonists followed; but the ground was soft; the thicket was difficult to penetrate; the companies were soon thrown into disorder. Each man fired at every bush he saw shake, thinking an Indian might lay concealed behind it, and several were thus wounded by their own friends. When night came on, the assailants retired with the loss of sixteen men.

The swamp continued to be watched and guarded, but Philip broke through, not without some loss, and escaped into the country of the Nipmucks, in the interior of Massachusetts. That tribe had already commenced hostilities by attacking Mendon. They waylaid and killed Captain Hutchinson, a son of the famous Mrs. Hutchinson, and sixteen out of a party of twenty sent from Boston to Brookfield to parley with them. Attacking Brookfield itself, they burned it, except one fortified house. The inhabitants were saved by Major Willard, who, on information of their danger, came with a troop of horse from Lancaster, thirty miles through the woods, to their rescue. A body of troops presently arrived from the eastward, and were stationed for some time at Brookfield.

The colonists now found that by driving Philip to extremity they had roused a host of unexpected enemies. The River Indians, anticipating an intended attack upon them, joined the assailants. Deerfield and Northfield, the northernmost towns on the Connecticut River, settled within a few years past, were attacked, and several of the inhabitants killed and wounded. Captain Beers, sent from Hadley to their relief with a convoy of provisions, was surprised near Northfield and slain, with twenty of his men. Northfield was abandoned, and burned by the Indians.

"The English at first," says Gookin, "thought easily to chastise the insolent doings and murderous practice of the heathen; but it was found another manner of thing than was expected; for our men could see no enemy to shoot at, but yet felt their bullets out of the thick bushes where they lay in ambush. The English wanted not courage or resolution, but could not discover nor find an enemy to fight with, yet were galled by the enemy." In the arts of ambush and surprise, with which the Indians were so familiar, the colonists were without practice. It is to the want of this experience, purchased at a very dear rate in the course of the war, that we must ascribe the numerous surprises and defeats from which the colonists suffered at its commencement.

Driven to the necessity of defensive warfare, those in command on the river determined to establish a magazine and garrison at Hadley. Captain Lathrop, who had been despatched from the eastward to the assistance of the river towns, was sent with eighty men, the flower of the youth of Essex county, to guard the wagons intended to convey to Hadley three thousand bushels of unthreshed wheat, the produce of the fertile Deerfield meadows. Just before arriving at Deerfield, near a small stream still known as Bloody Brook, under the shadow of the abrupt conical Sugar Loaf, the southern termination of the Deerfield Mountain, Lathrop fell into an ambush, and, after a brave resistance, perished there with all his company. Captain Moseley, stationed at Deerfield, marched to his assistance, but arrived too late to help him. Deerfield was abandoned, and burned by the Indians. Springfield, about the same time, was set on fire, but was partially saved by the arrival, with troops from Connecticut, of Major Treat, successor to the lately deceased Mason in the chief command of the Connecticut forces. An attack on Hatfield was vigorously repelled by the garrison.

Meanwhile, hostilities were spreading; the Indians on the Merrimac began to attack the towns in their vicinity; and the whole of Massachusetts was soon in the utmost alarm. Except in the immediate neighborhood of Boston, the country still remained an immense forest, dotted by a few openings. The frontier settlements could not be defended against a foe familiar with localities, scattered in small parties, skilful in concealment, and watching with patience for some unguarded or favorable moment. Those settlements were mostly broken up, and the inhabitants, retiring toward Boston, spread everywhere dread and intense hatred of "the bloody heathen."

Even the praying Indians and the small dependent and tributary tribes became objects of suspicion and terror. They had been employed at first as scouts and auxiliaries, and to good advantage; but some few, less confirmed in the faith, having deserted to the enemy, the whole body of them were denounced as traitors. Eliot the apostle, and Gookin, superintendent of the subject Indians, exposed themselves to insults, and even to danger, by their efforts to stem this headlong fury, to which several of the magistrates opposed but a feeble resistance. Troops were sent to break up the praying villages at Mendon, Grafton, and others in that quarter. The Natick Indians, "those poor despised sheep of Christ," as Gookin affectionately calls them, were hurried off to Deer Island, in Boston harbor, where they suffered excessively from a severe winter. A part of the praying Indians of Plymouth colony were confined, in like manner, on the islands in Plymouth harbor.

Not content with realities sufficiently frightful, superstition, as usual, added bugbears of her own. Indian bows were seen in the sky, and scalps in the moon. The northern lights became an object of terror. Phantom horsemen careered among the clouds or were heard to gallop invisible through the air. The howling of wolves was turned into a terrible omen. The war was regarded as a special judgment in punishment of prevailing sins. Among these sins the General Court of Massachusetts, after consultation with the elders, enumerated: Neglect in the training of the children of church members; pride, in men's wearing long and curled hair; excess in apparel; naked breasts and arms, and superfluous ribbons; the toleration of Quakers; hurry to leave meeting before blessing asked; profane cursing and swearing; tippling-houses; want of respect for parents; idleness; extortion in shopkeepers and mechanics; and the riding from town to town of unmarried men and women, under pretence of attending lectures—"a sinful custom, tending to lewdness."

Penalties were denounced against all these offences; and the persecution of the Quakers was again renewed. A Quaker woman had recently frightened the Old South congregation in Boston by entering that meeting-house clothed in sackcloth, with ashes on her head, her feet bare, and her face blackened, intending to personify the small-pox, with which she threatened the colony, in punishment for its sins.

About the time of the first collision with Philip, the Tarenteens, or Eastern Indians, had attacked the settlements in Maine and New Hampshire, plundering and burning the houses, and massacring such of the inhabitants as fell into their hands. This sudden diffusion of hostilities and vigor of attack from opposite quarters made the colonists believe that Philip had long been plotting and had gradually matured an extensive conspiracy, into which most of the tribes had deliberately entered for the extermination of the whites. This belief infuriated the colonists and suggested some very questionable proceedings.

It seems, however, to have originated, like the war itself, from mere suspicions. The same griefs pressed upon all the tribes; and the struggle once commenced, the awe which the colonists inspired thrown off, the greater part were ready to join in the contest. But there is no evidence of any deliberate concert; nor, in fact, were the Indians united. Had they been so, the war would have been far more serious. The Connecticut tribes proved faithful, and that colony remained untouched. Uncas and Ninigret continued friendly; even the Narragansetts, in spite of so many former provocations, had not yet taken up arms. But they were strongly suspected of intention to do so, and were accused by Uncas of giving, notwithstanding their recent assurances, aid and shelter to the hostile tribes.

An attempt had lately been made to revive the union of the New England colonies. At a meeting of commissioners, those from Plymouth presented a narrative of the origin and progress of the present hostilities. Upon the strength of this narrative the war was pronounced "just and necessary," and a resolution was passed to carry it on at the joint expense, and to raise for that purpose a thousand men, one-half to be mounted dragoons. If the Narragansetts were not crushed during the winter, it was feared they might break out openly hostile in the spring; and at a subsequent meeting a thousand men were ordered to be levied to coöperate in an expedition specially against them.

The winter was unfavorable to the Indians; the leafless woods no longer concealed their lurking attacks. The frozen surface of the swamps made the Indian fastnesses accessible to the colonists. The forces destined against the Narragansetts—six companies from Massachusetts, under Major Appleton; two from Plymouth, under Major Bradford; and five from Connecticut, under Major Treat—were placed under the command of Josiah Winslow, Governor of Plymouth since Prince's death—son of that Edward Winslow so conspicuous in the earlier history of the colony. The Massachusetts and Plymouth forces marched to Petasquamscot, on the west shore of Narragansett Bay, where they made some forty prisoners.

Being joined by the troops from Connecticut, and guided by an Indian deserter, after a march of fifteen miles through a deep snow they approached a swamp in what is now the town of South Kingston, one of the ancient strongholds of the Narragansetts. Driving the Indian scouts before them, and penetrating the swamp, the colonial soldiers soon came in sight of the Indian fort, built on a rising ground in the morass, a sort of island of two or three acres, fortified by a palisade and surrounded by a close hedge a rod thick. There was but one entrance, quite narrow, defended by a tree thrown across it, with a block-house of logs in front and other on the flank.

It was the "Lord's day," but that did not hinder the attack. As the captains advanced at the heads of their companies the Indians opened a galling fire, under which many fell. But the assailants pressed on and forced the entrance. A desperate struggle ensued. The colonists were once driven back, but they rallied and returned to the charge, and, after a two-hours' fight, became masters of the fort. Fire was put to the wigwams, near six hundred in number, and all the horrors of the Pequot massacre were renewed. The corn and other winter stores of the Indians were consumed, and not a few of the old men, women, and children perished in the flames. In this bloody contest, long remembered as the "Swamp Fight," the colonial loss was terribly severe. Six captains, with two hundred thirty men, were killed or wounded; and at night, in the midst of a snow-storm, with a fifteen-miles' march before them, the colonial soldiers abandoned the fort, of which the Indians resumed possession. But their wigwams were burned; their provisions destroyed; they had no supplies for the winter; their loss was irreparable. Of those who survived the fight many perished of hunger.

Even as a question of policy this attack on the Narragansetts was more than doubtful. The starving and infuriated warriors, scattered through the woods, revenged themselves by attacks on the frontier settlements. Lancaster was burned, and forty of the inhabitants killed or taken; among the rest, Mrs. Rolandson, wife of the minister, the narrative of whose captivity is still preserved. Groton, Chelmsford, and other towns in that vicinity were repeatedly attacked. Medfield, twenty miles from Boston, was furiously assaulted, and, though defended by three hundred men, half the houses were burned. Weymouth, within eighteen miles of Boston, was attacked a few days after. These were the nearest approaches which the Indians made to that capital.

For a time the neighborhood of the Narragansett country was abandoned. The Rhode Island towns, though they had no part in undertaking the war, yet suffered the consequences of it. Warwick was burned and Providence was partially destroyed. Most of the inhabitants sought refuge in the islands; but the aged Roger Williams accepted a commission as captain for the defence of the town he had founded. Walter Clarke was presently chosen governor in Coddington's place, the times not suiting a Quaker chief magistrate.

The whole colony of Plymouth was overrun. Houses were burned in almost every town, but the inhabitants, for the most part, saved themselves in their garrisons, a shelter with which all the towns now found it necessary to be provided. Captain Pierce, with fifty men and some friendly Indians, while endeavoring to cover the Plymouth towns, fell into an ambush and was cut off. That same day, Marlborough was set on fire; two days after, Rehoboth was burned. The Indians seemed to be everywhere. Captain Wadsworth, marching to the relief of Sudbury, fell into an ambush and perished with fifty men. The alarm and terror of the colonists reached again a great height. But affairs were about to take a turn. The resources of the Indians were exhausted; they were now making their last efforts.

A body of Connecticut volunteers, under Captain Denison, and of Mohegan and other friendly Indians, Pequots and Niantics, swept the entire country of the Narragansetts, who suffered, as spring advanced, the last extremities of famine. Canochet, the chief sachem, said to have been a son of Miantonomoh, but probably his nephew, had ventured to his old haunts to procure seed-corn with which to plant the rich intervals on the Connecticut, abandoned by the colonists. Taken prisoner, he conducted himself with all that haughty firmness esteemed by the Indians as the height of magnanimity. Being offered his life on condition of bringing about a peace he scorned the proposal. His tribe would perish to the last man rather than become servants to the English. When ordered to prepare for death he replied: "I like it well; I shall die before my heart is soft or I shall have spoken anything unworthy of myself." Two Indians were appointed to shoot him, and his head was cut off and sent to Hartford.

The colonists had suffered severely. Men, women, and children had perished by the bullets of the Indians or fled naked through the wintry woods by the light of their blazing houses, leaving their goods and cattle a spoil to the assailants. Several settlements had been destroyed and many more had been abandoned; but the oldest and wealthiest remained untouched. The Indians, on the other hand, had neither provisions nor ammunition. While attempting to plant corn and catch fish at Montague Falls, on the Connecticut River, they were attacked with great slaughter by the garrison of the lower towns, led by Captain Turner, a Boston Baptist, and at first refused a commission on that account, but, as danger increased, pressed to accept it.

Yet this enterprise was not without its drawbacks. As the troops returned, Captain Turner fell into an ambush and was slain with thirty-eight men. Hadley was attacked on a lecture-day, while the people were at meeting; but the Indians were repulsed by the bravery of Goffe, one of the fugitive regicides, long concealed in that town. Seeing this venerable unknown man come to their rescue, and then suddenly disappear, the inhabitants took him for an angel.

Major Church, at the head of a body of two hundred volunteers, English and Indians, energetically hunted down the hostile bands in Plymouth colony. The interior tribes about Mount Wachusett were invaded and subdued by a force of six hundred men, raised for that purpose. Many fled to the north to find refuge in Canada—guides and leaders, in after-years, of those French and Indian war parties by which the frontiers of New England were so terribly harassed. Just a year after the fast at the commencement of the war, a thanksgiving was observed for success in it.

No longer sheltered by the River Indians, who now began to make their peace, and even attacked by bands of the Mohawks, Philip returned to his own country, about Mount Hope, where he was still faithfully supported by his female confederate and relative, Witamo, squaw-sachem of Pocasset. Punham, also, the Shawomet vassal of Massachusetts, still zealously carried on the war, but was presently killed. Philip was watched and followed by Church, who surprised his camp, killed upward of a hundred of his people, and took prisoners his wife and boy.

The disposal of this child was a subject of much deliberation. Several of the elders were urgent for putting him to death. It was finally resolved to send him to Bermuda, to be sold into slavery—a fate to which many other of the Indian captives were subjected. Witamo shared the disasters of Philip. Most of her people were killed or taken. She herself was drowned while crossing a river in her flight, but her body was recovered, and the head, cut off, was stuck upon a pole at Taunton, amid the jeers and scoffs of the colonial soldiers, and the tears and lamentations of the Indian prisoners.

Philip still lurked in the swamps, but was now reduced to extremity. Again attacked by Church, he was killed by one of his own people, a deserter to the colonists. His dead body was beheaded and quartered, the sentence of the English law upon traitors. One of his hands was given to the Indian who had shot him, and on the day appointed for a public thanksgiving his head was carried in triumph to Plymouth.

The popular rage against the Indians was excessive. Death or slavery was the penalty for all known or suspected to have been concerned in shedding English blood. Merely having been present at the Swamp Fight was adjudged by the authorities of Rhode Island sufficient foundation for sentence of death, and that, too, notwithstanding they had intimated an opinion that the origin of the war would not bear examination. The other captives who fell into the hands of the colonists were distributed among them as ten-year servants. Roger Williams received a boy for his share. Many chiefs were executed at Boston and Plymouth on the charge of rebellion; among others, Captain Tom, chief of the Christian Indians at Natick, and Tispiquin, a noted warrior, reputed to be invulnerable, who had surrendered to Church on an implied promise of safety.

A large body of Indians, assembled at Dover to treat of peace, were treacherously made prisoners by Major Waldron, who commanded there. Some two hundred of these Indians, claimed as fugitives from Massachusetts, were sent by water to Boston, where some were hanged and the rest shipped off to be sold as slaves. Some fishermen of Marblehead having been killed by the Indians at the eastward, the women of that town, as they came out of meeting on a Sunday, fell upon two Indian prisoners who had just been brought in, and murdered them on the spot.

The same ferocious spirit of revenge which governed the contemporaneous conduct of Berkeley in Virginia toward those concerned in Bacon's rebellion swayed the authorities of New England in their treatment of the conquered Indians. By the end of the year the contest was over in the South, upward of two thousand Indians having been killed or taken. But some time elapsed before a peace could be arranged with the Eastern tribes, whose haunts it was not so easy to reach.

In this short war of hardly a year's duration the Wampanoags and Narragansetts had suffered the fate of the Pequots. The Niantics alone, under the guidance of their aged sachem Ninigret, had escaped destruction. Philip's country was annexed to Plymouth, though sixty years afterward, under a royal order in council, it was transferred to Rhode Island. The Narragansett territory remained as before, under the name of King's Province, a bone of contention between Connecticut, Rhode Island, the Marquis of Hamilton, and the Atherton claimants. The Niantics still retained their ancient seats along the southern shores of Narragansett Bay. Most of the surviving Narragansetts, the Nipmucks, and the River Indians, abandoned their country and migrated to the north and west. Such as remained, along with the Mohegans and other subject tribes, became more than ever abject and subservient.

The work of conversion was now again renewed, and, after such overwhelming proofs of Christian superiority, with somewhat greater success. A second edition of the Indian Old Testament, which seems to have been more in demand than the New, was presently published, revised by Eliot, with the assistance of John Cotton, son of the "Great Cotton," and minister of Plymouth. But not an individual exists in our day by whom it can be understood. The fragments of the subject tribes, broken in spirit, lost the savage freedom and rude virtues of their fathers without acquiring the laborious industry of the whites. Lands were assigned them in various places, which they were prohibited by law from alienating. But this very provision, though humanely intended, operated to perpetuate their indolence and incapacity. Some sought a more congenial occupation in the whale fishery, which presently began to be carried on from the islands of Nantucket and Martha's Vineyard. Many perished by enlisting in the military expeditions undertaken in future years against Acadia and the West Indies. The Indians intermarried with the blacks, and thus confirmed their degradation by associating themselves with another oppressed and unfortunate race. Gradually they dwindled away. A few hundred sailors and petty farmers, of mixed blood, as much African as Indian, are now the sole surviving representatives of the aboriginal possessors of Southern New England.

On the side of the colonists the contest had also been very disastrous. Twelve or thirteen towns had been entirely ruined and many others partially destroyed. Six hundred houses had been burned, near a tenth part of all in New England. Twelve captains, and more than six hundred men in the prime of life, had fallen in battle. There was hardly a family not in mourning. The pecuniary losses and expenses of the war were estimated at near a million of dollars.

GROWTH OF PRUSSIA UNDER THE GREAT ELECTOR

HIS VICTORY AT FEHRBELLIN

A.D. 1675

THOMAS CARLYLE

It was the good-fortune of Frederick William, Elector of Brandenburg, who is known in history as the "Great Elector," to lay a firm foundation for Prussian monarchy. Under his father, George William, the Tenth Elector, Brandenburg had lost much of its former importance. When Frederick William came into his inheritance in 1640 he found a weak and disunited state, little more than a group of provinces, with foreign territories lying between them, and governed by differing laws.

The great problem before the Elector was how to become actual ruler of his ill-joined possessions, and his first aim was to weld them together, that he might make himself absolute monarch. By forming an army of mercenaries he established his authority. His whole life was occupied with warlike affairs. He remained neutral during the last stages of the Thirty Years' War, but was always prepared for action. He freed Prussia from Polish control and drove the Swedes from Brandenburg.

This last was his most famous success. It was won by his victory over the Swedes under Wrangel, at Fehrbellin. Carlyle's characteristic narrative and commentary on this and other triumphs of the Great Elector place him before the reader as one of the chief personages of the Hohenzollern race and a leading actor in European history.

BRANDENBURG had sunk very low under the Tenth Elector, in the unutterable troubles of the times, but it was gloriously raised up again by his Son Friedrich Wilhelm, who succeeded in 1640. This is he whom they call the "Great Elector" ("*Grosse Kurfuerst*"), of whom there is much writing and celebrating in Prussian Books. As for the epithet, it is not uncommon among petty German populations, and many times does not mean too much: thus Max of Bavaria, with his Jesuit Lambkins and Hyacinths, is by Bavarians called "Maximilian the Great." Friedrich Wilhelm, both by his intrinsic qualities and the success he met with, deserves it better than most. His success, if we look where he started and where he ended, was beyond that of any other man in his day. He found Brandenburg annihilated, and he left Brandenburg sound and flourishing—a great country, or already on the way toward greatness: undoubtedly a most rapid, clear-eyed, active man. There was a stroke in him swift as lightning, well aimed mostly, and of a respectable weight withal, which shattered asunder a whole world of impediments for him by assiduous repetition of it for fifty years.

There hardly ever came to sovereign power a young man of twenty under more distressing, hopeless-looking circumstances. Political significance Brandenburg had none—a mere Protestant appendage dragged about by a Papist Kaiser. His Father's Prime Minister was in the interest of his enemies; not Brandenburg's servant, but Austria's. The very Commandants of his Fortresses, Commandant of Spandau more especially, refused to obey Friedrich Wilhelm on his accession—"were bound to obey the Kaiser in the first place." He had to proceed softly as well as swiftly, with the most delicate hand, to get him of Spandau by the collar, and put him under lock and key, as a warning to others.

For twenty years past Brandenburg had been scoured by hostile armies, which, especially the Kaiser's part of which, committed outrages new in human history. In a year or two hence Brandenburg became again the theatre of business. Austrian Gallas, advancing thither again (1644) with intent "to shut up Tortenson and his Swedes in Jutland," where they had been chastising old Christian IV, now meddlesome again for the last time, and never a good neighbor to Sweden, Gallas could by no means do what he intended; on the contrary, he had to run from Tortenson what feet could do, was hunted, he and his *Merode*-Bruder (beautiful inventors of the "Marauding" Art), "till they pretty much all died (*crepirten*)," says Kohler. No great loss to society, the death of these Artists, but we can fancy what their life, and especially what the process of their dying, may have cost poor Brandenburg again.

Friedrich Wilhelm's aim, in this as in other emergencies, was sun-clear to himself, but for most part dim to everybody else. He had to walk very warily, Sweden on one hand of him, suspicious Kaiser on the other; he had to wear semblances, to be ready with evasive words and advance noiselessly by many circuits. More delicate operation could not be imagined; but advance he did, advance and arrive. With extraordinary talent, diligence, and felicity, the young man wound himself out of this first fatal position; got those foreign Armies pushed out of his country, and kept them out. His first concern had been to find some vestige of revenue, to put that upon a clear footing, and by loans or otherwise to scrape a little ready money together, on the strength of which a small body of soldiers could be collected about him, and drilled into real ability to fight and obey. This as a basis; on this followed all manner of things, freedom from Swedish-Austrian invasions as the first thing.

He was himself, as appeared by and by, a fighter of the first quality when it came to that, but never was willing to fight if he could help it; preferred rather to shift, manœuvre, and negotiate, which he did in a most vigilant, adroit, and masterly manner. But by degrees he had grown to have, and could maintain it, an Army of twenty-four thousand men, among the best troops then in being. With or without his will, he was in all the great Wars of his time—the time of Louis XIV—who kindled Europe four times over, thrice in our Kurfuerst's day. The Kurfuerst's Dominions, a long, straggling country, reaching from Memel to Wesel, could hardly keep out of the way of any war that might rise. He made himself available, never against the good cause of Protestantism and German Freedom, yet always in the place and way where his own best advantage was to be had. Louis XIV had often much need of him; still oftener, and more pressingly, had Kaiser Leopold, the little Gentleman "in scarlet stockings, with a red feather in his hat," whom Mr. Savage used to see majestically walking about, with Austrian lip that said nothing at all. His twenty-four thousand excellent fighting-men, thrown in at the right time, were often a thing that could turn the balance in great questions. They required to be allowed for at a high rate, which he well knew how to adjust himself for exacting and securing always.

When the Peace of Westphalia (1648) concluded that Thirty-Years' Conflagration, and swept the ashes of it into order again, Friedrich Wilhelm's right to Pommern was admitted by everybody, and well insisted on by himself; but right had to yield to reason of state, and he could not get it. The Swedes insisted on their expenses; the Swedes held Pommern, had all along held it —in pawn, they said, for their expenses. Nothing for it but to give the Swedes the better half of Pommern—*Fore*-Pommern so they call it, "Swedish Pomernia" thenceforth), which lies next the Sea; this, with some Towns and cuttings over and above, was Sweden's share. Friedrich Wilhelm had to put up with *Hinder*-Pommern, docked furthermore of the Town of Stettin, and of other valuable cuttings, in favor of Sweden, much to Friedrich Wilhelm's grief and just anger, could he have helped it.

They gave him Three secularized Bishoprics, Magdeburg, Halberstadt, Minden with other small remnants, for compensation, and he had to be content with these for the present. But he never gave up the idea of Pommern. Much of the effort of his life was spent upon recovering Fore-Pommern; thrice eager upon that, whenever lawful opportunity offered. To no purpose, then; he never could recover Swedish Pommern; only his late descendants, and that by slowish degrees, could recover it all. Readers remember that Burgermeister of Stettin, with the helmet and sword flung into the grave and picked out again, and can judge whether Brandenburg got its good luck quite by lying in bed.

Once, and once only, he had a voluntary purpose toward War, and it remained a purpose only. Soon after the Peace of Westphalia, old Pfalz-Neuburg, the same who got the slap on the face, went into tyrannous proceedings against the Protestant part of his subjects in Juelic-Cleve, who called to Friedrich Wilhelm for help. Friedrich Wilhelm, a zealous Protestant, made remonstrances, retaliations; ere long the thought struck him, "Suppose, backed by the Dutch, we threw out this fantastic old gentleman, his Papistries, and pretended claims and self, clear out of it?" This was Friedrich Wilhelm's thought, and he suddenly marched troops into the Territory with that view. But Europe was in alarm; the Dutch grew faint. Friedrich Wilhelm saw it would not do. He had a conference with old Pfalz-Neuburg: "Young gentleman, we remember how your Grandfather made free with us and our august countenance! Nevertheless, we—" In fine, the "statistics of Treaties" was increased by One, and there the matter rested till calmer times.

In 1666 an effective Partition of these litigated Territories was accomplished; Prussia to have the Duchy of Cleve-Proper, the Counties of Mark and Ravensberg, with other Patches and Pertinents; Neuburg, what was the better share, to have Juelich Duchy and Berg Duchy. Furthermore, if either of the Lines failed, in no sort was a collateral to be admitted; but Brandenburg was to inherit Neuburg, or Neuburg Brandenburg, as the case might be. A clear Bargain this at last, and in the times that had come it proved executable so far; but if the reader fancies the Lawsuit was at last out in this way, he will be a simple reader. In the days of our little Fritz,[1] the Line of Pfalz-Neuburg was evidently ending; but that Brandenburg, and not a collateral, should succeed it, there lay the quarrel open still, as if it had never been shut, and we shall hear enough about it.

Friedrich Wilhelm's first actual appearance in War, Polish-Swedish War (1655–1660), was involuntary in the highest degree; forced upon him for the sake of his Preussen, which bade fair to be lost or ruined without blame of his or its. Nevertheless, here too he made his benefit of the affair. The big King of Sweden had a standing quarrel, with his big cousin of Poland, which broke out into hot War; little Preussen lay between them, and was like to be crushed in the collision. Swedish King was Karl Gustav, Christina's Cousin, Charles XII's Grandfather: a great and mighty man, lion of the North in his time; Polish King was one John Casimir; chivalrous enough, and with clouds of forward Polish chivalry about him, glittering with barbaric gold. Friedrich III, Danish King for the first time being, he also was much involved in the thing. Fain would Friedrich Wilhelm have kept out of it, but he could not. Karl Gustav as good as forced him to join; he joined; fought along with Karl Gustav an illustrious Battle, "Battle of Warsaw," three days long (July 28–30, 1656), on the skirts of Warsaw; crowds "looking from the upper windows" there; Polish chivalry, broken at last, going like chaff upon the winds, and John Casimir nearly ruined.

Shortly after which, Friedrich Wilhelm, who had shone much

[1] Frederick the Great.

in the Battle, changed sides. An inconsistent, treacherous man? Perhaps not, O reader; perhaps a man advancing "in circuits," the only way he has; spirally, face now to east, now to west, with his own reasonable private aim sun-clear to himself all the while.

John Casimir agreed to give up the "Homage of Preussen" for this service; a grand prize for Friedrich Wilhelm. What the Teutsch Ritters strove for in vain, and lost their existence in striving for, the shifty Kurfuerst has now got: Ducal Prussia, which is also called East Prussia, is now a free sovereignty, and will become as "Royal" as the other Polish part, or perhaps even more so, in the course of time—Karl Gustav, in a high frame of mind, informs the Kurfuerst that he has him on his books, and will pay the debt one day.

A dangerous debtor in such matters, this Karl Gustav. In these same months, busy with the Danish part of the Controversy, he was doing a feat of war which set all Europe in astonishment. In January, 1658, Karl Gustav marches his Army, horse, foot, and artillery, to the extent of Twenty thousand, across the Baltic ice, and takes an island without shipping—Island of Fuenen, across the Little Belt—three miles of ice, and a part of the sea *open*, which has to be crossed on planks; nay, forward from Fuenen, when once there, he achieves ten whole miles more of ice, and takes Zealand itself, to the wonder of all mankind: an imperious, stern-browed, swift-striking man, who had dreamed of a new Goth Empire: the mean Hypocrites and Fribbles of the South to be coerced again by noble Norse valor, and taught a new lesson; has been known to lay his hand on his sword while apprising an Embassador (Dutch High Mightiness) what his royal intentions were: "not the sale or purchase of groceries, observe you, Sir! My aims go higher." Charles XII's Grandfather, and somewhat the same type of man.

But Karl died short while after; left his big, wide-raging Northern Controversy to collapse in what way it could. Sweden and the fighting parties made their "Peace of Oliva" (Abbey of Oliva, near Dantzig, May 1, 1660), and this of Preussen was ratified, in all form, among other points. No Homage more; nothing now above Ducal Prussia but the Heavens, and great times coming for it. This was one of the successfulest strokes of business ever done by Friedrich Wilhelm, who had been forced, by sheer compulsion, to embark in that big game. "Royal Prussia," the Western *Polish* Prussia—this too, as all Newspapers know, has in our times gone the same road as the other, which probably after all, it may have had in Nature, some tendency to do? Cut away, for reasons, by the Polish sword, in that Battle of Tannenberg, long since, and then, also for reasons, cut back again: that is the fact, not unexampled in human History.

Old Johann Casimir, not long after that Peace of Oliva, getting tired of his unruly Polish chivalry and their ways, abdicated, retired to Paris, and "lived much with Ninon de l'Enclos and her circle" for the rest of his life. He used to complain of his Polish chivalry that there was no solidity in them, nothing but outside glitter, with tumult and anarchic noise; fatal want of one essential talent, the talent of Obeying; and has been heard to prophesy that a glorious Republic, persisting in such courses, would arrive at results which would surprise it.

Onward from this time Friedrich Wilhelm figures in the world, public men watching his procedure, Kings anxious to secure him, Dutch Printsellers sticking up his Portraits for a hero-worshipping Public. Fighting hero, had the Public known it, was not his essential character, though he had to fight a great deal. He was essentially an Industrial man; great in organizing, regulating, in constraining chaotic heaps to become cosmic for him. He drains bogs, settles colonies in the waste places of his Dominions, cuts canals; unweariedly encourages trade and work. The Friedrich-Wilhelm's Canal, which still carries tonnage from the Oder to the Spree, is a monument of his zeal in this way; creditable, with the means he had. To the poor French Protestants in the Edict-of-Nantes Affair, he was like an empress Benefit of Heaven: one Helper appointed, to whom the help itself was profitable. He munificently welcomed them to Brandenburg; showed really a noble piety and human self-pity, as well as judgment; nor did Brandenburg and he want their reward. Some twenty thousand nimble French souls, evidently of the best French quality, found a home there; made "waste sands about Berlin into pot-herb gardens"; and in the spiritual Brandenburg, too, did something of horticulture, which is still noticeable.

Certainly this Elector was one of the shiftiest of men; not an unjust man either; a pious, God-fearing man rather, stanch to his Protestantism and his Bible; not unjust by any means, nor, on the other hand, by any means thin-skinned in his interpretings of justice: Fairplay to myself always, or occasionally even the Height of Fairplay. On the whole, by constant energy, vigilance, adroit activity, by an ever-ready insight and audacity to seize the passing fact by its right handle, he fought his way well in the world; left Brandenburg a flourishing and greatly increased Country, and his own name famous enough.

A thickset, stalwart figure, with brisk eyes, and high, strong, irregularly-Roman nose. Good bronze Statue of him, by Schlueter, once a famed man, still rides on the *Lange-Bruecke* (Long Bridge) at Berlin; and his Portrait, in huge frizzled Louis-Quatorze wig, is frequently met with in German Galleries. Collectors of Dutch Prints, too, know him; here a gallant, eagle-featured little gentleman, brisk in the smiles of youth, with plumes, with truncheon, caprioling on his war-charger, view of tents in the distance: there a sedate, ponderous wrinkly old man, eyes slightly puckered (eyes *busier* than mouth), a face well plowed by Time, and not found unfruitful; one of the largest, most laborious potent faces (in an ocean of circumambient periwig) to be met with in that Century. There are many Histories about him, too, but they are not comfortable to read. He also has wanted a sacred Poet, and found only a bewildering Dryasdust.

His two grand Feats that dwell in the Prussian memory are perhaps none of his greatest, but were of a kind to strike the imagination. They both relate to what was the central problem of his life—the recovery of Pommern from the Swedes. Exploit First is the famed Battle of Fehrbellin (Ferry of Belleen), fought on June 18, 1675. Fehrbellin is an inconsiderable Town still standing in those peaty regions, some five-and-thirty miles northwest of Berlin, and had for ages plied its poor Ferry over the oily-looking, brown sluggish stream called Rhin, or Rhein in those parts, without the least notice from mankind till this fell out. It is a place of pilgrimage to patriotic Prussians ever since Friedrich Wilhelm's exploit there. The matter went thus:

Friedrich Wilhelm was fighting, far south in Alsace, on Kaiser Leopold's side, in the Louis XIV War—that second one, which ended in the Treaty of Nimwegen. Doing his best there, when the Swedes, egged on by Louis XIV, made war upon him; crossed the Pomeranian marshes, troop after troop, and invaded his Brandenburg Territory with a force which at length amounted to sixteen thousand men. No help for the moment; Friedrich Wilhelm could not be spared from his post. The Swedes, who had at first professed well, gradually went into plunder, roving, harrying at their own will; and a melancholy time they made of it for Friedrich Wilhelm and his People. Lucky if temporary harm were all the ill they were likely to do; lucky if— He stood steady, however; in his solid manner finishing the thing in hand first, since that was feasible. He then even retired into winter-quarters to rest his men, and seemed to have left the Swedish sixteen thousand autocrats of the situation, who accordingly went storming about at a great rate.

Not so, however; very far, indeed, from so. Having rested his men for certain months, Friedrich Wilhelm silently, in the first days of June, 1675, gets them under march again; marches his Cavalry and he as first instalment, with best speed from Schweinfurt, which is on the River Mayn, to Magdeburg, a distance of two hundred miles. At Magdeburg, where he rests three days, waiting for the first handful of Foot and a field-piece or two, he learns that the Swedes are in three parties wide asunder, the middle party of them within forty miles of him. Probably stronger, even this middle one, than his small body (of "Six thousand Horse, Twelve hundred Foot, and three guns") —stronger, but capable, perhaps, of being surprised, of being cut in pieces before the others can come up? Rathenau is the nearest skirt of this middle party: thither goes the Kurfuerst, softly, swiftly, in the June night (June 16–17, 1675); gets into Rathenau by brisk stratagem; tumbles out the Swedish Horse regiment there, drives it back toward Fehrbellin.

He himself follows hard; swift riding enough in the summer night through those damp Havel lands, in the old Hohenzollern fashion; and, indeed, old Freisack Castle, as it chances—Freisack, scene of Dietrich von Quitzow and *Lazy Peg* long since—is close by. Follows hard, we say; strikes in upon this midmost party (nearly twice his number, but Infantry for most part);

and after fierce fight, done with good talent on both sides, cuts it into utter ruin, as proposed; thereby he has left the Swedish Army as a mere head and tail without body; has entirely demolished the Swedish Army. Same feat intrinsically as that done by Cromwell on Hamilton and the Scots in 1648. It was, so to speak, the last visit Sweden paid to Brandenburg, or the last of any consequence, and ended the domination of the Swedes in those quarters — a thing justly to be forever remembered by Brandenburg; on a smallish modern scale, the Bannockburn, Sempach, Marathon of Brandenburg.

Exploit Second was four years later—in some sort a corollary to this, and a winding up of the Swedish business. The Swedes, in further prosecution of their Louis XIV speculation, had invaded Preussen this time, and were doing sad havoc there. It was in the dead of winter—Christmas, 1678—more than four hundred miles off; and the Swedes, to say nothing of their own havoc, were in a case to take Koenigsberg, and ruin Prussia altogether, if not prevented. Friedrich Wilhelm starts from Berlin, with the opening Year, on his long march; the Horse-troops first, Foot to follow at their swiftest; he himself (his Wife, his ever-true "Louisa," accompanying, as her wont was) travels toward the end, at the rate of "sixty miles a day." He gets in still in time; finds Koenigsberg unscathed; nay, it is even said the Swedes are extensively falling sick, having after a long famine found infinite "pigs near Insterburg," in those remote regions, and indulged in the fresh pork overmuch.

I will not describe the subsequent manœuvres, which would interest nobody; enough if I say that on January 16, 1679, it had become of the highest moment for Friedrich Wilhelm to get from Carwe (Village near Elbing), on the shore of the *Frische Haf*, where he was, through Koenigsberg, to Gilge on the *Curische Haf*, where the Swedes are, in a minimum of time. Distance, as the crow flies, is about a hundred miles; road, which skirts the two *Hafs* (wide shallow *Washes*, as we should name them), is of rough quality and naturally circuitous. It is ringing frost to-day, and for days back. Friedrich Wilhelm hastily gathers all the sledges, all the horses of the district; mounts Four thousand men in sledges; starts with speed of light, in that fashion; scours along all day, and after the intervening bit of land, again along, awakening the ice-bound silences. Gloomy *Frische Haf*, wrapped in its Winter cloud-coverlids, with its wastes of tumbled sand, its poor frost-bound fishing-hamlets, pine hillocks—desolate-looking, stern as Greenland, or more so, says Busching, who travelled there in winter-time—hears unexpected human voices, and huge grinding and trampling; the Four thousand, in long fleet of sledges, scouring across it in that manner. All day they rush along—out of the rimy hazes of morning into the olive-colored clouds of evening again—with huge, loud-grinding rumble, and do arrive in time at Gilge. A notable streak of things, shooting across those frozen solitudes in the New Year, 1679; little short of Karl Gustav's feat, which we heard of in the other or Danish end of the Baltic, twenty years ago, when he took islands without ships.

This Second Exploit—suggested or not by that prior one of Karl Gustav on the ice—is still a thing to be remembered by Hohenzollerns and Prussians. The Swedes were beaten here on Friedrich Wilhelm's rapid arrival; were driven into disastrous, rapid retreat Northward, which they executed in hunger and cold, fighting continually, like Northern bears, under the grim sky, Friedrich Wilhelm sticking to their skirts, holding by their tail, like an angry bear-ward with steel whip in his hand; a thing which, on the small scale, reminds one of Napoleon's experiences. Not till Napoleon's huge fighting-flight, a Hundred and thirty-four years after, did I read of such a transaction in those parts. The Swedish invasion of Preussen has gone utterly to ruin.

And this, then, is the end of Sweden, and its bad neighborhood on these shores, where it has tyrannously sat on our skirts so long? Swedish Pommern; the Elector already had: last year, coming toward it ever since the Exploit of Fehrbellin, he had invaded Swedish Pommern; had besieged and taken Stettin, nay Stralsund too, where Wallenstein had failed; cleared Pommern altogether of its Swedish guests, who had tried next in Preussen, with what luck we see. Of Swedish Pommern the Elector might now say, "Surely it is mine; again mine, as it long was; well won a second time, since the first would not do." But no; Louis XIV proved a gentleman to his Swedes. Louis, now that the Peace of Nimwegen had come, and only the Elector of

Brandenburg was still in harness, said steadily, though anxious enough to keep well with the Elector, "They are my allies, these Swedes; it was on my bidding they invaded you: can I leave them in such a pass? It must not be." So Pommern had to be given back: a miss which was infinitely grievous to Friedrich Wilhelm. The most victorious Elector cannot hit always, were his right never so good.

Another miss which he had to put up with, in spite of his rights and his good services, was that of the Silesian Duchies. The Heritage-Fraternity with Liegnitz had at length, in 1675, come to fruit. The last Duke of Liegnitz was dead: Duchies of Liegnitz, of Brieg, Wohlau, are Brandenburg's, if there were right done; but Kaiser Leopold in the scarlet stockings will not hear of Heritage-Fraternity. "Nonsense!" answers Kaiser Leopold: "a thing suppressed at once, ages ago by Imperial power; flat *zero* of a thing at this time; and you, I again bid you, return me your Papers upon it." This latter act of duty Friedrich Wilhelm would not do, but continued insisting: "Jagerndorf, at least, O Kaiser of the world," said he, "Jagerndorf, there is no color for your keeping that!" To which the Kaiser again answers, "Nonsense!" and even falls upon astonishing schemes about it, as we shall see, but gives nothing. Ducal Preussen is sovereign, Cleve is at peace, Hinter-Pommern ours; this Elector has conquered much, but Silesia, and Vor-Pommern, and some other things he will have to do without. Louis XIV, it is thought, once offered to get him made King, but that he declined for the present.

His married and domestic life is very fine and human, especially with that Oranien-Nassau Princess, who was his first Wife (1646–1667) Princess Louisa of Nassau-Orange, Aunt to our own Dutch William, King William III, in time coming: an excellent, wise Princess, from whom came the Orange Heritages, which afterward proved difficult to settle. Orange was at last exchanged for the small Principality of Neufchatel in Switzerland, which is Prussia's ever since. "Oranienburg (*Orange-Burg*)," a Royal Country-house, still standing, some Twenty miles northward from Berlin, was this Louisa's place: she had trimmed it up into a little jewel of the Dutch type—pot-herb gardens, training-schools for girls, and the like—a favorite abode of hers when she was at liberty for recreation. But her life was busy and earnest; she was helpmate, not in name only, to an ever-busy man. They were married young, a marriage of love withal. Young Friedrich Wilhelm's courtship, wedding in Holland; the honest trustful walk and conversation of the two Sovereign Spouses, their journeyings together, their mutual hopes, fears, and manifold vicissitudes, till Death, with stern beauty, shut it in: all is human, true, and wholesome in it; interesting to look upon, and rare among sovereign persons.

Not but that he had his troubles with his womankind. Even with this his first Wife, whom he loved truly, and who truly loved him, there were scenes—the Lady having a judgment of her own about everything that passed, and the man being choleric withal. Sometimes, I have heard, "he would dash his hat at her feet," saying symbolically, "Govern you, then, Madam! Not the Kurfuerst Hat; a Coif is my wear, it seems!" Yet her judgment was good, and he liked to have it on the weightiest things, though her powers of silence might halt now and then. He has been known, on occasions, to run from his Privy Council to her apartment, while a complex matter was debating, to ask her opinion, hers, too, before it was decided. Excellent Louisa, Princess full of beautiful piety, good sense, and affection—a touch of the Nassau-Heroic in her. At the moment of her death, it is said, when speech had fled, he felt from her hand which lay in his, three slight, slight pressures: "Farewell!" thrice mutely spoken in that manner, not easy to forget in this world.

His second Wife, Dorothea, who planted the Lindens in Berlin, and did other husbandries, fell far short of Louisa in many things, but not in tendency to advise, to remonstrate, and plaintively reflect on the finished and unalterable. Dreadfully thrifty lady, moreover; did much in dairy produce, farming of town-rates, provision-taxes, not to speak again of that Tavern she was thought to have in Berlin, and to draw custom to it in an oblique manner! "Ah! I have not my Louisa now; to whom now shall I run for advice or help?" would the poor Kurfuerst at times exclaim.

He had some trouble, considerable trouble, now and then, with mutinous spirits in Preussen; men standing on antique Prussian franchises and parchments, refusing to see that the same were now antiquated incompatible, nor to say impossible, as the new Sovereign alleged, and carrying themselves very stiffly at times. But the Hohenzollerns had been used to such things; a Hohenzollern like this one would evidently take his measures, soft but strong, and even stronger to the needful pitch, with mutinous spirits. One Buergermeister of Koenigsberg, after much stroking on the back, was at length seized in open Hall by Electoral writ, soldiers having first gently barricaded the principal streets, and brought cannon to bear upon them. This Buergermeister, seized in such brief way, lay prisoner for life, refusing to ask his liberty, though it was thought he might have had it on asking.

Another gentleman, a Baron von Kalkstein, of old Teutsch-Ritter kin, of very high ways, in the Provincial Estates (*Staende*) and elsewhere, got into lofty, almost solitary, opposition, and at length, into mutiny proper, against the new "Non-Polish" Sovereign, and flatly refused to do homage at his accession—refused, Kalkstein did, for his share; fled to Warsaw; and very fiercely, in a loud manner, carried out his mutinies in the Diets and Court Conclaves there, his plea being, or plea for the time, "Poland is our liege lord" (which it was not always), "and we cannot be transferred to you except by our consent asked and given," which, too, had been a little neglected on the former occasion of transfer; so that the Great Elector knew not what to do with Kalkstein, and at length (as the case was pressing) had him kidnapped by his Embassador at Warsaw; had him "rolled in a carpet" there, and carried swiftly in the Embassador's coach, in the form of luggage, over the frontier, into his native Province, there to be judged, and, in the end (since nothing else would serve him), to have the sentence executed, and his head cut off; for the case was pressing. These things, especially this of Kalkstein, with a boisterous Polish Diet and parliamentary eloquence in the rear of him, gave rise to criticisms, and required management on the part of the Great Elector.

Of all his ancestors, our little Fritz, when he grew big, admired this one—a man made like himself in many points. He seems really to have loved and honored this one. In the year 1750 there had been a new Cathedral got finished at Berlin; the ancestral bones had to be shifted over from the vaults of the old one—the burying-place ever since Joachim II, that Joachim who drew his sword on Alba. King Friedrich, with some attendants, witnessed the operation, January, 1750. When the Great Kurfuerst's coffin came, he bade them open it; gazed in silence on the features for some time, which were perfectly recognizable; laid his hand on the hand long dead, and said, "*Messieurs, celui-ci a fait de grandes choses!*" ("This one did a grand work").

WILLIAM PENN RECEIVES THE GRANT OF PENNSYLVANIA

FOUNDING OF PHILADELPHIA

A.D. 1681

GEORGE E. ELLIS

Although European settlers had occupied portions of the present State of Pennsylvania for fifty years before William Penn arrived in that territory, the real foundation of the great commonwealth named after him is justly dated from his time.

Penn was an English "Friend," or Quaker, and was descended from a long line of sailors. He was born in London in 1644, his father being Admiral Sir William Penn of the English navy. The son was educated at Oxford University, and became a preacher of the Society of Friends. This calling brought him into collision with the authorities. He was several times arrested, and for a while was imprisoned in the Tower for "urging the cause of freedom with importunity."

Through the influence of his family and the growing weight of his own character, he escaped the heavier penalties inflicted upon some of his coreligionists, and, by the shrewdness and tact which he united with spiritual fervor, he rapidly advanced in public position.

In 1675 Penn became part proprietor of West New Jersey, where a colony of English Friends was settled. Five years later, through his influence at court and the aid of wealthy persons, he was enabled to purchase a large tract in East New Jersey, where he designed to establish a similar colony on a larger plan. But this project was soon superseded by a much greater one, of which the execution is here related.

THE interest of William Penn having been engaged for some time in the colonization of an American province, and the idea having become familiar to his mind of establishing there a Christian home as a refuge for Friends, and the scene for a fair trial of their principles, he availed himself of many favorable circumstances to become a proprietary himself. In various negotiations concerning New Jersey he had had a conspicuous share, and the information which his inquiring mind gathered from the adventures in the New World gave him all the knowledge which was requisite for his further proceedings. Though he had personal enemies in high places, and the project which he designed crossed the interests of the Duke of York[1] and of Lord Baltimore, yet his court influence was extensive, and he knew how to use it.

The favor of Charles II and of his brother the Duke of York had been sought by Penn's dying father for his son, and freely promised. But William Penn had a claim more substantial than a royal promise of those days. The crown was indebted to the estate of Admiral Penn for services, loans, and interest, to the amount of sixteen thousand pounds. The exchequer, under the convenient management of Shaftesbury, would not meet the claim. Penn, who was engaged in settling the estate of his father, petitioned the King, in June, 1680, for a grant of land in America as a payment for all these debts.

The request was laid before the privy council, and then before the committee of trade and plantations. Penn's success must have been owing to great interest made on his behalf; for both the Duke of York, by his attorney, and Lord Baltimore opposed him. As proprietors of territory bounding on the tract which he asked for, and as having been already annoyed by the conflict of charters granted in the New World, they were naturally unfairly biassed. The application made to the King succeeded after much debate. The provisions in the charter of Lord Baltimore were adopted by Penn with slight alterations. Sir William Jones objected to one of the provisions, which allowed a freedom from taxation, and the Bishop of London, as the ecclesiastical supervisor of plantations, proposed another provision, to prevent too great liberty in religious matters. Chief Justice North having reduced the patent to a satisfactory form, to guard the King's prerogative and the powers of Parliament, it was signed by writ of privy seal at Westminster, March 4, 1681. It made Penn the owner of about forty thousand square miles of territory.

This charter is given at length by Proud and other writers. The preamble states that the design of William Penn was to enlarge the British empire and to civilize and convert the savages.

[1] Afterward James II. He was proprietor of New York, and Lord Baltimore of Maryland.

The first section avers that his petition was granted on account of the good purposes of the son and the merits and services of the father. The bounds of the territory are thus defined: "All that tract or part of land, in America, with the islands therein contained, as the same is bounded on the east by Delaware River, from twelve miles distance northward of New Castle town, unto the three-and-fortieth degree of northern latitude, if the said river doth extend so far northward; but if the said river shall not extend so far northward, then, by the said river, so far as it doth extend; and from the head of the said river, the eastern bounds are to be determined by a meridian line to be drawn from the head of the said river, unto the said forty-third degree. The said land to extend westward five degrees in longitude to be computed from the said eastern bounds; and the said lands to be bounded on the north by the beginning of the three-and-fortieth degree of northern latitude, and on the south by a circle drawn at twelve miles' distance from New Castle, northward and westward, unto the beginning of the fortieth degree of northern latitude; and then by a straight line westward to the limits of longitude above mentioned."

Though these boundaries appear to be given with definiteness and precision, a controversy, notwithstanding, arose at once between Penn and Lord Baltimore, which outlasted the lives of both of them, and, being continued by their representatives, was not in fact closed until the Revolutionary War.

The charter vested the perpetual proprietaryship of this territory in William Penn and his heirs, on the fealty of the annual payment of two beaver-skins; it authorized him to make and execute laws not repugnant to those of England, to appoint judges, to receive those who wished to transport themselves, *to establish a military force*, to constitute municipalities, and to carry on a free commerce. It required that an agent of the proprietor should reside in or near London, and provided for the rights of the Church of England. The charter also disclaimed all taxation, except through the proprietor, the governor, the assembly, or Parliament, and covenanted that if any question of arms or conditions should arise it should be decided in favor of the proprietor. By a declaration to the inhabitants and planters of Pennsylvania, dated April 2d, the King confirmed the charter, to ratify it for all who might intend to emigrate under it, and to require compliance from all whom it concerned.

By a letter from Penn to his friend Robert Turner, written upon the day on which the charter was signed, we learn that the proprietor designed to call his territory "New Wales"; but the under-secretary, a Welshman, opposed it. Penn then suggested "Sylvania," as applicable to the forest region; but the secretary, acting under instructions, prefixed "Penn " to this title. The modest and humble Quaker offered the official twenty guineas as a bribe to leave off his name. Failing again, he went to the King and stated his objection; but the King said he would take the naming upon himself, and insisted upon it as doing honor to the old admiral.

Penn now resigned the charge of West New Jersey, and devoted himself to the preliminary tasks which should make his province available to himself and others. He sent over, in May, his cousin and secretary, Colonel William Markham, then only twenty-one years old, to make such arrangements for his own coming as might be necessary. This gentleman, who acted as Penn's deputy, carried over from him a letter, dated London, April 8, 1681, addressed "For the Inhabitants of Pennsylvania; to be read by my Deputy." This was a courteous announcement of his proprietaryship and intentions to the Dutch, Swedes, and English, who, to the number, probably, of about three thousand, were then living within his patent.

Penn's object being to obtain adventurers and settlers at once, he published *Some Account of the Province of Pennsylvania, in America, lately granted, under the Great Seal of England, to William Penn.* This was accompanied by a copy of the charter and a statement of the terms on which the land was to be sold, with judicious advice addressed to those who were disposed to transport themselves, warning them against mere fancy dreams, or the desertion of friends, and encouraging them by all reasonable expectations of success.

The terms of sale were, for a hundred acres of land, forty shillings purchase money, and one shilling as an annual quit-rent. This latter stipulation, made in perfect fairness, not unreasonable in itself, and ratified by all who of their own accord acceded to it, was, as we shall see, an immediate cause of disaffection, and has ever since been the basis of a calumny against the honored and most estimable founder of Pennsylvania.

Under date of July 11, 1681, Penn published *Certain Conditions or Concessions to be agreed upon by William Penn, Proprietary and Governor of the Province of Pennsylvania, and those who may become Adventurers and Purchasers in the same Province.* These conditions relate to dividing, planting, and building upon the land, saving mulberry- and oak-trees, and dealing with the Indians. These documents were circulated, and imparted sufficient knowledge of the country and its produce, so that purchasers at once appeared, and Penn went to Bristol to organize there a company called "The Free Society of Traders in Pennsylvania," who purchased twenty thousand acres of land, and prepared to establish various trades in the province.

Yet further to mature his plans, and to begin with a fair understanding among all who might be concerned in the enterprise, Penn drew up and submitted a sketch of the frame of government, providing for alterations, with a preamble for liberty of conscience. On the basis of contracts and agreements thus made and mutually ratified, three passenger ships, two from London and one from Bristol, sailed for Pennsylvania in September, 1681. One of them made an expeditious passage; another was frozen up in the Delaware; and the third, driven to the West Indies, was long delayed. They took over some of the ornamental work of a house for the proprietor.

The Governor also sent over three commissioners, whose instructions we learn from the original document addressed to them by Penn, dated September 30, 1681. These commissioners were William Crispin, John Bezar, and Nathaniel Allen. Their duty was that of "settling the colony." Penn refers them to his cousin Markham, "now on the spot." He instructs them to take good care of the people; to guard them from extortionate prices for commodities from the earlier inhabitants; to select a site by the river, and there to lay out a town; to have his letter to the Indians read to them in their own tongue; to make them presents from him—adding, "Be grave; they love not to be smiled upon"—and to enter into a league of amity with them. Penn also instructs the commissioners to select a site for his own occupancy, and closes with some good advice in behalf of order and virtue.

These commissioners probably did not sail until the latter part of October, as they took with them the letter to the Indians, to which Penn refers. This letter, bearing the date October 18, 1681, is a beautiful expression of feeling on the part of the proprietor. He does not address the Indians as heathen, but as his brethren, the children of the one Father. He announces to them his accession, as far as a royal title could legitimate it, to a government in their country; he distinguishes between himself and those who had ill treated the Indians, and pledges his love and service.

About this time William Penn was elected a fellow of the Royal Society in London, probably by nomination of his friend, Dr. John Wallis, one of its founders, and with the hope that his connection with the New World would enable him to advance its objects.

With a caution, which the experience of former purchases rendered essential, Penn obtained of the Duke of York a release of all his claims within the patent. His royal highness executed a quitclaim to William Penn and his heirs on August 21, 1682. The Duke had executed, in March, a ratification of his two former grants of East Jersey. But a certain fatality seemed to attend upon these transfers of ducal possessions. After various conflicts and controversies long continued, we may add, though by anticipation, that the proprietaryship of both the Jerseys was abandoned, and they were surrendered to the crown under Queen Anne, in April, 1702.

Penn also obtained of the Duke of York another tract of land adjoining his patent. This region, afterward called the "Territories," and the three "Lower Counties," now Delaware, had been successively held by the Swedes and Dutch, and by the English at New York. The Duke confirmed it to William Penn, by two deeds, dated August 24, 1682.

The last care on the mind of William Penn, before his embarkation, was to prepare proper counsel and instruction for his wife and children. This he did in the form of a letter written at Worminghurst, August 4, 1682. He knew not that he should ever see them again, and his heart poured forth to them the most touching utterances of affection. But it was not the heart alone which indited the epistle. It expressed the wisest counsels of prudence and discretion. All the important letters written by Penn contain a singular union of spiritual and worldly wisdom. Indeed, he thought these two ingredients to be but one element. He urged economy, filial love, purity, and industry, as well as piety, upon his children. He favored, though he did not insist upon, their receiving his religious views. We may express a passing regret that he who could give such advice to his children should not have had the joy to leave behind him anyone who could meet the not inordinate wish of his heart.

In the mean while his deputy, Markham, acting by his instructions, was providing him a new home by purchasing for him, of the Indians, a piece of land, the deed of which is dated July 15th, and endorsed with a confirmation, August 1st, and by commencing upon it the erection which was afterward known as Pennsbury Manor.

All his arrangements being completed, William Penn, at the age of thirty-eight, well, strong, and hopeful of the best results, embarked for his colony, on board the ship Welcome, of three hundred tons, Robert Greenaway master, on the last of August, 1682. While in the Downs he wrote a *Farewell Letter to Friends, the Unfaithful and Inquiring*, in his native land, dated August 30th, and probably many private letters. He had about one hundred fellow-passengers, mostly Friends from his own neighborhood in Sussex. The vessel sailed about September 1st, and almost immediately the small-pox, that desolating scourge of the passenger-ships of those days, appeared among the passengers, and thirty fell victims to it. The trials of that voyage, told to illustrate the Christian spirit which submissively encountered them, were long repeated from father to son and from mother to daughter.

In about six weeks the ship entered the Delaware River. The old inhabitants along the shores, which had been settled by the whites for about half a century, received Penn with equal respect and joy. He arrived at New Castle on October 27th. The day was not commemorated by annual observances until the year 1824, when a meeting for that purpose was held at an inn, in Lætitia court, where Penn had resided. While the ship and its company went up the river, the proprietor, on the next day, called the inhabitants, who were principally Dutch and

Swedes, to the court-house, where, after addressing them, he assumed and received the formal possession of the country. He renewed the commissions of the old magistrates, who urged him to unite the Territories to his government.

After a visit of ceremony to the authorities at New York and Long Island, with a passing token to his friends in New Jersey, Penn went to Upland to hold the first Assembly, which opened on December 4th. Nicholas Moore, an English lawyer, and president of the Free Society of Traders, was made speaker. After three days' peaceful debate, the Assembly ratified, with modifications, the laws made in England, with about a score of new ones of a local, moral, or religious character, in which not only the drinking of healths, but the talking of scandal, was forbidden. By suggestion of his friend and fellow-voyager, Pearson, who came from Chester, in England, Penn substituted that name for Upland. By an act of union, passed on December 7th, the three Lower Counties, or the Territories, were joined in the government, and the foreigners were naturalized at their own request.

On his arrival Penn had sent two messengers to Charles Calvert, Lord Baltimore, to propose a meeting and conference with him about their boundaries. On December 19th they met at West River with courtesy and kindness; but after three days they concluded to wait for the more propitious weather of the coming year. Penn, on his way back, attended a religious meeting at a private house, and afterward an official meeting at Choptank, on the eastern shore of the Chesapeake, and reached Chester again by December 29th, where much business engaged him. About twenty-three ships had arrived by the close of the year; none of them met with disaster, and all had fair passages. The new-comers found a comparatively easy sustenance. Provisions were obtained at a cheap rate of the Indians and of the older settlers. But great hardships were endured by some, and special providences are commemorated. Many found their first shelter in caves scooped out in the steep bank of the river. When these caves were deserted by their first occupants, the poor or the vicious made them a refuge; and one of the earliest signs both of prosperity and of corruption, in the colony, is disclosed in the mention that these rude coverts of the first devoted emigrants soon became tippling-houses and nuisances in the misuse of the depraved.

There has been much discussion of late years concerning the far-famed Treaty of Penn with the Indians. A circumstance, which has all the interest both of fact and of poetry, was confirmed by such unbroken testimony of tradition that history seemed to have innumerable records of it in the hearts and memories of each generation. But as there appears no document or parchment of such *criteria* as to satisfy all inquiries, historical scepticism has ventured upon the absurd length of calling in question the fact of the treaty. The Historical Society of Pennsylvania, with commendable zeal, has bestowed much labor upon the questions connected with the treaty, and the results which have been attained can scarcely fail to satisfy a candid inquirer. All claim to a peculiar distinction for William Penn, on account of the singularity of his just proceedings in this matter is candidly waived, because the Swedes, the Dutch, and the English had previously dealt thus justly with the natives. It is in comparison with Pizarro and Cortés that the colonists of all other nations in America appear to an advantage; but the fame of William Penn stands, and ever will stand, preëminent for unexceptionable justice and peace in his relations with the natives.

Penn had several meetings for conference and treaties with the Indians, besides those which he held for the purchase of lands. But unbroken and reverently cherished tradition, beyond all possibility of contradiction, has designated one great treaty held under a large elm-tree, at Shackamaxon (now Kensington), a treaty which Voltaire justly characterizes as "never sworn to, and never broken." In Penn's *Letter to the Free Society of Traders*, dated August 16, 1683, he refers to his conferences with the Indians. Two deeds, conveying land to him, are on record, both of which bear an earlier date than this letter; namely, June 23d and July 14th of the same year. He had designed to make a purchase in May; but having been called off to a conference with Lord Baltimore, he postponed the business till June. The "Great Treaty" was doubtless unconnected with the purchase of land, and was simply a treaty of amity and friendship, in confirmation of one previously held, by Penn's direction, by Markham, on the same spot; that being a place which the Indians were wont to use for this purpose. It is probable that the treaty was held on the last of November, 1682; that the Delawares, the Mingos, and other Susquehanna tribes formed a large assembly on the occasion; that written minutes of the conference were made, and were in possession of Governor Gordon, who states nine conditions as belonging to them in 1728, but are now lost; and that the substance of the treaty is given in Penn's *Letter to the Free Traders*. These results are satisfactory, and are sufficiently corroborated by known facts and documents. The Great Treaty, being distinct from a land purchase, is significantly distinguished in history and tradition.

The inventions of romance and imagination could scarcely gather round this engaging incident attractions surpassing in its own simple and impressive interest. Doubtless Clarkson has given a fair representation of it, if we merely disconnect from his account the statement that the Indians were armed, and all that confounds the treaty of friendship with the purchase of lands. Penn wore a sky-blue sash of silk around his waist, as the most simple badge. The pledges there given were to hold their sanctity "while the creeks and rivers run, and while the sun, moon, and stars endure."

While the whites preserved in written records the memory of such covenants, the Indians had their methods for perpetuating in safe channels their own relations. They cherished in grateful regard, they repeated to their children and to the whites, the terms of the Great Treaty. The Delawares called William Penn *Miquon*, in their own language, though they seem to have adopted the name given him by the Iroquois, *Onas;* both which terms signify a quill or pen. Benjamin West's picture of the treaty is too imaginative for a historical piece. He makes Penn of a figure and aspect which would become twice the years that had passed over his head. The elm-tree was spared in the war of the American Revolution, when there was distress for fire-wood, the British officer, Simcoe, having placed a sentinel beneath it for protection. It was prostrated by the wind on the night of Saturday, March 3, 1810. It was of gigantic size, and the circles around its heart indicated an age of nearly three centuries. A piece of it was sent to the Penn mansion at Stoke Poges, in England, where it is properly commemorated. A marble monument, with suitable inscriptions, was "placed by the Penn Society, A.D. 1827, to mark the site of the Great Elm Tree." Long may it stand!

Penn then made a visit to his manor of Pennsbury, up the Delaware. Under Markham's care, the grounds had been arranged, and a stately edifice of brick was in process of completion. The place had many natural beauties, and is said to have been arranged and decorated in consistency both with the office and the simple manners of the proprietor. There was a hall of audience for Indian embassies within, and luxurious gardens without. Hospitality had here a wide range, and Penn evidently designed it for a permanent abode.

With the help of his surveyor, Thomas Holme, he laid out the plan of his now beautiful city, and gave it its name of Christian signification, that brotherly love might pervade its dwellings. He purchased the land, where the city stands, of the Swedes who already occupied it, and who purchased it of the Indians, though it would seem that a subsequent purchase was made of the natives of the same site with adjacent territory some time afterward by Thomas Holme, acting as president of the council, while Penn was in England. The Schuylkill and the Delaware rivers gave to the site eminent attractions. The plan was very simple, the streets running north and south being designated by numbers, those running east and west by the names of trees. Provision was made for large squares to be left open, and for common water privileges. The building was commenced at once, and was carried on with great zeal and continued success.

LAST TURKISH INVASION OF EUROPE

SOBIESKI SAVES VIENNA

A.D. 1683

SUTHERLAND MENZIES

After the defeat of the Turks at Lepanto, in 1571, the Ottoman power in Europe slowly declined. But under the Sultan Mahomet IV the old Moslem ambition for European conquest reawoke, as if for a final effort. And such it proved to be. By the disaster before Vienna, in which John Sobieski, King of Poland, once more saved Europe from their incursions, the Turks were driven back within their own confines, where they have since, for the most part, remained, making many wars, but no successful inroads, upon European powers.

In 1682 the Hungarian magnates, who were resisting the oppression and persecution of their people by the Austrian Government, called upon the Turks for assistance. Listening to the proposals of Tekeli, the Hungarian leader, who had secured the aid of Louis XIV of France, Mahomet IV decided to break the truce he had made with Austria in 1665. In vain the Emperor Leopold I sent an embassy to Constantinople to dissuade the Sultan from his purpose.

EARLY in the spring of 1683 Sultan Mahomet marched forth from his capital with a large army, which at Belgrad he transferred to the command of the Grand Vizier Kara Mustapha. Tekeli formed a junction with the Turks at Essek. In vain did Ibrahim, the experienced Pacha of Buda, endeavor to persuade Kara Mustapha first of all to subdue the surrounding country, and to postpone until the following year the attack upon Vienna; his advice was scornfully rejected, and, indeed, the audacity of the Grand Vizier seemed justified by the scant resistance he had met with. He talked of renewing the conquests of Solyman: he assembled, it is said, seven hundred thousand men, one hundred thousand horses, and one thousand two hundred guns—an army more powerful than any the Turks had set on foot since the capture of Constantinople. All of which may be reduced to one hundred fifty thousand barbarian troops without discipline, the last conquering army which the degenerate race of the Osmanlis produced wherewith to invade Hungary.

Hostilities commenced in March, 1683; for the Turks, who had not been accustomed to enter upon a campaign before the summer season, had begun their march that year before the end of winter. Some prompt and easy successes exalted the ambition of Kara Mustapha; and in spite of the contrary advice of Tekeli, Ibrahim Pacha, and several other personages, he determined to besiege Vienna. He accordingly advanced direct upon that capital and encamped under its walls on July 14th. It was just at the moment that Louis XIV had captured Strasburg, and at which his army appeared ready to cross the Rhine: all Europe was in alarm, believing that an agreement existed between France and the Porte for the conquest and dismemberment of Germany. But it was not so. The Turks, without giving France any previous warning, had of themselves made their invasion of Hungary; Louis XIV was delighted at their success, but nevertheless disposed, if it went too far, to check them, in order to play the part of saviour of Christendom.

It was fortunate for the Emperor Leopold that he had upon the frontiers of Poland an ally of indomitable courage in King John Sobieski, and that he found the German princes loyal and prompt on this occasion, contrary to their custom, in sending him succor. Moreover, in Duke Charles of Lorraine he met with a skilful general to lead his army. Consternation and confusion prevailed, however, in Vienna, while the Emperor with his court fled to Linz. Many of the inhabitants followed him; but the rest, when the first moments of terror had passed, prepared for the defence, and the dilatoriness of the Turks, who amused themselves with pillaging the environs and neighboring *châteaux*, allowed the Duke of Lorraine to throw twelve thousand men as a garrison into the city; then, as he was unable with his slender force to bar the approach of the Turkish army, he kept aloof and waited for the King of Poland.

Leopold solicited succor on all sides, and the Pope made an appeal to the piety of the King of France. Louis XIV, on the contrary, was intriguing throughout Europe in order that the Christian princes should not quit their attitude of repose, and he only offered to the Diet of Ratisbon the aid of his arms on condition that it should recognize the recent usurpations decreed by the famous Chambers of Reunion,[1] and that it should elect his son king of the Romans. He reckoned, if it should accept his offers, to determine the Turks to retreat and to effect a peace which, by bringing the imperial crown into his house, would have been the death-stroke for Austria. All these combinations miscarried through the devotedness of the Poles.

When Leopold supplicated Sobieski to come to his aid, Louis XIV tried to divert him from it; he reassured him upon the projects of the Turks by a letter of the Sultan, he made him see his real enemies in Austria, Brandenburg, and that power of the North, which the Dutch gazettes had begun to call "His Russian Majesty"; he reminded him, in fine, that the house of Austria, saved by the French on the day of St. Gothard, had testified its gratitude to them by allowing the victors to die of hunger and by envenoming their difference with the Porte. But it was all useless; hatred of the infidels prevailed, and the Polish squadrons hurried to the deliverance of Vienna.

Count Rudiger de Starhemberg was made commandant of the city, and showed himself alike bold and energetic in everything that could contribute to its defence. The Turkish camp encircled Vienna and its suburbs, spreading over the country all round to the distance of six leagues. Two days afterward, Kara Mustapha opened the trenches, and his artillery battered the walls in order to make a breach. Great efforts, moreover, were made in digging mines, with the design of blowing up bastions or portions of the wall, so that the city might be carried by assault, wherein the Turks hoped to find an immense booty. But the besieged made an obstinate defence, and repaired during the night the damage done on the previous day. During sixty days forty mines and ten counter-mines were exploded; the Turks delivered eighteen assaults, the besieged made twenty-four sorties. Each inch of ground was only obtained by dint of a hard and long struggle, in which an equal stubbornness both in attack and defence was exhibited.

The hottest fighting took place at the "Label" bastion,

[1] The Chambers of Reunion were special courts established in France by Louis XIV (1680). These courts declared for the annexation to France of various territories along the eastern frontier.—ED.

around which there was not a foot of ground that had not been steeped in the blood of friend or foe. However, by degrees the Turks gained a few paces; at the end of August they were lodged in the ditches of the city; and on September 4th they sprung a mine under the "Bourg" bastion; one-half of the city was shaken thereby, and a breach was rent in the bastion wide enough for an assault to be delivered, but the enemy was repulsed. Next day the Turks attacked it with renewed courage, but the valor of the besieged baffled the assailants. On September 10th another mine was sprung under the same bastion, and the breach was so wide that a battalion might have entered it abreast. The danger was extreme, for the garrison was exhausted by fighting, sickness, and incessant labor. The Count de Starhemberg despatched courier after courier to the Duke of Lorraine for succor: "There is not a moment to be lost, Monseigneur," he wrote, "not a moment;" and Vienna, exhausted, saw not yet her liberators arrive. At length, on the 14th, when the whole city was in a stupor in the immediate expectation of an attack, a movement was observed in the enemy's camp which announced that succor was at hand. At five o'clock in the afternoon the Christian army was descried surmounting the Hill of Kahlen, and it made its presence known by a salvo of artillery. John Sobieski had arrived at the head of a valiant army. The Electors of Saxony and of Bavaria with many princes, dukes, and margraves of Germany had brought with them fresh troops. Charles of Lorraine might then dare to march against the Moslems, although he had yet only forty-six thousand men.

The army of Sobieski reached Klosterenburg, Koenigstetten, St. André, the Valley of Hagen and Kirling, where it effected its junction with the Austrians and the Saxons who had arrived there in passing by Hoeflin. On Sunday, September 15th, in the earliest rays of a fine autumnal day, the holy priest Marco d'Aviano celebrated mass in the chapel of Kahlenberg, and the King of Poland served him during the sacrifice. Afterward, Sobieski made his son kneel down and dubbed him a knight in remembrance of the great occasion on which he was going to be present; then, turning toward his officers, he reminded them of the victory of Choczim, adding that the triumph they were about to achieve under the walls of Vienna would not only save a city, but Christendom. Next morning the Christian army descended the Hill of Kahlen in order of battle. A salvo of five cannon-shot gave the signal for the fight. Sobieski commanded the right wing, the Duke of Lorraine the left, under whose orders served Prince Eugene of Savoy, then aged nineteen. The Elector of Bavaria was in the centre. The village of Naussdorf, situated upon the Danube, was attacked by the Saxon and imperial troops which formed the left wing, and carried after an obstinate resistance. Toward noon the King of Poland, having descended into the plain with the right wing, at the head of his Polish cavalry, attacked the innumerable squadrons of Turkish horse. Flinging himself upon the enemy's centre with all the fury of a hurricane, he spread confusion in their ranks; but his courage carried him too far; he was surrounded and was on the point of being overwhelmed by numbers. Then, shouting for aid, the German cavalry, which had followed him, charged the enemy at full gallop, delivered the King, and soon put the Turks to flight on all sides. The right wing had decided the victory; by seven o'clock in the evening the deliverance of Vienna was achieved. The bodies of more than ten thousand infidels strewed the field of battle.

But all those combats were mere preludes to the great battle which must decide the fortune of the war. For the Turkish camp, with its thousands of tents, could still be seen spreading around as far as the eye could reach, and its artillery continued to play upon the city. The victorious commander-in-chief was holding a council of war to decide whether to give battle again on that same day, or wait till the morrow to give his troops an interval of rest, when a messenger came with the announcement that the enemy appeared to be in full flight; and it proved to be the fact. A panic had seized the Turks, who fled in disorder, abandoning their camp and baggage; and soon even those who were attacking the city were seen in full flight with the rest of the army.

The booty found in the Turkish camp was immense: three hundred pieces of heavy artillery, five thousand tents, that of the Grand Vizier with all the military chests and the chancery. The treasures amounted to fifteen million crowns; the tent of the Vizier alone yielded four hundred thousand crowns. Two millions also were found in the military chest; arms studded with precious stones, the equipments of Kara Mustapha, fell into the hands of the victors. In their flight the Mussulmans threw away arms, baggage, and banners, with the exception of the holy standard of the Prophet, which, nevertheless, the imperials pretended to have seized. The King of Poland received for his share four million florins; and in a letter to his wife—the sole delight of his soul, his dear and well-beloved Mariette—he speaks of that booty and of the happiness of having delivered Vienna. "All the enemy's camp," he wrote, "with the whole of his artillery and all his enormous riches, have fallen into our hands. We are driving before us a host of camels, mules, and Turkish prisoners."

Count Starhemberg received the King of Poland in the magnificent tent of the Grand Vizier and greeted him as a deliverer. Next day Sobieski, accompanied by the Elector of Bavaria and the different commanders, traversed the city on horseback, preceded by a great banner of cloth of gold and two tall gilded staves bearing the horse-tails which had been planted in front of the Grand Vizier's tent, as a symbol of supreme command. In the Loretto chapel of the Augustins the hero threw himself upon his face before the altar and chanted the *Te Deum*. Vienna was delivered; the flood of Ottomans, that had beaten against its walls one hundred fifty-four years previously, had returned more furiously, more menacing still, against that dignified protectress of European civilization, but this time it had been repelled never to return.

Thus vanished the insane hopes of the Grand Vizier. If Demetrius Cantemir may be believed, Kara Mustapha had desired to capture Vienna to appropriate it to himself and found in the West an empire of which he would have been the sovereign. "That subject," says the historian, "who only held his power from the Sultan, despised in his heart the Sultan himself; and as he found himself at the head of all the disciplined troops of the empire, he looked upon his master as a shadow denuded of strength and substance, who, being very inferior in courage to him, could never oppose to him an army like that which was under his command. For all that concerned the Emperor of Germany, he appeared still less to be feared: being a prince bare and despoiled so soon as he should have lost Vienna. It was thus that Kara Mustapha reasoned within himself.

"Already he casts his eyes over the treasures which he has in his possession; with the money of the Sultan he has also brought his own; all that of the German princes is going to be his; for he believes that it is amassed in the city he is besieging. If he needs support, he reckons upon the different governors of Hungary as devoted to his interests; these are his creatures, whom he has put into their posts during the seven years of his vizierate; not one of those functionaries dare offer an obstacle to the elevation of his benefactor. Ibrahim Pacha, Beylerbey of Buda, keeps him in suspense by reason of the influence that his fame gives him over the army and over Hungary; he must be won over before all else, as well as the chief officers of the janizaries and the spahis. Ibrahim shall be made King of Hungary. The different provinces comprised in that kingdom shall be divided into *timars* for appanage of the spahis, and all the rest of the soldiery shall have establishments in the towns, as so many new colonies; to them shall be assigned the lands of the old inhabitants, who will be driven out or reduced to slavery. He reserves for himself the title of Sultan, his share shall be all Germany as far as the frontiers of France, with Transylvania and Poland, which he intends to render subject or at least make tributary the year following." Such are the projects that Cantemir attributes to Kara Mustapha; the intervention of Sobieski caused these chimerical plans quickly to vanish.

The Emperor Leopold, who returned to Vienna on September 16th, instead of expressing his thanks and gratitude to the commanders who had rescued his capital, received them with the haughty and repulsive coldness prescribed by the etiquette of the imperial court. Sobieski nevertheless continued his services by pursuing the retreating Turks. Awakened from his dream of self-exaltation, the Grand Vizier retook the road toward Turkey, directing his steps to the Raab, where he rallied the remnants of his army. Thence he marched toward Buda, and attacked by the way the Styrian town of Lilenfeld; he was repulsed by the prelate Matthias Kalweis, and avenged himself for that fresh check by devastating Lower Styria. He crossed the Danube by a bridge of boats at Parkany; but the Poles vigorously disputed the passage with him, and he again lost more than eight thousand men taken or slain by the Christians. Shortly after, the fortress of Gran opened its gates to Kara Mustapha. The Grand Vizier barbarously put to death the officers who had signed the capitulation; he threw upon his generals the responsibility of his reverses, and thought to stifle in blood the murmurs of his accusers. The army marched in disorder as though struck with a panic terror. Kara Mustapha wished that a Jew whom he despatched to Belgrad should be escorted by a troop of horsemen. "I have no need of an escort," replied the Jew: "I have only to wear my cap in the German fashion, and not a Turk will touch me."

The enemies of the Grand Vizier, however, conspired to effect his ruin at Constantinople; and the results of the campaign justified the predictions of the party of peace. Mahomet IV, enraged at these disasters, sent his grand chamberlain to Belgrad with orders to bring back the head of the Vizier (1683): it was, in fact, brought to the Sultan in a silver dish.

MONMOUTH'S REBELLION

A.D. 1685

GILBERT BURNET

James II was scarcely seated on the English throne in 1685 when serious disturbances began in his realm. The King had inherited the peculiar traits of the Stuarts. His first purpose was to overcome the Parliamentary power and make himself absolute ruler. He was likewise a Roman Catholic, and one of his objects was the suppression of English Protestantism.

During the first days of his reign the Protestant peasants in the west of England rose in revolt. They supported the claims of James Fitzroy, Duke of Monmouth, to the throne. Monmouth was the (reputed) illegitimate son of Charles II and Lucy Walters. With other exiled malcontents, English and Scotch, he had taken refuge in Holland. One of those exiled was the Earl of Argyle, whose father had figured prominently on the side of the Scottish Presbyterians against Charles I.

Owing to national jealousy, the English and Scotch in Holland could not act in unison, but all were determined to strike against James. Two expeditions were planned—one under Argyle, who expected to find forces awaiting him in Scotland; the other under Monmouth, whose adherents were to join him in the west of England.

Argyle's attempt miscarried through disagreement among the leaders, and the Earl was taken and beheaded, June 30, 1685. What befell the enterprise of Monmouth is told by Bishop Burnet, a contemporary historian. Monmouth was executed July 15, 1685, and in the trials known as the "Bloody Assizes," presided over by the brutal George Jeffreys, some three hundred of the Duke's followers were condemned to death, and more than a thousand otherwise punished.

AS soon as Lord Argyle sailed for Scotland, Monmouth set about his design with as much haste as possible. Arms were brought and a ship was freighted for Bilbao in Spain. He pawned all his jewels, but these could not raise much, and no money was sent to him out of England. So he was hurried into an ill-designed invasion. The whole company consisted but of eighty-two persons. They were all faithful to one another. But some spies whom Shelton, the new envoy, set on work, sent him the notice of a suspected ship sailing out of Amsterdam with arms.

Shelton neither understood the laws of Holland nor advised with those who did; otherwise he would have carried with him an order from the admiralty of Holland, that sat at The Hague, to be made use of as the occasion should require. When he came to Amsterdam, and applied himself to the magistrates there, desiring them to stop and search the ship that he named, they found the ship was already sailed out of their port and their jurisdiction went no further. So he was forced to send to the admiralty at The Hague. But those on board, hearing what he was come for, made all possible haste. And, the wind favoring them, they got out of the Texel before the order desired could be brought from The Hague. After a prosperous course, the Duke landed at Lyme in Dorsetshire (June 11, 1685); and he with his small company came ashore with some order, but with too much daylight, which discovered how few they were.

The alarm was brought hot to London, where, upon the general report and belief of the thing, an act of attainder passed both Houses in one day; some small opposition being made by the Earl of Anglesey, because the evidence did not seem clear enough for so severe a sentence, which was grounded on the notoriety of the thing. The sum of five thousand pounds was set on his head. And with that the session of Parliament ended; which was no small happiness to the nation, such a body of men being dismissed with doing so little hurt. The Duke of Monmouth's manifesto was long and ill-penned—full of much black and dull malice.

It charged the King with the burning of London, the popish plot, Godfrey's murder, and the Earl of Essex's death; and to crown all, it was pretended that the late King was poisoned by his orders: it was set forth that the King's religion made him incapable of the crown; that three subsequent houses of commons had voted his exclusion: the taking away of the old charters, and all the hard things done in the last reign, were laid to his charge: the elections of the present parliament were also set forth very odiously, with great indecency of style; the nation was also appealed to, when met in a free parliament, to judge of the Duke's own pretensions; [1] and all sort of liberty, both in temporals and spirituals, was promised to persons of all persuasions.

[1] He asserted that his mother had been the lawful wife of his father. —ED.

Upon the Duke of Monmouth's landing, many of the country people came in to join him, but very few of the gentry. He had quickly men enough about him to use all his arms. The Duke of Albemarle, as lord lieutenant of Devonshire, was sent down to raise the militia, and with them to make head against him. But their ill-affection appeared very evident; many deserted, and all were cold in the service. The Duke of Monmouth had the whole country open to him for almost a fortnight, during which time he was very diligent in training and animating his men. His own behavior was so gentle and obliging that he was master of all their hearts as much as was possible. But he quickly found what it was to be at the head of undisciplined men, that knew nothing of war, and that were not to be used with rigor. Soon after their landing, Lord Grey was sent out with a small party. He saw a few of the militia, and he ran for it; but his men stood, and the militia ran from them. Lord Grey brought a false alarm, that was soon found to be so, for the men whom their leader had abandoned came back in good order. The Duke of Monmouth was struck with this when he found that the person on whom he depended most, and for whom he designed the command of the horse, had already made himself infamous by his cowardice. He intended to join Fletcher with him in that command. But an unhappy accident made it not convenient to keep him longer about him. He sent him out on another party, and he, not being yet furnished with a horse, took the horse of one who had brought in a great body of men from Taunton. He was not in the way, so Fletcher not seeing him to ask his leave, thought that all things were to be in common among them that could advance the service.

After Fletcher had ridden about as he was ordered, as he returned, the owner of the horse he rode on—who was a rough and ill-bred man—reproached him in very injurious terms for taking out his horse without his leave. Fletcher bore this longer than could have been expected from one of his impetuous temper. But the other persisted in giving him foul language, and offered a switch or a cudgel, upon which he discharged his pistol at him and shot him dead. He went and gave the Duke of Monmouth an account of this, who saw it was impossible to keep him longer about him without disgusting and losing the country people who were coming in a body to demand justice. So he advised him to go aboard the ship and to sail on to Spain whither she was bound. By this means he was preserved for that time.

Ferguson ran among the people with all the fury of an enraged man that affected to pass for an enthusiast, though all his performances that way were forced and dry. The Duke of Monmouth's great error was that he did not in the first heat venture on some hardy action and then march either to Exeter or Bristol; where as he would have found much wealth, so he would have gained some reputation by it. But he lingered in exercising his men and stayed too long in the neighborhood of Lyme.

By this means the King had time both to bring troops out of Scotland, after Argyle was taken, and to send to Holland for the English and Scotch regiments that were in the service of the states; which the Prince sent over very readily and offered his own person, and a greater force, if it were necessary. The King received this with great expressions of acknowledgment and kindness. It was very visible that he was much distracted in his thoughts, and that, what appearance of courage soever he might put on, he was inwardly full of apprehensions and fears. He dare not accept of the offer of assistance that the French made him; for by that he would have lost the hearts of the English nation, and he had no mind to be so much obliged to the Prince of Orange or to let him into his counsels or affairs. Prince George committed a great error in not asking the command of the army; for the command, how much soever he might have been bound to the counsels of others, would have given him some lustre; whereas his staying at home in such times of danger brought him under much neglect.

The King could not choose worse than he did when he gave the command to the Earl of Feversham, who was a Frenchman by birth—and nephew to M. de Turenne. Both his brothers changing religion—though he continued still a Protestant—made that his religion was not much trusted to. He was an honest, brave, and good-natured man, but weak to a degree not easy to be conceived. And he conducted matters so ill that every step he made was like to prove fatal to the King's service. He had no parties abroad. He got no intelligence, and was almost surprised and like to be defeated, when he seemed to be under no apprehension, but was abed without any care or order. So that if the Duke of Monmouth had got but a very small number of good soldiers about him, the King's affairs would have fallen into great disorder.

The Duke of Monmouth had almost surprised Lord Feversham and all about him while they were abed. He got in between two bodies, into which the army lay divided. He now saw his error in lingering so long. He began to want bread, and to be so straitened that there was a necessity of pushing for a speedy decision. He was so misled in his march that he lost an hour's time, and when he came near the army there was an inconsiderable ditch, in the passing which he lost so much more time that the officers had leisure to rise and be dressed, now they had the alarm. And they put themselves in order. Yet the Duke of Monmouth's foot stood longer and fought better than could have been expected; especially, when the small body of horse they had, ran upon the first charge, the blame of which was cast on Lord Grey.

The foot being thus forsaken and galled by the cannon, did run at last. About a thousand of them were killed on the spot, and fifteen hundred were taken prisoners. Their numbers, when fullest, were between five and six thousand.

The Duke of Monmouth left the field[1] too soon for a man of courage who had such high pretensions; for a few days before he had suffered himself to be called king, which did him no service, even among those that followed him. He rode toward Dorsetshire; and when his horse could carry him no further he changed clothes with a shepherd and went as far as his legs could carry him, being accompanied only by a German whom he had brought over with him. At last, when he could go no farther, they lay down in a field where there was hay and straw, with which they covered themselves, so that they hoped to lie there unseen till night. Parties went out on all hands to take prisoners. The shepherd was found by Lord Lumley in the Duke of Monmouth's clothes. So this put them on his track, and having some dogs with them, they followed the scent, and came to the place where the German was first discovered. And he immediately pointed to the place

[1] This engagement took place at Ledgemoor, Somerset, July 6, 1685. —Ed.

Duke of Monmouth prostrates himself at the feet of King James II, praying for mercy

Painting by J. Pettie, A. R. A.

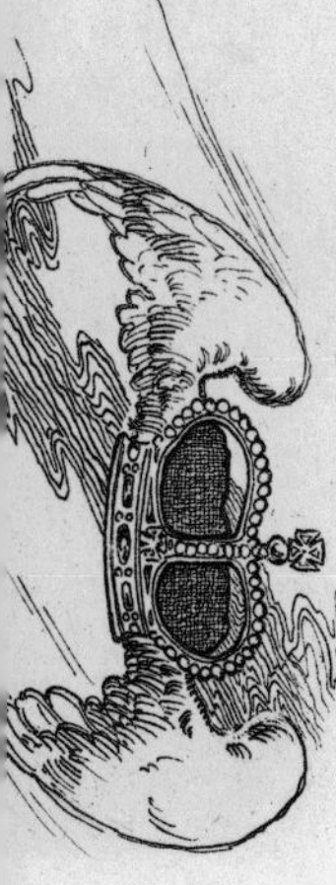

where the Duke of Monmouth lay. So he was taken in a very indecent dress and posture.

His body was quite sunk with fatigue, and his mind was now so low that he begged his life in a manner that agreed ill with the courage of the former parts of it. He called for pen, ink, and paper, and wrote to the Earl of Feversham, and both to the Queen and the Queen dowager, to intercede with the King for his life. The King's temper, as well as his interest, made it so impossible to hope for that, that it showed a great meanness in him to ask it in such terms as he used in his letters. He was carried up to Whitehall, where the King examined him in person, which was thought very indecent, since he was resolved not to pardon him.[1] He made new and unbecoming submissions, and insinuated a readiness to change his religion; for, he said, the King knew what his first education was in religion. There were no discoveries to be got from him; for the attempt was too rash to be well concerted, or to be so deep laid that many were involved in the guilt of it. He was examined on Monday, and orders were given for his execution on Wednesday.

Turner and Ken, the Bishops of Ely and of Bath and Wells, were ordered to wait on him. But he called for Dr. Tennison. The bishops studied to convince him of the sin of rebellion. He answered, he was sorry for the blood that was shed in it, but he did not seem to repent of the design. Yet he confessed that his father had often told him that there was no truth in the reports of his having married his mother. This he set under his hand, probably for his children's sake, who were then prisoners in the Tower, that so they might not be ill-used on his account. He showed a great neglect of his duchess. And her resentments for his course of life with Lady Wentworth wrought so much on her that she seemed not to have any of that tenderness left that became her sex and his present circumstances, for when he desired to speak privately with her she would have witnesses to hear

[1] The Duke of Monmouth pressed extremely that the King would see him, whence the King concluded he had something to say to him that he would tell to nobody else; but when he found it ended in nothing but lower submission than he either expected or desired, he told him plainly he had put it out of his power to pardon him by having proclaimed himself king. Thus may the most innocent actions of a man's life be sometimes turned to his disadvantage.—Ed.

all that passed, to justify herself, and to preserve her family. They parted very coldly. He only recommended to her the rearing of their children in the Protestant religion.

The bishops continued still to press on him a deep sense of the sin of rebellion; at which he grew so uneasy that he desired them to speak to him of other matters. They next charged him with the sin of living with Lady Wentworth, as he had done. In that he justified himself; he had married his duchess too young to give a true consent; he said that lady was a pious worthy woman, and that he had never lived so well, in all respects, as since his engagements with her. All the pains they took to convince him of the unlawfulness of that course of life had no effect. They did certainly very well in discharging their consciences and speaking so plainly to him. But they did very ill to talk so much of this matter and to make it so public, as they did, for divines ought not to repeat what they say to dying penitents no more than what the penitents say to them. By this means the Duke of Monmouth had little satisfaction in them and they had as little in him.

He was much better pleased with Dr. Tennison, who did very plainly speak to him with relation to his public actings and to his course of life; but he did it in a softer and less peremptory manner. And having said all that he thought proper, he left those points, in which he saw he could not convince him, to his own conscience, and turned to other things fit to be laid before a dying man. The Duke begged one day more of life with such repeated earnestness that as the King was much blamed for denying so small a favor, so it gave occasion to others to believe that he had some hope from astrologers that if he outlived that day he might have a better fate. As long as he fancied there was any hope, he was too much unsettled in his mind to be capable of anything.

But when he saw all was to no purpose and that he must die he complained a little that his death was hurried on so fast. But all on a sudden he came into a composure of mind that surprised those that saw it. There was no affectation in it. His whole behavior was easy and calm, not without a decent cheerfulness. He prayed God to forgive all his sins, unknown as well as known. He seemed confident of the mercies of God, and that he was going to be happy with him. And he went to the place of execution on Tower Hill with an air of undisturbed courage that was grave and composed. He said little there, only that he was sorry for the blood that was shed, but he had ever meant well to the nation. When he saw the axe he touched it and said it was not sharp enough. He gave the hangman but half the reward he intended, and said if he cut off his head cleverly, and not so butcherly as he did the Lord Russell's, his man would give him the rest.

The executioner was in great disorder, trembling all over; so he gave him two or three strokes without being able to finish the matter and then flung the axe out of his hand. But the sheriff forced him to take it up; and at three or four more strokes he severed his head from his body and both were presently buried in the chapel of the Tower. Thus lived and died this unfortunate young man. He had several good qualities in him, and some that were as bad. He was soft and gentle even to excess and too easy to those who had credit with him. He was both sincere and good-natured, and understood war well. But he was too much given to pleasure and to favorites.

REVOCATION OF THE EDICT OF NANTES

A.D. 1685

BON LOUIS HENRI MARTIN

It was one of the glories of Henry of Navarre to end the religious wars of France by publishing the Edict of Nantes (1598), which placed Catholics and Protestants on a practically equal footing as subjects. By the revocation of that edict, in 1685, Louis XIV opened the way for fresh persecution of the Huguenots. Of the hundreds of thousands whom the King and his agents then caused to flee the country and seek civil and religious liberty in other lands, many crossed the sea and settled in the colonies of North America, especially in South Carolina.

By revoking the Edict of Nantes Louis XIV arrayed against himself all the Protestant countries of Europe. By seizures of territory he also offended Catholic states. In 1686 the League of Augsburg combined the greater part of Europe for resisting his encroachments.

This period of the "Huguenots of the Dispersion" was marked by complicated strifes in politics, religion, and philosophy. It was one of the most reactionary epochs in French history. No writer has better depicted the time, with the severities, atrocities, and effects of the revocation of the great edict, than Martin, the celebrated historian of his country.

FOR many years the government of Louis XIV had been acting toward the Reformation as toward a victim entangled in a noose which is drawn tighter and tighter till it strangles its prey. In 1683 the oppressed had finally lost patience, and their partial attempts at resistance, disavowed by the most distinguished of their brethren, had been stifled in blood. After the truce of Ratisbon, declarations and decrees hostile to Protestantism succeeded each other with frightful rapidity; nothing else was seen in the official gazette. Protestant ministers were prohibited from officiating longer than three years in the same church (August, 1684); Protestant individuals were forbidden to give asylum to their sick coreligionists; the sick who were not treated at home were required to go to the hospitals, where they were put in the hands of churchmen. A beautiful and touching request, written by Pastor Claude, was in vain presented to the

King in January, 1685. Each day beheld some Protestant church closed for contraventions either imaginary or fraudulently fabricated by persecutors. It was enough that the child of a "convert" or a bastard (all bastards were reputed Catholic) should enter a Protestant church for the exercise of worship, to be interdicted there.

If this state of things had continued long, not a single Protestant church would have been left. The Protestant academy or university of Saumur, which had formed so many eminent theologians and orators, was closed; the ministers were subjected to the villein tax for their real estate (January, 1685). The quinquennial assembly of the clergy, held in May, presented to the King a multitude of new demands against the heretics; among others, for the establishment of penalties against the "converts" who did not fulfil their duties as Catholics. The penalty of death, which had been decreed against emigrants, was commuted into perpetual confinement in the galleys, by the request of the clergy. The first penalty had been little more than a threat; the second, which confounded with the vilest miscreants, unfortunates guilty of having desired to flee from persecution, was to be applied in the sternest reality! It was extended to Protestants living in France who should authorize their children to marry foreigners. It was interdicted to Reformers to follow the occupation of printer or bookseller. It was forbidden to confer on them degrees in arts, law, or medicine. Protestant orphans could have only Catholic guardians. Half of the goods of emigrants was promised to informers. It was forbidden to Reformers to preach or write against Catholicism (July, August, 1685).

A multitude of Protestant churches had been demolished, and the inhabitants of places where worship had been suppressed were prohibited from going to churches in places where it was still permitted. Grave difficulties resulted with respect to the principal acts of civil life, which, among Protestants as among Catholics, owed their authenticity only to the intervention of ministers of religion. A decree in council of September 15, 1685, enacted that, in places deprived of the exercise of worship, a pastor chosen by the intendant of the generality should celebrate, in the presence of relatives only, the marriages of Reformers; that their bans should be published to the congregations, and the registries of their marriages entered on the rolls of the local court. Similar decrees had been issued concerning baptisms and burials. Hitherto Protestantism had been struck right and left with all kinds of weapons, without any very definite method: these decrees seemed to indicate a definite plan; that is, the suppression of external worship, with a certain tolerance, at least provisionally, for conscience, and a kind of civil state separately constituted for obstinate Protestants.

This plan had, in fact, been debated in council. "The King," wrote Madame de Maintenon, August 13, 1684, "has it in mind to work for the *entire* conversion of heretics; he has frequent conferences for this purpose with M. le Tellier and M. de Châteauneuf (the secretary of state charged with the affairs of the so-called Reformed religion), in which they wish to persuade me to take part. M. de Châteauneuf has proposed means that are unsuitable. Things must not be hastened. *It is necessary to convert, not to persecute.* M. de Louvois prefers mild measures which do not accord with his nature and his eagerness to see things ended."

The means proposed by Châteauneuf was apparently the immediate revocation of the Edict of Nantes, which was judged premature. As to the "mildness" of Louvois, it was soon seen in operation. Louvois pretended to be moderate, lest the King, through scruples of humanity, should hesitate to confer on him the management of the affair. He had his plan ready: it was to recur to the "salutary constraint" already tried in 1681 by the instrumentality of soldiers to the Dragonade. Colbert was no longer at hand to interpose obstacles to this.

Louvois had persuaded the King that in the moral situation of Protestant communities it would be enough "to show them the troops," to compel them to abjure. The troops had been "shown," therefore, to the Reformers of Béarn; the intendant of that province, Foucault, had come to Paris to concert with the minister the management of the enterprise; Louvois could not have found a fitter instrument than this pitiless and indefatigable man, who had the soul of an inquisitor under the garb of a pliant courtier. On his return from Paris, Foucault, seconded by the Parliament of Pau and the clergy, began by the demolition, on account of "contraventions," of fifteen out of twenty Protestant churches that remained in Béarn, and the "conversion" of eleven hundred persons in two months (February–April, 1685). He then called for the assistance of the army to complete the work, promising "to keep a tight rein over the soldiers, so that they should do no violence." This was for the purpose of allaying the scruples of the King. The troops were therefore concentrated in the cities and villages filled with Reformers; the five remaining Protestant churches shared the fate of the rest, and the pastors were banished, some to a distance of six leagues from their demolished churches, others beyond the jurisdiction of the Parliament of Pau.

Terror flew before the soldiers; as soon as the scarlet uniforms and the high caps of the dragoons were descried, corporations, whole cities, sent their submission to the intendant. An almost universal panic chilled all hearts. The mass of Reformers signed or verbally accepted a confession of the Catholic faith, suffered themselves to be led to the church, bowed their heads to the benediction of the bishop or the missionary, and cannon and bonfires celebrated the "happy reconciliation." Protestants who had hoped to find a refuge in liberty of conscience without external worship saw this hope vanish. Foucault paid no attention to the decrees in council that regulated the baptisms, marriages, and burials of Protestants, because, he said in a despatch to the minister, "in the present disposition to general and speedy conversion, this would expose those who waver, and harden the obstinate." The council issued a new order confirmatory of the preceding ones, and specially for Béarn. Foucault, according to his own words, "did not judge proper to execute it." This insolence went unpunished. Success justified everything. Before the end of August the twenty-two thousand Protestants of Béarn were "converted," save a few hundred. Foucault, in his *Memoirs*, in which he exhibits his triumphs with cynicism, does not, however, avow all the means. Although he confesses that "the distribution of money drew many souls to the Church," he does not say how he kept his promise of preventing the "soldiers from doing any violence." He does not recount the brutalities, the devastations, the tortures resorted to against the refractory, the outrages to women, nor how these soldiers took turns from hour to hour to hinder their hosts from sleeping during entire weeks till these unfortunates, stupefied, delirious, signed an abjuration.

The King saw only the result. The resolution was taken to send everywhere these "booted missionaries" who had succeeded so well in Béarn. Louvois sent, on the part of the King, July 31st, a command to the Marquis de Boufflers, their general, to lead them into Guienne, and "to quarter them all on the Reformers"; "observing to endeavor to diminish the number of Reformers in such a manner that in each community the Catholics shall be twice or three times more numerous than they; so that when, in due time, his majesty shall wish no longer to permit the exercise of this religion in his kingdom, he may no longer have to apprehend that the small number that shall remain can undertake anything." The troops were to be withdrawn as fast as this object should be obtained in each place, without undertaking to convert all at once. The ministers should be driven out of the country, and by no means should they be retained by force; the pastors absent, the flocks could more easily be brought to reason. The soldiers were to commit "no other disorders than to levy (daily) twenty sous for each horseman or dragoon, and ten sous for each foot-soldier." Excesses were to be severely punished. Louvois, in another letter, warned the general not to yield to all the suggestions of the ecclesiastics, nor even of the intendants. They did not calculate on being able to proceed so rapidly as in Béarn.

These instructions show precisely, not what was done, but what the King wished should be done. The subalterns, sure of immunity in case of success, acted more in accordance with the spirit of Louvois than according to the words dictated by Louis. The King, when by chance he heard that his orders had been transcended, rarely chastised the transgressor, lest it might be "said to the Reformers that his majesty disapproves of whatsoever has been done to convert them." Louis XIV, therefore, cannot repudiate, before history, his share of this terrible responsibility.

The result exceeded the hopes of the King and of Louvois. Guienne yielded as easily as Béarn. The Church of Montauban, the head-quarters of the Reformation in this region, was "reunited" in great majority, after several days of military vexations; Bergerac held out a little longer; then all collective resistance ceased. The cities and villages, for ten or twelve leagues around, sent to the military leaders their promises of abjuration. In three weeks there were sixty thousand conversions in the district of Bordeaux or Lower Guienne, twenty thousand in that of Montauban or Upper Guienne. According to the reports of Boufflers, Louvois, September 7th, reckoned that before the end of the month there would not remain in Lower Guienne ten thousand Reformers out of the one hundred fifty thousand found there August 15th. "There is not a courier," wrote Madame de Maintenon, September 26th, "that does not bring the King great causes of joy; to wit, news of conversions by thousands." The only resistance that they deigned to notice here and there was that of certain provincial gentlemen, of simple and rigid habits, less disposed than the court nobility to sacrifice their faith to interest and vanity.

Guienne subjected, the army of Béarn was marched, a part into Limousin, Saintonge, and Poitou, a part into Languedoc. Poitou, already "dragooned" in 1681 by the intendant Marillac, had just been so well labored with by Marillac's successor, Lamoignon de Basville, aided by some troops, that Foucault, sent from Béarn into Poitou, found nothing more to glean. The King even caused Louvois to recommend that they should not undertake to convert all the Reformers at once, lest the rich and powerful families, who had in their hands the commerce of those regions, should avail themselves of the proximity of the sea to take flight (September 8th). Basville, a great administrator, but harshly inflexible, was sent from Poitou into Lower Languedoc, in the first part of September, in order to coöperate there with the Duke de Noailles, governor of the province. The intendant of Lower Languedoc, D'Aguesseau, although he had zealously coöperated in all the restrictive measures of the Reformed worship, had asked for his recall as soon as he had seen that the King was determined on the employment of military force; convinced that this determination would not be less fatal to religion than to the country, he retired, broken-hearted, his spirit troubled for the future.

The conversion of Languedoc seemed a great undertaking.

The mass of Protestants, nearly all concentrated in Lower Languedoc, and in the mountainous regions adjoining, was estimated at more than two hundred forty thousand souls; these people, more ardent, more constant than the mobile and sceptical Gascons, did not seem capable of so easily abandoning their belief. The result, however, was the same as elsewhere. Nîmes and Montpellier followed the example of Montauban. The quartering of a hundred soldiers in their houses quickly reduced the notables of Nîmes; in this diocese alone, the principal centre of Protestantism, sixty thousand souls abjured in three days. Several of the leading ministers did the same. From Nîmes the Duc de Noailles led the troops into the mountains. Cévennes and Gevaudan submitted to invasion like the rest, as the armed mission advanced from valley to valley. These cantons were still under the terror of the sanguinary repressions of 1683, and had been disarmed, as far as it was possible, as well as all Lower Languedoc. Noailles, in the earlier part of October, wrote to Louvois that he would answer "upon his head" that, before the end of November, the province would contain no more Huguenots. If we are to believe his letters, prepared for the eyes of the King, everything must have taken place "with all possible wisdom and discipline"; but the Chancellor d'Aguesseau, in the "life" of his father, the intendant, teaches us what we are to think of it. "The manner in which this miracle was wrought," he says, "the singular facts that were recounted to us day by day, would have sufficed to pierce a heart less religious than that of my father!" Noailles himself, in a confidential letter, announced to Louvois that he would ere long send "some capable men to answer about any matters which he desired to know, and about which he could not write." There was a half tacit understanding established between the minister, the military chiefs, and the intendants. The King, in their opinion, desired the end without sufficiently desiring the means.

Dauphiny, Limousin, La Rochelle, that holy Zion of the Huguenots, all yielded at the same time. Louis was intoxicated. It had sufficed for him to say a word, to lay his hand upon the hilt of his sword, to make those fierce Huguenots, who had formerly worn out so many armies, and had forced so many kings to capitulate before their rebellions, fall at his feet and the feet of the Church. Who would henceforth dare to doubt his divine mission and his infallible genius!

Not that Louis, nor especially those that surrounded him, precisely believed that terror produced the effects of *grace*, or that these innumerable conversions were sincere; but they saw in this the extinction of all strong conviction among the heretics, the moral exhaustion of an expiring sect. "The children at least will be Catholics, if the fathers are hypocrites," wrote Madame de Maintenon. At present it was necessary to complete the work and to prevent dangerous relapses in these subjugated multitudes. It was necessary to put to flight as quickly as possible the "false pastors" who might again lead their old flocks astray, and to make the law conform to the fact, by solemnly revoking the concessions formerly wrung by powerful and armed heresy from the feebleness of the ruling power. Louis had long preserved some scruples about the violation of engagements entered into by his grandfather Henry IV; but his last doubts had been set at rest, several months since, by a "special council of conscience," composed of two theologians and two jurisconsults, who had decided that he might and should revoke the Edict of Nantes. The names of the men who took upon themselves the consequences of such a decision have remained unknown: doubtless the confessor La Chaise was one of the theologians; who was the other? The Archbishop of Paris, Harlai, was not, perhaps, in sufficient esteem, on account of his habits. The great name of the Bishop of Meaux naturally presents itself to the mind; but neither the correspondence of Bossuet nor the documents relating to his life throw any light on this subject, and we know not whether a direct and material responsibility must be added to the moral responsibility with which the maxims of Bossuet and the spirit of his works burden his memory.

After the "council of conscience," the council of the King was convened for a definitive deliberation in the earlier part of October. Some of the ministers, apparently the two Colberts, Seignelai, and Croissi, insinuated that it would be better not to be precipitate. The Dauphin, a young prince of twenty-four, who resembled, in his undefined character, his grandfather more than his father, and who was destined to remain always as it were lost in the splendid halo of Louis the Great, attempted an intervention that deserves to rescue his name from oblivion. "He represented, from an anonymous memorial that had been addressed to him the evening before, that it was, perhaps, to be apprehended that the Huguenots might take up arms;" "that in case they did not dare to do this, a great number would leave the kingdom, which would injure commerce and agriculture, and thereby even weaken the state." The King replied that he had foreseen all and provided for all, that nothing in the world would be more painful to him than to shed a drop of the blood of his subjects, but that he had armies and good generals whom he would employ, in case of necessity, against rebels who desired their own destruction. As to the argument of interest, he judged it little worthy of consideration, compared with the advantages of an undertaking that would restore to religion its splendor, to the state its tranquillity, and to authority all its rights. The suppression of the Edict of Nantes was resolved upon without further opposition.

Father la Chaise and Louvois, according to their ecclesiastical and military correspondence, had promised that it should not even cost the drop of blood of which the King spoke. The aged Chancellor le Tellier, already a prey to the malady that was to bring him to his grave, drew up with trembling hand the fatal declaration, which the King signed October 17th.

Louis professed in this preamble to do nothing but continue the pious designs of his grandfather and his father for the reunion of their subjects to the Church. He spoke of the "perpetual and irrevocable" edict of Henry IV as a temporary regulation. "Our cares," he said, "since the truce that we facilitated for this purpose, have had the effect that we proposed to ourselves, since the better and the greater part of our subjects of the so-called Reformed religion have embraced the Catholic; and inasmuch as by reason of this the execution of the Edict of Nantes" "remains useless, we have judged that we could not do better, in order wholly to efface the memory of evils that this false religion had caused in our kingdom, than entirely to revoke the said Edict of Nantes and all that has been done since in favor of the said religion."

The order followed to demolish unceasingly all the churches

of the said religion situated in the kingdom. It was forbidden to assemble for the exercise of the said religion, in any place, private house or tenement, under penalty of confiscation of body and goods. All ministers of the said religion who would not be converted were enjoined to leave the kingdom in a fortnight, and divers favors were granted to those who should be converted. Private schools for instruction of children in the said religion were interdicted. Children who should be born to those of the said religion should for the future be baptized by the parish curates, under penalty of a fine of five hundred livres, and still more, if there were occasion, to be paid by the parents, and the children should then be brought up in the Catholic religion. A delay of four months was granted to fugitive Reformers to reënter the kingdom and recover possession of their property; this delay passed, the property should remain confiscated. It was forbidden anew to Reformers to leave the kingdom, under penalty of the galleys for men, and confiscation of body and goods for women. The declarations against backsliders were confirmed.

A last article, probably obtained by the representations of the Colberts, declared that the Reformers, "till it should please God to enlighten them like others, should be permitted to dwell in the kingdom, in strict loyalty to the King, to continue there their commerce and enjoy their goods, without being molested or hindered under pretext of the said religion."

The Edict of Revocation was sent in haste to the governors and intendants, without waiting for it to be registered, which took place in the Parliament of Paris, October 22d. The intendants were instructed not to allow the ministers who should abandon the country to dispose of their real estate, or to take with them their children above seven years of age: a monstrous dismemberment of the family wrought by an arbitrary will that recognized neither natural nor civil rights! The King recommended a milder course toward noblemen, merchants, and manufacturers; he did not desire that obstinacy should be shown "in compelling them to be converted immediately without exception" "by any considerable violence."

The tone of the ministerial instructions changed quickly on the reception of despatches announcing the effect of the edict in the provinces. This effect teaches us more in regard to the situation of the dragooned people than could the most sinister narratives. The edict which proscribed the Reformed worship, which interdicted the perpetuation of the Protestant religion by tearing from it infants at their birth, was received as a boon by Protestants who remained faithful to their belief. They saw, in the last article of the edict, the end of persecution, and, proud of having weathered the storm, they claimed the tolerance that the King promised them, and the removal of their executioners. The new converts, who, persuaded that the King desired to force all his subjects to profess his religion, had yielded through surprise, fear, want of constancy in suffering, or through a worthier motive, the desire of saving their families from the license of the soldiers, manifested their regret and their remorse, and were no longer willing to go to mass.

All the leaders of the dragonades, the Noailles, the Foucaults, the Basvilles, the Marillacs, complained bitterly of a measure that was useless to them as to the demolition of Protestant churches and the prohibition of worship, and very injurious as to the progress of conversions. They had counted on rooting out the worship by converting all the believers. The revocation of the Edict of Nantes sinned, therefore, in their eyes by excess of moderation! Louvois hastened to reassure them in this respect, and authorized them to act as if the last article of the edict did not exist. "His majesty," he said, "desires that the extremest rigors of the law should be felt by those who will not make themselves of his religion, and those who shall have the foolish glory of wishing to remain the last must be pushed to the last extremity." "Let the soldiers," he said elsewhere, "be allowed to live very licentiously!" (November, 1685).

The King, however, did not mean it thus, and claimed that persecution should be conducted with method and gravity. But men do not stop at pleasure in evil: one abyss draws on another. The way had been opened to brutal and cynical passions, to the spirit of denunciation, to low and mean fanaticism; the infamies with which the subaltern agents polluted themselves recoiled upon the chiefs who did not repress them, and on this proud government that did not blush to add to the odium of persecution the shame of faithlessness! The chiefs of the dragonades judged it necessary to restrain the bad converts by making example of the obstinate; hence arose an inundation of horrors in which we see, as Saint Simon says, "the orthodox imitating against heretics the acts of pagan tyrants against confessors and martyrs." Everything, in fact, was allowed the soldiers but rape and murder; and even this restriction was not always respected; besides, many of the unfortunate died or were maimed for life in consequence of the treatment to which they had been subjected; and the obscene tortures inflicted on women differed little from the last outrage, but in a perversity more refined.

All the diabolic inventions of the highwaymen of the Middle Ages to extort gold from their captives were renewed here and there to secure conversions: the feet of the victims were scorched, they were strappadoed, suspended by the feet; young mothers were tied to the bedposts, while their infants at the breast were writhing with hunger before their eyes. "From torture to abjuration, and from this to communion, there was often not twenty-four hours' distance, and their executioners were their guides and witnesses. Nearly all the bishops lent themselves to this sudden and impious practice." Among the Reformed whom nothing could shake, those who encouraged others to resistance by the influence of their character or social position were sent to the Bastille or other state prisons; some were entombed in subterranean dungeons—in those dark pits, stifling or deadly cold, invented by feudal barbarism. The remains of animals in a state of putrefaction were sometimes thrown in after them, to redouble the horror! The hospital of Valence and the tower of Constance at Aigues-Mortes have preserved, in Protestant martyrology, a frightful renown. The women usually showing themselves more steadfast than the men, the most obstinate were shut up in convents; infamous acts took place there; yet they were rare. It must be said to the honor of the sex, often too facile to the suggestions of fanaticism, that the nuns showed much more humanity and true religion than the priests and monks. Astonished to see Huguenot women so different from the idea they had formed of them, they almost became the protectors of victims that had been given them to torment.

The abduction of children put the final seal to the persecution. The Edict of Revocation had only declared that children subsequently born should be brought up in the Catholic religion. An edict of January, 1686, prescribed that children from five to sixteen years of age should be taken from their heretical relatives and put in the hands of Catholic relatives, or, if they had none, of Catholics designated by the judges! The crimes that we have just indicated might, in strictness, be attributed to the passions of subaltern agents; but this mighty outrage against the family and nature must be charged to the Government alone.

With the revocation, the dragonade was extended, two places partially excepted, over all France. When the great harvest had been sufficiently gathered in the South and West, the reapers were sent elsewhere. The battalions of converters marched from province to province till they reached the northern frontier, carrying everywhere the same terror. Metz, where the Protestants were numerous, was particularly the theatre of abominable excesses. Paris and Alsace were alone, to a certain extent, preserved. Louvois did not dare to show such spectacles to the society of Versailles and Paris; the King would not have endured it. The people of Paris demolished the Protestant church of Charenton, an object of their ancient animosity; the ruling power weighed heavily upon the eight or nine thousand Huguenots who remained in the capital, and constrained two-thirds of them, by intimidation, to a feigned conversion; but there were no striking acts of violence, except perhaps the banishment of thirty elders of the consistory to different parts of the kingdom, and the soldiers did not make their appearance. The lieutenant of police, La Reinie, took care to reassure the leading merchants, and the last article of the Edict of Revocation was very nearly observed in Paris and its environs. As to Lutheran Alsace, it had nothing in common with the system of the Edict of Nantes and the French Calvinists: the Treaty of Westphalia, the capitulation of Strasburg, all the acts that bound it to France, guaranteed to it a separate religious state. An attempt was indeed made to encroach upon Lutheranism by every means of influence and by a system of petty annoyances; but direct attacks were limited to a suppression of public worship in places where the population was two-thirds Catholic. The political events that soon disturbed Europe compelled the French Government to be circumspect toward the people of this recently conquered frontier.

The converters indemnified themselves at the expense of another frontier population, that was not dependent on France. The Vaudois, the first offspring of the Reformation, had always kept possession of the high Alpine valleys, on the confines of Piedmont and Dauphiny, in spite of the persecutions that they had repeatedly endured from the governments of France and Piedmont. The Piedmontese Vaudois had their Edict of Nantes; that is, liberty of worship in the three valleys of St. Martin, La Luzerne, and La Perouse. When the dragonade invaded Dauphiny, the Vaudois about Briançon and Pignerol took refuge in crowds with their brethren in the valleys subject to Piedmont. The French Government was unwilling to suffer them to remain in this asylum. The Duke Victor Amadeus II enjoined the refugees to quit his territory (November 4th). The order was imperfectly executed, and Louis XIV demanded more. The Duke, by an edict of February 1, 1686, prohibited the exercise of heretical worship, and ordered the schools to be closed under penalty of death. The *barbes* (ministers), schoolmasters, and French refugees were to leave the states of the Duke in a fortnight, under the same penalty. The Vaudois responded by taking up arms, without reflecting on the immense force of their oppressors. The three valleys were assailed at the same time by French and Piedmontese troops. The French were commanded by the governor of Casale, Catinat, a man of noble heart, an elevated and philosophic mind, who deplored his fatal mission, and attempted to negotiate with the insurgents, but Catinat could neither persuade to submission these men resolved to perish rather than renounce their faith, nor restrain the fury of his soldiers exasperated by the vigor of the resistance. The valleys of St. Martin and La Perouse were captured, and the victors committed frightful barbarities. Meanwhile the Piedmontese, after having induced the mountaineers, who guarded the entrance of the valley of La Luzerne, to lay down their arms, by false promises, slaughtered three thousand women, children, and old men at the Pré de la Tour! The remotest recesses of the Alps were searched; a multitude of unfortunates were exterminated singly: more than ten thousand were dragged as prisoners to the fortresses of Piedmont, where most of them died of want. A handful of the bravest succeeding in maintaining themselves among the rocks, where they could not be captured, and, protected by the intervention of Protestant powers, and especially of the Swiss, finally obtained liberty to emigrate, both for themselves and their coreligionists.

There has often been seen in history much greater bloodshed than that caused by the Revocation of the Edict of Nantes, scenes of destruction planned more directly and on a vaster scale by governments, and sometimes the same contrast between an advanced state of civilization and acts of barbarity; but no spectacle wounds moral sense and humanity to the same degree as this persecution carried on coldly and according to abstract ideas, without the excuse of struggle and danger, without the ardent fever of battle and revolution. The very virtues of the persecutors are here but an additional monstrosity: doubtless, there is also seen, at a later period, among the authors of another reign of terror, this same contrast that astounds and troubles the conscience of posterity; but they, at least, staked each day their own lives against the lives of their adversaries, and, with their lives, the very existence of the country involved in their cause!

A million and a half of Frenchmen were in terror and despair; yet songs of victory resounded around Louis the Great. The aged Le Tellier lifted to heaven the hand that had just signed the Revocation, and parodied, on the occasion of an edict that recalls the times of Decius and Diocletian, the canticle by which Simeon hailed the birth of the Redeemer. He died a fanatic, after having lived a cold and astute politician (October 31, 1685); he died, and the most eloquent voices of the Gallican Church broke forth in triumphal hymns, as over the tomb of a victorious hero! "Let us publish this miracle of our days," exclaimed Bossuet, in that funeral oration of Le Tellier, wherein he nevertheless exhibited apprehensions of new combats and of a sombre future for the Church; "let us pour forth our hearts in praise of the piety of Louis; let us lift our acclamations to heaven, and let us say to this new Constantine, to this new Theodosius, to this new Marcianus, to this new Charlemagne: 'You have strengthened the faith, you have exterminated the heretics; this is the meritorious work of your reign, its peculiar characteristic. Through you heresy is no more: God alone could have wrought this wonder.'" The gentle Fléchier himself echoed Bossuet, with the whole corps of the clergy with the great mass of the people. Paris and Versailles, that did not witness the horror of the details, that saw only the general prestige and the victory of unity, were deaf to the doleful reports that came from the provinces, and applauded the "new Constantine."

"This is the grandest and finest thing that ever was conceived and accomplished," wrote Madame de Sévigné. All the corporations, courts of justice, academies, universities, municipal bodies, vied with each other in every species of laudatory allusion; medals represented the King crowned by Religion "for having brought back to the Church two millions of Calvinists"; the number of victims was swollen in order to swell the glory of the persecutor. Statues were erected to the "destroyer of heresy." This concert of felicitations was prolonged for years; the influence of example, the habit of admiring, wrung eulogies even from minds that, it would seem, ought to have remained strangers to this fascination; every writer thought he must pay his tribute; even La Bruyere, that sagacious observer and excellent writer, whose acute and profound studies of manners appeared in 1687; and La Fontaine himself, the poet of free-thought and of universal freedom of action.

The Government redoubled its rigor. The penalty of death was decreed against ministers reëntering the kingdom without permission, and the galleys against whomsoever should give them asylum; penalty of death against whomsoever should take part in a meeting (July 1, 1686). And this penalty was not simply a dead letter! Whenever the soldiers succeeded in surprising Protestants assembled for prayer in any solitary place, they first announced their presence by a volley; those who escaped the bullet and the sword were sent to the gallows or the galleys. Measures almost as severe were employed to arrest emigration. Seamen were forbidden to aid the Reformers to escape under penalty of a fine for the first offence, and of corporal punishment for a second offence (November 5, 1685). They went further: ere long, whoever aided the flight of emigrants became liable to the galleys for life, like emigrants themselves (May 7, 1686). Armed barks cruised along all the coasts; all the passes of the frontier were guarded; the peasants everywhere had orders to rush upon the fugitives. Some of the emigrants perished in attempting to force an exit; a host of others was brought back manacled; they dared not place them all under the galley-master's lash; they feared the effects of their despair and of their numbers, if they should mass them in the royal galleys; they crowded the prisons with those who were unwilling to purchase pardon by abjuration. The misfortunes of the first emigrants served to render their coreligionists, not more timid, but more adroit; a multitude of pilgrims, of mendicants dragging their children after them, of nomadic artisans of both sexes and of all trades, incessantly took their way toward all the frontiers; innumerable disguises thus protected the "flight of Israel out of Egypt." Reformers selected the darkest winter nights to embark, in frail open boats, on the Atlantic or stormy Channel; the waves were seen to cast upon the shores of England families long tossed by tempests and dying with cold and hunger.

By degrees, the guards stationed along the shores and the frontiers were touched or seduced, and became saviors and guides to fugitives whom they were set to arrest. Then perpetual confinement in the galleys was no longer sufficient against the accomplices of the *desertes;* for the galleys an edict substituted death; death, which fell not upon those guilty of the pretended crime of desertion, was promised to their abettors (October 12, 1687). Some were given up to capital punishment; many, nevertheless, continued their perilous assistance to emigrants, and few betrayed them. Those Reformers whom the authority wished most to retain in the kingdom, the noblemen, the rich citizens, manufacturers, and merchants, were those who escaped easiest, being best able to pay for the interested compassion of the guards. It is said that the fugitives carried out of France sixty millions in five years. However this may be, the loss of men was much more to be regretted than the loss of money. The vital energy of France did not cease for many years to ooze away through this ever-open ulcer of emigration.

It is difficult to estimate, even approximately, the number of Protestants who abandoned their country, become to them a barbarous mother. Vauban estimated it at a hundred thousand, from 1684 to 1691. Benoit, the Calvinist historian of the Edict of Nantes, who published his book in 1695, estimates it at two hundred thousand; the illustrious refugee Basnage speaks vaguely of three or four hundred thousand. Others give figures much more exaggerated, while the Duke of Burgundy, in the memoir that we have cited above, reduces the emigration to less than sixty-eight thousand souls in the course of twenty years; but the truly inconceivable illusions preserved by this young prince, concerning the moral and political results of the Revocation, do not allow us to put confidence in his testimony; he was deceived, took pleasure in being deceived, and closed his ear to whomsoever desired to undeceive him. The amount from two hundred thousand to two hundred fifty thousand, from the Revocation to the commencement of the following century, that is, to the revolt of Cévennes, seems most probable. But it is not so much by the quantity as by the quality of the emigrants that the real loss of France must be measured. France was incomparably more weakened than if two hundred thousand citizens had been taken at hazard from the Catholic mass of the nation. The Protestants were very superior, on the average, if not to the Catholic middle class of Paris and the principal centres of French civilization, at least to the mass of the people, and the emigrants were the best of the Protestants. A multitude of useful men, among them many superior men, left a frightful void in France, and went to swell the forces of Protestant nations. France declined both by what she lost and what her rivals gained. Before 1689 nine thousand sailors, the best in the kingdom, as Vauban says, twelve thousand soldiers, six hundred officers, had gone to foreign countries.

The most skilful chiefs and agents of contemporaneous industry went in multitudes to settle in foreign lands. Industrial capacities, less striking than literary capacities, inflicted losses on France still more felt and less reparable. France was rich enough in literary glory to lose much without being impoverished; such was not the case with respect to industry; France was to descend in a few years, almost in a few months, from that economical supremacy which had been conquered for her by long efforts of a protective administration; populous cities beheld the branches of commerce that constituted their prosperity rapidly sinking, by the disappearance of the principal industrial families, and these branches taking root on the other side of the frontiers. Thus fell, never to rise again, the Norman hat trade—already suffering on account of regulations that fettered the Canadian fur trade. Other branches, in great number, did not disappear entirely, but witnessed the rise of a formidable competition in foreign lands, where they had hitherto remained unknown; these were so many outlets closed, so many markets lost for our exportation, lately so flourishing. A suburb of London (Spitalfields) was peopled with our workmen in silk, emigrated from Lyons and Touraine, which lost three-fourths of their looms; the manufacture of French silk was also established in Holland, with paper-making, cloth manufacture, etc. Many branches of industry were transplanted to Brandenburg, and twenty thousand Frenchmen carried the most refined arts of civilization to the coarse population thinly scattered among the sands and firs of that sombre region. French refugees paid for the hospitality of the Elector Frederick by laying the foundation of the high destinies of Berlin, which on their arrival was still but a small city of twelve or fifteen thousand souls, and which, thenceforth, took a start which nothing was to arrest. Like the Hebrews after the fall of Jerusalem, the Huguenot exiles scattered themselves over the entire world: some went to Ireland, carrying the cultivation of flax and hemp; others, led by a nephew of Duquesne, founded a small colony at the Cape of Good Hope.

France was impoverished, not only in Frenchmen who exiled themselves, but in those, much more numerous, who remained in spite of themselves, discouraged, ruined, whether they openly resisted persecution or suffered some external observances of Catholicism to be wrung from them, all having neither energy in work nor security in life; it was really the activity of more than a million of men that France lost, and of the million that produced most.

The great enterprise, the miracle of the reign, therefore miscarried; the new temple that Louis had pretended to erect to unity fell to ruin as it rose from the ground, and left only an open chasm in place of its foundation. Everything that had been undertaken by the governing power of France for a century in the direction of national, civil, and territorial unity had gloriously succeeded; as soon as the governing power left this legitimate field of unity to invade the domain of conscience and of human individuality, it raised before itself insurmountable obstacles;

it concerned itself in contests wherein it was equally fatal to conquer or be conquered, and gave the first blow to the greatness of France. What a contrast between the pretensions of Louis that he could neither be mistaken nor deceived, that he saw everything, that he accomplished everything, and the illusions with which he was surrounded in regard to the facility of success and the means employed! The nothingness of absolute power, and of government by one alone, was thus revealed under the reign of the "Great King!"

THE ENGLISH REVOLUTION

FLIGHT OF JAMES II

A.D. 1688

GILBERT BURNET — H. D. TRAILL

With the accession of William and Mary to the throne of England not only did the Stuart line come to an end, but the Protestant religion was finally established in the kingdom. By the Declaration of Right, upon which their title rested, it was decreed that after the death of William and Mary no person holding the Roman Catholic faith should ever be king or queen of England. Assumption of the throne by a Roman Catholic should release the people from their allegiance.

William III (William of Orange) was a nephew of James II. He had greatly distinguished himself as leader of the Dutch against the invasions of Louis XIV, when the English people, tired of the tyranny of James II, and also fearing that he might be succeeded by a Catholic, decided to choose a Protestant for their sovereign. William was married (1677) to Mary, eldest child of James II. Could they have been sure that she would succeed her father, the English people would gladly have had Mary for their sole ruler, though European interests demanded the elevation to larger power of the Prince of Orange as the great antagonist of Louis XIV. William was accordingly invited to take possession of the English throne conjointly with Mary. The Prince of Orange landed at Torbay, November 5, 1688.

This revolution, one of the least violent in all history, is best described by Bishop Burnet, who accompanied William of Orange from Holland to England, and in 1689 was made Bishop of Salisbury. He is not less eminent as the historian of his time than as a theologian and prelate of the English Church.

Having made his preparations for sailing, William was annoyed by many delays occasioned by the hesitation of his subordinates. Traill's account of the convention which William summoned for settlement of the crown, gives in a wholly modern way the particulars of the formal accession of William and Mary.

GILBERT BURNET

ALL this while the men-of-war were still riding at sea, it being a continued storm for some weeks. The Prince[1] sent out several advice-boats with orders to them to come in. But they could not come up to them. On October 27th there was for six

[1] William of Orange.

hours together a most dreadful storm; so that there were few among us that did not conclude that the best part of the fleet, and by consequence that the whole design, were lost. Many that have passed for heroes yet showed then the agonies of fear in their looks and whole deportment. The Prince still retained his usual calmness, and the same tranquillity of spirit that I had observed in him in his happiest days. On the 28th it calmed a little, and our fleet came all in, to our great joy. The rudder of one third-rate was broken; and that was all the hurt that the storm had done. At last the much-longed-for east wind came. And so hard a thing it was to set so vast a body in motion that two days of this wind were lost before all could be quite ready.

On November 1 (O. S.), we sailed out with the evening tide, but made little way that night, that so our fleet might come out and move in order. We tried next day till noon if it were possible to sail northward, but the wind was so strong and full in the east that we could not move that way. About noon the signal was given to steer westward. This wind not only diverted us from that unhappy course, but it kept the English fleet in the river; so that it was not possible for them to come out, though they were come down as far as to the Gunfleet. By this means we had the sea open to us, with a fair wind and a safe navigation. On the 3d we passed between Dover and Calais, and before night came in sight of the Isle of Wight. The next day, being the day in which the Prince was both born and married, he fancied if he could land that day it would look auspicious to the army and animate the soldiers. But we all, who considered that the day following, being gunpowder-treason day, our landing that day might have a good effect on the minds of the English nation, were better pleased to see that we could land no sooner.

Torbay was thought the best place for our great fleet to lie in, and it was resolved to land the army where it could be best done near it; reckoning that being at such a distance from London we could provide ourselves with horses, and put everything in order before the King could march his army toward us, and that we should lie some time at Exeter for the refreshing of our men. I was in the ship, with the Prince's other domestics, that went in the van of the whole fleet. At noon on the 4th, Russel came on board us with the best of all the English pilots that they had brought over. He gave him the steering of the ship, and ordered him to be sure to sail so that next morning we should be short of Dartmouth; for it was intended that some of the ships should land there, and that the rest should sail into Torbay. The pilot thought he could not be mistaken in measuring our course, and believed that he certainly kept within orders, till the morning showed us we were past Torbay and Dartmouth. The wind, though it had abated much of its first violence, was yet still full in the east; so now it seemed necessary for us to sail on to Plymouth, which must have engaged us in a long and tedious campaign in winter through a very ill country.

Nor were we sure to be received at Plymouth. The Earl of Bath, who was governor, had sent by Russel a promise to the Prince to come and join him; yet it was not likely that he would be so forward as to receive us at our first coming. The delays he made afterward, pretending that he was managing the garrison, whereas he was indeed staying till he saw how the matter was likely to be decided, showed us how fatal it had proved, if we had been forced to sail on to Plymouth. But while Russel was in no small disorder, after he saw the pilot's error (upon which he bade me go to my prayers, for all was lost), and as he was ordering the boat to be cleared to go aboard the Prince, on a sudden, to all our wonder, it calmed a little. And then the wind turned into the south, and a soft and happy gale of wind carried in the whole fleet in four hours' time into Torbay. Immediately as many landed as conveniently could. As soon as the Prince and Marshal Schomberg got to shore, they were furnished with such horses as the village of Broxholme could afford, and rode up to view the grounds, which they found as convenient as could be imagined for the foot in that season. It was not a cold night; otherwise the soldiers, who had been kept warm aboard, might have suffered much by it.

As soon as I landed, I made what haste I could to the place where the Prince was; who took me heartily by the hand, and asked me if I would not now believe in predestination. I told him I would never forget that providence of God which had appeared so signally on this occasion.[1] He was cheerfuller than or-

[1] Light is thrown on this passage by the following curious account given in M'Cormick's *Life of Carstares:* "Mr. Carstares set out along

dinary. Yet he returned soon to his usual gravity. The Prince sent for all the fishermen of the place and asked them which was the properest place for landing his horse, which all apprehended would be a tedious business and might hold some days. But next morning he was showed a place, a quarter of a mile below the village, where the ships could be brought very near the land, against a good shore, and the horses would not be put to swim above twenty yards. This proved to be so happy for our landing, though we came to it by mere accident, that if we had ordered the whole island round to be sounded we could not have found a properer place for it. There was a dead calm all that morning; and in three hours' time all our horse were landed, with as much baggage as was necessary till we got to Exeter. The artillery and heavy baggage were left aboard, and ordered to Topsham, the seaport to Exeter. All that belonged to us was so soon and so happily landed that by the next day at noon we were in full march, and marched four miles that night. We had from thence twenty miles to Exeter, and we resolved to make haste thither.

But as we were now happily landed, and marching, we saw new and unthought-of characters of a favorable providence of

with his highness in quality of his domestic chaplain, and went aboard of his own ship. It is well known that, upon their first setting out from the coast of Holland, the fleet was in imminent danger by a violent tempest, which obliged them to put back for a few days. Upon that occasion, the vessel which carried the Prince and his retinue narrowly escaped shipwreck, a circumstance which some who were around his person were disposed to interpret into a bad omen of their success. Among these, Dr. Burnet happening to observe that it seemed predestined that they should not set foot on English ground, the Prince said nothing ; but, upon stepping ashore at Torbay, in the hearing of Mr. Carstares, he turned about to Dr. Burnet, and asked him what he thought of the doctrine of predestination now ?" Cunningham, according to the translation of the Latin MS. of his *History of England*, says that "Dr. Burnet, who understood but little of military affairs, asked the Prince of Orange which way he intended to march, and when ? and desired to be employed by him in whatever service he should think fit. The Prince only asked what he now thought of predestination ? and advised, if he had a mind to be busy, to consult the canons." The Bishop omits mentioning the proximate cause of the Prince's question, and says nothing about his declining the offer of his services, which indeed it is not likely that he did, at least so uncivilly.

God watching over us. We had no sooner got thus disengaged from our fleet than a new and great storm blew from the west; from which our fleet, being covered by the land, could receive no prejudice; but the King's fleet had got out as the wind calmed, and in pursuit of us was come as far as the Isle of Wight, when this contrary wind turned upon them. They tried what they could to pursue us; but they were so shattered by some days of this storm that they were forced to go into Portsmouth, and were no more fit for service that year. This was a greater happiness than we were then aware of: for Lord Dartmouth assured me some time after, that, whatever stories we had heard and believed, either of officers or seamen, he was confident they would all have fought very heartily. But now, by the immediate hand of Heaven, we were masters of the sea without a blow. I never found a disposition to superstition in my temper: I was rather inclined to be philosophical upon all occasions; yet I must confess that this strange ordering of the winds and seasons just to change as our affairs required it, could not but make a deep impression on me as well as on all that observed it. Those famous verses of Claudian seemed to be more applicable to the Prince than to him they were made on:

> "Heaven's favorite, for whom the skies do fight,
> And all the winds conspire to guide thee right!"

The Prince made haste to Exeter, where he stayed ten days, both for refreshing his troops and for giving the country time to show its affection. Both the clergy and magistrates of Exeter were very fearful and very backward. The Bishop and the dean ran away. And the clergy stood off, though they were sent for and very gently spoken to by the Prince. The truth was, the doctrines of passive obedience and non-resistance had been carried so far and preached so much that clergymen either could not all on the sudden get out of that entanglement into which they had by long thinking and speaking all one way involved themselves, or they were ashamed to make so quick a turn. Yet care was taken to protect them and their houses everywhere, so that no sort of violence or rudeness was offered to any of them. The Prince gave me full authority to do this, and I took so particular a care of it that we heard of no complaints. The army was kept under such an exact discipline that everything was paid for where it was demanded, though the soldiers were contented with such moderate entertainment that the people generally asked but little for what they did eat. We stayed a week at Exeter before any of the gentlemen of the country about came in to the Prince. Every day some persons of condition came from other parts. The first were Lord Colchester, Mr. Wharton, the eldest sons of the Earl of Rivers, and Lord Wharton, Mr. Russel, Lord Russel's brother, and the Earl of Abingdon.

The King came down to Salisbury, and sent his troops twenty miles farther. Of these, three regiments of horse and dragoons were drawn on by their officers, Lord Cornbury and Colonel Langston, on design to come over to the Prince. Advice was sent to the Prince of this. But because these officers were not sure of their subalterns, the Prince ordered a body of his men to advance and assist them in case any resistance was made. They were within twenty miles of Exeter, and within two miles of the body that the Prince had sent to join them, when a whisper ran about among them that they were betrayed. Lord Cornbury had not the presence of mind that so critical a thing required. So they fell in confusion, and many rode back. Yet one regiment came over in a body, and with them about a hundred of the other two.

This gave us great courage, and showed us that we had not been deceived in what was told us of the inclinations of the King's army. Yet, on the other hand, those who studied to support the King's spirit by flatteries, told him that in this he saw that he might trust his army, since those who intended to carry over those regiments were forced to manage it with so much artifice, and dared not discover their design either to officers or soldiers, and that as soon as they perceived it the greater part of them had turned back. The King wanted support; for his spirits sunk extremely. His blood was in such fermentation that he was bleeding much at the nose, which returned oft upon him every day. He sent many spies over to us. They all took his money, and came and joined themselves to the Prince, none of them returning to him. So that he had no intelligence brought him of what the Prince was doing but what common reports brought him, which magnified our numbers and made him think we were coming near him while we were still at Exeter. He heard that the city of London was very unquiet.

News was brought him that the Earls of Devonshire and Danby, and Lord Lumley, were drawing great bodies together, and that both York and Newcastle had declared for the Prince. Lord Delamere had raised a regiment in Cheshire. And the body of the nation did everywhere discover their inclinations for the Prince so evidently that the King saw he had nothing to trust to but his army. And the ill-disposition among them was so apparent that he reckoned he could not depend on them. So that he lost both heart and head at once. But that which gave him the last and most confounding stroke was that Lord Churchill and the Duke of Grafton left him and came and joined the Prince at Axminster, twenty miles on that side of Exeter.

After this he could not know on whom he could depend. The Duke of Grafton was one of King Charles' sons by the Duchess of Cleveland. He had been some time at sea, and was a gallant but rough man. He had more spirit than anyone of that spurious race. He made answer to the King, about this time, that was much talked of. The King took notice of somewhat in his behavior that looked factious, and he said he was sure he could not pretend to act upon principles of conscience; for he had been so ill-bred that, as he knew little of religion, so he regarded it less. But he answered the King that, though he had little conscience, yet he was of a party that had conscience. Soon after that, Prince George, the Duke of Ormond, and Lord Drumlanerick, the Duke of Queensbury's eldest son, left him and came over to the Prince, and joined him when he was come as far as the Earl of Bristol's house at Sherburn.

When the news came to London the Princess was so struck with the apprehensions of the King's displeasure, and of the ill-effects that it might have, that she said to Lady Churchill that she could not bear the thoughts of it, and would leap out of window rather than venture on it. The Bishop of London was then lodged very secretly in Suffolk Street. So Lady Churchill, who knew where he was, went to him and concerted with him the method of the Princess' withdrawing from the court. The Princess went sooner to bed than ordinary. And about midnight she went down a back stairs from her closet, attended only by Lady

Churchill,[1] in such haste that they carried nothing with them. They were waited for by the Bishop of London, who carried them to the Earl of Dorset's, whose lady furnished them with everything. And so they went northward as far as Northampton, where that Earl attended on them with all respect, and quickly brought a body of horse to serve for a guard to the Princess. And in a little while a small army was formed about her, who chose to be commanded by the Bishop of London, of which he too easily accepted, and was by that exposed to much censure.

These things put the King in an inexpressible confusion. He saw himself now forsaken not only by those whom he had trusted and favored most, but even by his own children. And the army was in such distraction that there was not any one body that seemed entirely united and firm to him. A foolish ballad was made at that time treating the papists, and chiefly the Irish, in a very ridiculous manner, which had a burden, said to be Irish words, *lero, lero, lilibulero,* that made an impression on the army that cannot be well imagined by those who saw it not. The whole army, and at last all people both in city and country, were singing it perpetually. And perhaps never had so slight a thing so great an effect.

But now strange counsels were suggested to the King and Queen. The priests and all the violent papists saw a treaty was now opened. They knew that they must be the sacrifice.

[1] And Mrs. Berkeley, afterward Lady Fitzharding. The back stairs were made a little before for that purpose. The Princess pretended she was out of order, upon some expostulations that had passed between her and the Queen, in a visit she received from her that night, therefore said she would not be disturbed till she rang her bell. Next morning, when her servants had waited two hours longer than her usual time of rising, they were afraid something was the matter with her, and finding the bed open, and her highness gone, they ran screaming to my father's lodgings, which were the next to hers, and told my mother the Princess was murdered by the priests; thence they went to the Queen, and old Mistress Buss asked her in a very rude manner what she had done with her mistress. The Queen answered her very gravely, she supposed their mistress was where she liked to be, but did assure them she knew nothing of her, but did not doubt they would hear of her again very soon. Which gave them little satisfaction, upon which there was a rumor all over Whitehall that the Queen had made away with the Princess.—*Dartmouth.*

The whole design of popery must be given up, without any hope of being able in an age to think of bringing it on again. Severe laws would be made against them. And all those who intended to stick to the King, and to preserve him, would go into those laws with a particular zeal; so that they and their hopes must be now given up and sacrificed forever. They infused all this into the Queen. They said she would certainly be impeached, and witnesses would be set up against her and her son; the King's mother had been impeached in the Long Parliament; and she was to look for nothing but violence. So the Queen took up a sudden resolution of going to France with the child. The midwife, together with all who were assisting at the birth, were also carried over, or so disposed of that it could never be learned what became of them afterward.

The Queen prevailed with the King not only to consent to this, but to promise to go quickly after her. He was only to stay a day or two after her, in hope that the shadow of authority that was still left in him might keep things so quiet that she might have an undisturbed passage. So she went to Portsmouth. And thence, in a man-of-war, she went over to France, the King resolving to follow her in disguise. Care was also taken to send all the priests away. The King stayed long enough to get the Prince's answer. And when he had read it he said he did not expect so good terms. He ordered the lord chancellor to come to him next morning. But he had called secretly for the great seal. And the next morning, being December 10th, about three in the morning he went away in disguise with Sir Edward Hales, whose servant he seemed to be. They passed the river, and flung the great seal into it; which was some months after found by a fisherman near Foxhall. The King went down to a miserable fisher-boat that Hales had provided for carrying them over to France.

Thus a great king, who had yet a good army and a strong fleet, did choose rather to abandon all than either to expose himself to any danger with that part of the army that was still firm to him or to stay and see the issue of a parliament. Some put this mean and unaccountable resolution on a want of courage. Others thought it was the effect of an ill-conscience, and of some black thing under which he could not now support himself.

And they who censured it the most moderately said that it showed that his priests had more regard for themselves than for him; and that he considered their interests more than his own; and that he chose rather to wander abroad with them and to try what he could do by a French force to subdue his people than to stay at home and be shut up within the bounds of law, and be brought under an incapacity of doing more mischief; which they saw was necessary to quiet those fears and jealousies for which his bad government had given so much occasion. It seemed very unaccountable, since he was resolved to go, that he did not choose rather to go in one of his yachts or frigates than to expose himself in so dangerous and ignominious a manner. It was not possible to put a good construction on any part of the dishonorable scene which he then acted.

With this his reign ended: for this was a plain deserting of his people and exposing the nation to the pillage of an army which he had ordered the Earl of Feversham to disband. And the doing this without paying them was letting so many armed men loose upon the nation; who might have done much mischief if the execution of those orders that he left behind him had not been stopped. I shall continue the recital of all that passed in this *interregnum*, till the throne, which he now left empty, was filled.

He was not got far, when some fishermen of Feversham, who were watching for such priests and other delinquents as they fancied were making their escape, came up to him. And they, knowing Sir Edward Hales, took both the King and him, and brought them to Feversham. The King told them who he was.[1] And that flying about brought a vast crowd together to look on this astonishing instance of the uncertainty of all worldly greatness, when he who had ruled three kingdoms and might have been the arbiter of all Europe was now in such mean hands, and so low an equipage. The people of the town were extremely disordered with this unlooked-for accident; and, though for a while

[1] And desired they would send to Eastwell for the Earl of Winchelsea; which Sir Basil Dixwell put a stop to by telling him surely they were good enough to take care of him. Which occasioned the King's saying he found there was more civility among the common people than some gentlemen, when he was returned to Whitehall.—*Dartmouth.*

they kept him as a prisoner, yet they quickly changed that into as much respect as they could possibly pay him. Here was an accident that seemed of no great consequence. Yet all the strugglings which that party have made ever since that time to this day, which from him were called afterward the Jacobites, did rise out of this; for if he had got clear away, by all that could be judged, he would not have had a party left; all would have agreed that here was a desertion, and that therefore the nation was free and at liberty to secure itself. But that following upon this gave them a color to say that he was forced away and driven out. Till now he scarce had a party but among the papists. But from this incident a party grew up that has been long very active for his interests.

As soon as it was known at London that the King was gone, the 'prentices and the rabble, who had been a little quieted when they saw a treaty on foot between the King and the Prince, now broke out again upon all suspected houses, where they believed there were either priests or papists. They made great havoc of many places, not sparing the houses of ambassadors. But none was killed, no houses burned, nor were any robberies committed. Never was so much fury seen under so much management. Jeffreys finding the King was gone, saw what reason he had to look to himself, and, apprehending that he was now exposed to the rage of the people whom he had provoked with so particular a brutality, he had disguised himself to make his escape. But he fell into the hands of some who knew him. He was insulted by them with as much scorn and rudeness as they could invent. And, after many hours tossing him about, he was carried to the lord mayor, whom they charged to commit him to the Tower, which Lord Lucas had then seized, and in it had declared for the Prince. The lord mayor was so struck with the terror of this rude populace, and with the disgrace of a man who had made all people tremble before him, that he fell into fits upon it, of which he died soon after.

Upon the news of the King's desertion, it was proposed that the Prince should go on with all possible haste to London. But that was not advisable. For the King's army lay so scattered through the road all the way to London that it was not fit for him to advance faster than his troops marched before him;

otherwise, any resolute officer might have seized or killed him. Though, if it had not been for that danger a great deal of mischief that followed would have been prevented by his speedy advance; for now began that turn to which all the difficulties that did afterward disorder our affairs may be justly imputed. Two gentlemen of Kent came to Windsor the morning after the Prince came thither. They were addressed to me; and they told me of the accident at Feversham, and desired to know the Prince's pleasure upon it. I was affected with this dismal reverse of the fortune of a great prince more than I think fit to express. I went immediately to Benthink and wakened him, and got him to go to the Prince and let him know what had happened, that some order might be presently given for the security of the King's person, and for taking him out of the hands of a rude multitude who said they would obey no orders but such as came from the Prince.

The Prince ordered Zuylestein to go immediately to Feversham, and to see the King safe and at full liberty to go whithersoever he pleased. But as soon as the news of the King's being at Feversham came to London, all the indignation that people had formerly conceived against him was turned to pity and compassion. The privy council met upon it. Some moved that he should be sent for. Others said he was king, and might send for his guards and coaches as he pleased, but it became not them to send for him. It was left to his general, the Earl of Feversham, to do what he thought best. So he went for him with his coaches and guards. And, as he came back through the city, he was welcomed with expressions of joy by great numbers; so slight and unstable a thing is a multitude, and so soon altered. At his coming to Whitehall, he had a great court about him. Even the papists crept out of their lurking-holes, and appeared at court with much assurance. The King himself began to take heart. And both at Feversham, and now at Whitehall, he talked in his ordinary high strain, justifying all that he had done; only he spoke a little doubtfully of the business of Magdalen College. But when he came to reflect on the state of his affairs, he saw it was so soon broken that nothing was now left to deliberate upon. So he sent the Earl of Feversham to Windsor without demanding any passport, and ordered him to desire the Prince to come to St.

James' to consult with him of the best way for settling the nation.

When the news of what had passed at London came to Windsor, the Prince thought the privy council had not used him well, who after they had sent to him to take the government upon him, had made this step without consulting him. Now the scene was altered and new counsels were to be taken. The Prince heard the opinions, not only of those who had come along with him, but of such of the nobility as were now come to him, among whom the Marquis of Halifax was one. All agreed that it was not convenient that the King should stay at Whitehall. Neither the King, nor the Prince, nor the city, could have been safe if they had been both near one another. Tumults would probably have arisen out of it. The guards and the officious flatterers of the two courts would have been unquiet neighbors. It was thought necessary to stick to the point of the King's deserting his people, and not to give up that by entering upon any treaty with him. And since the Earl of Feversham, who had commanded the army against the Prince, was come without a passport he was for some days put in arrest.

It was a tender point now to dispose of the King's person. Some proposed rougher methods: the keeping him a prisoner, at least till the nation was settled, and till Ireland was secured. It was thought his being kept in custody would be such a tie on all his party as would oblige them to submit and be quiet. Ireland was in great danger. And his restraint might oblige the Earl of Tyrconnel to deliver up the government, and to disarm the papists, which would preserve that kingdom and the Protestants in it. But, because it might raise too much compassion and perhaps some disorder if the King should be kept in restraint within the kingdom, therefore the sending him to Breda was proposed. The Earl of Clarendon pressed this vehemently on account of the Irish Protestants, as the King himself told me, for those that gave their opinions in this matter did it secretly and in confidence to the Prince. The Prince said he could not deny but that this might be good and wise advice, but it was that to which he could not hearken; he was so far satisfied with the grounds of this expedition that he could act against the King in a fair and open war; but for his person, now that he had him in his power, he could not put such a hardship on him as to make him a prisoner; and he knew the Princess' temper so well that he was sure she would never bear it: nor did he know what disputes it might raise, or what effect it might have upon the Parliament that was to be called; he was firmly resolved never to suffer anything to be done against his person; he saw it was necessary to send him out of London, and he would order a guard to attend upon him who should only defend and protect his person, but not restrain him in any sort.

A resolution was taken of sending the Lords Halifax, Shrewsbury, and Delamere to London, who were first to order the English guards that were about the court to be drawn off and sent to quarters out of town, and when that was done the Count of Solms with the Dutch guards was to come and take all the posts about the court. This was obeyed without any resistance or disorder, but not without much murmuring. It was midnight before all was settled. And then these lords sent to the Earl of Middleton to desire him to let the King know that they had a message to deliver to him from the Prince. He went in to the King, and sent them word from him that they might come with it immediately. They came and found him abed. They told him the necessity of affairs required that the Prince should come presently to London; and he thought it would conduce to the safety of the King's person and the quiet of the town that he should retire to some house out of town, and they proposed Ham.

The King seemed much dejected, and asked if it must be done immediately. They told him he might take his rest first, and they added that he should be attended by a guard who should only guard his person, but should give him no sort of disturbance. Having said this, they withdrew. The Earl of Middleton came quickly after them and asked them if it would not do as well if the King should go to Rochester; for since the Prince was not pleased with his coming up from Kent it might be perhaps acceptable to him if he should go thither again. It was very visible that this was proposed in order to a second escape.

They promised to send word immediately to the Prince of Orange, who lay that night at Sion, within eight miles of London. He very readily consented to it. And the King went next day to Rochester, having ordered all that which is called the moving wardrobe to be sent before him, the Count of Solms ordering everything to be done as the King desired. A guard went with him that left him at full liberty, and paid him rather more respect than his own guards had done of late. Most of that body, as it happened, were papists. So when he went to mass they went in and assisted very reverently. And when they were asked how they could serve in an expedition that was intended to destroy their own religion, one of them answered, his soul was God's, but his sword was the Prince of Orange's. The King was so much delighted with this answer that he repeated it to all that came about him. On the same day the Prince came to St. James'. It happened to be a very rainy day. And yet great numbers came to see him. But, after they had stood long in the wet, he disappointed them; for he, who loved neither shows nor shoutings, went through the park. And even this trifle helped to set people's spirits on edge.

The revolution was thus brought about with the universal applause of the whole nation; only these last steps began to raise a fermentation. It was said, here was an unnatural thing to waken the King out of his sleep, in his own palace, and to order him to go out of it when he was ready to submit to everything. Some said he was now a prisoner, and remembered the saying of King Charles I, that the prisons and the graves of princes lay not far distant from one another; the person of the King was now struck at, as well as his government, and this specious undertaking would now appear to be only a disguised and designed usurpation. These things began to work on great numbers. And the posting of the Dutch guards where the English guards had been, gave a general disgust to the whole English army. They indeed hated the Dutch besides, on account of the good order and strict discipline they were kept under; which made them to be as much beloved by the nation as they were hated by the soldiery. The nation had never known such an inoffensive march of an army. And the peace and order of the suburbs, and the freedom of markets in and about London, were so carefully maintained that in no time fewer disorders had been committed than were heard of this winter.

None of the papists or Jacobites was insulted in any sort.

The Prince had ordered me, as we came along, to take care of the papists and to secure them from all violence. When he came to London he renewed these orders, which I executed with so much zeal and care that I saw all the complaints that were brought me fully redressed. When we came to London I procured passports for all that desired to go beyond the sea. Two of the popish bishops were put in Newgate. I went thither in the Prince's name. I told them the Prince would not take upon him yet to give any orders about prisoners; as soon as he did that, they should feel the effects of it. But in the mean while I ordered them to be well used, and to be taken care of, and that their friends might be admitted to come to them; so truly did I pursue the principle of moderation even toward those from whom nothing of that sort was to be expected.

Now that the Prince was come, all the bodies about the town came to welcome him. The bishops came the next day. Only the Archbishop of Canterbury, though he had once agreed to it, yet would not come. The clergy of London came next. The city, and a great many other bodies, came likewise, and expressed a great deal of joy for the deliverance wrought for them by the Prince's means. Old Sergeant Maynard came with the men of the law. He was then near ninety, and yet he said the liveliest thing that was heard of on that occasion. The Prince took notice of his great age, and said that he had outlived all the men of the law of his time; he answered he had liked to have outlived the law itself if his highness had not come over.

The first thing to be done after the compliments were over was to consider how the nation was to be settled. The lawyers were generally of opinion that the Prince ought to declare himself king, as Henry VII had done. This, they said, would put an end to all disputes, which might otherwise grow very perplexing and tedious; and they said he might call a Parliament which would be a legal assembly if summoned by the king in fact, though his title was not yet recognized. This was plainly contrary to his declaration, by which the settlement of the nation was referred to a parliament; such a step would make all that the Prince had hitherto done pass for an aspiring ambition only to raise himself; and it would disgust those who had been hitherto the best affected to his designs, and make them less concerned in the quarrel if, instead of staying till the nation should offer him the crown, he would assume it as a conquest.

These reasons determined the Prince against that proposition. He called all the peers and the members of the three last parliaments that were in town, together with some of the citizens of London. When these met it was told them that, in the present distraction, the Prince desired their advice about the best methods of settling the nation. It was agreed in both these Houses, such as they were, to make an address to the Prince, desiring him to take the administration of the Government into his hands in the *interim.* The next proposition passed not so unanimously; for, it being moved that the Prince should be likewise desired to write missive letters to the same effect, and for the same persons to whom writs were issued out for calling a parliament, that so there might be an assembly of men in the form of a parliament, though without writs under the great seal, such as that was that had called home King Charles II.

To this the Earl of Nottingham objected that such a convention of the states could be no legal assembly unless summoned by the King's writ. Therefore he moved that an address might be made to the King to order the writs to be issued. Few were of his mind. The matter was carried the other way, and orders were given for those letters to be sent round the nation.

The King continued a week at Rochester. And both he himself and everybody else saw that he was at full liberty, and that the guard about him put him under no sort of restraint. Many that were zealous for his interests went to him and pressed him to stay and to see the issue of things: a party would appear for him; good terms would be got for him; and things would be brought to a reasonable agreement. He was much distracted between his own inclinations and the importunities of his friends. The Queen, hearing what had happened, writ a most vehement letter to him, pressing his coming over, remembering him of his promise, which she charged on him in a very earnest if not in an imperious strain. This letter was intercepted. I had an account of it from one that read it. The Prince ordered it to be conveyed to the King, and that determined him. So he gave secret orders to prepare a vessel for him, and drew a paper, which he left on his table, reproaching the nation for their forsaking him. He declared that though he was going to seek for foreign aid to restore him to his throne, yet he would not make use of it to overthrow either the religion established or the laws of the land. And so he left Rochester very secretly on the last day of this memorable year and got safe over to France.

H. D. TRAILL

The convention for filling the vacant throne met on January 22d, when Halifax was chosen president in the Lords; Powle speaker of the Commons. A letter from William, read in both Houses, informed their members that he had endeavored to the best of his power to discharge the trust reposed in him, and that it now rested with the convention to lay the foundation of a firm security for their religion, laws, and liberties. The Prince then went on to refer to the dangerous condition of the Protestants in Ireland, and the present state of things abroad, which obliged him to tell them that next to the danger of unreasonable divisions among themselves, nothing could be so fatal as too great a delay in their consultations. And he further intimated that as England was already bound by treaty to help the Dutch in such exigencies as, deprived of the troops which he had brought over, and threatened with war by Louis XIV, they might easily be reduced to, so he felt confident that the cheerful concurrence of the Dutch in preserving this kingdom would meet with all the returns of friendship from Protestants and Englishmen whenever their own condition should require assistance.

To this the two Houses replied with an address thanking the Prince for his great care in the administration of the affairs of the kingdom to this time, and formally continuing to him the same commission, recommending to his particular care the present state of Ireland. William's answer to this address was characteristic both of his temperament and his preoccupation. "My lords and gentlemen," he said, "I am glad that what I have done hath pleased you; and since you desire me to continue the administration of affairs, I am willing to accept it. I must recommend to you the consideration of affairs abroad which makes it fit for you to expedite your business, not only for making a settlement at home on a good foundation, but for the safety of Europe."

On the 28th the Commons resolved themselves into a committee of the whole House, and Richard Hampden, son of the great John, was voted into the chair. The honor of having been the first to speak the word which was on everybody's lips belongs to Gilbert Dolben, son of a late archbishop of York, who "made a long speech tending to prove that the King's deserting his kingdom without appointing any person to administer the government amounted in reason and judgment of law to a demise." Sir Robert Howard, one of the members for Castle Rising, went a step further, and asserted that the throne was vacant. The extreme Tories made a vain effort to procure an adjournment, but the combination against them of Whigs and their own moderates was too strong for them, and after a long and stormy debate the House resolved "That King James II, having endeavored to subvert the constitution by breaking the original contract between the King and people, and by the advice of Jesuits and other wicked persons having violated the fundamental laws and withdrawn himself out of the kingdom, has abdicated the government, and that the throne is thereby vacant."

This resolution was at once sent up to the Lords. Before, however, they could proceed to consider it, another message arrived from the Commons to the effect that they had just voted it inconsistent with the safety and welfare of this Protestant nation to be governed by a popish king.

To this resolution the Peers assented with a readiness which showed in advance that James had no party in the Upper House, and that the utmost length to which the Tories in that body were prepared to go was to support the proposal of a regency. The first resolution of the Commons was then put aside in order that this proposal might be discussed. It was Archbishop Sancroft's plan, who, however, did not make his appearance to advocate it, and in his absence it was supported by Rochester and Nottingham, while Halifax and Danby led the opposition to it. After a day's debate it was lost by the narrow majority of two, forty-nine peers declaring in its favor and fifty-one against it.

The Lords then went into committee on the Commons' resolution, and at once proceeded, as was natural enough, to dispute the clause in its preamble which referred to the original contract between the King and the people. No Tory, of course, could really have subscribed to the doctrine implied in these words; but it was doubtless as hard in those days as in these to interest an assembly of English politicians in affirmations of abstract political principle, and some Tories probably thought it not worth while to multiply causes of dissent with the Lower House by attacking a purely academic recital of their resolution. Anyhow, the numbers of the minority slightly fell off, only forty-six Peers objecting to the phrase, while fifty-three voted that it should stand. The word "deserted" was then substituted without a division for the word "abdicated," and, the hour being late, the Lords adjourned.

The real battle, of course, was now at hand, and to anyone who assents to the foregoing criticisms it will be evident that it was far less of a conflict on a point of constitutional principle, and far more of a struggle between the parties of two distinct—one cannot call them rival—claimants to the throne than high-flying Whig writers are accustomed to represent it. It would, of course, be too much to say that the Whigs insisted on declaring the vacancy of the throne, *only* because they wished to place William on it, and that the Tories contended for a demise of the crown, *only* because they wished an English princess to succeed to the throne rather than a Dutch prince. Still, it is pretty certain that, but for this conflict of preferences, the two political parties, who had made so little difficulty of agreeing in the declaration that James had ceased to reign, would never have found it so hard to concur in its almost necessary sequence that the throne was vacant.

The debate on the last clause of the resolution began, and it soon became apparent that the Whigs were outnumbered. The forty-nine peers who had supported the proposal of a regency—which implied that the royal title was still in James—were bound, of course, to oppose the proposition that the throne was vacant; and they were reënforced by several peers who held that that title had already devolved upon Mary. An attempt to compromise the dispute by omitting the words pronouncing the throne vacant, and inserting words which merely proclaimed the Prince and Princess of Orange king and queen, was rejected by fifty-two votes to forty-seven; and the original clause was then put, and negatived by fifty-five votes to forty-one.

Thus amended by the substitution of "deserted" for "abdicated," and the omission of the words "and that the throne is thereby vacant," the resolution was sent back to the Commons, who instantly and without a division disagreed with the amendments. The situation was now becoming critical. The prospect of a deadlock between the two branches of the convention threw London into a ferment; crowds assembled in Palace Yard; petitions were presented in that tumultuous fashion which converts supplication into menace. To their common credit, however, both parties united in resistance to these attempts at popular coercion; and William himself interposed to enjoin a stricter police of the capital. On Monday, February 4th, the Lords resolved to insist on their amendments; on the following day the Commons reaffirmed their disagreement with them by two hundred eighty-two votes to one hundred fifty-one. A free conference between the two Houses was then arranged, and met on the following day.

But the dispute, like many another in our political history, had meanwhile been settled out of court. Between the date of the peers' vote and the conference Mary had communicated to Danby her high displeasure at the conduct of those who were setting up her claims in opposition to those of her husband; and William, who had previously maintained an unbroken silence, now made, unsolicited, a declaration of a most important and, indeed, of a conclusive kind. If the convention, he said, chose to adopt the plan of a regency, he had nothing to say against it, only they must look out for some other person to fill the office, for he himself would not consent to do so. As to the alternative proposal of putting Mary on the throne and allowing him to reign by her courtesy, "No man," he said, "can esteem a woman more than I do the Princess; but I am so made that I cannot think of holding anything by apron strings; nor can I think it reasonable to have any share in the government unless it be put in my own person, and that for the term of my life. If you think fit to settle it otherwise I will not oppose you, but will go back to Holland, and meddle no more in your affairs."

These few sentences of plain-speaking swept away the clouds

of intrigue and pedantry as by a wholesome gust of wind. Both political parties at once perceived that there was but one possible issue from the situation. The conference was duly held, and the constitutional question was, with great display of now unnecessary learning, solemnly debated; but the managers for the two Houses met only to register a foregone conclusion. The word "abdicated" was restored; the vacancy of the throne was voted by sixty-two votes to forty-seven; and it was immediately proposed and carried without a division that the Prince and Princess of Orange should be declared king and queen of England.

It now only remained to give formal effect to this resolution, and in so doing to settle the conditions whereon the crown, which the convention had now distinctly recognized itself as conferring upon the Prince and Princess, should be conferred. A committee appointed by the Commons to consider what safeguards should be taken against the aggressions of future sovereigns had made a report in which they recommended not only a solemn enunciation of ancient constitutional principles, but the enactment of new laws. The Commons, however, having regard to the importance of prompt action, judiciously resolved on carrying out only the first part of the programme. They determined to preface the tender of the crown to William and Mary by a recital of the royal encroachments of the past reigns, and a formal assertion of the constitutional principles against which such encroachments had offended. This document, drafted by a committee of which the celebrated Somers, then a scarcely known young advocate, was the chairman, was the famous "Declaration of Right." The grievances which it recapitulated in its earlier portion were as follows:

(1) The royal pretension to dispense with and suspend laws without consent of Parliament; (2) the punishment of subjects, as in the "Seven Bishops'" case, for petitioning the crown; (3) the establishment of the illegal court of high commission for ecclesiastical affairs; (4) the levy of taxes without the consent of Parliament; (5) the maintenance of a standing army in time of peace without the same consent; (6) the disarmament of Protestants while papists were both armed and employed contrary to law; (7) the violation of the freedom of election; (8)

the prosecution in the king's bench of suits only cognizable in Parliament; (9) the return of partial and corrupt juries; (10) the requisition of excessive bail; (11) the imposition of excessive fines; (12) the infliction of illegal and cruel punishments; (13) the grants of the estates of accused persons before conviction.

Then after solemnly reaffirming the popular rights from which these abuses of the prerogative derogated, the declaration goes on to recite that, having an "entire confidence" William would "preserve them from the violation of the rights which they have here asserted, the Three Estates do resolve that William and Mary, Prince and Princess of Orange, be and be declared king and queen: to hold the crown and royal dignity, to them the said Prince and Princess during their lives and the life of the survivor of them; and the sole and full exercise of the royal power be only in and exercised by the said Prince of Orange, in the names of the said Prince and Princess during their lives, and, after their deceases, the said crown and royal dignity of the said kingdoms and dominions to the heirs of the body of the said Princess; and, for default of such issue, to the Princess Anne of Denmark and the heirs of her body; and, for the default of such issue, to the issue of the said Prince of Orange." Then followed an alteration required by the scrupulous conscience of Nottingham in the terms of the oath of allegiance.

On February 12th Mary arrived from Holland. On the following day, in the Banqueting House at Whitehall, the Prince and Princess of Orange were waited on by both Houses of convention in a body. The declaration was read by the clerk of the crown; the sovereignty solemnly tendered to them by Halifax, in the name of the Estates; and on the same day they were proclaimed king and queen in the usual places in the cities of London and Westminster.

PETER THE GREAT MODERNIZES RUSSIA

SUPPRESSION OF THE STRELTSI

A.D. 1689

ALFRED RAMBAUD

It is the glory of Peter the Great to have changed the character of his country and elevated its position among European nations. By opening Russia to the influence of Western civilization he prepared the way for the advent of that vast empire as one of the world's great powers.

Peter I Alexeievitch was born in Moscow June 9 (N. S.), 1672. After a joint reign with his half-brother Ivan (1682–1696), he ruled alone until his death, February 8 (N. S.), 1725. He is distinguished among princes as a ruler who temporarily laid aside the character of royalty "in order to learn the art of governing better." By his travels under a common name and in a menial disguise, he acquired fruits of observation which proved of greater practical advantage in his career than comes to sovereigns from training in the knowledge of the schools. His restless and inquiring spirit was never subdued by the burdens of state, and his matured powers proved equal to the demands laid upon him by the great formative work which he was called to accomplish for his people.

The character and early career of this extraordinary man are here set forth by Rambaud in a masterly sketch, showing the first achievements which laid the foundation of Peter's constructive policies.

ALEXIS MIKHAILOVITCH, Czar of Russia, had by his first wife, Maria Miloslavski, two sons, Feodor and Ivan, and six daughters; by his second wife, Natalia Narychkine, one son (who became Peter I) and two daughters. As he was twice married, and the kinsmen of each wife had, according to custom, surrounded the throne, there existed two factions in the palace, which were brought face to face by his death and that of his eldest son, Feodor. The Miloslavskis had on their side the claim of seniority, the number of royal children left by Maria, and, above all, the fact that Ivan was the elder of the two surviving sons; but unluckily for them, Ivan was notoriously imbecile both in body and mind.

On the side of the Narychkines was the interest excited by the precocious intelligence of Peter, and the position of legal head of all the royal family, which, according to Russian law, gave to Natalia Narychkine her title of czarina dowager. Both factions had for some time taken their measures and recruited their partisans. Who should succeed Feodor? Was it to be the son of the Miloslavski, or the son of the Narychkine? The Miloslavskis were first defeated on legal grounds. Taking the incapacity of Ivan into consideration, the boyars and the Patriarch Joachim proclaimed the young Peter, then nine years old, Czar. The Narychkines triumphed: Natalia became czarina regent, recalled from exile her foster-father, Matveef, and surrounded herself by her brothers and uncles.

The Miloslavskis' only means of revenge lay in revolt, but they were without a head; for it was impossible for Ivan to take the lead. The eldest of his six sisters was thirty-two years of age, the youngest nineteen; the most energetic of them was Sophia, who was twenty-five. These six princesses saw themselves condemned to the dreary destiny of the Russian *czarevni*, and were forced to renounce all hopes of marriage, with no prospects but to grow old in the seclusion of the *terem*, subjected by law to the authority of a step-mother. All their youth had to look forward to was the cloister. They, however, only breathed in action; and though imperial etiquette and Byzantine manners, prejudices, and traditions forbade them to appear in public, even Byzantine traditions offered them models to follow. Had not Pulcheria, daughter of an emperor, reigned at Constantinople in the name of her brother, the incapable Theodosius? Had she not contracted a nominal marriage with the brave Marcian, who was her sword against the barbarians?

Here was the ideal that Sophia could propose to herself; to be a *czardievitsa*, a "woman-emperor." To emancipate herself from the rigorous laws of the terem, to force the "twenty-seven locks" of the song, to raise the *fata* that covered her face, to appear in public and meet the looks of men, needed energy, cunning, and patience that could wait and be content to proceed by successive efforts. Sophia's first step was to appear at Feodor's funeral, though it was not the custom for any but the widow and the heir to be present. There her litter encountered that of

Natalia Narychkine, and her presence forced the Czarina-mother to retreat. She surrounded herself with a court of educated men, who publicly praised her, encouraged and excited her to action. Simeon Polotski and Silvester Medviedef wrote verses in her honor, recalled to her the example of Pulcheria and Olga, compared her to the Virgin Queen, Elizabeth of England, and even to Semiramis; we might think we were listening to Voltaire addressing Catharine II. They played on her name Sophia (wisdom), and declared she had been endowed with the quality as well as the title. Polotski dedicated to her the *Crown of Faith*, and Medviedef his *Gifts of the Holy Spirit*.

The terem offered the strangest contrasts. There acted they the *Malade Imaginaire*, and the audience was composed of the heterogeneous assembly of popes, monks, nuns, and old pensioners that formed the courts of the ancient czarinas. In this shifting crowd there were some useful instruments of intrigue. The old pensioners, while telling their rosaries, served as emissaries between the palace and the town, carried messages and presents to the turbulent *streltsi*,[1] and arranged matters between the czarian ladies and the soldiers. Sinister rumors were skilfully disseminated through Moscow: Feodor, the eldest son of Alexis, had died, the victim of conspirators; the same lot was doubtless reserved for Ivan. What was to become of the poor czarevni, of the blood of kings? At last it was publicly announced that a brother of Natalia Narychkine had seized the crown and seated himself on the throne, and that Ivan had been strangled. Love and pity for the son of Alexis, and the indignation excited by the news of the usurpation, immediately caused the people of Moscow to revolt, and the ringleaders cleverly directed the movement. The tocsin sounded from four hundred churches of the "holy city"; the regiments of the streltsi took up arms and marched, followed by an immense crowd, to the Kremlin, with drums beating, matches lighted, and dragging cannon behind them. Natalia Narychkine had only to show herself on the "Red Staircase," accompanied by her son Peter, and Ivan who was reported dead. Their mere appearance sufficed to contra-

[1] The streltsi were an ancient Muscovite guard composed of citizens rendering hereditary military service in the different cities and fortified posts. At this time many of them were ripe for revolt.

dict all the calumnies. The streltsi hesitated, seeing they had been deceived. A clever harangue of Matveef, who had formerly commanded them, and the exhortations of the patriarch, shook them further. The revolt was almost appeased; the Miloslavskis had missed their aim, for they had not yet succeeded in putting to death the people of whom they were jealous.

Suddenly Prince Michael Dolgorouki, chief of the *prikaz* of the streltsi, began to insult the rioters in the most violent language. This ill-timed harangue awoke their fury; they seized Dolgorouki, and flung him from the top of the Red Staircase onto their pikes. They stabbed Matveef, under the eyes of the Czarina; then they sacked the palace, murdering all who fell into their hands. Athanasius Narychkine, a brother of Natalia, was thrown from a window onto the points of their lances. The following day the *émeute* recommenced; they tore from the arms of the Czarina her father Cyril and her brother Ivan; the latter was tortured and sent into a monastery. Historians show us Sophia interceded for the victims on her knees, but an understanding between the rebels and the Czarevna did exist; the streltsi obeyed orders.

The following days were consecrated to the purifying of the palace and the administration, and the seventh day of the revolt they sent their commandant, the prince-boyar, Khovanski, to declare that they would have two czars—Ivan at the head, and Peter as coadjutor; and if this were refused, they would again rebel. The boyars of the *douma* deliberated on this proposal, and the greater number of the boyars were opposed to it. In Russia the absolute power had never been shared, but the orators of the terem cited many examples both from sacred and profane history: Pharaoh and Joseph, Arcadius and Honorius, Basil II and Constantine VIII; and the best of all the arguments were the pikes of the streltsi (1682).

Sophia had triumphed: she reigned in the name of her two brothers, Ivan and Peter. She made a point of showing herself in public, at processions, solemn services, and dedications of churches. At the Ouspienski Sobor, while her brothers occupied the place of the czar, she filled that of the czarina; only *she* raised the curtains and boldly allowed herself to be incensed by the patriarch. When the *raskolniks* challenged the heads of the orthodox church to discussion, she wished to preside and hold the meeting in the open air, at the Lobnoe Miesto on the Red Place. There was, however, so much opposition that she was forced to call the assembly in the Palace of Facets, and sat behind the throne of her two brothers, present though invisible. The double-seated throne used on those occasions is still preserved at Moscow; there is an opening in the back, hidden by a veil of silk, and behind this sat Sophia. This singular piece of furniture is the symbol of a government previously unknown to Russia, composed of two visible czars and one invisible sovereign.

The streltsi, however, felt their prejudices against female sovereignty awaken. They shrank from the contempt heaped by the Czarevna upon the ancient manners. Sophia had already become in their eyes a "scandalous person" (*pozornoe litzo*). Another cause of misunderstanding was the support she gave to the state church, as reformed by Nicon, while the streltsi and the greater part of the people held to the "old faith." She had arrested certain "old believers," who at the discussion in the Palace of Facets had challenged the patriarchs and orthodox prelates, and she had caused the ringleader to be executed. Khovanski, chief of the streltsi, whether from sympathy with the *raskol* or whether he wished to please his subordinates, affected to share their discontent. The court no longer felt itself safe at Moscow. Sophia took refuge with the Czarina and the two young princes in the fortified monastery of Troitsa, and summoned around her the gentlemen-at-arms. Khovanski was invited to attend, was arrested on the way, and put to death with his son. The streltsi attempted a new rising, but, with the usual fickleness of a popular militia, suddenly passed from the extreme of insolence to the extreme of humility. They marched to Troitsa, this time in the guise of suppliants, with cords round their necks, carrying axes and blocks for the death they expected. The patriarch consented to intercede for them, and Sophia contented herself with the sacrifice of the ringleaders.

Sophia, having got rid of her accomplices, governed by aid of her two favorites—Chaklovity, the new commandant of the streltsi, whom she had drawn from obscurity, and who was completely devoted to her, and Prince Vasili Galitsyne. Galitsyne has become the hero of a historic school which opposes his genius to that of Peter the Great, in the same way as in France Henry, Duke of Guise, has been exalted at the expense of Henry IV. He was the special favorite, the intimate friend, of Sophia, the director of her foreign policy, and her right hand in military affairs. Sophia and Galitsyne labored to organize a holy league between Russia, Poland, Venice, and Austria against the Turks and Tartars. They also tried to gain the countenance of the Catholic powers of the West; and in 1687 Jacob Dolgorouki and Jacob Mychetski disembarked at Dunkirk as envoys to the court of Louis XIV. They were not received very favorably: the King of France was not at all inclined to make war against the Turks; he was, on the other hand, the ally of Mahomet IV, who was about to besiege Vienna while Louis blockaded Luxemburg. The whole plan of the campaign was, however, thrown out by the intervention of Russia and John Sobieski in favor of Austria. The Russian ambassadors received orders to reëmbark at Havre, without going farther south.

The government of the Czarevna still persisted in its warlike projects. In return for an active coöperation against the Ottomans, Poland had consented to ratify the conditions of the Treaty of Androussovo, and to sign a perpetual peace (1686). A hundred thousand Muscovites, under the command of Prince Galitsyne, and fifty thousand Little Russian Cossacks, under the orders of the hetman Samoilovitch, marched against the Crimea (1687). The army suffered greatly in the southern steppes, as the Tartars had fired the grassy plains. Galitsyne was forced to return without having encountered the enemy. Samoilovitch was accused of treason, deprived of his command, and sent to Siberia; and Mazeppa, who owed to Samoilovitch his appointment as secretary-at-war, and whose denunciations had chiefly contributed to his downfall, was appointed his successor.

In the spring of 1689 the Muscovite and Ukranian armies, commanded by Galitsyne and Mazeppa, again set out for the Crimea. The second expedition was hardly more fortunate than the first: they got as far as Perekop, and were then obliged to retreat without even having taken the fortress. This double defeat did not hinder Sophia from preparing for her favorite a triumphal entry into Moscow. In vain Peter forbade her to leave the palace; she braved his displeasure and headed the procession, accompanied by the clergy and the images and followed by the army of the Crimea, admitted the generals to kiss her hand and distributed glasses of brandy among the officers. Peter left Moscow in anger, and retired to the village of Preobrajenskoe. The foreign policy of the Czarevna was marked by another display of weakness. By the Treaty of Nertchinsk she restored to the Chinese empire the fertile regions of the Amur, which had been conquered by a handful of Cossacks, and razed the fortress of Albazine, where those adventurers had braved all the forces of the East. On all sides Russia seemed to retreat before the barbarians.

Meanwhile Peter was growing. His precocious faculties, his quick intelligence, and his strong will awakened alike the hopes of his partisans and the fears of his enemies. As a child he only loved drums, swords, and muskets. He learned history by means of colored prints brought from Germany. Zotof, his master, whom he afterward made "the archpope of fools," taught him to read. Among the heroes held up to him as examples we are not surprised to find Ivan the Terrible, whose character and position offer so much analogy to his own. "When the Czarevitch was tired of reading," says M. Zabieline, "Zotof took the book from his hand and, to amuse him, would himself read the great deeds of his father, Alexis Mikhailovitch, and those of the Czar, Ivan Vasilievitch, their campaigns, their distant expeditions, their battles and sieges: how they endured fatigues and privations better than any common soldier; what benefits they had conferred on the empire, and how they extended the frontiers of Russia."

Peter also learned Latin, German, and Dutch. He read much and widely, and learned a great deal, though without method. Like Ivan the Terrible, he was a self-taught man. He afterward complained of not having been instructed according to rule. This was perhaps a good thing. His education, like that of Ivan IV, was neglected, but at least he was not subjected to the enervating influence of the terem—he was not cast in that dull mould which turned out so many idiots in the royal family. He "roamed at large, and wandered in the streets with his comrades." The streets of Moscow at that period were, according to M. Zabieline, the worst school of profligacy and debauchery that can be imagined; but they were, on the whole, less bad for Peter than the palace. He met there something besides mere jesters: he encountered new elements which had as yet no place in the terem, but contained the germ of the regeneration of Russia. He came across Russians who, if unscrupulous, were also unprejudiced, and who could aid him in his bold reform of the ancient society. He there became acquainted with Swiss, English, and German adventurers—with Lefort, with Gordon, and with Timmermann, who initiated him into European civilization.

His court was composed of Leo Narychkine, of Boris Galitsyne, who had undertaken never to flatter him; of Andrew Matveef, who had marked taste for everything European; and of Dolgorouki, at whose house he first saw an astrolabe. He played at soldiers with his young friends and his grooms, and formed them into the "battalion of playmates," who manœuvred after the European fashion, and became the kernel of the future regular army. He learned the elements of geometry and fortification, and constructed small citadels, which he took or defended with his young warriors in those fierce battles which sometimes counted their wounded or dead, and in which the Czar of Russia was not always spared. An English boat stranded on the shore of Yaousa caused him to send for Franz Timmermann, who taught him to manage a sailing-boat, even with a contrary wind. He who formerly, like a true boyar of Moscow, had such a horror of the water that he could not make up his mind to cross a bridge, became a determined sailor: he guided his boat first on the Yaousa, then on the lake of Pereiaslavl. Brandt, the Dutchman, built him a whole flotilla; and already, in spite of the terrors of his mother, Natalia, Peter dreamed of the sea.

"The child is amusing himself," the courtiers of Sophia affected to observe; but these amusements disquieted her. Each day added to the years of Peter seemed to bring her nearer to the cloister. In vain she proudly called herself "autocrat"; she saw her stepmother, her rival, lifting up her head. Galitsyne confined himself to regretting that they had not known better how to profit by the revolution of 1682, but Chaklovity, who knew he must fall with his mistress, said aloud, "It would be wiser to put the Czarina to death than to be put to death by her." Sophia could only save herself by seizing the throne—but who would help her to take it? The streltsi? But the result of their last rising had chilled them considerably. Sophia herself, while trying to bind this formidable force, had broken it, and the streltsi had not forgotten their chiefs beheaded at Troitsa. Now what did the emissaries of Sophia propose to them? Again to attack the palace; to put Leo Narychkine and other partisans of Peter to death; to arrest his mother, and to expel the patriarch. They trusted that Peter and Natalia would perish in the tumult. The streltsi remained indifferent when Sophia, affecting to think her life threatened, fled to the Dievitchi monastery, and sent them letters of entreaty. "If thy days are in peril," tranquilly replied the streltsi, "there must be an inquiry." Chaklovity could hardly collect four hundred of them at the Kremlin.

The struggle began between Moscow and Preobrajenskoe, the village with the prophetical name (the "Transfiguration" or "Regeneration"). Two streltsi warned Peter of the plots of his sister, and for the second time he sought an asylum at Troitsa. It was then seen who was the true czar; all men hastened to range themselves around him: his mother, his armed squires, the "battalion of playmates," the foreign officers, and even the streltsi of the regiment of Soukharef. The patriarch also took the side of the Czar, and brought him moral support, as the foreign soldiers had brought him material force. The partisans of Sophia were cold and irresolute; the streltsi themselves demanded that her favorite Chaklovity should be surrendered to the Czar. She had to implore the mediation of the patriarch. Chaklovity was first put to the torture and made to confess his plot against the Czar, and then decapitated. Medviedef was at first only condemned to the knout and banishment for heresy, but he acknowledged he had intended to take the place of the patriarch and to marry Sophia; he was dishonored by being imprisoned with two sorcerers, condemned to be burned alive in a cage, and was afterward beheaded. Galitsyne was deprived of his property, and exiled to Poustozersk. Sophia remained in the Dievitchi Monastyr, subjected to a hard captivity. Though Ivan continued to reign conjointly with his brother, yet Peter, who was then only seventeen, governed alone, surrounded by his mother, the Narychkines, and the Dolgoroukis (1689).

Sophia had freed herself from the seclusion of the terem, as Peter had emancipated himself from the seclusion of the palace to roam the streets and navigate rivers. Both had behaved scandalously, according to the ideas of the time—the one haranguing soldiers, presiding over councils, walking with her veil raised; the other using the axe like a carpenter, rowing like a Cossack, brawling with foreign adventurers, and fighting with his grooms in mimic battles. But to the one her emancipation was only a means of obtaining power; to the other the emancipation of Russia, like the emancipation of himself, was the end. He wished the nation to shake off the old trammels from which he had freed himself. Sophia remained a Byzantine, Peter aspired to be a European. In the conflict between the Czarevna and the Czar, progress was not on the side of the Dievitchi Monastyr.

The first use the Czar made of his liberty was to hasten to Archangel. There, deaf to the advice and prayers of his mother, who was astounded at this unexpected taste for salt water, he gazed on that sea which no czar had ever looked on. He ate with the merchants and the officers of foreign navies; he breathed the air which had come from the West. He established a dockyard, built boats, dared the angry waves of this unknown ocean, and almost perished in a storm, which did not prevent the "skipper Peter Alexeievitch" from again putting to sea, and bringing the Dutch vessels back to the Holy Cape. Unhappily, the White Sea, by which, since the time of Ivan IV, the English had entered Russia, is frost-bound in winter. In order to open permanent communications with the West, with civilized countries, it was necessary for Peter to establish himself on the Baltic or the Black Sea. Now the first belonged to the Swedes, and the second to the Turks, as the Caspian did to the Persians. Who was first to be attacked? The treaties concluded with Poland and Austria, as well as policy and religion, urged the Czar against the Turks, and Constantinople has always been the point of attraction for orthodox Russia.

Peter shared the sentiments of his people, and had the enthusiasm of a crusader against the infidel. Notwithstanding his ardent wish to travel in the West, he took the resolution not to appear in foreign lands till he could appear as a victor. Twice had Galitsyne failed against the Crimea; Peter determined to attack the barbarians by the Don, and besiege Azov. The army was commanded by three generals, Golovine, Gordon, and Lefort, who were to act with the "bombardier of the Preobrajenski regiment, Peter Alexeievitch." This regiment, as well as three others which had sprung from the "amusements" of Preobrajenskoe—the Semenovski, the Botousitski, and the regiment of Lefort—were the heart of the expedition. It failed because the Czar had no fleet with which to invest Azov by sea, because the new army and its chiefs wanted experience, and because Jansen, the German engineer, ill-treated by Peter, passed over to the enemy. After two assaults the siege was raised. This check appeared the more grave because the Czar himself was with the army, because the first attempt to turn from the "amusements" of Preobrajenskoe to serious warfare had failed, and because this failure would furnish arms against innovations, against the Germans and the heretics, against the new tactics. It might even compromise, in the eyes of the people, the work of regeneration (1695).

Although Peter had followed the example of Galitsyne, and entered Moscow in triumph, he felt he needed revenge. He sent for good officers from foreign countries. Artillerymen arrived from Holland and Austria, engineers from Prussia, and Admiral Lima from Venice. Peter hurried on the creation of a fleet with feverish impatience. He built of green wood twenty-two galleys, a hundred rafts, and seventeen hundred boats or barks. All the small ports of the Don were metamorphosed into dock-yards; twenty-six thousand workmen were assembled there from all parts of the empire. It was like the camp of Boulogne. No misfortune—neither the desertion of the laborers, the burnings of the dock-yards, nor even his own illness—could lessen his activity. Peter was able to write that, "following the advice God gave to Adam, he earned his bread by the sweat of his brow." At last the "marine caravan," the Russian armada, descended the Don. From the slopes of Azov he wrote to his sister Natalia [1]: "In obedience to thy counsels, I do not go to meet the shells and balls; it is they who approach me, but tolerably courteously."

[1] His mother died in 1694, his brother Ivan in 1696.

Azov was blockaded by sea and land, and a breach was opened by the engineers. Preparations were being made for a general assault, when the place capitulated. The joy in Russia was great, and the streltsi's jealousy of the success of foreign tactics gave place to their enthusiasm as Christians for this victory over Islamism, which recalled those of Kazan and Astrakhan. The effect produced on Europe was considerable. At Warsaw the people shouted, "Long live the Czar!" The army entered Moscow under triumphal arches, on which were represented Hercules trampling a pacha and two Turks under foot, and Mars throwing to the earth a *mirza* and two Tartars. Admiral Lefort and Schein the generalissimo took part in the *cortège*, seated on magnificent sledges; while Peter, promoted to the rank of captain, followed on foot. Jansen, destined to the gibbet, marched among the prisoners (1696).

Peter wished to profit by this great success to found the naval power of Russia. By the decision of the *douma* three thousand families were established at Azov, besides four hundred Kalmucks, and a garrison of Moscow streltsi. The patriarch, the prelates, and the monasteries taxed themselves for the construction of one vessel to every eight thousand serfs. The nobles, the officials, and the merchants were seized with the fever of this holy war, and brought their contributions toward the infant navy. It was proposed to unite the Don and the Volga by means of a canal. A new appeal was made to the artisans and sailors of Europe. Fifty young nobles of the court were sent to Venice, England, and the Low Countries to learn seamanship and shipbuilding. But it was necessary that the Czar himself should be able to judge of the science of his subjects; he must counteract Russian indolence and prejudice by the force of a great example; and Peter, after having begun his career in the navy at the rank of "skipper," and in the army at that of bombardier, was to become a carpenter of Saardam. He allowed himself, as a reward for his success at Azov, the much-longed-for journey to the West.

In 1697 Admiral Lefort and Generals Golovine and Vosnitsyne prepared to depart for the countries of the West, under the title of "the great ambassadors of the Czar." Their suite was composed of two hundred seventy persons—young nobles, soldiers, interpreters, merchants, jesters, and buffoons. In the cortège was a young man who went by the name of Peter Mikhailof. This *incognito* would render the position of the Czar easier, whether in his own personal studies or in delicate negotiations. On the journey to Riga Peter allowed himself to be insulted by the governor, but laid up the recollection for future use. At Koenigsburg the Prussian, Colonel Sternfeld, delivered to "M. Peter Mikhailof" "a formal brevet of master of artillery." The great ambassadors and their travelling companion were cordially received by the courts of Courland, Hanover, and Brandenburg.

Sophia Charlotte of Hanover, afterward Queen of Prussia, has left us some curious notes about the Czar, then twenty-seven years of age. He astonished her by the vivacity of his mind and the promptitude and point of his answers, not less than by the grossness of his manners, his bad habits at table, his wild timidity, like that of a badly brought-up child, his grimaces, and a frightful twitching which at times convulsed his whole face. Peter had then a beautiful brown skin, with great piercing eyes, but his features already bore traces of toil and debauchery. "He must have very good and very bad points," said the young Electress; and in this he represented contemporary Russia. "If he had received a better education," adds the Princess, "he would have been an accomplished man." The suite of the Czar were not less surprising than their master; the Muscovites danced with the court ladies, and took the stiffening of their corsets for their bones. "The bones of these Germans are devilish hard!" said the Czar.

Leaving the great embassy on the road Peter travelled quickly and reached Saardam. The very day of his arrival he took a lodging at a blacksmith's, procured himself a complete costume like those worn by Dutch workmen, and began to wield the axe. He bargained for a boat, bought it, and drank the traditional pint of beer with its owner. He visited cutleries, ropewalks, and other manufactories, and everywhere tried his hand at the work: in a paper manufactory he made some paper. However, in spite of the tradition, he only remained eight days at Saardam. At Amsterdam his eccentricities were no less astonishing. He neither took any rest himself nor allowed others to do so; he exhausted all his *ciceroni*, always repeating, "I must see it." He inspected the most celebrated anatomical collections; engaged artists, workmen, officers, and engineers; and bought models of ships and collections of naval laws and treaties. He entered familiarly the houses of private individuals, gained the good-will of the Dutch by his *bonhomie*, penetrated into the recesses of the shops and stalls, and remained lost in admiration over a dentist.

But, amid all these distractions, he never lost sight of his aim. "We labor," he wrote to the patriarch Adrian, "in order thoroughly to master the art of the sea; so that, having once learned it, we may return to Russia and conquer the enemies of Christ, and free by his grace the Christians who are oppressed. This is what I shall long for to my last breath." He was vexed at making so little progress in shipbuilding, but in Holland everyone had to learn by personal experience. A naval captain told him that in England instruction was based on principles, and these he could learn in four months; so Peter crossed the sea, and spent three months in London and the neighboring towns. There he took into his service goldsmiths and gold-beaters, architects and bombardiers. He then returned to Holland, and, his ship being attacked by a violent tempest, he reassured those who trembled for his safety by the remark, "Did you ever hear of a czar of Russia who was drowned in the North Sea?"

Though much occupied with his technical studies, he had not neglected policy; he had conversed with William III, but did not visit France in this tour, for "Louis XIV," says St. Simon, "had procured the postponement of his visit"; the fact being that his alliance with the Emperor and his wars with the Turks were looked on with disfavor at Versailles. He went to Vienna to study the military art, and dissuaded Leopold from making peace with the Sultan. Peter wished to conquer Kertch in order to secure the Straits of Ienikale. He was preparing to go to Venice, when vexatious intelligence reached him from Moscow.

The first reforms of Peter, his first attempts against the national prejudices and customs, had raised him up a crowd of enemies. Old Russia did not allow herself quietly to be set aside by the bold innovator. There was in the interior a sullen and resolute resistance, which sometimes gave birth to bloody scenes.

The revolt of the streltsi, the insurrection of Astrakhan, the rebellion of the Cossacks, and later the trial of his son and first wife are only episodes of the great struggle. Already the priests were teaching that Antichrist was born. Now it had been prophesied that Antichrist should be born of an adulteress, and Peter was the son of the *second* wife of Alexis, therefore his mother Natalia was the "false virgin," the adulterous woman of the prophecies. The increasingly heavy taxes that weighed on the people were another sign that the time had come. Others, disgusted by the taste shown by the Czar for German clothes and foreign languages and adventures, affirmed that he was not the son of Alexis, but of Lefort the Genevan, or that his father was a German surgeon. They were scandalized to see the Czar, like another Gregory Otrepief, expose himself to blows in his military "amusements." The lower orders were indignant at the abolition of the long beards and national costume, and the *raskolniks* [1] at the authorization of "the sacrilegious smell of tobacco."

The journey to the west completed the general dissatisfaction. Had anyone ever before seen a czar of Moscow quit Holy Russia to wander in the kingdoms of foreigners? Who knew what adventures might befall him among the *niemtsi* and the *bousourmanes?* for the Russian people hardly knew how to distinguish between the Turks and the Germans, and were wholly ignorant of France and England. Under an unknown sky, at the extremity of the world, on the shores of the "ocean sea," what dangers might he not encounter? Then a singular legend was invented about the travels of the Czar. It was said that he went to Stockholm disguised as a merchant, and that the Queen had recognized him and had tried in vain to capture him. According to another version, she had plunged him in a dungeon, and delivered him over to his enemies, who wished to put him in a cask lined with nails and throw him into the sea. He had only been saved by a streletz who had taken his place. Some asserted that Peter was still kept there; and in 1705 the streltsi and raskolniks of Astrakhan still gave out that it was a false czar who had come back to Moscow—the true czar was a prisoner at Stockholm, attached to a stake.

[1] Dissenters from the orthodox church of Russia (Greek Church).—Ed.

In the midst of this universal disturbance, caused by the absence of Peter, there were certain symptoms peculiarly disquieting. The Muscovite army grew more and more hostile to the new order of things. In 1694 Peter had discovered a fresh conspiracy, having for its object the deliverance of Sophia; and at the very moment of his departure from Russia he had to put down a plot of streltsi and Cossacks headed by Colonel Tsykler. Those of the streltsi who had been sent to form the garrison of Azov pined for their wives, their children, and the trades they had left in Moscow. When in the absence of the Czar they were sent from Azov to the frontiers of Poland, they again began to murmur. "What a fate is ours! It is the boyars who do all the mischief; for three years they have kept us from our homes."

Two hundred deserted and returned to Moscow; but the douma, fearing their presence in the already troubled capital, expelled them by force. They brought back to their regiments a letter of Sophia. "You suffer," she wrote; "later it will become worse. March on Moscow. What is it you wait for? There is no news of the Czar." It was repeated through the army that the Czar had died in foreign lands, and that the boyars wished to put his son Alexis to death. It was necessary to march on Moscow and exterminate the nobles.

The military sedition was complicated by the religious fanaticism of the raskolniks and the demagogic passions of the popular army. Four regiments revolted and deserted. Generals Schein and Gordon, with their regular troops, hastened after them, came up with them on the banks of the Iskra, and tried to persuade them to return to their duty. The streltsi replied by a petition setting forth all their grievances: "Many of them had died during the expedition to Azov, suggested by Lefort, a German, a heretic; they had endured fatiguing marches over burning plains, their only food being bad meat; their strength had been exhausted by severe tasks, and they had been banished to distant garrisons. Moscow was now a prey to all sorts of horrors. Foreigners had introduced the custom of shaving the beard and smoking tobacco. It was said that these niemtsi meant to seize the town. On this rumor, the streltsi had arrived, and also because Romodanovski wished to disperse and put them to the sword without anyone knowing why." A few cannon-shots were sufficient to scatter the rebels. A large number were arrested; torture, the gibbet, and the dungeon awaited the captives.

When Peter hastened home from Vienna he decided that his generals and his douma had been too lenient. He had old grievances against the streltsi; they had been the army of Sophia, in opposition to the army of the Czar; he remembered the invasion of the Kremlin, the massacre of his mother's family, her terrors in Troitsa, and the conspiracies which all but delayed his journey to the west. At the very time that he was travelling in Europe for the benefit of his people, these incorrigible mutineers had forced him to renounce his dearest projects and had stopped him on the road to Venice. He resolved to take advantage of the opportunity by crushing his enemies *en masse*, and by making the Old Russia feel the weight of a terror that would recall the days of Ivan IV. The long beards had been the standard of revolt—they should fall. On August 26th he ordered all the gentlemen of his court to shave themselves, and himself applied the razor to his great lords. The same day the Red Place was covered with gibbets. The patriarch Adrian tried in vain to appease the anger of the Czar by presenting to him the wonder-working image of the Mother of God. "Why hast thou brought out the holy icon?" exclaimed the Czar. "Retire and restore it to its place. Know that I venerate God and his Mother as much as thyself, but know also that it is my duty to protect the people and punish the rebels."

On October 30th there arrived at the Red Place the first instalment of two hundred thirty prisoners: they came in carts, with lighted torches in their hands, nearly all already broken by torture, and followed by their wives and children, who ran behind chanting a funeral wail. Their sentence was read, and they were slain, the Czar ordering several officers to help the executioner. John George Korb, the Austrian agent, who as an eye-witness has left us an authentic account of the executions, heard that five rebel heads had been sent into the dust by blows from an axe wielded by the noblest hand in Russia." The terrible carpenter of Saardam worked and obliged his boyars to work at this horrible employment. Seven other days were employed in this way; a thousand victims were put to death. Some were broken on the wheel, and others died by various modes of torture. The removal of the corpses was forbidden: for five months Moscow had before its eyes the spectacle of the dead bodies hanging from the battlements of the Kremlin and the other ramparts; and for five months the streltsi suspended to the bars of Sophia's prison presented her the petition by which they had entreated her to reign. Two of her confidants were buried alive; she herself, with Eudoxia Lapoukhine, Peter's wife, who had been repudiated for her obstinate attachment to the ancient customs, had their heads shaved and were confined in monasteries. After the revolt of the inhabitants of Astrakhan, who put their waywode to death, the old militia was completely abolished, and the way left clear for the formation of new troops.

TYRANNY OF ANDROS IN NEW ENGLAND

THE "BLOODLESS REVOLUTION"

A.D. 1689

CHARLES W. ELLIOTT

When the spirit of the English Revolution of 1688 crossed the Atlantic and stirred the New England colonists to throw off the Stuart tyranny represented by Andros, a long step was taken in the development of early American self-government. The Charter Oak tradition, whether or not resting on actual occurrences, correctly typifies the temper of that self-government as it has ever manifested itself in the crises of patriotic development in this country. And the ending of theocratic government, as here recorded of Massachusetts, foreshadowed the further growth of democracy in America.

Sir William Andros, an Englishman, was colonial governor of New York from 1674 to 1681, and of New England, including New York, from 1686 to 1689. His rule "was on the model dear to the heart of his royal master—a harsh despotism, but neither strong nor wise; it was wretched misgovernment and stupid, blundering oppression." What poor success Andros had in his attempt to force such a rule upon people of the English race who had already accustomed themselves to a large measure of independence and self-government Elliott's account briefly but fully shows.

WHILE colonies are poor they are neglected by the parent state; when they are able to pay taxes then she is quite ready to "govern them"; she is willing to appoint various dependents to important offices, and to allow the colonies to pay liberal salaries; she likes also to tax them to the amount of the surplus production which is transferred to the managers in the mother-country. Surprising as this is, it is what many call "government," and is common everywhere. England has been no exception to this, and her practice in New England was of this character till, in the year 1776, the back of the people was so galled that it threw its rider with violence.

At various times attempts had been made to destroy the

Massachusetts charter. At the restoration of Charles II, in 1660, the enemies of the Puritans roused themselves. All who scented the breath of liberty in those Western gales—all who had been disappointed of fond hopes in those infant states—all who had felt in New England, too, the iron hand of ecclesiastical tyranny, who chafed in the religious manacles which there, as everywhere else, were imposed upon the minority—all united against them; and in 1664 commissioners were sent over with extraordinary powers. The colony withstood them to the best of its ability; but at last, in 1676, a *quo warranto* was issued, and judgment was obtained in England against the Massachusetts charter.

In 1683 the quo warranto was brought over by Edward Randolph, who had been appointed collector of the port of Boston in 1681, but had not been allowed to act. He was the "messenger of death" to the hopes of the colony. The deputies refused to appear in England and plead, and judgment was entered up against them at last, in 1685, and the charter was abrogated. Charles died, and the bitter and bigoted James II came to the throne in 1684. The colonists then had rumors that Colonel Kirke, the fiercest hater of the Nonconformists in England, was coming over as governor, which filled them with dread. The colony now seemed to be at the mercy of the churchmen, or, worse than that, of the papists, for such was James. Mr. Rawson, secretary of the colony, about this time wrote, "Our condition is awful."

Mr. Joseph Dudley was appointed governor and acted for a short time, but was succeeded by Sir Edmund Andros, who arrived December 19, 1686, with a commission from James II, to take upon himself the absolute government of all New England. Andros was supposed to be a bigoted papist, and he certainly carried matters with a high hand; the poisoned chalice of religious despotism, which these Pilgrims had commended to the lips of Roger Williams, the Browns, Mrs. Hutchinson, Gorton, Clarke, and the Quakers, was now offered to their own lips, and the draught was bitter.

First, the press was muzzled; then marriage was no longer free. The minister Moody (1684) was imprisoned six months in New Hampshire for refusing to administer the communion to Cranfield and others, according to the manner and form set forth in the *Book of Common Prayer.* The Congregational ministers were as mere laymen, and danger menaced public worship and the meeting-houses. But this last extremity was saved them by the necessity which James was under of securing the triumph of *his* church in Protestant England, the first step toward which was the proclamation of religious toleration. This, of course, secured the colonists, and the pilgrims were saved that fearful misery of being driven out from their own cherished altars. Andros carried things with as high a hand in Massachusetts as his master did in England; absolute subjection they both insisted on. Besides the denial of political and religious rights, the practice of arbitrary taxation was asserted by Andros, and all titles to lands were questioned; in the brutal phrase of the time, it was declared that "the calf died in the cow's belly"; that is, having no rights as a state, they had none as individuals; so fees, fines, and expenditures impoverished the people and enriched the officials. All seemed lost in Massachusetts.

Andros went down to Hartford, in Connecticut, with his suite, and with sixty troops took possession of the government there and demanded the charter. Through the day (October 31, 1687) the authorities remonstrated and postponed. When they met Andros again in the evening the people collected, much excited. There seemed no relief. Their palladium, their charter, was demanded, and before them stood Andros, with soldiers and drawn swords, to compel his demand. There was then no hope, and the roll of parchment—the charter, with the great royal seal upon it—was brought forth and laid upon the table, in the midst of the excited people. Suddenly, without warning, all lights were extinguished! There were darkness and silence, followed by wonder, movement, and confusion. What meant this very unparliamentary conduct, or was it a gust of wind which had startled all? Lights were soon obtained, and then—

"Where is the charter?" was the question that went round the assembly.

"What means this?" cried Andros, in anger.

But no man knew where the charter had disappeared to; neither threats nor persuasion brought it to light. What could Andros do? Clearly nothing, for the authorities had done all that could be asked: they had produced the charter in the presence of Andros, and now it had disappeared from his presence. He had come upon a fool's errand, and some sharp Yankee (Captain Wadsworth) had outwitted him. Where was the charter? Safely hidden in the heart of the great oak, at Hartford, on the grounds of Samuel Wyllys. There it remained beyond the reach of tyranny.

The tree known as the "Charter Oak" stood for over a century and a half from that day. The Indians had always prayed that the tree might be spared; they have our thanks.

Andros wrote on the last page of their records, *Finis*, and disappeared—but that was not the end of Connecticut.

It was a dark time for liberty in New England, and a dark day for liberty in Old England; for there James II and his unscrupulous ministers were corruptly, grossly, and illegally trampling down the rights of manhood. Andros was doing it in New England, and he found in Dudley, Stoughton, Clark, and others, sons of New England, ready feet. In 1688 Randolph writes, "We are as arbitrary as the great Turk"; which seems to have been true. The hearts of the best men in both countries sank within them, and they cried in their discouragement, "O Lord! how long!"

Thus matters stood when, during the spring of 1688–1689, faint rumors of the landing of William, Prince of Orange, in England, came from Virginia. Could this be true? It brought Andros up to Boston (April), where he gave orders to have the soldiers ready against surprise.

Liberty is the most ardent wish of a brave and noble people, and is too often betrayed by confidence in cultivated and designing and timid men. Liberty was the wish of the people of New England; and for the want of brave men then and since then they suffered.

When, on April 4th, John Winslow brought from Virginia the rumor of the English Revolution and the landing of the Prince of Orange, it went through their blood like the electric current, and thrilled from the city along the byways into every home. Men got on their horses and rode onward to the next house to carry the tidings that the popish King was down and William was up, and that there was hope; through town and country the questions were eagerly asked: "Shall we get our old charter?

Shall we regain our rights?" "What is there for us to do?" cried the people.

Andros put out a proclamation that all persons should be in readiness to resist the forces of the Prince of Orange should they come. But the old magistrates and leaders silently prayed for his success; the people, less cautious and more determined, said to one another: "Let us do something. Why not act?" and this went from mouth to mouth till their hatred of Andros, and the remembrance to his dastardly oppressions, blazed into a consuming fire.

"On April 18, 1689," wrote an onlooker, "I knew not anything of what was intended until it was begun, yet being at the north end of the town, where I saw boys running along the streets with clubs in their hands encouraging one another to fight, I began to mistrust what was intended, and hasting toward the Town Dock I soon saw men running for their arms; but before I got to the Red Lion I was told that Captain George and the master of the frigate were seized and secured in Mr. Colman's house at the North End; and when I came to the Town Dock I understood that Bullivant and some others were laid hold of, and then immediately the drums began to beat, and the people hastened and ran, some with and some for arms," etc.

So it was begun, no one knew by whom; but men remembered yet their old liberties and were ready to risk something to regain them; they remembered, too, their present tyrants and longed to punish them. But in all this, men of property took no part—they are always timid. It was the "mob" that acted.

Governor Andros was at the fort with some soldiers, and sent for the clergymen to come to him, who declined. The people and train-bands rallied together at the Town House, where old Governor Bradstreet and some other principal men met to consult as to what should be done. The King's frigate in the harbor ran up her flags, and the lieutenant swore he would die before she should be taken, and he opened her ports and ran out her guns; but Captain George (prisoner in Boston) sent him word not to fire a shot, for the people would tear him in pieces if he did. In the afternoon the soldiers and people marched to the fort, took possession of a battery, turned its guns upon the fort and demanded its surrender. They did not wait for its surrender, but stormed in through the portholes, and Captain John Nelson, a Boston merchant, cried out to Andros, "I demand your surrender." Andros was surprised at the anger of an outraged people, and knew not what to do, but at last gave up the fort, and was lodged prisoner in Mr. Usher's house.

The next day he was forcedto give up the castle in the harbor, and the guns of the battery from the shore were brought to bear upon the frigate. But the captain prayed that she might not be forced to surrender, because all the officers and crew would lose their wages; so she was dismantled for present security. All through the day people came pouring in from the country, well armed and hot with rage against Andros and his confederates; and the cooler men trembled lest some unnecessary violence might be done; so Captain Fisher, of Dedham, led Andros by the collar of the coat back to the fort for safety.

On the 20th Bradstreet and other leading men met, and formed a kind of provisional council. They carefully abstained from resuming their old charter, partly from fear and partly from doubt, and called upon the towns to send up deputies. When these met, on May 22, 1689, forty out of fifty-four were for "resuming," but a majority of the council opposed it, and time was spent in disputes; but at last the old Governor and magistrates accepted the control of affairs, though they would not consent to resume the charter. Thus the moment for action passed, and the colony lost that chance for reëstablishing its old rights.

Rhode Island and Connecticut resumed their charters, which had never been legally vacated. Mr. Threat was obliged to take again the office of governor of Connecticut, when the amazing reports of the revolution and seizure of the Governor in Massachusetts reached them. They issued loyal addresses to William and Mary, in which they said: "Great was that day when the Lord who sitteth upon the floods did divide his and your adversaries like the waters of Jordan, and did begin to magnify you like Joshua, by the deliverance of the English dominions from popery and slavery."

Andros escaped, but was apprehended at Rhode Island, and sent back to Boston, and in February, 1689, with Dudley and some others, he was sent away to England.

Increase Mather, the agent of the Massachusetts Bay Colony,

with the aid of friends in England, endeavored to gain the restoration of the old charter from King William, but was unsuccessful; a new one was granted (1691), which contained many of the old privileges; but the King would not grant them the power of appointing their own governor; that power was reserved; and appeals from the colony courts to England were allowed. The Governor and the King both had a veto upon all colonial legislation. By it all religions except the Roman Catholic were declared free, and Plymouth was annexed to Massachusetts.

Thus two important elements of a free government were lost to Massachusetts; and powers which had been exercised over fifty years were, for nigh a hundred years, taken away. In Connecticut and Rhode Island they continued to elect their own rulers and to exercise all the powers of government. The new charter was brought over by Sir William Phipps, the new governor appointed by the King, who arrived on May 14, 1692.

Thus ended the rule of the theocracy in Massachusetts, and from this time forward the ministers and church-members possessed no more power than the rest of the people.

MASSACRE OF LACHINE

A.D. 1689

FRANÇOIS XAVIER GARNEAU

Just after Count Frontenac's first administration of Canada (1672–1682), when the colony of New France was under the rule of De la Barre and his successor, the Marquis de Denonville, Montreal and its immediate vicinity suffered from the most terrible and bloody of all the Indian massacres of the colonial days. The hatred of the Five Nations for the French, stimulated by the British colonists of New York, under its governor, Colonel Dongan, was due to French forays on the Seneca tribes, and to the capture and forwarding to the royal galleys in France of many of the betrayed Iroquois chiefs. At this period the English on the seaboard began to extend their trade into the interior of the continent and to divert commerce from the St. Lawrence to the Hudson. This gave rise to keen rivalries between the two European races, and led the English to take sides with the Iroquois in their enmity to the French. The latter, at Governor Denonville's instigation, sought to settle accounts summarily with the Iroquois, believing that the tribes of the Five Nations could never be conciliated, and that it was well to extirpate them at once. Soon the Governor put his fell purpose into effect. With a force of two thousand men, in a fleet of canoes, he entered the Seneca country by the Genesee River, and for ten days ravaged the Iroquois homes and put many of them cruelly to death. Returning by the Niagara River he erected and garrisoned a fort at its mouth and then withdrew to Quebec. A terrible revenge was taken on the French colonists for these infamous acts, as the following article by M. Garneau shows.

THE situation of the colonists of New France during the critical era of M. Denonville's administration was certainly anything but enviable. They literally "dwelt in the midst of alarms," yet their steady courage in facing perils, and their endurance of privations when unavoidable, were worthy of admiration. A lively idea of what they had to resist or to suffer may be found by reading the more particular parts of the Governor's despatches to Paris. For instance, in one of these he wrote in reference to the raids of the Iroquois: "The savages are just so many animals of prey, scattered through a vast forest, whence they are ever ready to issue, to raven and kill in the adjoining countries. After their ravages, to go in pursuit of them is a constant but almost bootless task. They have no settled place whither they can be traced with any certainty; they must be watched everywhere, and long waited for, with fire-arms ready primed. Many of their lurking-places could be reached only by blood-hounds or by other savages as our trackers, but those in our service are few, and the native allies we have are seldom trustworthy; they fear the enemy more than they love us, and they dread, on their own selfish account, to drive the Iroquois to extremity. It has been resolved, in the present strait, to erect a fort in every seigniory, as a place of shelter for helpless people and live-stock, at times when the open country is overrun with ravagers. As matters now stand, the arable grounds lie wide apart, and are so begirt with bush that every thicket around serves as a point for attack by a savage foe; insomuch that an army, broken up into scattered posts, would be needful to protect the cultivators of our cleared lands." [1]

Nevertheless, at one time hopes were entertained that more peaceful times were coming. In effect, negotiations with the Five Nations were recommenced; and the winter of 1687–1688 was passed in goings to and fro between the colonial authorities and the leaders of the Iroquois, with whom several conferences were holden. A correspondence, too, was maintained by the Governor with Colonel Dongan at New York; the latter intimating in one of his letters that he had formed a league of all the Iroquois tribes, and put arms in their hands, to enable them to defend British colonial territory against all comers.

The Iroquois confederation itself sent a deputation to Canada, which was escorted as far as Lake St. François by twelve hundred warriors—a significant demonstration enough. The envoys, after having put forward their pretensions with much stateliness and yet more address, said that, nevertheless, their people did not mean to press for all the advantages they had the right and the power to demand. They intimated that they were perfectly aware of the comparative weakness of the colony; that the Iroquois could at any time burn the houses of the inhabitants, pillage their stores, waste their crops, and afterward eas-

[1] Letter to M. Seignelai, August 10, 1688.

ily raze the forts. The Governor-general, in reply to these—not quite unfounded—boastings and arrogant assumptions, said that Colonel Dongan claimed the Iroquois as English subjects, and admonished the deputies that, if such were the case, then they must act according to his orders, which would necessarily be pacific, France and England not now being at war; whereupon the deputies responded, as others had done before, that the confederation formed an independent power; that it had always resisted French as well as English supremacy over its subjects; and that the coalesced Iroquois would be neutral, or friends or else enemies to one or both, at discretion; "for we have never been conquered by either of you," they said; adding that, as they held their country immediately from God, they acknowledge no other master.

It did not appear, however, that there was a perfect accordance among the envoys on all points, for the deputies from Onnontaguez, the Onneyouths, and Goyogouins agreed to a truce on conditions proposed by M. Denonville; namely, that all the native allies of the French should be comprehended in the treaty. They undertook that deputies [others than some of those present?] should be sent from the Agniers and Tsonnouthouan cantons, who were then to take part in concluding a treaty; that all hostilities should cease on every side, and that the French should be allowed to revictual, undisturbed, the fort of Cataracoui. The truce having been agreed to on those bases, five of the Iroquois remained (one for each canton), as hostages for its terms being observed faithfully. Notwithstanding this precaution, several roving bands of Iroquois, not advertised, possibly, of what was pending, continued to kill our people, burn their dwellings, and slaughter live-stock in different parts of the colony; for example, at St. François, at Sorel, at Contrecœur, and at St. Ours. These outrages, however, it must be owned, did not long continue, and roving corps of savages, either singly or by concert, drew off from the invaded country and allowed its harassed people a short breathing-time at least.

The native allies of the French, on the other hand, respected the truce little more than the Iroquois. The Abenaquis invaded the Agniers canton, and even penetrated to the English settlements, scalping several persons. The Iroquois of the Sault and of La Montagne did the like; but the Hurons of Michilimackinac, supposed to be those most averse to the war, did all they could, and most successfully, too, to prevent a peace being signed.

While the negotiations were in progress, the "Machiavel of the wilderness," as Raynal designates a Huron chief, bearing the native name of Kondiarak, but better known as Le Rat in the colonial annals, arrived at Frontenac (Kingston), with a chosen band of his tribe, and became a means of complicating yet more the difficulties of the crisis. He was the most enterprising, brave, and best-informed chief in all North America; and, as such, was one courted by the Governor in hopes of his becoming a valuable auxiliary to the French, although at first one of their most formidable enemies. He now came prepared to battle in their favor, and eager to signalize himself in the service of his new masters. The time, however, as we may well suppose, was not opportune, and he was informed that a treaty with the Iroquois being far advanced, and their deputies on the way to Montreal to conclude it, he would give umbrage to the Governor-general of Canada should he persevere in the hostilities he had been already carrying on.

The Rat was taken aback on hearing this to him unwelcome news, but took care to hide his surprise and uttered no complaint. Yet was he mortally offended that the French should have gone so far in the matter without the concert of their native allies, and he at once resolved to punish them, in his own case, for such a marked slight. He set out secretly with his braves, laid an ambuscade near Famine Cove for the approaching deputation of Iroquois, murdered several and made the others his prisoners. Having done so, he secretly gloried in the act, afterward saying that he had "killed the peace." Yet in dealing with the captives he put another and a deceptive face on the matter; for, on courteously questioning them as to the object of their journey, being told that they were peaceful envoys, he affected great wonder, seeing that it was Denonville himself who had sent him on purpose to waylay them!

To give seeming corroboration to his astounding assertions, he set the survivors at liberty, retaining one only to replace one of his men who was killed by the Iroquois in resisting the Hurons' attack. Leaving the deputies to follow what course they thought fit, he hastened with his men to Michilimackinac, where he presented his prisoner to M. Durantaye, who, not as yet officially informed, perhaps, that a truce existed with the Iroquois, consigned him to death, though he gave Durantaye assurance of who he really was; but when the victim appealed to the Rat for confirmation of his being an accredited envoy, that unscrupulous personage told him he must be out of his mind to imagine such a thing! This human sacrifice offered up, the Rat called upon an aged Iroquois, then and long previously a Huron captive, to return to his compatriots and inform them from him that while the French were making a show of peace-seeking, they were, underhand, killing and making prisoners of their native antagonists.

This artifice, a manifestation of the diabolic nature of its author, had too much of the success intended by it, for, although the Governor managed to disculpate himself in the eyes of the more candid-minded Iroquois leaders, yet there were great numbers of the people who could not be disabused, as is usual in such cases, even among civilized races. Nevertheless the enlightened few, who really were tired of the war, agreed to send a second deputation to Canada; but when it was about to set out, a special messenger arrived, sent by Andros, successor of Dongan, enjoining the chiefs of the Iroquois confederation not to treat with the French without the participation of his master, and announcing at the same time that the King of Great Britain had taken the Iroquois nations under his protection. Concurrently with this step, Andros wrote to Denonville that the Iroquois territory was a dependency holden of the British, and that he would not permit its people to treat upon those conditions already proposed by Dongan.

This transaction took place in 1688; but before that year concluded, Andros' "royal master" was himself superseded, and living an exile in France.[1] Whether instructions sent from England previously warranted the polity pursued by Andros or not,

[1] In 1688 Andros was appointed Governor of New York and New England. The appointment of this tyrant, and the annexation of the colony to the neighboring ones, were measures particularly odious to the people.—Ed.

his injunctions had the effect of instantly stopping the negotiations with the Iroquois, and prompting them to recommence their vengeful hostilities. War between France and Britain being proclaimed next year, the American colonists of the latter adopted the Iroquois as their especial allies, in the ensuing contests with the people of New France.

Andros, meanwhile, who adopted the policy of his predecessor so far as regarded the aborigines if in no other respect, not only fomented the deadly enmity of the Iroquois for the Canadians, but tried to detach the Abenaquis from their alliance with the French, but without effect in their case; for this people honored the countrymen of the missionaries who had made the Gospel known to them, and their nation became a living barrier to New France on that side, which no force sent from New England could surmount; insomuch that the Abenaquis, some time afterward, having crossed the borders of the English possessions, and harassed the remoter colonists, the latter were fain to apply to the Iroquois to enable them to hold their own.

The declaration of Andros, and the armings of the Iroquois, now let loose on many parts of Canada, gave rise to a project as politic, perhaps, as it was daring, and such as communities when in extremity have adopted with good effect; namely, to divert invasion by directly attacking the enemies' neighboring territories. The Chevalier de Callières, with whom the idea originated, after having suggested to Denonville a plan for making a conquest of the province of New York, set out for France, to bring it under the consideration of the home government, believing that it was the only means left to save Canada to the mother-country.

It was high time, indeed, that the destinies of Canada were confided to other directors than the late and present ones, left as the colony had been, since the departure of M. de Frontenac, in the hands of superannuated or incapable chiefs. Any longer persistency in the policy of its two most recent governors might have irreparably compromised the future existence of the colony. But worse evils were in store for the latter days of the Denonville administration; a period which, take it altogether, was one of the most calamitous which our forefathers passed through.

At the time we have now reached in this history an unexpected as well as unwonted calm pervaded the country, yet the Governor had been positively informed that a desolating inroad by the collective Iroquois had been arranged, and that its advent was imminent; but as no precursive signs of it appeared anywhere to the general eyes, it was hoped that the storm, said to be ready to burst, might yet be evaded. None being able to account for the seeming inaction of the Iroquois, the Governor applied to the Jesuits for their opinion on the subject. The latter expressed their belief that those who had brought intelligence of the evil intention of the confederacy had been misinformed as to facts, or else exaggerated sinister probabilities. The prevailing calm was therefore dangerous as well as deceitful, for it tended to slacken preparations which ought to have been made to lessen the apprehensions of coming events which threw no shadow before.

The winter and the spring of the year 1688–1689 had been passed in an unusually tranquil manner, and the summer was pretty well advanced when the storm, long pent up, suddenly fell on the beautiful island of Montreal, the garden of Canada. During the night of August 5th, amid a storm of hail and rain, fourteen hundred Iroquois traversed Lake St. Louis, and disembarked silently on the upper strand of that island. Before daybreak next morning the invaders had taken their station at Lachine in platoons around every considerable house within a radius of several leagues. The inmates were buried in sleep—soon to be the dreamless sleep that knows no waking, for too many of them.

The Iroquois wait only for the signal from their leaders to fall on. It is given. In short space the doors and the windows of the dwellings are driven in; the sleepers dragged from their beds; men, women, children all struggling in the hands of their butchers. Such houses as the savages cannot force their way into, they fire; and as the flames reach the persons of those within, intolerable pain drives them forth to meet death beyond the threshold, from beings who know no pity. The more fiendish murderers even forced parents to throw their children into the flames. Two hundred persons were burned alive; others died under prolonged tortures. Many were reserved to perish similarly, at a future time. The fair island upon which the sun shone brightly erewhile, was lighted up by fires of woe; houses, plantations, and crops were reduced to ashes, while the ground reeked with blood up to a line a short league apart from Montreal city. The ravagers crossed to the opposite shore, the desolation behind them being complete, and forthwith the parish of Le Chenaie was wasted by fire and many of its people massacred.

The colonists for many leagues around the devoted region seem to have been actually paralyzed by the brain-blow thus dealt their compatriots by the relentless savages, as no one seems to have moved a step to arrest their course; for they were left in undisturbed possession of the country during several weeks. On hearing of the invasion, Denonville lost his self-possession altogether. When numbers of the colonists, recovering from their stupor, came up armed desiring to be led against the murderers of their countrymen, he sent them back or forbade them to stir! Several opportunities presented themselves for disposing of parties of the barbarians, when reckless from drink after their orgies, or when roving about in scattered parties feeble in number; but the Governor-general's positive orders to refrain from attacking them withheld the uplifted hand from striking.

In face of a prohibition so authoritative, the soldiers and the inhabitants alike could only look on and wait till the savages should find it convenient to retire. Some small skirmishing, indeed, there was at a few distant points between the people and their invaders. Thus a party of men, partly French and partly natives, led by Larobeyre, an ex-lieutenant, on the way to reënforce Fort Roland, where Chevalier de Vaudreuil commanded, were set upon and all killed or dispersed. More than half of the prisoners taken were burned by their conquerors. Larobeyre, being wounded and not able to fire, was led captive by the Iroquois to their country, and roasted at a slow fire in presence of the assembled tribe of his captors. Meantime the resistance to the barbarians being little or none in the regions they overran, they slew most of the inhabitants they met in their passage; while their course was marked, wherever they went, by lines of flame.

Their bands moved rapidly from one devoted tract to another; yet wherever they had to face concerted resistance—which in some cases, at least, put a fitting obstacle in the way of their intended ravagings—they turned aside and sought an easier prey elsewhere. In brief, during ten entire weeks or more, did they wreak their wrath, almost unchecked, upon the fairest region of Canada, and did not retire thence till about mid-October.

The Governor-General having sent a party of observation to assure himself of the enemy having decamped, this detachment observed a canoe on the Lake of the Two Mountains, bearing twenty-two of the retiring Iroquois. The Canadians, who were of about the same number, embarked in two boats and, nearing the savages, coolly received their fire; but in returning the discharge, each singled out his man, when eighteen of the Iroquois were at once laid low.

However difficult it may have been to put the people of a partially cleared country, surrounded with forests, on their guard against such an irruption as the foregoing, it is difficult to account for their total unpreparedness without imputing serious blame to Denonville and his subalterns in office. That he exercised no proper influence, in the first place, was evident, and the small use he made of the means he had at his disposal when the crisis arrived was really something to marvel at. He was plainly unequal to the occasion, and his incapacity in every particular made it quite impossible for his presence, as chief of the colony, to be endured any longer. There is little doubt that had he not been soon recalled by royal order, the colonists themselves would have set him aside. The latter season of his inglorious administration took the lugubrious name "the Year of the Massacre." [1]

The man appointed through a happy inspiration to supersede M. de Denonville had now reached the Lower Canadian waters. He was no other than the Count de Frontenac. It appears that the King, willing to cover, with a handsome pretext, the recall of Denonville, in a letter dated May 31st, advertised him that, war having been rekindled in Europe, his military tal-

[1] The Five Nations, being at war with the French, made a sudden descent on Montreal, burned and sacked the town, killed one hundred of the inhabitants, carrying away a number of prisoners whom they burned alive, and then returned to their own country with the loss of only a few of their number. Had the English followed up the success of their allies, all Canada might have been easily conquered.—ED.

ents would be of the greatest use in home service. By this time De Frontenac was called to give counsel regarding the projects of the Chevalier de Callières, and assist in preparing the way for their realization if considered feasible. Meanwhile he undertook to resume his duties as governor-general of New France; but a series of events delayed his arrival in Canada till the autumn of 1689.

He landed at Quebec on October 18th, at 8 P.M., accompanied by De Callières, amid the heartiest demonstrations of popular welcome. The public functionaries and armed citizens in waiting, with torch-bearers, escorted him through the city, which was spontaneously illuminated, to his quarters. His return was hailed by all, but by none more than the Jesuits, who had, in fact for years before, labored to obtain his recall. The nobles, the merchants, the business class, gave him so hearty a reception as to convince him that real talent such as his must in the end rise superior to all the conjoined efforts of faction, public prejudices, and the evil passions of inferior minds.

War was declared against Britain in the month of June. M. de Frontenac, on resuming the reins of government, had to contend both against the Anglo-American colonies and the Five Nations. His energy and skill, however, overcame all obstacles; the war was most glorious for the Canadians, so few in number compared with their adversaries; and far from succumbing to their enemies, they carried the war into the adversaries' camp and struck at the heart of their most remote possessions.

SIEGE OF LONDONDERRY AND BATTLE OF THE BOYNE

A.D. 1689–1690

TOBIAS G. SMOLLETT

Londonderry, capital of the county of the same name in Ireland, is a city of historic celebrity by reason of the successful defence there made (April–August, 1689) by the Irish Protestants against the besieging forces of James II. The battle of the Boyne (July 1, 1690) is of less importance in a military sense than for the reason that it virtually ended the war which James II carried into Ireland in his unsuccessful attempt to regain his throne from William and Mary. On account of this result, and still more by reason of the hereditary antagonisms which have so long survived it, this battle still retains a peculiar fame in history.

In Ireland, where the Roman Catholics were numerous, there was strong opposition to the government of William and Mary. The fugitive James II had supporters who controlled the Irish army. Some resistance was made by the English and Scotch colonists in Ireland, but little head was made against the Catholic party, which supported James, until William entered the country with his forces.

In the following narrative Smollett speaks of an "intended massacre" of the Protestants at Londonderry. The people of that city were of Anglo-Saxon blood. Although belonging to various Protestant churches, they were united in their hostility to the Irish and to the Catholic faith. They were alarmed at the close of 1688 by rumors of a plan for their own extirpation by the papists. News of the approach of the Earl of Antrim with a regiment, under orders from the Lord Deputy, filled the city with consternation. What followed there is graphically told in the words of the historian. A better account of a military action than that which Smollett gives of the Battle of the Boyne it would be hard to find.

ON the first alarm of an intended massacre, the Protestants of Londonderry had shut their gates against the regiment commanded by the Earl of Antrim, and resolved to defend themselves against the Lord Deputy; they transmitted this resolution to the Government of England, together with an account of the danger they incurred by such a vigorous measure, and implored immediate assistance; they were accordingly supplied with some arms and ammunition, but did not receive any considerable reënforcement till the middle of April, when two regiments arrived at Loughfoyl under the command of Cunningham and Richards.

By this time King James had taken Coleraine, invested Kilmore, and was almost in sight of Londonderry. George Walker, rector of Donaghmore, who had raised a regiment for the defence of the Protestants, conveyed this intelligence to Lundy, the governor; this officer directed him to join Colonel Crafton, and take post at the Longcausey, which he maintained a whole night against the advanced guard of the enemy, until, being overpowered by numbers, he retreated to Londonderry and exhorted the governor to take the field, as the army of King James was not yet completely formed. Lundy assembling a council of war, at which Cunningham and Richards assisted, they agreed that as the place was not tenable, it would be imprudent to land the two regiments; and that the principal officers should withdraw themselves from Londonderry, the inhabitants of which would obtain the more favorable capitulation in consequence of their retreat; an officer was immediately despatched to King James with proposals of a negotiation; and Lieutenant-general Hamilton agreed that the army should halt at the distance of four miles from the town.

Notwithstanding this preliminary, James advanced at the head of his troops, but met with such a warm reception from the besieged that he was fain to retire to St. John's Town in some disorder. The inhabitants and soldiers in garrison at Londonderry were so incensed at the members of the council of war who had resolved to abandon the place that they threatened immediate vengeance. Cunningham and Richards retired to their ships, and Lundy locked himself in his chamber. In vain did Walker and Major Baker exhort him to maintain his government; such was his cowardice or treachery that he absolutely refused to be concerned in the defence of the place, and he was suffered to escape in disguise, with a load of matches on his back; but he was afterward apprehended in Scotland, from whence he was sent to London to answer for his perfidy or misconduct.

After his retreat the townsmen chose Mr. Walker and Major Baker for their governors with joint authority; but this office they would not undertake until it had been offered to Colonel

Cunningham, as the officer next in command to Lundy; he rejected the proposal, and with Richards returned to England, where they were immediately cashiered. The two new governors, thus abandoned to their fate, began to prepare for a vigorous defence: indeed their courage seems to have transcended the bounds of discretion, for the place was very ill-fortified; their cannon, which did not exceed twenty pieces, were wretchedly mounted; they had not one engineer to direct their operations; they had a very small number of horse; the garrison consisted of people unacquainted with military discipline; they were destitute of provisions; they were besieged by a king, in person, at the head of a formidable army, directed by good officers, and supplied with all the necessary implements for a siege or battle.

The town was invested on April 20th; the batteries were soon opened, and several attacks were made with great impetuosity, but the besiegers were always repulsed with considerable loss; the townsmen gained divers advantages in repeated sallies, and would have held their enemies in the utmost contempt had they not been afflicted with a contagious distemper, as well as reduced to extremity by want of provisions; they were even tantalized in their distress, for they had the mortification to see some ships, which had arrived with supplies from England, prevented from sailing up the river by the batteries the enemy had raised on both sides, and a boom with which they had blocked up the channel.

At length a reënforcement arrived in the Lough, under the command of General Kirke, who had deserted his master, and been employed in the service of King William. He found means to convey intelligence to Walker that he had troops and provisions on board for their relief, but found it impracticable to sail up the river. He promised, however, that he would land a body of forces at the Inch, and endeavor to make a diversion in their favor, when joined by the troops at Inniskillen, which amounted to five thousand men, including two thousand cavalry. He said he expected six thousand men from England, where they were embarked before he set sail; he exhorted them to persevere in their courage and loyalty, and assured them that he would come to their relief at all hazards. The assurances enabled them to bear their miseries a little longer, though their numbers daily diminished. Major Baker dying, his place was filled by Colonel Michelburn, who now acted as colleague to Mr. Walker.

King James having returned to Dublin to be present at the Parliament, the command of his army devolved to the French general, Rosene,[1] who was exasperated by such an obstinate opposition by a handful of half-starved militia. He threatened to raze the town to its foundations and destroy the inhabitants without distinction of age or sex unless they would immediately submit themselves to their lawful sovereign. The governors treated his menaces with contempt, and published an order that no person, on pain of death, should talk of surrendering. They had now consumed the last remains of their provisions, and supported life by eating the flesh of horses, dogs, cats, rats, mice, and tallow, starch, and salted hides; and even this loathsome food began to fail. Rosene, finding them deaf to all his proposals, threatened to wreak his vengeance on all the Protestants of that county and drive them under the walls of Londonderry, where they should be suffered to perish by famine. The Bishop of Meath being informed of this design, complained to King James of the barbarous intention, entreating his majesty to prevent its being put into execution; that Prince assured him that he had already ordered Rosene to desist from such proceedings; nevertheless, the Frenchman executed his threats with the utmost rigor.

Parties of dragoons were detached on this cruel service. After having stripped all the Protestants for thirty miles round, they drove these unhappy people before them like cattle, without even sparing the enfeebled old men, nurses with infants at their breasts, and tender children. About four thousand of these miserable objects were driven under the walls of Londonderry. This expedient, far from answering the purpose of Rosene, produced a quite contrary effect. The besieged were so exasperated at this act of inhumanity that they resolved to perish rather than submit to such a barbarian. They erected a gibbet in sight of the enemy, and sent a message to the French general importing that they would hang all the prisoners they had taken during the siege unless the Protestants whom they had driven under the walls should be immediately dismissed. This threat produced a negotiation,

[1] James was assisted in his attempt by a small body of French troops, England having entered the Grand Alliance against Louis XIV.—ED.

in consequence of which the Protestants were released after they had been detained three days without tasting food. Some hundreds died of famine or fatigue; and those who lived to return to their own habitations found them plundered and sacked by the papists, so that the greater number perished for want, or were murdered by straggling parties of the enemy. Yet these very people had for the most part obtained protection from King James, to which no respect was paid by his general.

The garrison of Londonderry was now reduced from seven thousand to five thousand seven hundred men, and these were driven to such extremity of distress that they began to talk of killing the popish inhabitants and feeding on their bodies. Kirke, who had hitherto lain inactive, ordered two ships laden with provisions to sail up the river, under convoy of the Dartmouth (frigate); one of these, called the Mountjoy, broke the enemy's boom, and all the three—after having sustained a very hot fire from both sides of the river—arrived in safety at the town, to the inexpressible joy of the inhabitants.

The army of James was so dispirited by the success of this enterprise that they abandoned the siege in the night, and retired with precipitation, after having lost about nine thousand men before the place. Kirke no sooner took possession of the town than Walker was prevailed upon to embark for England, with an address of thanks from the inhabitants to their majesties for the seasonable relief they had received.

King James trusted so much to the disputes in the English Parliament that he did not believe his son-in-law would be able to quit that kingdom, and William had been six days in Ireland before he received intimation of his arrival. This was no sooner known than he left Dublin under the guard of the militia, commanded by Luttrel, and, with a reënforcement of six thousand infantry which he had lately received from France, joined the rest of his forces, which now almost equalled William's army in number, exclusive of about fifteen thousand men who remained in different garrisons. He occupied a very advantageous post on the bank of the Boyne, and, contrary to the advice of his general officers, resolved to stand battle. They proposed to strengthen their garrisons, and retire to the Shannon, to wait the effect of the operations at sea.

Louis had promised to equip a powerful armament against the English fleet, and send over a great number of small frigates to destroy William's transports, as soon as their convoy should be returned to England; the execution of this scheme was not at all difficult, and must have proved fatal to the English army, for their stores and ammunition were still on board; the ships sailed along the coast as the troops advanced in their march; and there was not one secure harbor into which they could retire on any emergency. James, however, was bent on hazarding an engagement, and expressed uncommon confidence and alacrity. Besides the river, which was deep, his front was secured by a morass and a rising ground; so that the English army could not attack him without manifest disadvantage.

King William marched up to the opposite bank of the river, and as he reconnoitred their situation was exposed to the fire of some field-pieces, which the enemy purposely planted against his person. They killed a man and two horses close by him, and the second bullet rebounding from the earth, grazed on his right shoulder, so as to carry off part of his clothes and skin and produce a considerable contusion. This accident, which he bore without the least emotion, created some confusion among his attendants, which, the enemy perceiving, concluded he was killed, and shouted aloud in token of their joy; the whole camp resounded with acclamation, and several squadrons of their horse were drawn down toward the river as if they intended to pass it immediately and attack the English army. The report was instantly communicated from place to place until it reached Dublin; from thence it was conveyed to Paris, where, contrary to the custom of the French court, the people were encouraged to celebrate the event with bonfires and illuminations.

William rode along the line to show himself to the army after this narrow escape. At night he called a council of war, and declared his resolution to attack the enemy in the morning. Schomberg [1] at first opposed his design, but, finding the King determined, he advised that a strong detachment of horse and foot should that night pass the Boyne at Slane bridge and take post

[1] The Duke of Schomberg, who commanded for William, had accompanied him to England in 1688. The Duke is further spoken of below. "Young Schomberg" was his son.—ED.

between the enemy and the pass at Duleck, that the action might be the more decisive; this counsel being rejected, the King determined that early in the morning Lieutenant-general Douglas with the right wing of the infantry, and young Schomberg with the horse, should pass at Slane bridge, while the main body of the foot should force their passage at Old bridge, and the left at certain fords between the enemy's camp and Drogheda. The Duke, perceiving that his advice was not relished by the Dutch generals, retired to his tent, where, the order of battle being brought to him, he received it with an air of discontent, saying it was the first that had ever been sent to him in that manner. The proper dispositions being made, William rode quite through the army by torchlight, and then retired to his tent after having given orders to his soldiers to distinguish themselves from the enemy by wearing green boughs in their hats during the action.

At six o'clock in the morning, General Douglas, with young Schomberg, the Earl of Portland, and Auverquerque, marched to Slane bridge, and passed the river with very little opposition. When they reached the farther bank they perceived the enemy drawn up in two lines, to a considerable number of horse and foot, with a morass in their front, so that Douglas was obliged to wait for reënforcements. This being arrived, the infantry was led on to the charge through the morass, while Count Schomberg rode round it with his cavalry, to attack the enemy in flank. The Irish, instead of waiting the assault, faced about, and retreated toward Duleck with some precipitation; yet not so fast but that Schomberg fell in among their rear, and did considerable execution. King James, however, soon reënforced his left wing from the centre; and the Count was in his turn obliged to send for assistance.

At this juncture King William's main body, consisting of the Dutch guards, the French regiments,[1] and some battalions of English, passed the river, which was waist-high, under a general discharge of artillery. King James had imprudently removed his cannon from the other side; but he had posted a strong body of musketeers along the bank, behind hedges, houses, and some works raised for the occasion; these poured in a close fire on the English troops before they reached the shore; but it produced

[1] French Protestants or Huguenots.—Ed.

very little effect. Then the Irish gave way, and some battalions landed without further opposition; yet before they could form, they were charged with great impetuosity by a squadron of the enemy's horse, and a considerable body of their cavalry and foot, commanded by General Hamilton, advanced from behind some little hillocks to attack those that were landed as well as to prevent the rest from reaching the shore; his infantry turned their backs and fled immediately; but the horse charged with incredible fury, both on the bank and in the river, so as to put the unformed regiments in confusion.

Then the Duke of Schomberg passed the river in person, put himself at the head of the French Protestants, and pointing to the enemy, "Gentlemen," said he, "those are your persecutors." With these words he advanced to the attack, where he himself sustained a violent onset from a party of the Irish horse, which had broken through one of the regiments and were now on their return. They were mistaken for English, and allowed to gallop up to the Duke, who received two severe wounds in the head; but the French troops, now sensible of their mistake, rashly threw in their fire on the Irish while they were engaged with the Duke, and, instead of saving, shot him dead on the spot.

The death of this general had wellnigh proved fatal to the English army, which was immediately involved in tumult and disorder; while the infantry of King James rallied and returned to their posts with a face of resolution. They were just ready to fall on the centre when King William, having passed with the left wing, composed of the Danish, Dutch, and Inniskillen horse, advanced to attack them on the right: they were struck with such a panic at his appearance that they made a sudden halt, and then facing about retreated to the village of Dunmore. There they made such a vigorous stand that the Dutch and Danish horse, though headed by the King in person, recoiled; even the Inniskillens gave way, and the whole wing would have been routed had not a detachment of dragoons, belonging to the regiment of Cunningham and Levison, dismounted and lined the hedges on each side of the ditch through which the fugitives were driven; there they did such execution on the pursuers as soon checked their ardor. The horse, which were broken, had now time to rally, and, returning to the charge, drove the enemy before them in their turn.

In this action General Hamilton, who had been the life and soul of the Irish during the whole engagement, was wounded and taken, an incident which discouraged them to such a degree that they made no further efforts to retrieve the advantage they had lost. He was immediately brought to the King, who asked him if he thought the Irish would make any further resistance, and he replied, "On my honor I believe they will, for they have still a good body of horse entire." William, eying him with a look of disdain, repeated, "Your honor, your honor!" but took no other notice of his having acted contrary to his engagement, when he was permitted to go to Ireland on promise of persuading Tyrconnel to submit to the new government. The Irish now abandoned the field with precipitation; but the French and Swiss troops, that acted as their auxiliaries under De Lauzun, retreated in good order, after having maintained the battle for some time with intrepidity and perseverance.

As King William did not think proper to pursue the enemy, the carnage was not great; the Irish lost a thousand five hundred men and the English about one-third of that number; though the victory was dearly purchased, considering the death of the gallant Duke of Schomberg, who fell, in the eighty-second year of his age, after having rivalled the best generals of that time in military reputation. He was the descendant of a noble family, in the Palatinate, and his mother was an Englishwoman, daughter of Lord Dudley. Being obliged to leave his country on account of the troubles by which it was agitated, he commenced a soldier of fortune, and served successively in the armies of Holland, England, France, Portugal, and Brandenburg; he attained to the dignity of mareschal in France, grandee in Portugal, generalissimo in Prussia, and duke in England. He professed the Protestant religion; was courteous and humble in his deportment; cool, penetrating, resolute, and sagacious, nor was his probity inferior to his courage.

This battle also proved fatal to the barve Caillemote, who had followed the Duke's fortunes, and commanded one of the Protestant regiments. After having received a mortal wound, he was carried back through the river by four soldiers, and, though almost in the agonies of death, he, with a cheerful countenance, encouraged those who were crossing to do their duty, exclaiming, "*À la gloire, mes enfants, à la gloire!*" ("To glory, my lads, to glory!"

The third remarkable person who lost his life on this occasion was Walker, the clergyman, who had so valiantly defended Londonderry against the whole army of King James; he had been very graciously received by King William, who gratified him with a reward of five thousand pounds and a promise of further favor; but, his military genius still predominating, he attended his royal patron in this battle, and, being shot, died in a few minutes.

The persons of distinction who fell on the other side were the Lords Dongan and Carlingford; Sir Neile O'Neile and the Marquis of Hocquincourt. James, himself, stood aloof during the action on the hill of Dunmore, surrounded with some squadrons of horse, and seeing victory declare against him retired to Dublin without having made the least effort to reassemble his broken forces. Had he possessed either spirit or conduct his army might have been rallied and reënforced from his garrisons, so as to be in a condition to keep the field and even to act on the offensive; for his loss was inconsiderable, and the victor did not attempt to molest his troops in their retreat, an omission which has been charged to him as a flagrant instance of misconduct. Indeed, through the whole of this engagement William's personal courage was much more conspicuous than his military skill.

SALEM WITCHCRAFT TRIALS

A.D. 1692

RICHARD HILDRETH

Among the people of Massachusetts during the century which saw the Pilgrims seek religious liberty there, a delusion broke out which not only spread horror through the community and caused suffering and disgrace even in the most respectable families, but has baffled all later attempts at explanation. The witchcraft madness, as manifested there and elsewhere in the world, has remained alike the puzzle of history and the riddle of psychology.

Historically, witchcraft is classed with other occult phenomena or practices connected with supposed supernatural influences. The famous trials and executions for witchcraft which took place in and near Salem, Massachusetts, toward the end of the seventeenth century, owed their special prominence to their peculiar localization and environment. Otherwise they might have been regarded as nothing more than incidents of a once general course in criminal procedure. Thousands in Europe had already suffered similar condemnation, and the last recorded execution for witchcraft in Great Britain did not occur till 1722. Even so late as 1805 a woman was imprisoned for this "crime" in Scotland.

Hildreth's account skilfully condenses the essential matters relating to this strange episode in Massachusetts history.

THE practice of magic, sorcery, and spells, in the reality of which all ignorant communities have believed, had long been a criminal offence in England. A statute of the thirty-third year of Henry VIII made them capital felonies. Another statute of the first year of James I, more specific in its terms, subjected to the same penalty all persons "invoking any evil spirit, or consulting, covenanting with, entertaining, employing, feeding, or rewarding any evil spirit, or taking up dead bodies from their graves to be used in any witchcraft, sorcery, charm, or enchantment, or killing or otherwise hurting any person by such infernal arts."

That second Solomon, before whom the illustrious Bacon bowed with so much reverence, was himself a firm believer in witchcraft. He professed, indeed, to be an adept in the art of detecting witches, an art which became the subject of several learned treatises, one of them from James' own royal pen. During the Commonwealth England had abounded with professional witch-detectors, who travelled from county to county, and occasioned the death of many unfortunate persons. The "Fundamentals" of Massachusetts contained a capital law against witchcraft, fortified by that express declaration of Scripture, "Thou shalt not suffer a witch to live."

Yet, among other evidences of departure from ancient landmarks, and of the propagation even to New England of a spirit of doubt, were growing suspicions as to the reality of that every-day supernaturalism which formed so prominent a feature of the Puritan theology. The zeal of Increase Mather against this rising incredulity had engaged him, while the old charter was still in existence, to publish a book of *Remarkable Providences*, in which were enumerated, among other things, all the supposed cases of witchcraft which had hitherto occurred in New England, with arguments to prove their reality.

What at that time had given the matter additional interest was the case of a bewitched or haunted house at Newbury. An intelligent neighbor, who had suggested that a mischievous grandson of the occupant might perhaps be at the bottom of the mystery, was himself accused of witchcraft and narrowly escaped. A witch, however, the credulous townspeople were resolved to find, and they presently fixed upon the wife of the occupant as the culprit. Seventeen persons testified to mishaps experienced in the course of their lives, which they charitably chose to ascribe to the ill-will and diabolical practices of this unfortunate old woman. On this evidence she was found guilty by the jury; but the magistrates, more enlightened, declined to order her execution. The deputies thereupon raised a loud complaint at this delay of justice. But the firmness of Governor Bradstreet, supported as he was by the moderate party, and the abrogation of the charter which speedily followed, saved the woman's life.

This same struggle of opinion existed also in the mother-country, where the rising sect of "freethinkers" began to deny and deride all diabolical agencies. Nor was this view confined to professed freethinkers. The latitudinarian party in the

Church, a rapidly growing body, leaned perceptibly the same way. The "serious ministers," on the other hand, led by Richard Baxter, their acknowledged head, defended with zeal the reality of witchcraft and the personality and agency of the devil, to deny which they denounced as little short of atheism. They supported their opinions by the authority of Sir Matthew Hale, lord chief justice of England, as distinguished for piety as for knowledge of the law, under whose instructions two alleged witches, at whose trials he had presided shortly after the Restoration, had been found guilty and executed. The accounts of those trials, published in England on occasion of this controversy and republished at Boston, had tended to confirm the popular belief. The doubts by which Mather had been alarmed were yet confined to a few thinking men. Read with a forward and zealous faith, these stories did not fail to make a deep impression on the popular imagination.

While Andros was still governor, shortly after Increase Mather's departure for England, four young children, members of a pious family in Boston, the eldest a girl of thirteen, the youngest a boy not five, had begun to behave in a singular manner, barking like dogs, purring like cats, seeming to become deaf, blind, or dumb, having their limbs strangely distorted, complaining that they were pinched, pricked, pulled, or cut—acting out, in fact, the effects of witchcraft, according to the current notions of it and the descriptions in the books above referred to. The terrified father called in Dr. Oakes, a zealous leader of the ultra-theocratic party—presently sent to England as joint agent with Mather—who gave his opinion that the children were bewitched. The oldest girl had lately received a bitter scolding from an old Irish indented servant, whose daughter she had accused of theft.

This same old woman, from indications no doubt given by the children, was soon fixed upon as being the witch. The four ministers of Boston and another from Charlestown having kept a day of fasting and prayer at the troubled house, the youngest child was relieved. But the others, more persevering and more artful, continuing as before, the old woman was presently arrested and charged with bewitching them. She had for a long time been reputed a witch, and she even seems to have flattered herself that she was one. Indeed, her answers were so "senseless" that the magistrates referred it to the doctors to say if she were not "crazed in her intellects." On their report of her sanity, the old woman was tried, found guilty, and executed.

Though Increase Mather was absent on this interesting occasion, he had a zealous representative in his son, Cotton Mather, by the mother's side grandson of the "Great Cotton," a young minister of twenty-five, a prodigy of learning, eloquence, and piety, recently settled as colleague with his father over Boston North Church. Cotton Mather had an extraordinary memory, stuffed with all sorts of learning. His application was equal to that of a German professor. His lively imagination, trained in the school of Puritan theology, and nourished on the traditionary legends of New England, of which he was a voracious and indiscriminate collector, was still further stimulated by fasts, vigils, prayers, and meditations almost equal to those of any Catholic saint. Of a temperament ambitious and active, he was inflamed with a great desire of "doing good." Fully conscious of all his gifts, and not a little vain of them, like the Jesuit missionaries in Canada, his contemporaries, he believed himself to be often, during his devotional exercises, in direct and personal communication with the Deity.

In every piece of good-fortune he saw a special answer to his prayers; in every mortification or calamity, the special personal malice of the devil and his agents. Yet both himself and his father were occasionally troubled with "temptations to atheism," doubts which they did not hesitate to ascribe to diabolical influence. The secret consciousness of these doubts of their own was perhaps one source of their great impatience at the doubts of others.

Cotton Mather had taken a very active part in the late case of witchcraft; and, that he might study the operations of diabolical agency at his leisure, and thus be furnished with evidence and arguments to establish its reality, he took the eldest of the bewitched children home to his own house. His eagerness to believe invited imposture. His excessive vanity and strong prejudices made him easy game. Adroit and artful beyond her years, the girl fooled him to the top of his bent. His ready pen was soon furnished with materials for "a story all made up of wonders," which, with some other matters of the same sort, and a sermon preached on the occasion, he presently published, under the title of *Memorable Providences relating to Witchcrafts and Possessions*, with a preface in which he warned all "Sadducees" that he should regard their doubts for the future as a personal insult.

Cotton Mather was not the only dupe. "The old heresy of the sensual Sadducees, denying the being of angels either good or evil," says the recommendatory preface to this book, signed by the other four ministers of Boston, "died not with them, nor will it, whilst men, abandoning both faith and reason, count it their wisdom to credit nothing but what they see or feel. How much this fond opinion hath gotten ground in this debauched age is awfully observable; and what a dangerous stroke it gives to settle men in atheism is not hard to discern. God is therefore pleased, besides the witness borne to this truth in Sacred Writ, to suffer devils sometimes to do such things in the world as shall stop the mouths of gainsayers, and extort a confession from them."

They add their testimony to the truth of Mather's statements, which they commend as furnishing "clear information" that there is "both a God and a devil, and witchcraft." The book was presently republished in London, with a preface by Baxter, who pronounced the girl's case so "convincing" that "he must be a very obdurate Sadducee who would not believe it."

Mather's sermon, prefixed to this narrative, is a curious specimen of fanatical declamation. "Witchcraft," he exclaims, "is a renouncing of God, and the advancement of a filthy devil into the throne of the Most High. Witchcraft is a renouncing of Christ, and preferring the communion of a loathsome, lying devil before all the salvation of the Lord Redeemer. Witchcraft is a siding with hell against heaven and earth, and therefore a witch is not to be endured in either of them. 'Tis a capital crime, and is to be prosecuted as a species of devilism that would not only deprive God and Christ of all his honor, but also plunder man of all his comfort. Nothing too vile can be said of, nothing too hard can be done to, such a horrible iniquity as witchcraft is!"

Such declamations from such a source, giving voice and authority to the popular superstition, prepared the way for the tragedy that followed. The suggestion, however, that Cotton Mather, for purposes of his own, deliberately got up this witchcraft delusion, and forced it upon a doubtful and hesitating people, is utterly absurd. And so is another suggestion, a striking exhibition of partisan extravagance, that because the case of the four Boston children happened during the government of Andros, therefore the responsibility of that affair rests on him, and not on the people of Massachusetts. The Irish woman was tried under a Massachusetts law, and convicted by a Massachusetts jury; and, had Andros interfered to save her life, to the other charges against him would doubtless have been added that of friendship for witches.

Cotton Mather seems to have acted, in a degree, the part of a demagogue. Yet he is not to be classed with those tricky and dishonest men, so common in our times, who play upon popular prejudices which they do not share, in the expectation of being elevated to honors and office. Mather's position, convictions, and temperament alike called him to serve on this occasion as the organ, exponent, and stimulator of the popular faith.

The bewitched girl, as she ceased to be an object of popular attention, seems to have returned to her former behavior. But the seed had been sown on fruitful ground. After an interval of nearly four years, three young girls in the family of Parris, minister of Salem village, now Danvers, began to exhibit similar pranks. As in the Boston case, a physician pronounced them bewitched, and Tituba, an old Indian woman, the servant of Parris, who undertook, by some vulgar rites, to discover the witch, was rewarded by the girls with the accusation of being herself the cause of their sufferings. The neighboring ministers assembled at the house of Parris for fasting and prayer. The village fasted; and presently a general fast was ordered throughout the colony. The "bewitched children," thus rendered objects of universal sympathy and attention, did not long want imitators. Several other girls and two or three women of the neighborhood began to be afflicted in the same way, as did also John, the Indian husband of Tituba, warned, it would seem, by the fate of his wife.

Parris took a very active part in discovering the witches; so did Noyes, minister of Salem, described as "a learned, a charitable, and a good man." A town committee was soon formed for the detection of the witches. Two of the magistrates, resident at Salem, entered with great zeal into the matter. The accusations, confined at first to Tituba and two other friendless women, one crazed, the other bedrid, presently included two female members of Parris' church, in which, as in so many other churches, there had been some sharp dissensions. The next Sunday after this accusation Parris preached from the verse, "Have I not chosen you twelve, and one is a devil?" At the announcement of this text the sister of one of the accused women rose and left the meeting-house. She, too, was accused immediately after, and the same fate soon overtook all who showed the least disposition to resist the prevailing delusion.

The matter had now assumed so much importance that the Deputy-governor—for the provisional government was still in operation—proceeded to Salem village, with five other magistrates, and held a court in the meeting-house. A great crowd was present. Parris acted at once as clerk and accuser, producing the witnesses, and taking down the testimony. The accused were held with their arms extended and hands open, lest by the least motion of their fingers they might inflict torments on their victims, who sometimes affected to be struck dumb, and at others to be knocked down by the mere glance of an eye. They were haunted, they said, by the spectres of the accused, who tendered them a book, and solicited them to subscribe a league with the devil; and when they refused, would bite, pinch, scratch, choke, burn, twist, prick, pull, and otherwise torment them. At the mere sight of the accused brought into court, "the afflicted" would seem to be seized with a fit of these torments, from which, however, they experienced instant relief when the accused were compelled to touch them—infallible proof to the minds of the gaping assembly that these apparent sufferings were real and the accusations true. The theory was that the touch conveyed back into the witch the malignant humors shot forth from her eyes; and learned references were even made to Descartes, of whose new philosophy some rumors had reached New England, in support of this theory.

In the examinations at Salem village meeting-house some

very extraordinary scenes occurred. "Look there!" cried one of the afflicted; "there is Goody Procter on the beam!" This Goody Procter's husband, notwithstanding the accusation against her, still took her side, and had attended her to the court; in consequence of which act of fidelity some of "the afflicted" began now to cry out that he too was a wizard. At the exclamation above cited, "many, if not all, the bewitched had grievous fits."

Question by the Court: "Ann Putnam, who hurts you?"

Answer: "Goodman Procter, and his wife, too."

Then some of the afflicted cry out, "There is Procter going to take up Mrs. Pope's feet!" and "immediately her feet are taken up."

Question by the Court: "What do you say, Goodman Procter, to these things?"

Answer: "I know not: I am innocent."

Abigail Williams, another of the afflicted, cries out, "There is Goodman Procter going to Mrs. Pope!" and "immediately said Pope falls into a fit."

A magistrate to Procter: "You see the devil will deceive you; the children," so all the afflicted were called, "could see what you were going to do before the woman was hurt. I would advise you to repentance, for you see the devil is bringing you out."

Abigail Williams cries out again, "There is Goodman Procter going to hurt Goody Bibber!" and "immediately Goody Bibber falls into a fit." Abigail Williams and Ann Putnam both "made offer to strike at Elizabeth Procter; but when Abigail's hand came near, it opened, whereas it was made up into a fist before, and came down exceedingly lightly as it drew near to said Procter, and at length, with open and extended fingers, touched Procter's hood very lightly; and immediately Abigail cries out, 'My fingers, my fingers, my fingers burn!' and Ann Putnam takes on most grievously of her head, and sinks down."

Such was the evidence upon which people were believed to be witches, and committed to prison to be tried for their lives! Yet, let us not hurry too much to triumph over the past. In these days of animal magnetism, have we not ourselves seen imposture as gross, and even in respectable quarters a headlong credulity just as precipitate? We must consider also that the judgments of our ancestors were disturbed, not only by wonder, but by fear.

Encouraged by the ready belief of the magistrates and the public, "the afflicted" went on enlarging the circle of their accusations, which presently seemed to derive fresh corroboration from the confessions of some of the accused. Tituba had been flogged into a confession; others yielded to a pressure more stringent than blows. Weak women, astonished at the charges and contortions of their accusers, assured that they were witches beyond all doubt, and urged to confess as the only possible chance for their lives, were easily prevailed upon to repeat any tales put into their mouths: their journeys through the air on broomsticks to attend witch sacraments—a sort of travesty on the Christian ordinance—at which the devil appeared in the shape of a "small black man"; their signing the devil's book, renouncing their former baptism, and being baptized anew by the devil, who "dipped" them in "Wenham Pond," after the Anabaptist fashion.

Called upon to tell who were present at these sacraments, the confessing witches wound up with new accusations; and by the time Phipps arrived in the colony, near a hundred persons were already in prison. The mischief was not limited to Salem. An idea had been taken up that the bewitched could explain the causes of sickness; and one of them, carried to Andover for that purpose, had accused many persons of witchcraft, and thrown the whole village into the greatest commotion. Some persons also had been accused in Boston and other towns.

It was one of Governor Phipps' first official acts to order all the prisoners into irons. This restraint upon their motions might impede them, it was hoped, in tormenting the afflicted. Without waiting for the meeting of the General Court, to whom that authority properly belonged, Phipps hastened, by advice of his counsel, to organize a special court for the trial of the witches. Stoughton, the Lieutenant-governor, was appointed president; but his cold and hard temper, his theological education, and unyielding bigotry were ill qualifications for such an office. His associates, six in number, were chiefly Boston men, possessing a high reputation for wisdom and piety, among them Richards, the late agent, Wait Winthrop, brother of Fitz-John Winthrop, and grandson of the former Governor, and Samuel Sewell, the two latter subsequently, in turn, chief-justices of the province.

The new court, thus organized, proceeded to Salem, and commenced operations by the trial of an old woman who had long enjoyed the reputation of being a witch. Besides "spectral evidence," that is, the tales of the afflicted, a jury of women, appointed to make an examination, found upon her a wart or excrescence, adjudged to be "a devil's teat." A number of old stories were also raked up of dead hens and foundered cattle and carts upset, ascribed by the neighbors to her incantations. On this evidence she was brought in guilty, and hanged a few days after, when the court took an adjournment to the end of the month.

The first General Court under the new charter met meanwhile, and Increase Mather, who had returned in company with Phipps, gave an account of his agency. From a House not well pleased with the loss of the old charter he obtained a reluctant vote of thanks, but he received no compensation for four years' expenses, which had pressed very heavily upon his narrow income. After passing a temporary act for continuing in force all the old laws, among others the capital law against witchcraft, an adjournment was had, without any objection or even reference, so far as appears, to the special court for the trial of the witches, which surely would have raised a great outcry had it been established for any unpopular purpose.

According to a favorite practice of the old Government, now put in use for the last time, Phipps requested the advice of the elders as to the proceedings against the witches. The reply, drawn up by the hand of Cotton Mather, acknowledges with thankfulness "the success which the merciful God has given to the sedulous and assiduous endeavors of our honorable rulers to defeat the abominable witchcrafts which have been committed in the country, humbly praying that the discovery of those mysterious and mischievous wickednesses may be perfected." It advises, however, "critical and exquisite caution" in relying too much on "the devil's authority," that is, on spectral evidence, or "apparent changes wrought in the afflicted by the presence of the accused"; neither of which, in the opinion of the ministers, could be trusted as infallible proof. Yet it was almost entirely on this sort of evidence that all the subsequent convictions were had. Stoughton, unfortunately, had espoused the opinion—certainly a plausible one—that it was impossible for the devil to assume the appearance of an innocent man, or for persons not witches to be spectrally seen at witches' meetings; and some of the confessing witches were prompt to flatter the chief justice's vanity by confirming a doctrine so apt for their purposes.

At the second session of the special court five women were tried and convicted. The others were easily disposed of; but in the case of Rebecca Nurse, one of Parris' church-members, a woman hitherto of unimpeachable character, the jury at first gave a verdict of acquittal. At the announcement of this verdict "the afflicted" raised a great clamor. The "honored Court" called the jury's attention to an exclamation of the prisoner during the trial, expressive of surprise at seeing among the witnesses two of her late fellow-prisoners: "Why do these testify against me? They used to come among us!" These two witnesses had turned confessors, and these words were construed by the court as confirming their testimony of having met the prisoner at witches' meetings. The unhappy woman, partially deaf, listened to this colloquy in silence. Thus pressed by the Court, and hearing no reply from the prisoner, the jury changed their verdict and pronounced her guilty. The explanations subsequently offered in her behalf were disregarded. The Governor, indeed, granted a reprieve, but the Salem committee procured its recall, and the unhappy woman, taken in chains to the meeting-house, was solemnly excommunicated, and presently hanged with the others.

At the third session of the court six prisoners were tried and convicted, all of whom were presently hanged except Elizabeth Procter, whose pregnancy was pleaded in delay. Her true and faithful husband, in spite of a letter to the Boston ministers, denouncing the falsehood of the witnesses, complaining that confessions had been extorted by torture, and begging for a trial at Boston or before other judges, was found guilty, and suffered with the rest. Another of this unfortunate company was John Willard, employed as an officer to arrest the accused, but whose imprudent expression of some doubts on the subject had caused him to be accused also. He had fled, but was pursued and taken, and was now tried and executed. His behavior, and that of Procter, at the place of execution, made, however, a deep impression on many minds.

A still more remarkable case was that of George Burroughs, a minister whom the incursions of the Eastern Indians had lately driven from Saco back to Salem village, where he had formerly preached, and where he now found among his former parishioners enemies more implacable even than the Indians. It was the misfortune of Burroughs to have many enemies, in part, perhaps, by his own fault. Encouragement was thus found to accuse him. Some of the witnesses had seen him at witches' meetings; others had seen the apparitions of his dead wives, which accused him of cruelty. These witnesses, with great symptoms of horror and alarm, even pretended to see these dead wives again appearing to them in open court. Though small of size, Burroughs was remarkably strong, instances of which were given in proof that the devil helped him. Stoughton treated him with cruel insolence, and did his best to confuse and confound him.

What insured his condemnation was a paper he handed to the jury, an extract from some author, denying the possibility of witchcraft. Burroughs' speech from the gallows affected many, especially the fluent fervency of his prayers, concluding with the Lord's Prayer, which no witch, it was thought, could repeat correctly. Several, indeed, had been already detected by some slight error or mispronunciation in attempting it. The impression, however, which Burroughs might have produced was neutralized by Cotton Mather, who appeared on horseback among the crowd, and took occasion to remind the people that Burroughs, though a preacher, was no "ordained" minister, and that the devil would sometimes assume even the garb of an angel of light.

At a fourth session of the court six women were tried and found guilty. At another session shortly after, eight women and one man were convicted, all of whom received sentence of death. An old man of eighty, who refused to plead, was pressed to death —a barbarous infliction prescribed by the common law for such cases.

Ever since the trials began, it had been evident that confession was the only avenue to safety. Several of those now found guilty confessed and were reprieved; but Samuel Woodwell, having retracted his confession, along with seven others who persisted in their innocence, was sent to execution. "The afflicted" numbered by this time about fifty; fifty-five had confessed themselves witches and turned accusers; twenty persons had already suffered death; eight more were under sentence; the jails were full of prisoners, and new accusations were added every day. Such was the state of things when the court adjourned to the first Monday in November.

Cotton Mather employed this interval in preparing his *Wonders of the Invisible World*, containing an exulting account of the late trials, giving full credit to the statements of the afflicted and the confessors, and vaunting the good effects of the late executions in "the strange deliverance of some that had lain for many years in a most sad condition, under they knew not what evil hand."

While the witch trials were going on, the Governor had hastened to Pemaquid, and in accordance with instructions brought with him from England, though at an expense to the province which caused loud complaints, had built there a strong stone fort. Colonel Church had been employed, in the mean time, with four hundred men, in scouring the shores of the Penobscot and the banks of the Kennebec.

Notwithstanding some slight cautions about trusting too much to spectral evidence, Mather's book, which professed to be published at the special request of the Governor, was evidently intended to stimulate to further proceedings. But, before its publication, the reign of terror had already reached such a height as to commence working its own cure. The accusers, grown bold with success, had begun to implicate persons whose character and condition had seemed to place them beyond the possibility of assault. Even "the generation of the children of God" were in danger. One of the Andover ministers had been implicated; but two of the confessing witches came to his rescue by declaring that they had surreptitiously carried his shape to a witches' meeting, in order to create a belief that he was there. Hale, minister of Beverly, had been very active against the witches; but when his own wife was charged, he began to hesitate. A son of Governor Bradstreet, a magistrate of Andover, having refused to issue any more warrants, was himself accused, and his brother soon after, on the charge of bewitching a dog. Both were obliged to fly for their lives. Several prisoners, by the favor of friends, escaped to Rhode Island, but, finding themselves in danger there, fled to New York, where Governor Fletcher gave them protection. Their property was seized as forfeited by their flight. Lady Phipps, applied to in her husband's absence on behalf of an unfortunate prisoner, issued a warrant to the jailer in her own name, and had thus, rather irregularly, procured his discharge. Some of the accusers, it is said, began to throw out insinuations even against her.

The extraordinary proceedings on the commitments and trials; the determination of the magistrates to overlook the most obvious falsehoods and contradictions on the part of the afflicted and the confessors, under pretence that the devil took away their memories and imposed upon their brain, while yet reliance was placed on their testimony to convict the accused; the partiality exhibited in omitting to take any notice of certain accusations; the violent means employed to obtain confessions, amounting sometimes to positive torture; the total disregard of retractions made voluntarily, and even at the hazard of life—all these circumstances had impressed the attention of the more rational part of the community; and, in this crisis of danger and alarm, the meeting of the General Court was most anxiously awaited.

When that body assembled, a remonstrance came in from Andover against the condemnation of persons of good fame on the testimony of children and others "under diabolical influences." What action was taken on this remonstrance does not appear. The court was chiefly occupied in the passage of a number of acts, embodying some of the chief points of the old civil and criminal laws of the colony. The capital punishment of witchcraft was specially provided for in the very terms of the English act of Parliament. Heresy and blasphemy were also continued as capital offences. By the organization of the Superior Court under the charter, the special commission for the trial of witches was superseded. But of this Superior Court

Stoughton was appointed chief justice, and three of his four colleagues had sat with him in the special court.

There is no evidence that these judges had undergone any change of opinion; but when the new court proceeded to hold a special term at Salem for the continuation of the witch trials a decided alteration in public feeling became apparent. Six women of Andover renounced their confessions, and sent in a memorial to that effect. Of fifty-six indictments laid before the grand jury, only twenty-six were returned true bills. Of the persons tried, three only were found guilty. Several others were acquitted, the first instances of the sort since the trials began.

The court then proceeded to Charlestown, where many were in prison on the same charge. The case of a woman who for twenty or thirty years had been reputed a witch, was selected for trial. Many witnesses testified against her; but the spectral evidence had fallen into total discredit, and was not used. Though as strong a case was made out as any at Salem, the woman was acquitted, with her daughter, granddaughter, and several others. News presently came of a reprieve for those under sentence of death at Salem, at which Stoughton was so enraged that he left the bench, exclaiming, "Who it is that obstructs the course of justice I know not; the Lord be merciful to the country!" nor did he again take his seat during that term.

At the first session of the Superior Court at Boston the grand jury, though sent out to reconsider the matter, refused to find a bill even against a confessing witch.

The idea was already prevalent that some great mistakes had been committed at Salem. The reality of witchcraft was still insisted upon as zealously as ever, but the impression was strong that the devil had used "the afflicted" as his instruments to occasion the shedding of innocent blood. On behalf of the ministers, Increase Mather came out with his *Cases of Conscience concerning Witchcraft*, in which, while he argued with great learning that spectral evidence was not infallible, and that the devil might assume the shape of an innocent man, he yet strenuously maintained as sufficient proof confession, or "the speaking such words or the doing such things as none but such as have familiarity with the devil ever did or can do." As to such as falsely confessed themselves witches, and were hanged in consequence, Mather thought that was no more than they deserved.

King William's veto on the witchcraft act prevented any further trials; and presently, by Phipps' order, all the prisoners were discharged. To a similar veto Massachusetts owes it that heresy and blasphemy ceased to appear as capital crimes on her statute-book.

The Mathers gave still further proof of faith unshaken by discovering an afflicted damsel in Boston, whom they visited and prayed with, and of whose case Cotton Mather wrote an account circulated in manuscript. This damsel, however, had the discretion to accuse nobody, the spectres that beset her being all veiled. Reason and common-sense at last found an advocate in Robert Calef, a citizen of Boston, sneered at by Cotton Mather as "a weaver who pretended to be a merchant." And afterward, when he grew more angry, as "a coal sent from hell" to blacken his character—a man, however, of sound intelligence and courageous spirit. Calef wrote an account, also handed about in manuscript, of what had been said and done during a visitation of the Mathers to this afflicted damsel, an exposure of her imposture and their credulity, which so nettled Cotton Mather that he commenced a prosecution for slander against Calef, which, however, he soon saw reason to drop.

Calef then addressed a series of letters to Mather and the other Boston ministers, in which he denied and ridiculed the reality of any such compacts with the devil as were commonly believed in under the name of witchcraft. The witchcraft spoken of in the Bible meant no more, he maintained, than "hatred or opposition to the word and worship of God, and seeking to seduce therefrom by some sign"—a definition which he had found in some English writer on the subject, and which he fortified by divers texts.

It was, perhaps, to furnish materials for a reply to Calef that a circular from Harvard College, signed by Increase Mather as president, and by all the neighboring ministers as fellows, invited reports of "apparitions, possessions, enchantments, and all extraordinary things, wherein the existence and agency of the invisible world is more sensibly demonstrated," to be used "as some fit assembly of ministers might direct." But the "invisible world" was fast ceasing to be visible, and Cotton Mather laments that in ten years scarce five returns were received to this circular.

Yet the idea of some supernatural visitation at Salem was but very slowly relinquished, being still persisted in even by those penitent actors in the scene who confessed and lamented their own delusion and blood-guiltiness. Such were Sewell, one of the judges; Noyes, one of the most active prosecutors; and several of the jurymen who had sat on the trials. The witnesses upon whose testimony so many innocent persons had suffered were never called to any account. When Calef's letters were presently published in London, together with his account of the supposed witchcraft, the book was burned in the college yard at Cambridge by order of Increase Mather. The members of the Boston North Church came out also with a pamphlet in defence of their pastors. Hale, minister of Beverly, in his *Modest Inquiry into the Nature of Witchcraft,* and Cotton Mather, in his *Magnalia,* though they admit there had been "a going too far" in the affair at Salem, are yet still as strenuous as ever for the reality of witchcraft.

Nor were they without support from abroad. Dr. Watts, then one of the chief leaders of the English Dissenters, wrote to Cotton Mather, "I am persuaded there was much agency of the devil in those affairs, and perhaps there were some real witches, too." Twenty years elapsed before the heirs of the victims, and those who had been obliged to fly for their lives, obtained some partial indemnity for their pecuniary losses. Stoughton and Cotton Mather, though they never expressed the least regret or contrition for their part in the affair, still maintained their places in the public estimation. Just as the trials were concluded, Stoughton, though he held the King's commission as lieutenant-governor, was chosen a counsellor—a mark of confidence which the theocratic majority did not choose to extend to several of the moderate party named in the original appointment—and to this post he was annually reëlected as long as he lived; while Moody, because he had favored the escape of some of the accused, found it necessary to resign his pastorship of the First Church of Boston, and to return again to Portsmouth.

Yet we need less wonder at the pertinacity with which this

delusion was adhered to, when we find Addison arguing for the reality of witchcraft at the same time that he refuses to believe in any modern instance of it; and even Blackstone, half a century after, gravely declaring that "to deny the possibility, nay, actual existence of witchcraft and sorcery, is at once flatly to contradict the revealed word of God in various passages both of the Old and New Testament."

ESTABLISHMENT OF THE BANK OF ENGLAND

A.D. 1694

JOHN FRANCIS

Not only did the establishment of the Bank of England meet the demands of public exigency at the time; it also created an institution which was to become vitally important in the expanding life of the nation. This custodian of the public money and manager of the public debt of Great Britain is now the largest bank in the world. The only other financial institution that could show an equal record of long stability was the Bank of Amsterdam, which existed from 1609 to 1814.

The national debt of England began in 1693, when William III, in order to carry on the war against France, resorted to a system of loans. This debt, however, was not intended to be permanent; but when the Bank of England was established, the contracting of a permanent debt began. Its advantages and disadvantages to England have been discussed by many theorists and financial authorities. But of the extraordinary service rendered to Great Britain by the far-seeing Scotchman, William Paterson, originator of the plan of the Bank of England, there is no question, although, as Francis shows, the project at first met with opposition from many quarters.

THE important position assumed by England, toward the middle of the seventeenth century, renders the absence of a national bank somewhat surprising. Under the sagacious government of Cromwell the nation had increased in commercial and political greatness; and although several projects were issued for banks, one of which was to have branches in every important town throughout the country, yet, a necessity for their formation not being absolutely felt, the proposals were dismissed. During the Protectorate, however, Parliament, taking into consideration the rate of interest, which was higher in England than abroad, and that the trade was thereby rendered comparatively disadvantageous to the English merchant, reduced the legal rate from 8 to 6 per cent., and this measure, although it had been carried by the Parliament of Cromwell, almost every act of which proved odious in the eyes of the Stuarts, was nevertheless confirmed by the legislature of Charles II. In 1546 the payment of interest had been rendered legal, and fixed at 10 per cent. In 1624 the rate had been reduced to 8 per cent.; and with the advance of commercial prosperity it had been found advisable to lower it still further.

There were many reasons for the establishment of a national bank. It was necessary for the sake of a secure paper currency. It was required for the support of the national credit. It was desirable as a method of reducing the rate of interest paid by the state; a rate so high that, according to Anderson, men were induced to take their money out of trade, for the sake of securing it; an operation "big with mischief." The truth is that the times required it. The theorist may prove to demonstration the perfection of his theory; the speculator may show the certainty of its success: but unless it be a necessity called for by the onward progress of society, it must eventually fall to the ground.

That the want of such an establishment was felt is certain. But while such firms as Childs—the books of whom go back to the year 1620, and refer to prior documents; Hoares, dating from 1680; and Snows, from 1685—were able to assist the public demand, although at the exorbitant interest of the period, it does not occasion so much surprise that the attempt made to meet the increasing requirements of trade proved insufficient. In 1678, sixteen years previous to the foundation of the Bank of England, "proposals for a large model of a bank" were published; and, in 1683 a "national bank of credit" was brought forward. In a rare pamphlet entitled *Bank Credit; or the usefullness and security of The Bank of Credit, examined in a dialogue between a Country Gentleman and a London Merchant*, this idea is warmly defended. It was, however, simply to have one of credit, nor was it proposed to form a bank of deposit; although, by the following remark of the "Country Gentleman," it is evident that such an establishment on a secure scale was desirable. He says:

"Could they not without damage to themselves have secured the running cash of the nobility, gentry, merchants, and the traders of the city and kingdom, from all hazard, which would have been a great benefit to all concerned, who know not where to deposit their cash securely?"

After much trouble this bank of credit was established at Devonshire House, in Bishopsgate Street; its object, as we have related, being principally to advance money to tradesmen and manufacturers on the security of goods. Three-fourths of the value was lent on these, and bills for their amount given to the depositor. In order to render them current, an appointed number of persons in each trade was formed into a society to regulate commercial concerns. Any individual possessed of such bills might therefore obtain from this company goods or merchandise with as much ease as if he offered current coin.

The bank of credit does not appear to have flourished. The machinery was too complicated, and the risk of depreciation and the value of manufactures too great. It was next to impossible for such a company to exist after the Bank of England came with its low discount and free accommodations.

The wild spirit of speculation—that spirit which at various periods has created fearful crises in the commercial world—commenced in 1694. The fever which from time to time has flushed the mind of the moneyed man, and given a fierce excitement to the almost penniless adventurer, was then and in the following year in full operation. The great South Sea scheme in 1720 is ordinarily considered the earliest display of this reckless spirit. But a quarter of a century before, equal ingenuity and equal villany were exercised. Obscure men, whose sole capital was their enormous impudence, invented similar schemes, promised similar advantages, and used similar arts to entice the capitalists, which were employed with so much success at a later period.

The want of a great banking association was sure to be made a pretext. Two "land banks," and a "London bank" to be managed by the magistrates, with several other proposals, were therefore put promisingly forward. One of these was for another "bank of credit"; and a pamphlet published in 1694, under the title of *England's Glory*, will give some idea of its nature:

"If a person desires money to be returned at Coventry or York he pays it at the office in London, and receives a bill of credit after their form written upon marble paper, indenturewise, or on other as may be contrived to prevent counterfeiting." It was also proposed that the Government should share the profits; but neither of the projects was carried out.

The people neglected their calling. The legitimate desire of money grew into a fierce and fatal spirit of avarice. The arts so common at a later day were had recourse to. Project begat project, copper was to be turned into brass. Fortunes were to be realized by lotteries. The sea was to yield the treasures it had engulfed. Pearl-fisheries were to pay impossible percentages. "Lottery on lottery," says a writer of the day, "engine on engine, multiplied wonderfully. If any person got considerably by a happy and useful invention, others followed in spite of the patent, and published printed proposals, filling the daily newspapers therewith, thus going on to jostle one another, and abuse the credulity of the people."

Amid the many delusive and impracticable schemes were two important projects which have conferred great benefits on the English people. The first of these was the New River Company, the conception of Sir Hugh Middleton; the second was the corporation of the Bank of England. Nature and the great nations of antiquity suggested the former; the force and pressure of the times demanded the latter. It is from such demands that our chief institutions arise. By precept we may be taught their propriety; by example we may see their advantages. But until the necessity is personally felt they are sure to be neglected; and men wonder at their want of prescience and upbraid their shortsightedness when, with a sudden and sometimes startling success, the proposal they have slighted arises through the energy of another.

William Paterson, one of those men whose capacity is measured by failure or success, was the originator of the new bank; and it is perhaps unfortunate for his fame that no biography exists of this remarkable person. As the projector of the present Bank of Scotland, as the very soul of the celebrated Darien Company, and as the founder of the Bank of England, he deserves notice. A speculator as well as an adventurous man, he proved his belief in the practicability of the Darien scheme by accompanying that unfortunate expedition; and the formation of the Bank of England was the object of his desires and the subject of his thoughts for a long time previous to its establishment.

From that political change which had been so justly termed the "great revolution," to the establishment of the Bank of England, the new Government had been in constant difficulties; and the ministerial mode of procuring money was degrading to a great people. The duties in support of the war waged for liberty and Protestantism were required before they were levied. The city corporation was usually applied to for an advance; interest which varied probably according to the necessity of the borrower rather than to the real value of cash, was paid for the accommodation. The officers of the city went round in their turn to the separate wards, and borrowed in smaller amounts the money they had advanced to the state. Interest and premiums were thus often paid to the extent of 25 and even 30 per cent., in proportion to the exigency of the case, and the trader found his pocket filled at the expense of the public. Mr. Paterson gives a graphic description:

"The erection of this famous bank not only relieved the ministerial managers from their frequent processions into the city, for borrowing of money on the best and nearest public securities, at 10 or 12 per cent. per annum, but likewise gave life and currency to double or treble the value of its capital in other branches of the public credit, and so, under God, became the principal means of the success of the campaign in 1695; as, particularly, in reducing the important fortress of Namur, the first material step toward the peace concluded in 1679."

To remedy this evil the Bank of England was projected; and after much labor, William Paterson, aided by Mr. Michael Godfrey, procured from Government a consideration of the proposal. The King was abroad when the scheme was laid before the council, but the Queen occupied his place. Here considerable opposition occurred. Paterson found it more difficult to procure consent than he anticipated, and all those who feared an invasion of their interests united to stop its progress. The goldsmith foresaw the destruction of his monopoly, and he opposed it from self-interest. The Tory foresaw an easier mode of gaining money for the government he abhorred, with a firmer hold on the people for the monarch he despised, and his antagonism bore all the energy of political partisanship.

The usurer foresaw the destruction of his oppressive extortion, and he resisted it with the vigor of his craft. The rich man foresaw his profits diminished on government contracts, and he vehemently and virtuously opposed it on all public principles. Loud therefore were the outcries and great the exertions of all parties when the bill was first introduced to the House of Commons. But outcries are vain and exertions futile in opposition to a dominant and powerful party. A majority had been secured for the measure; and they who opposed its progress covered their defeat with vehement denunciations and vague prophecies. The prophets are in their graves, and their predictions only survive in the history of that establishment the downfall of which they proclaimed.

"The scheme of a national bank," says Smollett, "had been recommended to the ministry for the credit and security of the Government and the increase of trade and circulation. William Paterson was author of that which was carried into execution. When it was properly digested in the cabinet, and a majority in Parliament secured, it was introduced into the House of Commons. The supporters said it would rescue the nation out of the hands of extortioners; lower interest; raise the value of land; revive public credit; extend circulation; improve commerce; facilitate the annual supplies; and connect the people more closely with Government. The project was violently opposed by a strong party, who affirmed that it would become a monopoly, and engross the whole of the kingdom; that it might be employed to the worst purposes of arbitrary power; that it would weaken commerce by tempting people to withdraw their money from trade; that brokers and jobbers would prey on their fellow-creatures; encourage fraud and gambling; and corrupt the morals of the nation."

Previous governments had raised money with comparative ease because they were legitimate. That of William was felt to be precarious. It was feared by the money-lender that a similar convulsion to the one which had borne him so easily to the throne of a great nation might waft him back to the shores of that Holland he so dearly loved. Thus the very circumstances which made supplies necessary also made them scarce.

In addition to these things his person was unpopular. His phlegmatic Dutch habits contrasted unfavorably with those of the graceful Stuarts, whose evil qualities were forgotten in the remembrance of their showy characteristics. Neither his Dutch followers nor his Dutch manners were regarded with favor; and had it not been for his eminently kingly capacity, these things would have proved as dangerous to the throne as they tended to make the sovereign unpopular. In a pamphlet published a few years after the establishment of the new corporation is the following vivid picture of this monarch's government:

"In spite of the most glorious Prince and most vigilant General the world has ever seen, yet the enemy gained upon us every year; the funds were run down, the credit jobbed away in Change Alley, the King and his troops devoured by mechanics, and sold to usury, tallies lay bundled up like Bath fagots in the hands of brokers and stock-jobbers; the Parliament gave taxes, levied funds, but the loans were at the mercy of those men (the jobbers); and they showed their mercy, indeed, by devouring the King and the army, the Parliament, and indeed the whole nation; bringing their great Prince sometimes to that exigence through inexpressible extortions that were put upon him, that he has even gone into the fields without his equipage, nay even without his army; the regiments have been unclothed when the King had been in the field, and the willing, brave English spirits, eager to honor their country, and follow such a King, have marched even to battle without either stockings or shoes, while his servants have been every day working in Exchange Alley to get his men money of the stock-jobbers, even after all the horrible demands of discount have been allowed; and at last, scarce 50 per cent. of the money granted by Parliament has come into the hands of the Exchequer, and that late, too late for service, and by driblets, till the King has been tired with the delay."

This is a strange picture; beating even Mr. Paterson's account of the "processions in the city," and adds another convincing proof of the necessity which then existed for some establishment, capable of advancing money at a reasonable rate, on the security of Parliamentary grants.

The scheme proposed by William Paterson was too important not to meet with many enemies, and it appears from a pamphlet by Mr. Godfrey, the first deputy-governor, that "some pretended to dislike the bank only for fear it should disappoint their majesties of the supplies proposed to be raised." That "all the several companies of oppressors are strangely alarmed, and exclaim at the bank, and seemed to have joined in a confederacy against it." That "extortion, usury, and oppression were never so attacked as they are likely to be by the bank." That "others pretend the bank will join with the prince to make him absolute. That the concern have too good a bargain and that it would be prejudicial to trade." In Bishop Burnet's *History of His Own Times* we read an additional evidence of its necessity:

"It was visible that all the enemies of the Government set themselves against it with such a vehemence of zeal that this alone convinced all people that they saw the strength that our affairs would receive from it. I heard the Dutch often reckon the great advantage they had had from their banks, and they concluded that as long as England remained jealous of her Government, a bank could never be settled among us, nor gain credit among us to support itself, and upon that they judged that the superiority in trade must still be on their side."

All these varied interests were vainly exerted to prevent the bill from receiving the royal sanction; and the Bank of England, founded on the same principles which guarded the banks of Venice and Genoa, was incorporated by royal charter, dated July 27, 1694. From Mr. Gilbart's *History and Principles of Banking* we present the following brief analysis of this important act:

"The Act of Parliament by which the Bank was established is entitled 'An Act for granting to their majesties several duties upon tonnage of ships and vessels, and upon beer, ale, and other liquors, for securing certain recompenses and advantages in the said Act mentioned to such persons as shall voluntarily advance the sum of fifteen hundred thousand pounds toward carrying on the war with France.' After a variety of enactments relative to the duties upon tonnage of ships and vessels, and upon beer, ale, and other liquors, the Act authorizes the raising of 1,200,000 pounds by voluntary subscription, the subscribers to be formed into a corporation and be styled 'The Governor and Company of the Bank of England.'

"The sum of 300,000 pounds was also to be raised by subscription, and the contributors to receive instead annuities for one, two, or three lives. Toward the 1,200,000 pounds no one person was to subscribe more than 10,000 pounds before the first day of July, next ensuing, nor at any time more than 20,000 pounds. The Corporation were to lend their whole capital to the Government, for which they were to receive interest at the rate of 8 per cent. per annum, and 4000 pounds per annum for management; being 100,000 pounds per annum on the whole. The Corporation were not allowed to borrow or owe more than the amount of their capital, and if they did so the individual members became liable to the creditors in proportion to the amount of their stock. The Corporation were not to trade in any 'goods, wares, or merchandise whatever, but they were allowed to deal in bills of Exchange, gold or silver bullion, and to sell any goods, wares, or merchandise upon which they had advanced money, and which had not been redeemed within three months after the time agreed upon.' The whole of the subscription was filled in a few days; 25 per cent. paid down; and, as we have seen, a charter was issued on July 27, 1694, of which the following are the most important points:

"That the management and government of the corporation be admitted to the governor, deputy-governor, and twenty-four directors, who shall be elected between March 25th and April 25th of each year, from among the members of the company, duly qualified.

"That no dividend shall at any time be made by the said governor and company save only out of the interest, profit, or produce arising out of the said capital, stock, or fund, or by such dealing as is allowed by act of Parliament.

"They must be natural-born subjects of England, or naturalized subjects; they shall have in their own name and for their own use, severally, viz., the governor at least 4000 pounds, the deputy-governor 3000 pounds, and each director 2000 pounds of the capital stock of the said corporation.

"That thirteen or more of the said governors or directors (of which the governor or deputy-governor shall be always one) shall constitute a court of directors for the management of the affairs of the company, and for the appointment of all agents and servants which may be necessary, paying them such salaries as they may consider reasonable.

"Every elector must have, in his own name and for his own use, 500 pounds or more capital stock, and can only give one vote; he must, if required by any member present, take the oath of stock, or the declaration of stock if it be one of those people called Quakers.

"Four general courts to be held in every year in the months of September, December, April, and July. A general court may be summoned at any time, upon the requisition of nine proprietors duly qualified as electors.

"The majority of electors in general courts have the power to make and constitute by-laws and ordinances for the government of the corporation, provided that such by-laws and ordinances be not repugnant to the laws of the kingdom, and be confirmed and approved according to the statutes in such case made and provided."

When the payment was completed it was handed into the exchequer, and the bank procured from other quarters the funds which it required. It employed the same means which the bankers had done at the Exchange, with this difference, that the latter traded with personal property, while the bank traded with the deposits of their customers. It was from the circulation of a capital so formed that the bank derived its profits. It is evident, however, from the pamphlet of the first deputy-governor, that at this period they allowed interest to their depositors; and another writer, D'Avenant, makes it a subject of complaint: "It would be for the general good of trade if the bank were restrained from allowing interest for running cash; for the ease of having 3 and 4 per cent. without trouble must be a continual bar to industry."

First in Mercers' Hall, where they remained but a few months, and afterward in Grocers' Hall, since razed for the erection of a more stately structure, the Bank of England conducted its operations. Here, in one room, with almost primitive simplicity were gathered all who performed the duties of the establishment. "I looked into the great hall where the bank is kept," says the graceful essayist of the day, "and was not a little pleased to see the directors, secretaries, and clerks, with all the other members of that wealthy Corporation, ranged in their several stations according to the parts they hold in that just and regular economy." The secretaries and clerks altogether numbered but fifty-four, while their united salaries did not exceed four thousand three hundred fifty pounds. But the picture is a pleasant one, and though so much unlike present usages it is doubtful whether our forefathers did not derive more benefit from intimate association with and kindly feelings toward their inferiors than their descendants receive from the broad line of demarcation adopted at the present day.

The effect of the new corporation was almost immediately experienced. On August 8th, in the year of its establishment, the rate of discount on foreign bills was 6 per cent.; although this was the highest legal interest, yet much higher rates had been previously demanded. The name of William Paterson was not long upon the list of directors. The bank was established in 1694, and for that year only was its founder among those who managed its proceedings. The facts which led to his departure from the honorable post of director are difficult to collect; but it is not at all improbable that the character of Paterson was too speculative for those with whom he was joined in companionship. Sir John Dalrymple remarks, "The persons to whom he applied made use of his ideas, took the honor to themselves, were civil to him awhile, and neglected him afterward." Another writer says, "The friendless Scot was intrigued out of his post and out of the honors he had earned." These assertions must be received with caution; accusations against a great body are easily made; and it is rarely consistent with the dignity of the latter to reply; they are received as truths either because people are too idle to examine or because there is no opportunity of investigating them.

COLONIZATION OF LOUISIANA

A.D. 1699

CHARLES E. T. GAYARRÉ

It was not only as the beginning of what was to become an important State of the American Union, but also as a nucleus of occupation which led to an immense acquisition of territory by the United States, that the first settlement in Louisiana proved an event of great significance. Nothing in American history is of greater moment than the adding of the Louisiana Purchase (1803) to the United States domain. And the acquisition of that vast region, extending from New Orleans to British America, and westward from the Mississippi to the Rocky Mountains, had historic connection with the French settlement of 1699.

As early as 1630 the territory afterward known as Louisiana was mostly embraced in the Carolina grant by Charles I to Sir Robert Heath. It was taken into possession for the French King by La Salle in 1682, and named Louisiana in honor of Louis XIV. In 1698 Louis undertook to colonize the region of the lower Mississippi, and sent out an expedition under Pierre le Moyne, Sieur d'Iberville, a naval commander, who had served in the French wars of Canada, and aided in establishing French colonies in North America.

With two hundred colonists Iberville sailed (September 24, 1698) for the mouth of the Mississippi. Among his companions were his brothers, Sauvolle and Jean Baptiste le Moyne, Sieur de Bienville. The latter was long governor of Louisiana, and founded New Orleans. Of their arrival and subsequent operations in the lower Mississippi region, Gayarré, the Louisiana historian, gives a glowing and picturesque account.

ON February 27, 1699, Iberville and Bienville reached the Mississippi. When they approached its mouth they were struck with the gloomy magnificence of the sight. As far as the eye could reach, nothing was to be seen but reeds which rose five or six feet above the waters in which they bathed their roots. They waved mournfully under the blast of the sharp wind of the north, shivering in its icy grasp, as it tumbled, rolled, and gambolled on the pliant surface. Multitudes of birds of strange appearance, with their elongated shapes so lean that they looked like metamorphosed ghosts, clothed in plumage, screamed in the air, as if they were scared of one another. There was something agonizing in their shrieks that was in harmony with the desolation of the place. On every side of the vessel, monsters of the deep and huge alligators heaved themselves up heavily from their native or favorite element, and, floating lazily on the turbid waters, seemed to gaze at the intruders.

Down the river, and rumbling over its bed, there came a sort of low, distant thunder. Was it the voice of the hoary Sire of Rivers, raised in anger at the prospect of his gigantic volume of waters being suddenly absorbed by one mightier than he? In their progress it was with great difficulty that the travellers could keep their bark free from those enormous rafts of trees which the Mississippi seemed to toss about in mad frolic. A poet would have thought that the great river, when departing from the altitude of its birthplace, and as it rushed down to the sea through three thousand miles, had, in anticipation of a contest which threatened the continuation of its existence, flung its broad arms right and left across the continent, and, uprooting all its forests, had hoarded them in its bed as missiles to hurl at the head of its mighty rival when they should meet and struggle for supremacy.

When night began to cast a darker hue on a landscape on which the imagination of Dante would have gloated there issued from that chaos of reeds such uncouth and unnatural sounds as would have saddened the gayest and appalled the most intrepid. Could this be the far-famed Mississippi, or was it not rather old Avernus? It was hideous indeed—but hideousness refined into sublimity, filling the soul with a sentiment of grandeur. Nothing daunted, the adventurers kept steadily on their course. They knew that through those dismal portals they were to arrive at the most magnificent country in the world; they knew that awful screen concealed loveliness itself. It was a coquettish freak of nature, when dealing with European curiosity, as it came eagerly bounding to the Atlantic wave, to herald it through an avenue so sombre as to cause the wonders of the great valley of the Mississippi to burst with tenfold more force upon the bewildered gaze of those who, by the endurance of so many perils and fatigues, were to merit admittance into its Eden.

It was a relief for the adventurers when, after having toiled up the river for ten days, they at last arrived at the village of the Bayagoulas. There they found a letter of Tonty[1] to La Salle, dated in 1685. The letter, or rather that "speaking bark" as the Indians called it, had been preserved with great reverence. Tonty, having been informed that La Salle was coming with a fleet from France to settle a colony on the banks of the Mississippi, had not hesitated to set off from the northern lakes, with twenty Canadians and thirty Indians, and to come down to the Balize to meet his friend, who had failed to make out the mouth of the Mississippi, and had been landed by Beaujeu on the shores of Texas. After having waited for some time, and ignorant of what had happened, Tonty, with the same indifference to fatigues and dangers of an appalling nature, retraced his way back, leaving a letter to La Salle to inform him of his disappointment. Is there not something extremely romantic in the characters of the men of that epoch? Here is Tonty undertaking, with the most heroic unconcern, a journey of nearly three thousand miles, through such difficulties as it is easy for us to imagine, and leaving a letter to La Salle, as a proof of his visit, in the same way that one would, in these degenerate days of effeminacy, leave a card at a neighbor's house.

The French extended their explorations up to the mouth of the Red River. As they proceeded through that virgin country, with what interest they must have examined every object that met their eyes, and listened to the traditions concerning De Soto,[2] and the more recent stories of the Indians on La Salle and the iron-handed Tonty! A coat of mail which was presented as having belonged to the Spaniards, and vestiges of their encampment on the Red River, confirmed the French in the belief that there was much of truth in the recitals of the Indians.

On their return from the mouth of the Red River the two brothers separated when they arrived at Bayou Manchac. Bienville was ordered to go down the river to the French fleet, to give information of what they had seen and heard. Iberville went through Bayou Manchac to those lakes which are known under the names of Pontchartrain and Maurepas. Louisiana

[1] Henry de Tonty was an Italian explorer who accompanied La Salle in his descent of the Mississippi (1681–1682).—Ed.

[2] De Soto explored this region in 1541.—Ed.

had been named from a king: was it not in keeping that those lakes should be called after ministers?

From the Bay of St. Louis, Iberville returned to his fleet, where, after consultation, he determined to make a settlement at the Bay of Biloxi. On the east side, at the mouth of the bay, as it were, there is a slight swelling of the shore, about four acres square, sloping gently to the woods in the background, and on the bay. Thus this position was fortified by nature, and the French skilfully availed themselves of these advantages. The weakest point, which was on the side of the forest, they strengthened with more care than the rest, by connecting with a strong intrenchment the two ravines, which ran to the bay in a parallel line to each other. The fort was constructed with four bastions, and was armed with twelve pieces of artillery. When standing on one of the bastions which faced the bay, the spectator enjoyed a beautiful prospect. On the right, the bay could be seen running into the land for miles, and on the left stood Deer Island, concealing almost entirely the broad expanses of water which lay beyond. It was visible only at the two extreme points of the island, which both, at that distance, appeared to be within a close proximity of the mainland. No better description can be given than to say that the bay looked like a funnel to which the island was the lid, not fitting closely, however, but leaving apertures for egress and ingress. The snugness of the locality had tempted the French, and had induced them to choose it as the most favorable spot, at the time, for colonization. Sauvolle was put in command of the fort, and Bienville, the youngest of the three brothers, was appointed his lieutenant.

A few huts having been erected round the fort, the settlers began to clear the land, in order to bring it into cultivation. Iberville having furnished them with all the necessary provisions, utensils, and other supplies, prepared to sail for France. How deeply affecting must have been the parting scene! How many casualties might prevent those who remained in this unknown region from ever seeing again those who, through the perils of such a long voyage, had to return to their home! What crowding emotions must have filled up the breast of Sauvolle, Bienville, and their handful of companions, when they beheld the sails of Iberville's fleet fading in the distance, like transient clouds! Well may it be supposed that it seemed to them as if their very souls had been carried away, and that they felt a momentary sinking of the heart when they found themselves abandoned, and necessarily left to their own resources, scanty as they were, on a patch of land between the ocean on one side and on the other a wilderness, which fancy peopled with every sort of terrors. The sense of their loneliness fell upon them like the gloom of night, darkening their hopes and filling their hearts with dismal apprehensions.

But as the country had been ordered to be explored, Sauvolle availed himself of that circumstance to refresh the minds of his men by the excitement of an expedition into the interior of the continent. He therefore hastened to despatch most of them with Bienville, who, with a chief of the Bayagoulas for his guide, went to visit the Colapissas. They inhabited the northern shore of Lake Pontchartrain, and their domains embraced the sites now occupied by Lewisburg, Mandeville, and Fontainebleau. That tribe numbered three hundred warriors, who, in their distant hunting-excursions, had been engaged in frequent skirmishes with some of the British colonists in South Carolina. When the French landed, they were informed that, two days previous, the village of the Colapissas had been attacked by a party of two hundred Chickasaws, headed by two Englishmen. These were the first tidings which the French had of their old rivals, and which proved to be the harbinger of the incessant struggle which was to continue for more than a century between the two races, and to terminate by the permanent occupation of Louisiana by the Anglo-Saxon.

Bienville returned to the fort to convey this important information to Sauvolle. After having rested there for several days, he went to the Bay of Pascagoulas, and ascended the river which bears that name, and the banks of which were tenanted by a branch of the Biloxis, and by the Moelobites. Encouraged by the friendly reception which he met everywhere, he ventured farther, and paid a visit to the Mobilians, who entertained him with great hospitality. Bienville found them much reduced from what they had been, and listened with eagerness to the many tales of their former power, which had been rapidly declining since the crushing blow they had received from De Soto.

When Iberville ascended the Mississippi the first time, he had remarked Bayou Plaquemines and Bayou Chetimachas. The one he called after the fruit of certain trees which appeared to have exclusive possession of its banks, and the other after the name of the Indians who dwelt in the vicinity. He had ordered them to be explored, and the indefatigable Bienville, on his return from Mobile, obeyed the instructions left to his brother, and made an accurate survey of these two bayous. When he was coming down the river, at the distance of about eighteen miles below the site where New Orleans now stands, he met an English vessel of sixteen guns, under the command of Captain Bar. The English captain informed the French that he was examining the banks of the river, with the intention of selecting a spot for the foundation of a colony. Bienville told him that Louisiana was a dependency of Canada; that the French had already made several establishments on the Mississippi; and he appealed, in confirmation of his assertions, to their own presence in the river, in such small boats, which evidently proved the existence of some settlement close at hand. The Englishman believed Bienville, and sailed back. Where this occurrence took place the river makes a considerable bend, and it was from the circumstance which I have related that the spot received the appellation of the "English Turn"—a name which it has retained to the present day. It was not far from that place, the atmosphere of which appears to be fraught with some malignant spell hostile to the sons of Albion, that the English, who were outwitted by Bienville in 1699, met with a signal defeat in battle from the Americans in 1815. The diplomacy of Bienville and the military genius of Jackson proved to them equally fatal when they aimed at the possession of Louisiana.

Since the exploring expedition of La Salle down the Mississippi, Canadian hunters, whose habits and intrepidity Fenimore Cooper has so graphically described in the character of Leather-Stocking, used to extend their roving excursions to the banks of that river; and those holy missionaries of the Church, who, as the pioneers of religion, have filled the New World with their sufferings, and whose incredible deeds in the service of God afford so many materials for the most interesting of books, had come in advance of the pickaxe of the settler, and had domiciliated themselves among the tribes who lived near the waters of the Mississippi. One of them, Father Montigny, was residing with the Tensas, within the territory of the present parish of Tensas, in the State of Louisiana, and another, Father Davion, was the pastor of the Yazoos, in the present State of Mississippi.

Such were the two visitors who in 1699 appeared before Sauvolle, at the fort of Biloxi, to relieve the monotony of his cheerless existence, and to encourage him in his colonizing enterprise. Their visit, however, was not of long duration, and they soon returned to discharge the duties of their sacred mission.

Iberville had been gone for several months, and the year was drawing to a close without any tidings of him. A deeper gloom had settled over the little colony at Biloxi, when, on December 7th, some signal-guns were heard at sea, and the grateful sound came booming over the waters, spreading joy in every breast. There was not one who was not almost oppressed with the intensity of his feelings. At last, friends were coming, bringing relief to the body and to the soul! Every colonist hastily abandoned his occupation of the moment and ran to the shore. The soldier himself, in the eagerness of expectation, left his post of duty, and rushed to the parapet which overlooked the bay. Presently several vessels hove in sight, bearing the white flag of France, and, approaching as near as the shallowness of the beach permitted, folded their pinions, like water-fowl seeking repose on the crest of the billows.

It was Iberville returning with the news that, on his representations, Sauvolle had been appointed by the King governor of Louisiana; Bienville, lieutenant-governor; and Boisbriant, commander of the fort at Biloxi, with the grade of major. Iberville, having been informed by Bienville of the attempt of the English to make a settlement on the banks of the Mississippi, and of the manner in which it had been foiled, resolved to take precautionary measures against the repetition of any similar attempt. Without loss of time he departed with Bienville, on January 16, 1700, and running up the river, he constructed a small fort, on the first solid ground which he met, and which is said to have been at a distance of fifty-four miles from its mouth.

When so engaged, the two brothers one day saw a canoe rapidly sweeping down the river and approaching the spot where they stood. It was occupied by eight men, six of whom were rowers, the seventh was the steersman, and the eighth, from his appearance, was evidently of a superior order to that of his companions, and the commander of the party. Well may it be imagined what greeting the stranger received, when leaping on shore he made himself known as the Chevalier de Tonty, who had again heard of the establishment of a colony in Louisiana, and who, for the second time, had come to see if there was any truth in the report. With what emotion did Iberville and Bienville fold in their arms the faithful companion and friend of La Salle, of whom they had heard so many wonderful tales from the Indians, to whom he was so well known under the name of "Iron Hand"! With what admiration they looked at his person, and with what increasing interest they listened to his long recitals of what he had done and had seen on that broad continent, the threshold of which they had hardly passed!

After having rested three days at the fort, the indefatigable Tonty reascended the Mississippi, with Iberville and Bienville, and finally parted with them at Natchez. Iberville was so much pleased with that part of the bank of the river where now exists the city of Natchez that he marked it down as a most eligible spot for a town, of which he drew the plan, and which he called Rosalie, after the maiden name of the Countess Pontchartrain, the wife of the chancellor. He then returned to the new fort he was erecting on the Mississippi, and Bienville went to explore the country of the Yatasses, of the Natchitoches, and of the Ouachitas. What romance can be more agreeable to the imagination than to accompany Iberville and Bienville in their wild explorations, and to compare the state of the country in their time with what it is in our days?

When the French were at Natchez they were struck with horror at an occurrence, too clearly demonstrating the fierceness of disposition of that tribe which was destined in after years to become celebrated in the history of Louisiana. One of their temples having been set on fire by lightning, a hideous spectacle presented itself to the Europeans. The tumultuous rush of the Indians; the infernal howlings and lamentations of the men, women, and children; the unearthly vociferations of the priests, their fantastic dances and ceremonies around the burning edifice; the demoniac fury with which mothers rushed to the fatal spot, and, with the piercing cries and gesticulations of maniacs, flung their new-born babes into the flames to pacify their irritated deity—the increasing anger of the heavens—blackening with the impending storm, the lurid flashes of lightning darting as it were in mutual enmity from the clashing clouds—the low, distant growling of the coming tempest—the long column of smoke and fire shooting upward from the funeral pyre, and looking like one of the gigantic torches of Pandemonium—the war of the elements combined with the worst effects of frenzied superstition of man—the suddenness and strangeness of the awful scene—all the circumstances produced such an impression upon the French as to deprive them for a moment of the powers of volition and action. Rooted to the ground, they stood aghast with astonishment and indignation at the appalling scene. Was it a dream—a wild delirium of the mind? But no—the monstrous reality of the vision was but too apparent; and they threw themselves among the Indians, supplicating them to cease their horrible sacrifice to their gods, and joining threats to their supplications. Owing to this intervention, and perhaps because a sufficient number of victims had been offered, the priests gave the signal of retreat, and the Indians slowly withdrew from the accursed spot. Such was the aspect under which the Natchez showed themselves, for the first time, to their visitors: it was ominous presage for the future.

After these explorations Iberville departed again for France, to solicit additional assistance from the government, and left Bienville in command of the new fort on the Mississippi. It was very hard for the two brothers, Sauvolle and Bienville, to be thus separated, when they stood so much in need of each other's countenance, to breast the difficulties that sprung up around them with a luxuriance which they seemed to borrow from the vegetation of the country. The distance between the Mississippi and Biloxi was not so easily overcome in those days as in ours, and the means which the two brothers had of communing together were very scanty and uncertain.

Sauvolle died August 22, 1701, and Louisiana remained under the sole charge of Bienville, who, though very young, was fully equal to meet that emergency, by the maturity of his mind and by his other qualifications. He had hardly consigned his brother to the tomb when Iberville returned with two ships of the line and a brig laden with troops and provisions.

According to Iberville's orders, and in conformity with the King's instructions, Bienville left Boisbriant, his cousin, with twenty men, at the old fort of Biloxi, and transported the principal seat of the colony to the western side of the river Mobile, not far from the spot where now stands the city of Mobile. Near the mouth of that river there is an island, which the French had called Massacre Island from the great quantity of human bones which they found bleaching on its shores. It was evident that there some awful tragedy had been acted; but Tradition, when interrogated, laid her choppy finger upon her skinny lips, and answered not.

This uncertainty, giving a free scope to the imagination, shrouded the place with a higher degree of horror and with a deeper hue of fantastical gloom. It looked like the favorite ball-room of the witches of hell. The wind sighed so mournfully through the shrivelled-up pines, those vampire heads seemed incessantly to bow to some invisible and grisly visitors: the footsteps of the stranger emitted such an awful and supernatural sound, when trampling on the skulls which strewed his path, that it was impossible for the coldest imagination not to labor under some crude and ill-defined apprehension. Verily, the weird sisters could not have chosen a fitter abode. Nevertheless, the French, supported by their mercurial temperament, were not deterred from forming an establishment on that sepulchral island, which, they thought, afforded some facilities for their transatlantic communications.

In 1703 war had broken out between Great Britain, France, and Spain; and Iberville, a distinguished officer of the French navy, was engaged in expeditions that kept him away from the colony. It did not cease, however, to occupy his thoughts, and had become clothed, in his eye, with a sort of family interest. Louisiana was thus left, for some time, to her scanty resources; but, weak as she was, she gave early proofs of that generous spirit which has ever since animated her; and on the towns of

Pensacola and St. Augustine, then in possession of the Spaniards, being threatened with an invasion by the English of South Carolina, she sent to her neighbors what help she could in men, ammunition, and supplies of all sorts. It was the more meritorious as it was the *obolus* of the poor!

The year 1703 slowly rolled by and gave way to 1704. Still, nothing was heard from the parent country. There seemed to be an impassable barrier between the old and the new continent. The milk which flowed from the motherly breast of France could no longer reach the parched lips of her new-born infant; and famine began to pinch the colonists, who scattered themselves all along the coast, to live by fishing. They were reduced to the veriest extremity of misery, and despair had settled in every bosom, in spite of the encouragements of Bienville, who displayed the most manly fortitude amid all the trials to which he was subjected, when suddenly a vessel made its appearance. The colonists rushed to the shore with wild anxiety, but their exultation was greatly diminished when, on the nearer approach of the moving speck, they recognized the Spanish instead of the French flag. It was relief, however, coming to them, and proffered by a friendly hand. It was a return made by the governor of Pensacola for the kindness he had experienced the year previous. Thus the debt of gratitude was paid: it was a practical lesson. Where the seeds of charity are cast, there springs the harvest in time of need.

Good things, like evils, do not come singly, and this succor was but the herald of another one, still more effectual, in the shape of a ship from France. Iberville had not been able to redeem his pledge to the poor colonists, but he had sent his brother Chateaugué in his place, at the imminent risk of being captured by the English, who occupied, at that time, most of the avenues of the Gulf of Mexico. He was not the man to spare either himself or his family in cases of emergency, and his heroic soul was inured to such sacrifices. Grateful the colonists were for this act of devotedness, and they resumed the occupation of their tenements which they had abandoned in search of food. The aspect of things was suddenly changed; abundance and hope reappeared in the land, whose population was increased by the arrival of seventeen persons, who came, under the guidance of Chateaugué, with the intention of making a permanent settlement, and who, in evidence of their determination, had provided themselves with all the implements of husbandry. We, who daily see hundreds flocking to our shores, and who look at the occurrence with as much unconcern as at the passing cloud, can hardly conceive the excitement produced by the arrival of these seventeen emigrants among men who, for nearly two years, had been cut off from communication with the rest of the civilized world. A denizen of the moon, dropping on this planet, would not be stared at and interrogated with more eager curiosity.

This excitement had hardly subsided when it was revived by the appearance of another ship, and it became intense when the inhabitants saw a procession of twenty females, with veiled faces, proceeding arm in arm, and two by two, to the house of the Governor, who received them in state and provided them with suitable lodgings. What did it mean? Innumerable were the gossipings of the day, and part of the coming night itself was spent in endless commentaries and conjectures. But the next morning, which was Sunday, the mystery was cleared by the officiating priest reading from the pulpit, after mass, and for the general information, the following communication from the minister to Bienville: "His majesty sends twenty girls to be married to the Canadians and to the other inhabitants of Mobile, in order to consolidate the colony. All these girls are industrious and have received a pious and virtuous education. Beneficial results to the colony are expected from their teaching their useful attainments to the Indian females. In order that none should be sent except those of known virtue and of unspotted reputation, his majesty did intrust the Bishop of Quebec with the mission of taking these girls from such establishments as, from their very nature and character, would put them at once above all suspicions of corruption. You will take care to settle them in life as well as may be in your power, and to marry them to such men as are capable of providing them with a commodious home."

This was a very considerate recommendation, and very kind it was, indeed, from the great Louis XIV, one of the proudest monarchs that ever lived, to descend from his Olympian seat of majesty to the level of such details and to such minute instructions for ministering to the personal comforts of his remote

Louisianan subjects. Many were the gibes and high was the glee on that occasion; pointed were the jokes aimed at young Bienville on his being thus transformed into a matrimonial agent and *pater familiæ.* The intentions of the King, however, were faithfully executed, and more than one rough but honest Canadian boatman of the St. Lawrence and of the Mississippi closed his adventurous and erratic career and became a domestic and useful member of that little commonwealth, under the watchful influence of the dark-eyed maid of the Loire or of the Seine. Infinite are the chords of the lyre which delights the romantic muse; and these incidents, small and humble as they are, appear to me to be imbued with an indescribable charm, which appeals to her imagination.

PRUSSIA PROCLAIMED A KINGDOM

A.D. 1701

LEOPOLD VON RANKE

Few historical developments are more distinctly traceable or of greater importance than that of the margravate of Brandenburg into the kingdom of Prussia, the principal state of the present German empire. As far back as the tenth century the name Preussen (Prussia) was applied to a region lying east of Brandenburg, which in that century became a German margravate. At that time the inhabitants of Prussia were still heathens. In the thirteenth century they were converted to Christianity, having first been conquered by the Teutonic Knights in "a series of remorseless wars" continued for almost fifty years. German colonization followed the conquest.

In 1466 nearly the whole of Prussia was wrested from the Teutonic Knights and annexed to the Polish crown. Soon after the beginning of the Reformation the Teutonic Knights embraced Protestantism and the order became secularized. In 1525 the Knights formally surrendered to King Sigismund of Poland, their late grand master was created duke of Prussia, and this, with other former possessions of the order, was held by him as a vassal of the Polish crown. This relation continued until 1618, when the duchy of Prussia was united with Brandenburg, which had become a German electorate.

During the Thirty Years' War the enlarged electorate took little part in affairs, but suffered much from the ravages of the conflict. Under the electorate of George William, who died in 1640, Brandenburg became almost a desert, and in this impoverished condition was left to his son, Frederick William, the "Great Elector," who restored it to prosperity and strengthened its somewhat insecure sovereignty over the duchy of Prussia. The Great Elector died in 1688, and was succeeded by his son, Frederick III of Brandenburg. This Elector, through the series of events narrated by Ranke, became the founder of the Prussian monarchy, and is known in history as Frederick I. He founded the Academy of Sciences in Berlin and the University of Halle.

FREDERICK I, the next heir and successor to the "Great Elector," though far inferior to his father in native energy of character, cannot be accused of having flinched from the task imposed on him. Above all, the warlike fame of the Brandenburg troops suffered no diminution under his reign. His army took a very prominent and active part in the most important events of that period.

Prince William of Orange might, perhaps, have hesitated whether to try the adventure which made him king of England, had not the Dutch troops, which he was forced to withdraw from the Netherlands for his expedition, been replaced by some from Brandenburg. The fact has indeed been disputed, but on closer investigation its truth has been established, beyond doubt, that many other Brandenburg soldiers in his service and that of his republic followed him to England, where they contributed essentially to his success.

In the war which now broke out upon the Rhine the young Elector, Frederick, took the field himself, inflamed by religious enthusiasm, patriotism, and personal ambition. On one occasion, at the siege of Bonn, when he was anxious about the result, he stepped aside to the window and prayed to God that he might suffer no disgrace in this his first enterprise. He was successful in his attack upon Bonn, and cleared the whole lower Rhine of the hostile troops; he at the same time gained a high reputation for personal courage.

Long after, at the beginning of the War of the Spanish Succession, the presence of the Elector contributed in a great measure to the speedy termination of the first important siege—that of Kaiserswerth, a point from which the French threatened at once both Holland and Westphalia.

But it was not only when led by the Elector that his troops distinguished themselves by their courage; they fought most bravely at the battle of Hochstadt. Prince Eugene, under whose command they stood, could scarce find words strong enough to praise the "undaunted steadfastness" with which they first withstood the shock of the enemy's attack, and then helped to break through his tremendous fire. Two years later, at Turin, they helped to settle the affairs of Italy in the same manner as they had already done in those of Germany; headed by Prince Leopold of Anhalt, they climbed over the enemy's intrenchments, under the full fire of his artillery, shouting the old Brandenburg war-cry of "*Gah to*" ("Go on"). The warlike enterprise of Brandenburg never spread over a wider field than under Frederick I. Then it was that they first met the Turks in terrible battles; they showed themselves in the South of France at the siege of Toulon; in their camp the Protestant service was performed for the first time in the territories of the pope, and the inhabitants of the surrounding country came to look on and displayed a certain satisfaction at the sight. But the Netherlands were always the scene of their greatest achievements and at that time an excellent school for their further progress in the art of war; there they might at once study sieges under the Dutch commanders, Vauban and Coehorn, and campaigns under Marlborough, one of the greatest generals of all times.

Throughout all the years of his reign Frederick steadily adhered to the Great Alliance which his father had helped to form so long as that alliance continued to subsist; and, indeed, the interest which he took in the affairs of Europe at large was in the end of great advantage to himself and to his house. That very alliance was the original cause of his gaining a crown—the foundation of the Prussian monarchy. It will not be denied, even by those who think most meanly of the externals of rank and title, that the attainment of a higher step in the European hierarchy, as it then stood, was an object worth striving for.

The Western principalities and republics still formed a great corporation, at the head of which was the German Emperor. Even the crown of France had to submit to manifold and wearisome negotiations in order to obtain the predicate of "majesty," which until then had belonged exclusively to the Emperor. The other sovereigns then laid claim to the same dignity as that enjoyed by the King of France, and the Venetian republic to an equal rank with those, on the score of the kingdoms which she once possessed; and, accordingly, the electoral ambassadors to Vienna had to stand bareheaded while the Venetian covered his head. The electors and reigning dukes were but ill-pleased with such precedence, and in their turn laid claim to the designation of "serenissimus," and the title of "brother," for themselves, and the style of "excellency" for their ambassadors. But even the most powerful among the electors found it difficult to advance a single step in this matter, because whatever privileges were conceded to them were immediately claimed by all the rest, many of whom were mere barons of the empire. It is evident that Brandenburg was interested in being freed at once from these negotiations, which only served to impede and embarrass all really important business. There exists the distinct assertion of a highly placed official man that the royal title had been promised to the Elector, Frederick William: his son now centred his whole ambition in its attainment.

Frederick, while elector, was one of the most popular princes that ever reigned in Brandenburg. His contemporaries praise him for his avoidance of all dissipation, and his life entirely devoted to duty; while his subjects were still asleep, say they, the Prince was already busied with their affairs, for he rose very early. A poet of the time makes Phosphorus complain that he is ever anticipated by the King of Prussia. His manners were gracious, familiar, sincere, and deliberate. His conversation indicated "righteous and princely thoughts." Those essays, written by him, which we have read, exhibit a sagacious and careful treatment of the subjects under consideration. He shared in a very great degree the taste of his times for outward show and splendor; but in him it took a direction which led to something far higher than mere ostentation. The works of sculpture and architecture produced under his reign are monuments of a pure and severe taste; the capital of Prussia has seen none more beautiful. He complacently indulged in the contemplation of the greatness founded by his father, the possession of a territory four times as large as that of any other elector, and the power of bringing into the field an army which placed him on a level with kings. Now, however, he desired that this equality should be publicly recognized, especially as he had no lack of treasure and revenue wherewith to maintain the splendor and dignity of a royal crown. In the mind of the father, this ambition was combined with schemes of conquest; in the son it was merely a desire for personal and dynastic aggrandizement. It is certain that the origin of such a state as the kingdom of Prussia can be attributed to no other cause than to so remarkable a succession of so many glorious princes. Frederick was resolved to appear among them distinguished by some important service rendered to his house. "Frederick I," said he, "gained the electoral dignity for our house, and I, as Frederick III, would fain give it royal rank, according to the old saying that 'the third time makes perfect.'"

It was in the year 1693 that he first began seriously to act upon the project of obtaining a royal crown. He had just led some troops to Crossen which were to serve the Emperor against the Turks; but the imperial ministers neither arrived in due time to receive them, nor, when at length they made their appearance, did they bring with them the grants of certain privileges and expectancies which Frederick had looked for. In disgust at being treated with neglect at the very moment in which he was rendering the Emperor a very essential service, he went to Carlsbad, where he was joined by his ambassador to Vienna, who had been commissioned by the imperial ministers to apologize for the omissions of which they had been guilty. In concert with his ambassador, and his prime minister, Dankelmann, the brother of the former, Frederick resolved to make public the wish which he had hitherto entertained in secret, or only now and then let drop into conversation; the ambassador accordingly received instruction to present a formal memorial.

At that time, however, nothing could be done. The Count of Ottingen, who was hostile to the Protestant princes, was once more in favor at the court of Vienna; the peril from without had ceased to be pressing, and coalition had begun gradually to dissolve; the only result of the negotiation was a vague and general promise.

The Elector did not, however, give up his idea. The elevation of the Saxon house to the throne of Poland, the prospect enjoyed by his near kindred of Hanover of succeeding to that of England, and perhaps the very difficulties and opposition which he encountered, tended to sharpen his appetite for a royal crown. The misunderstandings which arose among the great European powers out of the approaching vacancy of the throne of Spain soon afforded him an excellent opportunity of renewing his demands. The court of Vienna was not to be moved by past, but by future, services.

It would be unnecessary to enter into the details of the negotiation on this subject; it suffices to say that the Prince devoted his whole energy to it, and never lost sight of any advantage afforded by his position. Suggestions of the most exaggerated kind were made to him; for instance, that he should lay his claims before the Pope, who possessed the power of granting the royal dignity in a far higher degree than the Emperor; while, on the other hand, some of the more zealous Protestants among his ministers were anxious to avoid even that degree of approach toward the Catholic element implied in a closer alliance with the Emperor, and desired that the Elector's elevation in rank should be made to depend upon some new and important acquisition of territory, such, for example, as that of Polish Prussia, which then seemed neither difficult nor improbable. Frederick, however, persisted in the opinion that he was entitled to the royal dignity merely on acccount of his sovereign dukedom of Prussia, and that the recognition of the Emperor was the most important step in the affair. He was convinced that, when the Emperor had once got possession of the Spanish inheritance, or concluded a treaty upon the subject, nothing more was to be hoped from him; but that now, while the Elector of Brandenburg was able to render him as effectual assistance as any power in Europe, some advantage might be wrung from him in return.

Influenced by these considerations, he resolved to lay proposals before the Emperor, which acquired uncommon significance from the circumstances under which they were made. At that very time, in March, 1700, England, Holland, and France had just concluded a treaty for the division of the Spanish monarchy, in which the right of inheritance of Austria was utterly disregarded, in order to preserve the European balance of power. Spain and the Indies were, indeed, to fall to the share of the young Archduke Charles, but he was to be deprived of Naples, Sicily, and Milan; and should the Archduke ever become Emperor of Germany, Spain and the Indies were to be given up to another prince, whose claims were far inferior to his. This treaty was received with disgust and indignation at Vienna, where the assistance of Heaven was solemnly implored, and its interference in the affair fully expected.

At this juncture Brandenburg offered to make common cause with the Emperor, not alone against France, but even against England and Holland, with whom it was otherwise closely allied. The only recompense was to be the concession of royal rank to the Elector.

The principal opposition to this offer arose out of the difference of confessions. It is also quite true that the Emperor's confessor, Pater Wolf, to whom the Elector wrote with his own hand, helped to overrule it, and took part in the negotiations. But the determining cause was, without doubt, the political state of affairs. A concession which involved no loss could not surely be thought too high a price to pay for the help of the most warlike of the German powers on so important an occasion. In the month of July, 1700, at the great conference, the imperial ministers came to the resolution that the wishes of the Elector should be complied with; and as soon as the conditions could be determined, involving the closest alliance both for the war and for the affairs of the empire, the treaty was signed on November 16, 1700. On the side of Brandenburg the utmost care was taken not to admit a word which might imply anything further than the assent and concurrence of the Emperor. The Elector affected to derive from his own power alone the right of assuming the royal crown. He would, nevertheless, have encountered much unpleasant oppositions in other quarters but for the concurrences which, very opportunely for him, now took place in France and Spain.

The last Spanish sovereign of the line of Hapsburg had died in the mean time; and on opening his will it was found to be entirely in favor of the King of France, whose grandson was appointed heir to the whole Spanish monarchy. Hereupon Louis XIV broke the treaty of partition which had recently been made under his own influence, and determined to seize the greater advantage, and to accept the inheritance. This naturally roused all the antipathies entertained by other nations against France, and England and Holland went over to the side of Austria. The opposition which these two powers had offered to the erection of a new throne was now silenced, and they beheld a common interest in the elevation of the house of Brandenburg.

Frederick had, moreover, already come to an understanding with the King of Poland, though not with the Republic; so that, thus supported, and with the consent of all his old allies, he could now celebrate the splendid coronation for which his heart had so long panted.

We will not describe here the ceremonial of January 18, 1701;

to our taste it seems overcharged when we read the account of it. But there is a certain grandeur in the idea of the sovereign's grasping the crown with his own hand; and the performance of the ceremony of anointing after, instead of before, the crowning, by two priests promoted to bishoprics for the occasion, was a protest against the dependence of the temporal on the spiritual power, such as perhaps never was made at any other coronation either before or since. The spiritual element showed itself in the only attitude of authority left to it in Protestant states: that of teaching and exhortation. The provost of Berlin demonstrated, from the examples of Christ and of David, that the government of kings must be carried on to the glory of God and the good of their people. He lays down as the first principle that all rulers should bear in mind, they have come into the world for the sake of their subjects, and not their subjects for the sake of them. Finally, he exhorts all his hearers to pray to God that he will deeply impress this conviction upon the hearts of all sovereign princes.

The institution of the order of the Black Eagle, which immediately preceded the coronation, was likewise symbolical of the duties of royalty. The words "*Suum cuique,*" on the insignia of the order, according to Lamberty, who suggested them, contain the definition of a good government, under which all men alike, good as well as bad, are rewarded according to their several deserts. The laurel and the lightning denote reward and punishment. The conception at least is truly royal. Leibnitz, who was at that time closely connected with the court, and who busied himself very much with this affair, justly observes that nothing is complete without a name, and that, although the Elector did already possess every royal attribute, he became truly a king only by being called so.

Although the new dignity rested only on the possession of Prussia, all the other provinces were included in the rank and title; those belonging to the German empire were thus in a manner chosen out from among the other German states, and united into a new whole, though, at the same time, care was taken in other respects to keep up the ancient connection with the empire. Thus we see that the elevation of the Elector to a royal title was an important, nay, even a necessary, impulse to the progress of Prussia, which we cannot even in thought separate from the whole combination of events.

The name of Prussia now became inseparable from an idea of military power and glory, which was increased by splendid feats of arms, such as those which we have already enumerated.

FOUNDING OF ST. PETERSBURG

A.D. 1703

K. WALISZEWSKI[1]

So radical and so vigorous were the changes made by Peter the Great in Russia that they roused the opposition of almost the entire nation. Moscow, the ancient capital, was the chief seat of this protesting conservatism; and Peter, resolved to teach his opponents how determined he was in his course and how helpless they were against his absolute power, formed the tremendous project of building a wholly new capital, one where no voice could be raised against him, where no traditions should environ him. He chose an icy desert plain looking out toward the waters which led to that Western Europe which he meant to imitate, if not to conquer.

No other man—one is almost tempted to say, no sane man—would have ventured to erect a capital city in such an impossible place and on the very frontier of his dominions. That Peter not only dared, but succeeded, though at an almost immeasurable cost, makes the creation of the great metropolis, St. Petersburg, one of the most remarkable events of history.

IT was the chances of the great northern war that led Peter to St. Petersburg. When he first threw down the gauntlet to Sweden he turned his eyes on Livonia—on Narva and Riga. But Livonia was so well defended that he was driven northward, toward Ingria. He moved thither grudgingly, sending, in the first instance, Apraxin, who turned the easily conquered province into a desert. It was not for some time, and gropingly, as it were, that the young sovereign began to see his way, and finally turned his attention and his longings to the mouth of the Neva. In former years Gustavus Adolphus had realized the strategical importance of a position which his successor, Charles XII, did not deem worthy of consideration, and had himself studied all its approaches. Peter not only took it to be valuable from the military and commercial point of view: he also found it most

[1] Translated from the Russian by Lady Mary Loyd.

attractive, and would fain have never left it. He was more at home there than anywhere else, and the historical legends, according to which it was true Russian ground, filled him with emotion. No one knows what inspired this fondness on his part. It may have been the vague resemblance of the marshy flats to the lowlands of Holland; it may have been the stirring of some ancestral instinct. According to a legend, accepted by Nestor, it was by the mouth of the Neva that the earliest Norman conquerors of the country passed on their journeys across the Varegian Sea—*their own sea*—and so to Rome.

Peter would seem to have desired to take up the thread of that tradition, nine centuries old; and the story of his own foundation of the town has become legendary and epic. One popular description represents him as snatching a halberd from one of his soldiers, cutting two strips of turf, and laying them crosswise with the words "Here there shall be a town!" Foundation-stones were evidently lacking, and sods had to take their place. Then, dropping the halberd, he seized a spade, and began the first embankment. At that moment an eagle appeared, hovering over the Czar's head. It was struck by a shot from a musket. Peter took the wounded bird, set it on his wrist, and departed in a boat to inspect the neighborhood. This occurred on May 16, 1703.

History adds that the Swedish prisoners employed on the work died in thousands. The most indispensable tools were lacking. There were no wheelbarrows, and the earth was carried in the corners of men's clothing. A wooden fort was first built on the island bearing the Finnish name of Ianni-Saari (Hare Island). This was the future citadel of St. Peter and St. Paul. Then came a wooden church, and the modest cottage which was to be Peter's first palace. Near these, the following year, there rose a Lutheran church, ultimately removed to the left bank of the river, into the Liteinaia quarter, and also a tavern, the famous inn of the Four Frigates, which did duty as a town hall for a long time before it became a place of diplomatic meeting. Then the cluster of modest buildings was augmented by the erection of a bazaar. The Czar's collaborators gathered round him, in cottages much like his own, and the existence of St. Petersburg became an accomplished fact.

But, up to the time of the battle of Poltava, Peter never thought of making St. Petersburg his capital. It was enough for him to feel he had a fortress and a port. He was not sufficiently sure of his mastery over the neighboring countries, not certain enough of being able to retain his conquest, to desire to make it the centre of his government and his own permanent residence. This idea was not definitely accepted till after his great victory. His final decision has been bitterly criticised, especially by foreign historians; it has been severely judged and remorselessly condemned. Before expressing any opinion of my own on the subject, I should like to sum up the considerations which have been put forward to support this unfavorable verdict.

The great victory, we are told, diminished the strategic importance of St. Petersburg, and almost entirely extinguished its value as a port; while its erection into the capital city of the empire was never anything but madness. Peter, being now the indisputable master of the Baltic shores, had nothing to fear from any Swedish attack in the Gulf of Finland. Before any attempt in that direction, the Swedes were certain to try to recover Narva or Riga. If in later years they turned their eyes to St. Petersburg, it was only because that town had acquired undue and unmerited political importance. It was easy of attack and difficult to defend. There was no possibility of concentrating any large number of troops there, for the whole country, forty leagues round, was a barren desert. In 1788 Catharine II complained that her capital was too near the Swedish frontier, and too much exposed to sudden movements, such as that which Gustavus III very nearly succeeded in carrying out. Here we have the military side of the question.

From the commercial point of view St. Petersburg, we are assured, did command a valuable system of river communication; but that commanded by Riga was far superior. The Livonian, Esthonian, and Courland ports of Riga, Libau, and Revel, all at an equal distance from St. Petersburg and Moscow, and far less removed from the great German commercial centres, enjoyed a superior climate, and were, subsequent to the conquest of the above-mentioned provinces, the natural points of contact between Russia and the West. An eloquent proof of this fact may be observed nowadays in the constant increase of their commerce, and the corresponding decrease of that of St. Petersburg, which has been artificially developed and fostered.

Besides this, the port of St. Petersburg, during the lifetime of its founder, never was anything but a mere project. Peter's ships were moved from Kronslot to Kronstadt. Between St. Petersburg and Kronstadt the Neva was not, in those days, more than eight feet deep, and Manstein tells us that all ships built at Petersburg had to be dragged, by means of machines fitted with cables, to Kronstadt, where they received their guns. Once these had been taken on board, the vessels could not get upstream again. The port of Kronstadt was closed by ice for six months out of the twelve, and lay in such a position that no sailing-ship could leave it unless the wind blew from the east. There was so little salt in its waters that the ship timbers rotted in a very short time, and, besides, there were no oaks in the surrounding forests, and all such timber had to be brought from Kasan. Peter was so well aware of all these drawbacks that he sought and found a more convenient spot for his ship-building yards at Rogerwick, in Esthonia, four leagues from Revel. But here he found difficulty in protecting the anchorage from the effects of hurricanes and from the insults of his enemies. He hoped to insure this by means of two piers, built on wooden caissons filled with stones. He thinned the forests of Livonia and Esthonia to construct it, and finally, the winds and the waves having carried everything away twice over, the work was utterly abandoned.

On the other hand, and from the very outset, the commercial activity of St. Petersburg was hampered by the fact that it was the Czar's capital. The presence of the court made living dear, and the consequent expense of labor was a heavy drawback to the export trade, which, by its nature, called for a good deal of manual exertion. According to a Dutch resident of that period, a wooden cottage, very inferior to that inhabited by a peasant in the Low Countries, cost from eight hundred to one thousand florins a year at St. Petersburg. A shopkeeper at Archangel could live comfortably on a quarter of that sum. The cost of transport, which amounted to between nine and ten copecks a pood (36.07 pounds), between Moscow and Archangel, five to six between Yaroslaff and Archangel, and three or four between Vologda and Archangel, came to eighteen, twenty, and thirty copecks a pood in the case of merchandise sent from any of these places to St. Petersburg. This accounts for the opposition of the foreign merchants at Archangel to the request that they should remove to St. Petersburg. Peter settled the matter in characteristic fashion, by forbidding any trade in hemp, flax, leather, or corn to pass through Archangel. This rule, though somewhat slackened, in 1714, at the request of the States-General of Holland, remained in force during the great Czar's reign. In 1718 hemp and some other articles of commerce were allowed free entrance into the port of Archangel, but only on condition that two-thirds of all exports should be sent to St. Petersburg. This puts the case from the maritime and commercial point of view.

As a capital city, St. Petersburg, we are told again, was ill-placed on the banks of the Neva, not only for the reasons already given, but for others, geographical, ethnical, and climatic, which exist even in the present day, and which make its selection an outrage on common-sense. Was it not, we are asked, a most extraordinary whim which induced a Russian to found the capital of his Slavonic empire among the Finns, against the Swedes—to centralize the administration of a huge extent of country in its remotest corner—to retire from Poland and Germany on the plea of drawing nearer to Europe, and to force everyone about him, officials, court, and diplomatic corps, to inhabit one of the most inhospitable spots, under one of the least clement skies, he could possibly have discovered? The whole place was a marsh—the Finnish word neva means "mud"; the sole inhabitants of the neighboring forests were packs of wolves. In 1714, during a winter night, two sentries, posted before the cannon-foundry, were devoured. Even nowadays, the traveller, once outside the town, plunges into a desert. Far away in every direction the great plain stretches; not a steeple, not a tree, not a head of cattle, not a sign of life, whether human or animal. There is no pasturage, no possibility of cultivation—fruit, vegetables, and even corn, are all brought from a distance. The ground is in a sort of intermediate condition between the sea and *terra firma*.

Up to Catharine's reign inundations were chronic in their occurrence. On September 11, 1706, Peter drew from his pocket the measure he always carried about him, and convinced himself that there were twenty-one inches of water above the floors of his cottage. In all directions he saw men, women, and children clinging to the wreckage of buildings, which was being carried down the river. He described his impressions in a letter to Menshikoff, dated from "Paradise," and declared it was "extremely amusing." It may be doubted whether he found many persons to share his delight. Communications with the town, now rendered easy by railways, were in those days not only difficult, but dangerous. Campredon, when he went from Moscow to St. Petersburg, in April, 1723, spent twelve hundred rubles. He lost part of his luggage, eight of his horses were drowned, and after having travelled for four weeks he reached his destination, very ill. Peter himself, who arrived before the French diplomat, had been obliged to ride part of the way, and to swim his horse across the rivers!

But in spite of all these considerations, the importance of which I am far from denying, I am inclined to think Peter's choice a wise one. Nobody can wonder that the idea of retaining Moscow as his capital was most repugnant to him. The existence of his work in those hostile surroundings—in a place which to this day has remained obstinately reactionary—could never have been anything but precarious and uncertain. It must, after his death at least, if not during his life, have been at the mercy of those popular insurrections before which the sovereign power, as established in the Kremlin, had already so frequently bowed. When Peter carried Muscovy out of her former existence, and beyond her ancient frontiers, he was logically forced to treat the seat of his government in the same manner. His new undertaking resembled, both in aspect and character, a marching and fighting formation, directed toward the west. The leader's place, and that of his chief residence, was naturally indicated at the head of his column. This once granted, and the principle of the translation of the capital to the western extremity of the Czar's newly acquired possessions admitted, the advantages offered by Ingria would appear to me to outweigh all the drawbacks previously referred to.

The province was, at that period, virgin soil sparsely inhabited by a Finnish population possessing neither cohesion nor historical consistency, and, consequently, docile and easily assimilated. Everywhere else—all along the Baltic coast, in Esthonia, in Carelia, and in Courland—though the Swedes might be driven out, the Germans still remained firmly settled; the neighborhood of their native country and of the springs of Teutonic culture enduing them with an invincible power of resistance. Riga in the present day, after nearly two centuries of Russian government, is a thoroughly German town. In St. Petersburg, Russia, as a country, became European and cosmopolitan, but the city itself is essentially Russian, and the Finnish element in its neighborhood counts for nothing.

In this matter, though Peter may not have clearly felt and thought it out, he was actuated by the mighty and unerring instinct of his genius. I am willing to admit that here, as in everything else, there was a certain amount of whim, and perhaps some childish desire to ape Amsterdam. I will even go further, and acknowledge that the manner in which he carried out his plan was anything but reasonable. Two hundred thousand laborers, we are told, died during the construction of the new city, and the Russian nobles ruined themselves to build palaces which soon fell out of occupation. But an abyss was opened between the past the reformer had doomed and the future on which he had set his heart, and the national life, thus violently forced into a new channel, was stamped, superficially at first, but more and more deeply by degrees, with the Western and European character he desired to impart.

Moscow, down to the present day, has preserved a religious, almost a monastic air; at every street corner chapels attract the passers-by, and the local population, even at its busiest, crosses itself and bends as it passes before the sacred pictures which rouse its devotion at every turn. St. Petersburg, from the very earliest days, presented a different and quite a secular appearance. At Moscow no public performance of profane music was permitted. At St. Petersburg the Czar's German musicians played every day on the balcony of his tavern. Toward the middle of the eighteenth century the new city boasted a French theatre and an Italian opera, and Schloezer noted that divine service was performed in fourteen languages! Modern Russia, governed, educated to a certain extent, intellectually speaking emancipated, and relatively liberal, could not have come into existence nor grown in stature elsewhere.

And to conclude: Peter was able to effect this singular change without doing too great violence to the historical traditions of his country. From the earliest days of Russian history, the capital had been removed from place to place—from Novgorod to Kiev, from Kiev to Vladimir, from Vladimir to Moscow. This phenomenon was the consequence of the immense area of the national territory, and the want of consistency in the elements of the national life. From the beginning to the end of an evolution which lasted centuries the centre of gravity of the disjointed, scattered, and floating forces of ancient Russia perpetually changed its place. Thus the creation of St. Petersburg was nothing but the working out of a problem in dynamics. The struggle with Sweden, the conquest of the Baltic provinces, and the yet more important conquest of a position in the European world naturally turned the whole current of the national energies and life in that direction. Peter desired to perpetuate this course. I am inclined to think he acted wisely.

BATTLE OF BLENHEIM

CURBING OF LOUIS XIV

A.D. 1704

SIR EDWARD SHEPHERD CREASY

Among the decisive battles of the world, that of Blenheim is regarded by historians as one of the most far-reaching in results. "The decisive blow struck at Blenheim," says Alison, "resounded through every part of Europe. It at once destroyed the vast fabric of power which it had taken Louis XIV so long to construct." And Creasy himself elsewhere declares: "Had it not been for Blenheim, all Europe might at this day suffer under the effect of French conquests resembling those of Alexander in extent and those of the Romans in durability."

It was the first great battle in the War of the Spanish Succession (1701-1714), which was carried on mainly in Italy, the Netherlands, and Germany. This war followed closely upon the War of the Palatinate, which ended with the Treaty of Ryswick, in 1697. To this peace Louis XIV of France—the most powerful monarch in Europe, who, in spite of his brutal conduct of the war, had really been a loser by it—gave his consent. Among the concessions made by him was his recognition—much against his own interest—of William III as the rightful King of England.

Louis gave his consent to the Treaty of Ryswick partly because of his interest in the question of the Spanish succession. Charles II of Spain—last of the Hapsburg line in that country—was childless, and there were three claimants for the throne; namely, Philip of Anjou, grandson of Louis XIV; the Electoral Prince of Bavaria; and Charles, son of Leopold I of Germany, Emperor of the Holy Roman Empire. The real stake was the "balance of power" in Europe. At last, after much wrangling and intrigue among the courts, Charles II bequeathed his throne to the Bavarian Prince, whose death, in 1699, left Europe still divided over the succession.

Finally, Louis XIV completely won Charles II to his side, and Philip of Anjou was named in Charles' will as his heir. Louis accepted for Philip, who was crowned at Madrid, in 1701, as Philip V, and Europe was stirred to wrath by the greed of the already too powerful French King. Turning now upon England, Louis, in violation of the Treaty of Ryswick, declared the son of the exiled James II rightful king of that country. The result of Louis' acts was the Grand Alliance of The Hague against France, formed between England, Holland, Prussia, the Holy Roman Empire, Portugal, and Savoy.

On the side of the allies in the war that followed, the great generals were the English Duke of Marlborough, Prince Eugene of Savoy, and Hensius, Pensioner of Holland. France had lost her best generals by death, and Louis was compelled to rely upon inferior men as leaders of his army. War was formally declared against France by the allies May 4, 1702. The early operations were carried on in Flanders, in Germany—on the Upper Rhine—and in Northern Italy.

MARLBOROUGH headed the allied troops in Flanders during the first two years of the war, and took some towns from the enemy, but nothing decisive occurred. Nor did any actions of importance take place during this period between the rival armies in Italy. But in the centre of that line from north to south, from the mouth of the Schelde to the mouth of the Po, along which the war was carried on, the generals of Louis XIV acquired advantages in 1703 which threatened one chief member of the Grand Alliance with utter destruction.

France had obtained the important assistance of Bavaria as her confederate in the war. The Elector of this powerful German state made himself master of the strong fortress of Ulm, and opened a communication with the French armies on the Upper Rhine. By this junction the troops of Louis were enabled to assail the Emperor in the very heart of Germany. In the autumn of 1703 the combined armies of the Elector and French King completely defeated the Imperialists in Bavaria; and in the following winter they made themselves masters of the important cities of Augsburg and Passau. Meanwhile the French army of the Upper Rhine and Moselle had beaten the allied armies opposed to them, and taken Treves and Landau. At the same time the discontents in Hungary with Austria again broke out into open insurrection, so as to distract the attention and complete the terror of the Emperor and his council at Vienna.

Louis XIV ordered the next campaign to be commenced by his troops on a scale of grandeur and with a boldness of enterprise such as even Napoleon's military schemes have seldom equalled. On the extreme left of the line of the war, in the Netherlands, the French armies were to act only on the defensive. The fortresses in the hands of the French there were so many and so strong that no serious impression seemed likely to be made by the allies on the French frontier in that quarter during one campaign, and that one campaign was to give France such triumphs elsewhere as would, it was hoped, determine the war. Large detachments were therefore to be made from the French force in Flanders, and they were to be led by Marshal Villeroy to the Moselle and Upper Rhine.

The French army already in the neighborhood of those rivers was to march under Marshal Tallard through the Black Forest, and join the Elector of Bavaria, and the French troops that were already with the Elector under Marshal Marsin. Meanwhile the French army of Italy was to advance through the Tyrol into Austria, and the whole forces were to combine between the Danube and the Inn. A strong body of troops was to be despatched into Hungary, to assist and organize the insurgents in that kingdom; and the French grand army of the Danube was then in collected and irresistible might to march upon Vienna and dictate terms of peace to the Emperor. High military genius was shown in the formation of this plan, but it was met and baffled by a genius higher still.

Marlborough had watched with the deepest anxiety the progress of the French arms on the Rhine and in Bavaria, and he saw the futility of carrying on a war of posts and sieges in Flanders, while death-blows to the empire were being dealt on the Danube. He resolved, therefore, to let the war in Flanders languish for a year, while he moved with all the disposable forces that he could collect to the central scenes of decisive operations. Such a march was in itself difficult; but Marlborough had, in the first instance, to overcome the still greater difficulty of obtaining the consent and cheerful coöperation of the allies, especially of the Dutch, whose frontier it was proposed thus to deprive of the larger part of the force which had hitherto been its protection.

Fortunately, among the many slothful, the many foolish, the many timid, and the not few treacherous rulers, statesmen, and generals of different nations with whom he had to deal, there were two men, eminent both in ability and integrity, who entered fully into Marlborough's projects and who, from the stations which they occupied, were enabled materially to forward them. One of these was the Dutch statesman Heinsius, who had been the cordial supporter of King William, and who now, with equal zeal and good faith, supported Marlborough in the councils of the allies; the other was the celebrated general, Prince Eugene, whom the Austrian cabinet had recalled from the Italian frontier to take the command of one of the Emperor's armies in Germany. To these two great men, and a few more, Marlborough communicated his plan freely and unreservedly; but to the general councils of his allies he only disclosed part of his daring scheme.

He proposed to the Dutch that he should march from Flanders to the Upper Rhine and Moselle with the British troops and part of the foreign auxiliaries, and commence vigorous operations against the French armies in that quarter, while General Auverquerque, with the Dutch and the remainder of the auxiliaries, maintained a defensive war in the Netherlands. Having with difficulty obtained the consent of the Dutch to this portion of his project, he exercised the same diplomatic zeal, with the same success, in urging the King of Prussia and other princes of the empire to increase the number of the troops which they supplied, and to post them in places convenient for his own intended movements.

Marlborough commenced his celebrated march on May 19th. The army which he was to lead had been assembled by his brother, General Churchill, at Bedburg, not far from Maestricht, on the Meuse; it included sixteen thousand English troops, and consisted of fifty-one battalions of foot, and ninety-two squadrons of horse. Marlborough was to collect and join with him on his march the troops of Prussia, Luneburg, and Hesse, quartered on the Rhine, and eleven Dutch battalions that were stationed at Rothweil. He had only marched a single day when the series of interruptions, complaints, and requisitions from the other leaders of the allies began, to which he seemed subjected throughout his enterprise, and which would have caused its failure in the hands of anyone not gifted with the firmness and the exquisite temper of Marlborough.

One specimen of these annoyances and of Marlborough's mode of dealing with them may suffice. On his encamping at Kupen on the 20th, he received an express from Auverquerque pressing him to halt, because Villeroy, who commanded the French army in Flanders, had quitted the lines which he had been occupying, and crossed the Meuse at Namur with thirty-six battalions and forty-five squadrons, and was threatening the town of Huy. At the same time Marlborough received letters from the Margrave of Baden and Count Wratislaw, who commanded the Imperialist forces at Stollhoffen, near the left bank of the Rhine, stating that Tallard had made a movement, as if intending to cross the Rhine, and urging him to hasten his march toward the lines of Stollhoffen. Marlborough was not diverted by these applications from the prosecution of his grand design.

Conscious that the army of Villeroy would be too much reduced to undertake offensive operations, by the detachments which had already been made toward the Rhine, and those which must follow his own march, he halted only a day to quiet the alarms of Auverquerque. To satisfy also the Margrave, he ordered the troops of Hompesch and Buelow to draw toward Philippsburg, though with private injunctions not to proceed beyond a certain distance. He even exacted a promise to the same effect from Count Wratislaw, who at this juncture arrived at the camp to attend him during the whole campaign.

Marlborough reached the Rhine at Coblenz, where he crossed that river, and then marched along its left bank to Broubach and Mainz. His march, though rapid, was admirably conducted, so as to save the troops from all unnecessary fatigue; ample supplies of provisions were ready, and the most perfect discipline was maintained. By degrees Marlborough obtained more reënforcements from the Dutch and the other confederates, and he also was left more at liberty by them to follow his own course. Indeed, before even a blow was struck, his enterprise had paralyzed the enemy and had materially relieved Austria from the pressure of the war. Villeroy, with his detachments from the French Flemish army, was completely bewildered by Marlborough's movements, and, unable to divine where it was that the English general meant to strike his blow, wasted away the early part of the summer between Flanders and the Moselle without effecting anything.[1]

Marshal Tallard, who commanded forty-five thousand French

[1] "Marshal Villeroy," says Voltaire, "who had wished to follow Marlborough on his first marches, suddenly lost sight of him altogether, and only learned where he really was on hearing of his victory at Donawert."

at Strasburg, and who had been destined by Louis to march early in the year into Bavaria, thought that Marlborough's march along the Rhine was preliminary to an attack upon Alsace; and the marshal therefore kept his forty-five thousand men back in order to protect France in that quarter. Marlborough skilfully encouraged his apprehensions by causing a bridge to be constructed across the Rhine at Philippsburg, and by making the Landgrave of Hesse advance his artillery at Mannheim, as if for a siege of Landau.

Meanwhile the Elector of Bavaria and Marshal Marsin, suspecting that Marlborough's design might be what it really proved to be, forbore to press upon the Austrians opposed to them or to send troops into Hungary; and they kept back so as to secure their communications with France. Thus, when Marlborough, at the beginning of June, left the Rhine and marched for the Danube, the numerous hostile armies were uncombined and unable to check him.

"With such skill and science," says Coxe, "had this enterprise been concerted that at the very moment when it assumed a specific direction the enemy was no longer enabled to render it abortive. As the march was now to be bent toward the Danube, notice was given for the Prussians, Palatines, and Hessians, who were stationed on the Rhine, to order their march so as to join the main body in its progress. At the same time directions were sent to accelerate the advance of the Danish auxiliaries, who were marching from the Netherlands."

Crossing the river Neckar, Marlborough marched in a southeastern direction to Mundelshene, where he had his first personal interview with Prince Eugene, who was destined to be his colleague on so many glorious fields. Thence, through a difficult and dangerous country, Marlborough continued his march against the Bavarians, whom he encountered on July 2d on the heights of the Schullenberg, near Donauwoerth. Marlborough stormed their intrenched camp, crossed the Danube, took several strong places in Bavaria, and made himself completely master of the Elector's dominions except the fortified cities of Munich and Augsburg. But the Elector's army, though defeated at Donauwoerth, was still numerous and strong; and at last Marshal Tallard, when thoroughly apprised of the real nature of Marlborough's movements, crossed the Rhine; and being suffered, through the supineness of the German general at Stollhoffen, to march without loss through the Black Forest, he united his powerful army at Biberach, near Augsburg, with that of the Elector and the French troops under Marshal Marsin, who had previously been cooperating with the Bavarians.

On the other hand, Marlborough recrossed the Danube, and on August 11th united his army with the Imperialist forces under Prince Eugene. The combined armies occupied a position near Hoechstaedt,[1] a little higher up the left bank of the Danube than Donauwoerth, the scene of Marlborough's recent victory, and almost exactly on the ground where Marshal Villars and the Elector had defeated an Austrian army in the preceding year. The French marshals and the Elector were now in position a little further to the east, between Blenheim and Lützingen, and with the little stream of the Nebel between them and the troops of Marlborough and Eugene. The Gallo-Bavarian army consisted of about sixty thousand men, and they had sixty-one pieces of artillery. The army of the allies was about fifty-six thousand strong, with fifty-two guns.

Although the French army of Italy had been unable to penetrate into Austria, and although the masterly strategy of Marlborough had hitherto warded off the destruction with which the cause of the allies seemed menaced at the beginning of the campaign, the peril was still most serious. It was absolutely necessary for Marlborough to attack the enemy before Villeroy should be roused into action. There was nothing to stop that general and his army from marching into Franconia, whence the allies drew their principal supplies; and besides thus distressing them, he might, by marching on and joining his army to those of Tallard and the Elector, form a mass which would overwhelm the force under Marlborough and Eugene. On the other hand, the chances of a battle seemed perilous, and the fatal consequences of a defeat were certain. The disadvantage of the allies in point of number was not very great, but still it was not to be disregarded; and the advantage which the enemy seemed to have in the composition of their troops was striking.

[1] The Battle of Blenheim is called by the Germans and the French the battle of Hoechstaedt.—ED.

Tallard and Marsin had forty-five thousand Frenchmen under them, all veterans and all trained to act together; the Elector's own troops also were good soldiers. Marlborough, like Wellington at Waterloo, headed an army of which the larger proportion consisted, not of English, but of men of many different nations and many different languages. He was also obliged to be the assailant in the action, and thus to expose his troops to comparatively heavy loss at the commencement of the battle, while the enemy would fight under the protection of the villages and lines which they were actively engaged in strengthening. The consequences of a defeat of the confederated army must have broken up the Grand Alliance, and realized the proudest hopes of the French King. Alison, in his admirable military history of the Duke of Marlborough, has truly stated the effects which would have taken place if France had been successful in the war; and when the position of the confederates at the time when Blenheim was fought is remembered—when we recollect the exhaustion of Austria, the menacing insurrection of Hungary, the feuds and jealousies of the German princes, the strength and activity of the Jacobite party in England, and the imbecility of nearly all the Dutch statesmen of the time, and the weakness of Holland if deprived of her allies—we may adopt his words in speculating on what would have ensued if France had been victorious in the battle, and "if a power, animated by the ambition, guided by the fanaticism, and directed by the ability of that of Louis XIV, had gained the ascendency in Europe.

"Beyond all question, a universal despotic dominion would have been established over the bodies, a cruel spiritual thraldom over the minds, of men. France and Spain, united under Bourbon princes and in a close family alliance—the empire of Charlemagne with that of Charles V—the power which revoked the Edict of Nantes and perpetrated the massacre of St. Bartholomew, with that which banished the Moriscoes and established the Inquisition, would have proved irresistible, and, beyond example, destructive to the best interests of mankind.

"The Protestants might have been driven, like the pagan heathens of old by the son of Pépin, beyond the Elbe; the Stuart race, and with them Romish ascendency, might have been reëstablished in England; the fire lighted by Latimer and Ridley might have been extinguished in blood; and the energy breathed by religious freedom into the Anglo-Saxon race might have expired. The destinies of the world would have been changed. Europe, instead of a variety of independent states, whose mutual hostility kept alive courage, while their national rivalry stimulated talent, would have sunk into the slumber attendant on universal dominion. The colonial empire of England would have withered away and perished, as that of Spain has done in the grasp of the Inquisition. The Anglo-Saxon race would have been arrested in its mission to overspread the earth and subdue it. The centralized despotism of the Roman Empire would have been renewed on Continental Europe; the chains of Romish tyranny, and with them the general infidelity of France before the Revolution, would have extinguished or perverted thought in the British Islands."

Marlborough's words at the council of war, when a battle was resolved on, are remarkable, and they deserve recording. We know them on the authority of his chaplain, Mr. (afterward Bishop) Hare, who accompanied him throughout the campaign, and in whose journal the biographers of Marlborough have found many of their best materials. Marlborough's words to the officers who remonstrated with him on the seeming temerity of attacking the enemy in their position were: "I know the danger, yet a battle is absolutely necessary, and I rely on the bravery and discipline of the troops, which will make amends for our disadvantages." In the evening orders were issued for a general engagement, and were received by the army with an alacrity which justified his confidence.

The French and Bavarians were posted behind the little stream called the Nebel, which runs almost from north to south into the Danube immediately in front of the village of Blenheim. The Nebel flows along a little valley, and the French occupied the rising ground to the west of it. The village of Blenheim was the extreme right of their position, and the village of Luetzingen, about three miles north of Blenheim, formed their left. Beyond Luetzingen are the rugged high grounds of the Godd Berg and Eich Berg, on the skirts of which some detachments were posted, so as to secure the Gallo-Bavarian position from being turned on the left flank. The Danube secured their right flank; and it was only in front that they could be attacked. The villages of Blenheim and Luetzingen had been strongly palisaded and intrenched; Marshal Tallard, who held the chief command, took his station at Blenheim; the Elector and Marshal Marsin commanded on the left.

Tallard garrisoned Blenheim with twenty-six battalions of French infantry and twelve squadrons of French cavalry. Marsin and the Elector had twenty-two battalions of infantry and thirty-six squadrons of cavalry in front of the village of Luetzingen. The centre was occupied by fourteen battalions of infantry, including the celebrated Irish brigade. These were posted in the little hamlet of Oberglau, which lies somewhat nearer to Luetzingen than to Blenheim. Eighty squadrons of cavalry and seven battalions of foot were ranged between Oberglau and Blenheim. Thus the French position was very strong at each extremity, but was comparatively weak in the centre. Tallard seems to have relied on the swampy state of the part of the valley that reaches from below Oberglau to Blenheim for preventing any serious attack on this part of his line.

The army of the allies was formed into two great divisions, the largest being commanded by the Duke in person, and being destined to act against Tallard, while Prince Eugene led the other division, which consisted chiefly of cavalry, and was intended to oppose the enemy under Marsin and the Elector. As they approached the enemy, Marlborough's troops formed the left and the centre, while Eugene's formed the right of the entire army. Early in the morning of August 13th the allies left their own camp and marched toward the enemy. A thick haze covered the ground, and it was not until the allied right and centre had advanced nearly within cannon-shot of the enemy that Tallard was aware of their approach. He made his preparations with what haste he could, and about eight o'clock a heavy fire of artillery was opened from the French right on the advancing left wing of the British. Marlborough ordered up some of his batteries to reply to it, and while the columns that were to form the allied left and centre deployed, and took up their proper stations in the line, a warm cannonade was kept up by the guns on both sides.

The ground which Eugene's columns had to traverse was peculiarly difficult, especially for the passage of the artillery, and it was nearly mid-day before he could get his troops into line opposite to Luetzingen. During this interval Marlborough ordered divine service to be performed by the chaplains at the head of each regiment, and then rode along the lines, and found both officers and men in the highest spirits and waiting impatiently for the signal for the attack. At length an aide-de-camp galloped up from the right with the welcome news that Eugene was ready. Marlborough instantly sent Lord Cutts, with a strong brigade of infantry to assault the village of Blenheim, while he himself led the main body down the eastward slope of the valley of the Nebel, and prepared to effect the passage of the stream.

The assault on Blenheim, though bravely made, was repulsed with severe loss, and Marlborough, finding how strongly that village was garrisoned, desisted from any further attempts to carry it, and bent all his energies to breaking the enemy's line between Blenheim and Oberglau. Some temporary bridges had been prepared, and planks and fascines had been collected; and by the aid of these, and a little stone bridge which crossed the Nebel near a hamlet called Unterglau, that lay in the centre of the valley, Marlborough succeeded in getting several squadrons across the Nebel, though it was divided into several branches, and the ground between them was soft, and, in places, little better than a mere marsh.

But the French artillery was not idle. The cannon-balls plunged incessantly among the advancing squadrons of the allies, and bodies of French cavalry rode frequently down from the western ridge, to charge them before they had time to form on the firm ground. It was only by supporting his men by fresh troops, and by bringing up infantry, who checked the advance of the enemy's horse by their steady fire, that Marlborough was able to save his army in this quarter from a repulse, which, succeeding the failure of the attack upon Blenheim, would probably have been fatal to the allies. By degrees, his cavalry struggled over the blood-stained streams; the infantry were also now brought across, so as to keep in check the French troops who held Blenheim, and who, when no longer assailed in front, had begun to attack the allies on their left with considerable effect.

Marlborough had thus at length succeeded in drawing up the whole left wing of his army beyond the Nebel, and was about to press forward with it, when he was called away to another part of the field by a disaster that had befallen his centre. The Prince of Holstein Beck had, with eleven Hanoverian battalions, passed the Nebel opposite to Oberglau, when he was charged and utterly routed by the Irish brigade which held that village. The Irish drove the Hanoverians back with heavy slaughter, broke completely through the line of the allies, and nearly achieved a success as brilliant as that which the same brigade afterward gained at Fontenoy.

But at Blenheim their ardor in pursuit led them too far. Marlborough came up in person, and dashed in upon the exposed flank of the brigade with some squadrons of British cavalry. The Irish reeled back, and as they strove to regain the height of Oberglau their column was raked through and through by the fire of three battalions of the allies, which Marlborough had summoned up from the reserve. Marlborough having reëstablished the order and communications of the allies in this quarter, now, as he returned to his own left wing, sent to learn how his colleague fared against Marsin and the Elector, and to inform Eugene of his own success.

Eugene had hitherto not been equally fortunate. He had made three attacks on the enemy opposed to him, and had been thrice driven back. It was only by his own desperate personal exertions, and the remarkable steadiness of the regiments of Prussian infantry, which were under him, that he was able to save his wing from being totally defeated. But it was on the southern part of the battle-field, on the ground which Marlborough had won beyond the Nebel with such difficulty, that the crisis of the battle was to be decided.

Like Hannibal, Marlborough relied principally on his cavalry for achieving his decisive successes, and it was by his cavalry that Blenheim, the greatest of his victories, was won. The battle had lasted till five in the afternoon. Marlborough had now eight thousand horsemen drawn up in two lines, and in the most perfect order for a general attack on the enemy's line along the space between Blenheim and Oberglau. The infantry was drawn up in battalions in their rear, so as to support them if repulsed, and to keep in check the large masses of the French that still occupied the village of Blenheim. Tallard now interlaced his squadrons of cavalry with battalions of infantry, and Marlborough, by a corresponding movement, brought several regiments of infantry and some pieces of artillery to his front line at intervals between the bodies of horse.

A little after five Marlborough commenced the decisive movement, and the allied cavalry, strengthened and supported by foot and guns, advanced slowly from the lower ground near the Nebel up the slope to where the French cavalry, ten thousand strong, awaited them. On riding over the summit of the acclivity, the allies were received with so hot a fire from the French artillery and small arms that at first the cavalry recoiled, but without abandoning the high ground. The guns and the infantry which they had brought with them maintained the contest with spirit and effect. The French fire seemed to slacken. Marlborough instantly ordered a charge along the line. The allied cavalry galloped forward at the enemy's squadrons, and the hearts of the French horsemen failed them. Discharging their carbines at an idle distance, they wheeled round and spurred from the field, leaving the nine infantry battalions of their comrades to be ridden down by the torrent of the allied cavalry.

The battle was now won. Tallard and Marsin, severed from each other, thought only of retreat. Tallard drew up the squadrons of horse that he had left, in a line extended toward Blenheim, and sent orders to the infantry in that village to leave it and join him without delay. But long ere his orders could be obeyed the conquering squadrons of Marlborough had wheeled to the left and thundered down on the feeble array of the French marshal. Part of the force which Tallard had drawn up for this last effort was driven into the Danube; part fled with their general to the village of Sonderheim, where they were soon surrounded by the victorious allies and compelled to surrender. Meanwhile Eugene had renewed his attack upon the Gallo-Bavarian left, and Marsin, finding his colleague utterly routed, and his own right flank uncovered, prepared to retreat. He and the Elector succeeded in withdrawing a considerable part of their troops in tolerable order to Dillingen; but the large body of French who garrisoned Blenheim were left exposed to certain destruction.

Marlborough speedily occupied all the outlets from the village with his victorious troops, and then, collecting his artillery round it, he commenced a cannonade that speedily would have destroyed Blenheim itself and all who were in it. After several gallant but unsuccessful attempts to cut their way through the allies, the French in Blenheim were at length compelled to surrender at discretion; and twenty-four battalions and twelve squadrons, with all their officers, laid down their arms and became the captives of Marlborough.

"Such," says Voltaire, "was the celebrated battle which the French called the battle of Hoechstaedt, the Germans Blindheim, and the English Blenheim. The conquerors had about five thousand killed and eight thousand wounded, the greater part being on the side of Prince Eugene. The French army was almost entirely destroyed: of sixty thousand men, so long victorious, there never reassembled more than twenty thousand effective. About twelve thousand killed, fourteen thousand prisoners, all the cannon, a prodigious number of colors and standards, all the tents and equipages, the general of the army, and one thousand two hundred officers of mark in the power of the conqueror, signalized that day!"

Ulm, Landau, Treves, and Traerbach surrendered to the allies before the close of the year. Bavaria submitted to the Emperor, and the Hungarians laid down their arms. Germany was completely delivered from France, and the military ascendency of the arms of the allies was completely established. Throughout the rest of the war Louis fought only in defence. Blenheim had dissipated forever his once proud visions of almost universal conquest.

UNION OF ENGLAND AND SCOTLAND

A.D. 1707

JOHN HILL BURTON

Although not one of the longest, the reign of Queen Anne was one of the most glorious, in English history. Not only was it signalized by the victorious deeds of Marlborough in the War of the Spanish Succession, but also by the union of the two kingdoms of England and Scotland, one of the principal events in British annals.

Before the union England and Scotland had no political partnership save that derived through the person of the sovereign by inheritance of both crowns. From the completion of the union in 1707 both countries have been not only under one royal head, but also represented in a single Parliament. At the beginning of Anne's reign the attitude of Scotland toward England was hostile, old antagonisms surviving in memory to intensify fresh irritations. Although William III, predecessor of Anne, had urged a union of the kingdoms, all negotiations to that end had failed. In 1703, and again in 1704, the Scottish Parliament had passed an act of security declaring in favor of the abrogation of the union of the crowns which had existed for a century. The English Parliament resorted to retaliatory measures.

By this time, however, the wiser statesmen in both countries saw that open hostilities could be averted only by a complete political union of the two kingdoms, and they used all their influence to bring it about. How this great historic reconciliation was accomplished, Burton, the eminent Scottish historian and jurist, shows with equal learning and impartiality.

THE English statute, responding by precautions and threats to the Scots Act of Security, contained clauses for furthering an incorporating union as the only conclusive settlement of accumulating difficulties. It provided that commissioners for England appointed by the Queen under the great seal shall have power "to treat and consult" with commissioners for the same purpose "authorized by authority of the Parliament of Scotland." The statute of the Parliament of Scotland completing the adjustment, with the short title "Act for a treaty with England," authorizes such persons "as shall be nominated and appointed by her majesty under the great seal of this kingdom" to treat and consult with "the commissioners for England."

The next great step was the appointment of the two commissions, thirty-one on either side. On the English were the two archbishops; for Scotland there was no clerical element. It was noticed that for England all the members not official were from the peerage, while in Scotland there seemed to be a desire to represent the peerage, the landed commoners, and the burgesses or city interest, in just proportions. At an early stage in the daily business, the English brought up a proposition about the reception of which they had considerable apprehension: that there should be "the same customs, excise, and all other taxes" throughout the United Kingdom—virtually a resolution that Scotland should be taxed on the English scale. This was easily passed by means of a solvent—due, no doubt, to the financial genius of Godolphin—that, on an accounting and proof of local or personal hardships arising from the adoption of uniformity, compensation in money should be made from the English treasury. But a more critical point was reached when, on April 24th, the chancellor of Scotland brought forward, among certain preliminary articles, one "that there be free communication, and intercourse of trade and navigation, between the two kingdoms and plantations thereunto belonging, under such regulations as in the progress of this treaty shall be found most for the advantage of both kingdoms." This was frankly accepted on the part of England, and faithfully adjusted in detail. It was felt to be a mighty sacrifice made to exercise indefinite but formidable calamities in another shape.

At this point in the progress of the union all interest resting on the excitements of political victory and defeat, or the chances of a bitter war, came to an end. There were a few small incidents in Scotland; but England was placidly indifferent. She had cheerfully paid a heavy stake as loser in the great game, and it would trouble her no more. The statesmen of the two countries knew that the union must pass unless the Jacobites of Scotland were joined by an invading French army; and that was not a likely casualty while Marlborough was hovering on the frontiers of France. There was a touch of the native haughtiness in this placid indifference of England. No doubt it helped in clearing the way to the great conclusion; but for many years after the fusing of the two nations into one, disturbing events showed that it had been better had the English known something about the national institutions and the temper of the people who had now a right to call themselves their fellow-countrymen.

It was expected that Scotland would be quietly absorbed into England—absorptions much more difficult in the first aspect were in continuous progress in Asia and America. The Englishman had great difficulty in reconciling himself to political and social conditions not his own, and his pride prompted him to demand that, if he left England, any part of the world honored by his presence should make an England for his reception. When expecting this on the other side of the border, he forgot that the Scot had too much of his own independence and obstinacy. True, the Scot, among the sweet uses of adversity, had imbibed more of the vagrant, and could adapt himself more easily to the usages and temper of other nations. But on the question of yielding up his own national usages and prejudices in his own country he was as obstinate as his mighty partner.

There was still a world of business to be transacted in details of the unattractive kind that belong to accountants' reports. These may be objects of vital and intense interest—as in the realizing of the assets in bankruptcies, where persons immediately interested in frantic excitement hunt out the array of small figures—two, three, four, or five—that tells them whether they are safe or ruined. But the interest is not of a kind to hold its intensity through after generations. On some items of the present accounting, however, there was, in the principle adopted, a fund of personal and political interest. The heavy debts of England had to be considered—and here, as in all pecuniary arrangements, England was freehanded. The Scots made an effort to retain their African Company, but they fortunately offered the alternative of purchasing the stock from the holders. On the alternative of retention the English commissioners were resolute in refusal and resistance, but they were ready to entertain the other; and they accepted it in a literal shape. To have bought the stock at its market value would have been a farce, after the ruin that had overcome the company. But if it could not be even said that England had ruined the company, the sacrifice had been made in the prevalence of English interests, and while there was yet a hold on England it should be kept. There was no difficulty in coming to a settlement satisfactory to the Scots, and willingly offered by the English. It was substantially payment of the loss on each share, as calculated from an examination of the company's books.

The adjustment of the several pecuniary claims thus created in favor of Scotland was simply the collective summation of the losses incurred by all the stockholders; and when the summation was completed the total was passed into a capital sum, called the "Equivalent." This sum total of the various items, with all their fractions, making up a fractional sum less than four hundred thousand pounds, might be otherwise described as a capital stock held by the shareholders of the old company trading to Africa and the Indies, each to the extent of his loss. Odious suspicions were, down to the present generation, propagated about an item or group of items in the Equivalent. A sum amounting to twenty thousand five hundred forty pounds seventeen shillings sevenpence had been made over by the English treasury, to be paid to influential Scotsmen as the price of their votes or influence in favor of England.

Fortunately this affair was closely investigated by the celebrated committee of inquiry that brought on Marlborough's dismissal and Walpole's imprisonment. It was found that the Scots treasury had been drained; and the crisis of the union was not a suitable time either for levying money or for leaving debts —the salaries of public offices especially—unpaid. England, therefore, lent money to clear away this difficulty. The transaction was irregular, and had not passed through the proper treasury forms. It was ascertained, however, that the money so lent had been repaid. In discussions of the affair, before those concerned were fully cleared of the odium of bribery, taunting remarks had been made on the oddity and sordid specialties of the items of payment. Thus the allowance to the Lord Banff was, in sterling money, eleven pounds two shillings. It would have had a richer sound, and perhaps resolved itself into round numbers, in Scots money; but as it is, there is no more to be said against it than that, as a debt in some way due to the Lord Banff, the exact English book-keeper had entered it down to its fraction.

There remained a few matters of adjustment of uniformities between the two countries for the advantage of both—such as a fixed standard for rating money in account. The Scots grumbled, rather than complained, about the English standard being always made the rule, and no reciprocity being offered. But the Scots were left considerable facilities for the use of their own customs for home purposes in pecuniary matters, and in weights and measures. If, for the general convenience of commerce and taxation, any uniformity was necessary, and the practice of the greater nation was a suitable standard for the other, it was the smaller sacrifice, and to both parties the easier arrangement, that those who were only an eighth part of the inhabitants of the island should yield to the overwhelming majority.

It was in keeping with the wisdom and tolerance prevailing throughout on the English side of the treaty that it should be first discussed in the Parliament of Scotland. If this was felt as a courtesy to Scotland it was an expediency for England. All opposition would be in Scotland, and it was well to know it at once, that disputes might be cleared off and a simple affirmative or negative presented to the Parliament of Scotland.

The Parliament of England has ever restrained vague oratory by a rule that there must always be a question of yes or no, fitted for a division as the text of a debate. In Scotland on this occasion, as on many others, there was at first a discussion of the general question; and when this, along with other sources of information, had given the servants of the Crown some assurance of the fate of the measure, there was a separate debate and division on the first article, understood on all hands to be a final decision. The debate was decorated by a work of oratorical art long admired in Scotland, and indeed worthy of admiration anywhere for its brilliancy and power. It was a great philippic—taking that term in its usual acceptation—as expressing a vehement torrent of bitter epigram and denunciatory climax.

The speech of John Hamilton, Lord Belhaven, "On the subject-matter of a union betwixt the two kingdoms of England and Scotland," was so amply dispersed in its day that if a collector of pamphlets on the union buys them in volumes he will generally find this speech in each volume. It is, no doubt, an effort of genius; but what will confer more interest on the following specimens selected from it is that it was an attempt to rouse the nation to action at this perilous and momentous crisis, and succeeded only in drawing attention and admiration as a fine specimen of rhetorical art:

"I think I see the present peers of Scotland, whose noble ancestors conquered provinces, overran countries, reduced and subjected towns and fortified places, exacted tribute through the greater part of England, now walking in the court of requests like so many English attorneys, laying aside their walking-swords when in company with the English peers, lest their self-defence should be found murder.

"I think I see the royal state of boroughs walking their desolate streets, hanging down their heads under disappointments, wormed out of all the branches of their old trade, uncertain what hand to turn to, necessitate to become 'prentices to their unkind neighbors, and yet after all finding their trade so fortified by companies and secured by prescriptions that they despair of any success therein. But above all, my lord, I think I see our ancient mother, Caledonia, like Cæsar, sitting in the midst of our senate, ruefully looking round her, covering herself with her royal garment, attending the fatal blow, and breathing out her last with a '*et tu quoque mi fili.*'"

The great remedy for all is an end of rancorous feuds and hatreds dividing Scotland; and this calls from him a glowing picture of the land that by union and industry has made itself too powerful to be a safe partner for humiliated Scotland:

"They are not under the afflicting hand of Providence as we are; their circumstances are great and glorious; their treaties are prudently managed both at home and abroad; their generals brave and valorous; their armies successful and victorious; their trophies and laurels memorable and surprising; their enemies subdued and routed. Their royal navy is the terror of Europe; their trade and commerce extended through the universe, encircling the whole world, and rendering their own capital city the emporium for the whole inhabitants of the earth."

The speech was for the country, not for the House. The great points about trade and virtual independence had been conceded by England, and a union was looked to rather as a refuge and a gain than as oppression and plunder. It has even been said that there was some inclination to receive the speech with irony; and Defoe, who seems to have been present on the occasion, gives this account of what followed:

"Mr. Seton, who made the first speech, stood up to answer the Lord Belhaven; but as he had already spoken, the order of the House—viz., 'that the same member could not speak twice in the same cause'—was urged against his speaking, and the Earl of Marchmont standing up at the same time, the lord chancellor gave place to him, who indeed made a short return to so long a speech, and which answer occasioned some laughter in the House. The Earl of Marchmont's speech was to this purpose, viz.: He had heard a long speech, and a very terrible one; but he was of opinion it required a short answer, which he gave in these terms: 'Behold he dreamed, but, lo! when he awoke, he found it was a dream.' This answer, some said, was as satisfactory to the members, who understood the design of that speech as if it had been answered vision by vision."

In the debates on the union, some Scots statesmen found a tactic, infinitely valuable to them in the united Parliament, of voting in a group. They were called the "New party," and nicknamed the "*Squadrone volante.*" In the correspondence already referred to, it was good news at St. Stephen's when it was announced that the New party had adopted the union. On the critical division the numbers stood one hundred eighteen for the article and eighty-three against it. The remainder of the clauses passed without division, a ready acceptance being given to amendments, that were virtually improvements, in giving effect to the spirit of details in the treaty; as where it was adjusted that, for trading purposes, vessels bought abroad for trade from the Scots harbors should be counted equivalent to vessels of Scottish build.

There was a considerable noisy excitement through the country, the Jacobites ever striving to rouse the people in the great towns to riot and sedition, and, when they found that impossible, spreading exaggerated accounts of the effects of their efforts. A mob was raised in Edinburgh, but it was appeased without the loss of life and with no other casualty save the frightening of the provost's wife. There were some eccentric movements among the Cameronians, rendered all the more grotesque by the Jacobites taking the leadership in them; and some of the more vehement clergy betook themselves to their own special weapons in the holding of a day of humiliation and prayer.

Ere the whole came to a conclusion, a point was yielded to the Presbyterian Church of Scotland. It was passed as a separate act before the Act of Union was passed—the separate act stipulating its repetition in any act adopting the Treaty of Union. It provided for the preservation of the discipline, worship, and ecclesiastical government of the establishment. It was further provided that every sovereign of the United Kingdom, on accession to the throne, should make oath in terms of this act. Hence it happens that this oath is taken immediately on the accession, the other oaths, including that for the protection of the Church of England, being postponed till the ceremony of the coronation. On October 16, 1706, there came a vote on the passing of the "Act ratifying and approving the Treaty of Union." This was carried in the Scots Parliament by one hundred ten to sixty-nine.

It was the determination of the Queen's ministers for England to carry the treaty as it came from Scotland, word for word; and they employed all their strength to do so. It was the policy of the English government and their supporters in the matter of the union, to avoid a Parliamentary debate upon it clause by clause at St. Stephen's.

To this end there was an endeavor to give it, as much as in the peculiar conditions could be given, the character of a treaty between two independent powers, each acting through its executive, that executive acknowledging the full power of Parliament to examine, criticise, and virtually judge the act done as a whole, but not admitting Parliamentary interference with the progress of the details. If there were an illogicality in the essence of a treaty where the executive—the Queen—was the common sovereign of both realms, the difficulty could be discarded as a pedantry, in a constitutional community where the sovereign acts through responsible advisers. Some slight touches of apprehension were felt in England when it was seen that the Scots Estates were not only voting the separate articles, but in some measure remodelling them.

The Estates were taking the privilege naturally claimed by

the weaker party to a bargain in protecting themselves while it was yet time. When all was adjusted, England, as the vast majority, could correct whatever had been done amiss in the preliminary adjustment of her interests, but poor Scotland would be entirely helpless. There was another reason for tolerating the alterations, in their being directed to the safety and completeness of the legal institutions left in the hands of Scotland untouched, as matters of entire indifference to England; still it weakened the hands of those who desired to evade a Parliamentary discussion on the several articles in England that this had been permitted in Scotland, and had become effective in the shape of amendments. John Johnston, who had been for some time secretary of state for Scotland—a son of the celebrated covenanting hero Archibald Johnston of Warriston—was then in London carefully looking at the signs of the times. He wrote to Scotland, saying: "You may, I think, depend on it that the alterations you have hitherto made will not break the union; but if you go on altering, it's like your alterations will be altered here, which will make a new session with you necessary, and in that case no man knows what may happen." All is well as yet (January 4th), and if there be no more serious alterations the English ministers will be able to give effect to their resolution "to pass the union here without making any alterations at all."

By what had been usually called a message from the throne, the attention of Parliament was directed to the treaty as it had come from Scotland, but the matter being of supreme importance the Queen was her own messenger. From the Commons she had to ask for a supply to meet the equivalent. To both Houses she said: "You have now an opportunity before you of putting the last hand to a happy union of the two kingdoms, which I hope will be a lasting blessing to the whole island, a great addition to its wealth and power, and a firm security to the Protestant religion. The advantages that will accrue to us all from a union are so apparent that I will add no more, but that I shall look upon it as a particular happiness if this great work, which has been so often attempted without success, can be brought to perfection in my reign."

The opportunity was taken to imitate the Scots in a separate preliminary act "for securing the Church of England as by law established." There was a desultory discussion in both Houses, with a result showing the overwhelming strength of the supporters of the union. In the House of Lords there were some divisions, and among these the largest number of votes mustered by the opposition was twenty-three, bringing out a majority of forty-seven by seventy votes for the ministry. The conclusion of the discussion was a vote of approval by each House.

The opposition, however, did not adopt their defeat. They were preparing to fight the battle over again, clause by clause, when a bill was brought in to convert the Articles of Union into an act of Parliament. The English House of Commons has always been supremely tolerant to troublesome and even mischievous members, so long as they adhere to the forms of the House—forms to be zealously guarded, since they were framed for averting hasty legislation and the possible domination of an intolerant majority. It was determined, however, that the impracticals and impedimenters should not have their swing on this occasion, when the descent of a French army to gather to its centre the Jacobitism still lingering in the country darkened the political horizon. Both Houses had a full opportunity for discussing the merits of every word in the treaty, and the risk of national ruin was not to be encountered because they had not expended all their loquacity, having expected another opportunity.

The tactic for evading the danger was credited to the ingenuity of Sir Simon Harcourt, the attorney-general. The two acts of ecclesiastical security and the articles of the treaty were all recited in the preamble of the bill under the command of the mighty "Whereas," the enacting part of the act was dropped into a single sentence, shorter than statutory sentences usually are. The opposition might throw out the measure, and the ministry with it, if they had strength to do so; but there had been sufficient discussion on the clauses, and there should be no more. In the descriptive words of Burnet: "This put those in great difficulties who had resolved to object to several articles, and to insist on demanding several alterations in them, for they could not come at any debate about them; they could not object to the recital, it being mere matter of fact; and they had not strength enough to oppose the general enacting clause; nor was it easy to come at particulars and offer provisos relating to them. The matter was carried on with such zeal that it passed through the House of Commons before those who intended to oppose it had recovered out of the surprise under which the form it was drawn in had put them."

There was thus but one question, that the bill do pass, and the opposition had not reaped encouragement to resist so great an issue. The Lords had, in their usual manner of dignified repose, managed to discuss the clauses, but it was rather a conversation, to see that all was in right order, and that no accident had happened to a measure of so vital moment, than a debate.

On March 6, 1707, the Queen came to the House of Lords, and in a graceful speech gave the royal assent to the act.

DOWNFALL OF CHARLES XII AT POLTAVA

TRIUMPH OF RUSSIA

A.D. 1709

K. WALISZEWSKI[1]

The battle of Poltava was selected by Sir Edward Creasy as one of the fifteen great decisive contests which have altered the fate of nations. His able narrative of the battle has been superseded in scholars' eyes by the more modern work of the great Russian authority, Waliszewski; but the importance of the event remains. It reversed the positions of Sweden and Russia in European politics, and placed Russia among the great countries of the modern world; Sweden among the little ones.

Before 1709 Sweden still held the rank to which Gustavus Adolphus had raised her in the Thirty Years' War. Her prestige had been a little dimmed by the victories of the "Great Elector" of Prussia; but her ally Louis XIV had saved her from any considerable diminution of the extensive territories which she held on the mainland to the south and east of the Baltic Sea. About 1700 the young and gallant warrior, Charles XII, the "Madman of the North," reasserted her prowess, made her once more the dictator of Northern Europe, one of the five great powers of the world.

Meanwhile Peter the Great was progressing but slowly with his transformation of Russia. His people had little confidence in him; his armies were half-barbaric hordes. When he ventured into war against Sweden Europe conceived but one possible result: these undisciplined barbarians would be annihilated. At first the expected occurred. Again and again large Russian armies were defeated by small bodies of Swedes; but with splendid tenacity Peter persisted in the face of revolt at home and defeat abroad. "The Swedes shall teach us to beat them" was his famous saying, and at Poltava he achieved his aim. From that time forward Russia's antagonism to her leader disappeared. His people followed him eagerly along the path to power.

IT WOULD appear that it was not till Peter's visit to Vienna, in 1698, that he conceived the idea of attacking Sweden. Up till that time his warlike impulse had rather been directed southward, and the Turk had been the sole object of his enmity. But

[1] Translated from the Russian by Lady Mary Loyd.

at Vienna he perceived that the Emperor, whose help he had counted on, had failed him, and forthwith the mobile mind of the young Czar turned to the right-about. A war he must have of some kind, it little mattered where, to give work to his young army. The warlike instincts and the greed of his predecessors, tempted sometimes by the Black Sea, sometimes by the Baltic and the border provinces of Poland, had, indeed, always swung and turned back and forward between the south and the north. These alternate impulses, natural enough in a nation so full of youth and strength, have, since those days, been most unnecessarily idealized, erected into a doctrine, and dignified as a work of unification. It must be acknowledged that every nation has at one time or the other thus claimed the right to resume the national patrimony at the expense of neighboring peoples, and Peter, by some lucky fate, remained in this respect within certain bounds of justice, of logic, and of truth. Absorbed and almost exhausted, as he soon became, by the desperate effort demanded by his war in the North, he forgot or imperilled much that the conquering ambition of his predecessors had left him in the South and West. He clung to the territory already acquired on the Polish side, retired from the Turkish border, and claimed what he had most right, relatively speaking, to claim in the matter of resumption, on his northwestern frontier.

On that frontier the coast country between the mouth of the Narva, or Narova, and that of the Siestra, watered by the Voksa, the Neva, the Igora, and the Louga, was really an integral part of the original Russian patrimony. It was one of the five districts (*piatiny*) of the Novgorod territory, and was still full of towns bearing Slavonic names, such as Korela, Ojeshek, Ladoga, Koporie, Iamy, and Ivangrod. It was not till 1616 that the Czar Michael Feodorovitch, during his struggle with Gustavus Adolphus, finally abandoned the seacoast for the sake of keeping his hold on Novgorod. But so strong was the hope of recovering the lost territory, in the hearts of his descendants, that, after the failure of an attempt on Livonia, in Alexis' reign, a boyar named Ordin-Nashtchokin set to work to build a number of warships at Kokenhausen, on the Dvina, which vessels were intended for the conquest of Riga. Peter had an impression, confused it may be, but yet powerful, of these historic traditions. This is proved by the direction in which he caused his armies to march after he had thrown down the gauntlet to Sweden. He strayed off the path, swayed, as he often was, by sudden impulses, but he always came back to the traditional aim of his forefathers—access to the sea, a Baltic port, "a window open upon Europe."

His interview with Augustus II at Rawa definitely settled his wavering mind. The *pacta conventa*, signed by the King of Poland when he ascended his throne, bound him to claim from the King of Sweden the territories which had formerly belonged to the republic of Poland. For this end the help of Denmark could be reckoned on. The Treaty of Roeskilde (1658), which had been forced on Frederick III, weighed heavily on his successors, and the eager glances fixed by the neighboring states on Holstein, after the death of Christian Albert, in 1694, threatened to end in quarrel. There were fair hopes, too, of the help of Brandenburg. When Sweden made alliance with Louis XIV and Madame de Maintenon, that country abandoned its historic position in Germany to Prussia. But Sweden still kept some footing, and was looked on as a rival.

Further, Augustus had a personal charm for Peter sufficient in itself to prove how much simplicity, inexperience, and boyish thoughtlessness still existed in that half-polished mind. The Polish sovereign, tall, strong, and handsome, an adept in all physical exercises, a great hunter, a hard drinker, and an indefatigable admirer of the fair sex, in whose person debauch of every kind took royal proportions, delighted the Czar and somewhat overawed him. He was more than inclined to think him a genius, and was quite ready to bind up his fortunes with his friend's. At the end of four days of uninterrupted feasting, they had agreed on the division of the spoils of Sweden, and had made a preliminary exchange of arms and clothing. The Czar appeared at Moscow a few weeks later wearing the King of Poland's waistcoat and belted with his sword.

In the beginning of 1700 Augustus and Frederick of Denmark attacked Sweden; but Peter, though bound by treaty to follow their example, neither moved nor stirred. Frederick was beaten, his very capital was threatened. So much the worse for him! Augustus seized on Dunamunde, but utterly failed before Riga. All the better for the Russians; Riga was left for them!

Another envoy came hurrying to Moscow. The Czar listened coolly to his reproaches, and replied that he would act as soon as news from Constantinople permitted it. Negotiations there were proceeding satisfactorily, and he hoped shortly to fulfil his promise, and to attack the Swedes in the neighborhood of Pskof. This was a point on which the allies had laid great stress, and Peter had studiously avoided contradicting them. It was quite understood between them that the Czar was not to lay a finger on Livonia. At last on August 8, 1700, a courier arrived with the longed-for despatch. Peace with Turkey was signed at last, and that very day the Russian troops received their marching orders. But they were not sent toward Pskof. They marched on Narva, in the very heart of the Livonian country.

The army destined to lay siege to Narva consisted of three divisions of novel formation, under the orders of three generals—Golovin, Weyde, and Repnin—with 10,500 Cossacks, and some irregular troops—63,520 men in all. Repnin's division, numbering 10,834 men, and the Little Russian Cossacks, stopped on the way, so that the actual force at disposal was reduced to about 40,000 men. But Charles XII, the new King of Sweden, could not bring more than 5300 infantry and 3130 cavalry to the relief of the town. And, being obliged, when he neared Wesemburg, to throw himself in flying column across a country which was already completely devastated, and, consequently, to carry all his supplies with him, his troops arrived in presence of an enemy five times as numerous as themselves, worn out, and completely exhausted by a succession of forced marches.

Peter never dreamed that he would find the King of Sweden in Livonia. He believed his hands were more than full enough elsewhere with the King of Denmark; he was quite unaware that the Peace of Travendal, which had been signed on the very day of the departure of the Russian troops, had been already forced upon his ally. He started off gayly at the head of his bombardier company, full of expectation of an easy victory. When he arrived before the town, on September 23d, he was astounded to find any preparations for serious defence. A regular siege had to be undertaken, and when, after a month of preparations, the Russian batteries at last opened fire, they made no impression whatever. The artillery was bad, and yet more badly served. A second month passed, during which Peter waited and hoped for some piece of luck, either for an offer to capitulate or for the arrival of Repnin's force. What did happen was that on the night of November 17th news came that within twenty-four hours the King of Sweden would be at Narva. That very night Peter fled from his camp, leaving the command to the Prince de Croy.

None of the arguments brought forward by the sovereign and his apologists in justification of this step appears to me to hold water. The necessity pleaded for an interview with the Duke of Poland, the Czar's desire to hasten on Repnin's march, are mere pitiful excuses. Langen and Hallart, the generals sent by Augustus to observe the military operations in Livonia, gravely reported that the Czar had been obliged to go to Moscow to receive a Turkish envoy—who was not expected for four months! The Emperor's envoy, Pleyer, is nearer the mark when he says the sovereign obeyed the entreaties of his advisers, who considered the danger too great for him to be permitted to remain. And Hallart himself, speaking of these same counsellors, whether ministers or generals, does not hesitate to declare, in his rough soldierly language, that "they have about as much courage as a frog has hair on his belly." The Russian army, disconcerted by the unexpected resistance of the Swedes, ill-prepared for resistance, ill-commanded, ill-lodged, and ill-fed, was already demoralized to the last extent. The arrival of Charles caused a panic, and from that panic Peter, the most impressionable of men, was the first to suffer.

The startling rapidity with which Charles had rid himself of the weakest of his three adversaries, under the very walls of Copenhagen, would have been less astonishing to Peter if the young sovereign had better realized the conditions under which he and his allies had begun a struggle in which, at first sight, their superiority appeared so disproportionate. King Frederick had reckoned without the powers which had guaranteed the recent Treaty of Altona, by which the safety of Holstein was insured; without the Hanoverian troops, and those of Luneburg, which at once brought succor to Toeningen; without the Anglo-Dutch fleet, which forced his to seek shelter under the walls of Copenhagen, and thus permitted the King of Sweden to cross the

Sound unmolested, and land quietly in Zealand; and finally, he reckoned—and for this he may well be excused—without that which was soon to fill all Europe with terror and amazement: the lucky star and the military genius of Charles XII.

This monarch, born in 1682, who had slain bears when he was sixteen, and at eighteen was a finished soldier, greedy for glory and battle and blood, was the last representative of that race of men who, between the sixteenth and seventeenth centuries, held all Central Europe in their iron grip; fierce warriors who steeped Germany and Italy in fire and blood, fought their way from town to town, and hamlet to hamlet; giving no truce and showing no mercy; who lived for war and by war; grew old and died in harness in a very atmosphere of carnage, with bodies riddled with wounds, with hands stained with abominable crimes, but with spirits calm and unflinching to the last. Standing on the threshold of the new period he was the superb and colossal incarnation of that former one, which, happily for mankind, was to disappear in his person.

Count Guiscard, who as envoy from the King of France accompanied him on his first campaign, describes him thus: "The King of Sweden is of tall stature; taller than myself by almost a head; he is very handsome, he has fine eyes and a good complexion, his face is long, his speech a little thick. He wears a small wig tied behind in a bag, a plain stock, without cravat, a very tight jerkin of plain cloth, with sleeves as narrow as our waistcoat sleeves, a narrow belt above his jerkin, with a sword of extraordinary length and thickness, and almost perfectly flat-soled shoes—a very strange style of dress for a prince of his age."

In order to reach Narva with his eight thousand men, Charles, after having crossed a tract of desert country, was obliged, at a place called Pyhaioggi, to cross a narrow valley divided by a stream, which, if it had been fortified, must have stopped him short. The idea occurred to Gordon, but Peter would not listen to him, and it was not till the very last moment that he sent Sheremetief, who found the Swedes just debouching into the valley, received several volleys of grape-shot and retired in disorder. The mad venture had succeeded. But Charles' farther advance involved the playing of a risky game. His men were worn out, his horses had not been fed for two whole days. Still he went on; he reached Narva, formed his Swedes into several attacking columns, led one himself, and favored by a sudden hurricane which drove showers of blinding snow into his adversaries' faces, threw himself into their camp and mastered the place in half an hour. The only resistance he met was offered by the two regiments of the guard. All the rest fled or surrendered. A few Russians were drowned in the Narva. "If the river had been frozen," said Charles discontentedly, "I do not know that we should have contrived to kill a single man."

It was a total breakdown; the army had disappeared, and the artillery. The very sovereign was gone, and with him the country's honor. That had sunk out of sight amid the scornful laughter with which Europe hailed this undignified defeat. The Czar was in full flight. All Peter's plans of conquest, his dreams of European expansion and of navigating the northern seas, his hopes of glory, his faith in his civilizing mission, had utterly faded. And he himself had collapsed upon their heaped-up ruins. Onward he fled, feeling the Swedish soldiers on his heels. He wept, he sued for peace, vowing he would treat at once and submit to any sacrifice; he sent imploring appeals to the States-General of Holland, to England and to the Emperor, praying for mediation.

But swiftly he recovered possession of his faculties. Then, raising his head—through the golden haze with which his insufficient education, the infatuation inherent to his semi-oriental origin, and his inexperience, had filled his eyes, through the rent of that mighty catastrophe and that cruel lesson—he saw and touched the truth at last! He realized what he must set himself to do if he was to become that which he fain would be. There must be no more playing at soldiers and sailors; no more of that farce of power and glory, in which, till now, he had been the chief actor; no more aimless adventure, undertaken in utter scorn of time and place. He must toil now in downright earnest; he must go forward, step by step; measure each day's effort, calculate each morrow's task, let each fruit ripen ere he essayed to pluck it; learn patience and dogged perseverance. He did it all. He found means within him and about him to carry out his task. The strong, long-enduring, long-suffering race of which he came endowed him with the necessary qualities, and gave him its own inexhaustible and never-changing devotion and self-sacrifice.

Ten armies may be destroyed, he will bring up ten others to replace them, no matter what the price. His people will follow him and die beside him to the last man, to the last morsel of bread snatched from its starving jaws. A month hence, the fugitive from Narva will belong to a vanished, forgotten, almost improbable past; the future victor of Poltava will have taken his place.

Of the Russian army, as it had originally taken the field, about twenty-three thousand men remained—a certain number of troops—the cavalry under Sheremetief's command, and Repnin's division. The Czar ordered fresh levies. He melted the church-bells into cannon. In vain the clergy raised the cry of sacrilege; he never faltered for a moment. He went hither and thither giving orders and active help; rating some, encouraging others, inspiring everyone with some of his own energy—that energy which his misfortune had spurred and strengthened. Yet, Byzantine as he was by nature, he could not resist the temptation to endeavor to mislead public opinion. Matvieief was given orders to draw up his own special description of the battle of Narva and its consequences, for the benefit of the readers of the *Gazette de Hollande* and of the memoranda which he himself addressed to the States-General.

The Swedes, according to this account, had been surrounded by a superior force within the Russian camp, and had there been forced to capitulate; after which event, certain Russian officers, who had desired to pay their respects to the King of Sweden, had been treacherously seized by his orders. Europe only laughed, but in later years this pretended capitulation, and the supposed Swedish violation of it, were to serve Peter as a pretext for violating others, to which he himself had willingly consented. At Vienna, too, Count Kaunitz listened with a smile while Prince Galitzin explained that the Czar "needed no victories to prove his military glory." Yet, when the vice-chancellor inquired what conditions the Czar hoped to obtain from his victorious adversary, the Russian diplomat calmly claimed the greater part of Livonia, with Narva, Ivangrod, Kolyvan, Koporie, and Derpt—and future events were to prove that he had not asked too much.

Before long this boldness began to reap its own reward. To

begin with, Charles XII made no immediate attempt to pursue his advantage on Russian soil; Peter had the joy of seeing him plunge into the depths of the Polish plains. The King of Sweden's decision, which, we are told, did not tally with his generals' opinion, has been severely criticised. Guiscard thought it perfectly justifiable, so long as the King had not rid himself of Augustus, by means of the peace which this Prince appeared more than willing to negotiate, through the mediation of Guiscard himself. But Charles turned a deaf ear to the French diplomat's prayers and remonstrances. He feared, declared Guiscard, "he might run short of enemies," and as he could not advance on Russia and leave the Saxons and Poles in his rear, he desired—and here doubtless he was right—first of all to insure his line of communication, and of possible retreat. Thus, by his own deed, he strengthened and cemented an alliance which had already been shaken by common defeat.

Augustus, repulsed by the Swedish King, threw himself into Peter's arms, and in February, 1701, the common destinies of the Czar and the King of Poland were once more bound together. A fresh treaty was signed at the Castle of Birze, close to Dunaburg.

The year 1701 was a hard one for Peter. The junction between the army, which he had contrived after some fashion to put on a war footing, and the Saxon troops of Augustus, only resulted in the complete defeat of the allied forces under the walls of Riga, on July 3d. In the month of June the Moscow Kremlin caught fire; the state offices (*prikaz*) with their archives, the provision-stores, and palaces, were all devoured by the flames. The bells fell from the tower of Ivan the Great, and the heaviest, which weighed over a hundred tons, was broken in the fall. But in midwinter Sheremetief contrived to surprise Schlippenbach with a superior force, and defeated him at Erestfer, December 29th.

Peter's delight, and his wild manifestations of triumph, may easily be imagined. He did not content himself with exhibiting the few Swedish prisoners who had fallen into his hands at Moscow, in a sort of imitation Roman triumph; his practical mind incited him to make use of them in another way, and Cornelius von Bruyn, who had lived long enough in the country to be thoroughly acquainted with its customs, calmly reports that the price of war captives, which had originally been three or four florins a head, rose as high as twenty and thirty florins. Even foreigners now ventured to purchase them, and entered into competition in the open market.

On July 18, 1702, Sheremetief won a fresh victory over Schlippenbach—30,000 Russians defeated 8000 Swedes. According to Peter's official account of the battle, 5000 of his enemies were left dead on the field, while Sheremetief lost only 400 men. This report made Europe smile, but the Livonians found it no laughing matter. Volmar and Marienburg fell into the hands of the victor, who ravaged the country in the most frightful fashion. The Russians had not as yet learned any other form of warfare, and, as we may suppose, the idea that he might ever possess these territories had not yet occurred to Peter. His mind, indeed, was absorbed elsewhere. His old fancies and whims were strong upon him, and he left Apraxin to rage on the banks of the Neva, in Ingria, on the very spot where his future capital was to stand, while he himself gave all his time and strength to the building of a few wretched ships at Archangel. It was not till September, when the ice had driven him out of the northern port, that he returned to the west and took up his former course. He reached the Lake of Ladoga, sent for Sheremetief, and the end he was to pursue for many a long year seems at last to have taken firm root in his hitherto unstable mind. He laid siege to Noteburg, where he found a garrison of only four hundred fifty men, and on December 11, 1702, he rechristened the little fortress he had captured, by a new and symbolic name, "Schluesselburg" (Key of the Sea).

Next came the capture of Nienschantz, at the very mouth of the Neva, in April, 1703, a personal success for the captain of Bombardiers, Peter Mikhailoff, who there brought his batteries into play. A month later the artilleryman had become a sailor, and had won Russia's first naval victory. Two regiments of the guard manned thirty boats, surrounded two small Swedish vessels, which, in their ignorance of the capture of Nienschantz, had ventured close to the town, took possession of them, and murdered their crews. The victor's letters to his friends are full of the wildest and most childish delight, and there was, we must admit, some reason for this joy. He had reconquered the historic estuary, through which, in the ninth century, the first Varegs had passed southward, toward Grecian skies. On the 16th of the following May wooden houses began to rise on one of the neighboring islets. These houses were to multiply, to grow into palaces, and finally to be known as St. Petersburg.

Peter's conquests and newly founded cities disturbed Charles XII but little. "Let him build towns; there will be all the more for us to take!" Peter and his army had so far, where Charles was concerned, had to do only with small detachments of troops, scattered apart and thus foredoomed to destruction. The Russians took advantage of this fact to pursue their successes, strengthening and intrenching themselves both in Ingria and Livonia. In July, 1704, Peter was present at the taking of Derpt. In August he had his revenge for his disaster at Narva, and carried the town after a murderous assault. Already in November, 1703, a longed-for guest had appeared in the mouth of the Neva, a foreign trading-vessel laden with brandy and salt. Menshikoff, the Governor of *Piterburg*, entertained the captain at a banquet, and presented him with five hundred florins for himself, and thirty crowns for each of his sailors.

Meanwhile Charles XII tarried in Poland, where Augustus' affairs were going from bad to worse. A diet convened at Warsaw in February, 1704, proclaimed his downfall. After the disappearance of James Sobieski, whose candidature was put a stop to by an ambuscade, into which the dethroned King lured the son of the deliverer of Vienna, Charles, who was all-powerful, put forward that of Stanislaus Lesczynski. Though he gave little thought just then to Russia and to the Russian sovereign, the Czar was beginning to be alarmed as to the consequences which the Swedish King's position in Poland and in Saxony might entail on himself. Charles was sure to end by retracing his steps, and an encounter between Sheremetief and Loewenhaupt, at Hemauerthorf in Courland (July 15, 1705), clearly proved that the Russian army, unless in the case of disproportionate numerical superiority over the enemy, was not yet capable of resisting well-commanded Swedish troops. On this occasion Sheremetief lost all his infantry and was himself severely wounded.

What then was Peter to do? He must work on, increase his resources, and add to his experience. If Sheremetief and his likes proved unequal to their task, he must find foreign generals and instructors, technical and other; he must keep patience, he must avoid all perilous encounters, he must negotiate, and try to obtain peace, even at the price of parting with some of the territory he had conquered. The years between 1705 and 1707 were busy ones for him.

A treaty of peace among his enemies took him by surprise and found him quite unprepared. He soon made good his mistakes, took a swift decision, and adopted the course which was infallibly to bring him final victory. He evacuated Poland, retired backward, and, pushing forward the preparations which Charles' long stay in Saxony had permitted him to carry on with great activity, he resolved that the battle should be fought on his ground, and at his chosen time. He took fresh patience, he resolved to wait, to wear out his adversary, to draw back steadily and leave nothing but a void behind him. Thus he would force the enemy to advance across the desert plains he had deliberately devastated, and run the terrible risk, which had always driven back the ancient foes of his country, whether Turks, Tartars, or Poles—a winter sojourn in the heart of Russia. This was to be the final round of the great fight. The Czar, as he expressed it, was to set ten Russians against every Swede, and time and space and cold and hunger were to be his backers.

Charles, the most taciturn general who ever lived, never revealed the secret inspiration which drove him to play his adversary's game, by marching afresh on Grodno. During 1707 he seemed to give the law to Europe, from his camp in Saxony. France, which had been vanquished at Blenheim and Ramillies, turned a pleading glance toward him, and the leader of the victorious allies, Marlborough himself, solicited his help.

Charles may have had an idea of making Grodno his base for a spring attack on the Czar's new conquests in the North. This supposition would seem to have been the one accepted by Peter, if we may judge by the orders given, just at this time, to insure the safety of Livonia and Ingria, by completing their devastation; and these very orders may have induced the King of Sweden to abandon his original design, in favor of another, the wisdom of which is still contested by experts, but which, it cannot be denied, was of noble proportions. Charles, too, had found an ally to set against those natural ones with which Russia had furnished the Czar, and he had found him within the borders of the Czar's country. The name of this ally was Mazeppa.

The stormy career of the famous hetman, so dramatic, both from the historic and domestic point of view—from that adventure with the *pan* Falbowski, so naïvely related by Pasek, down to the romance with Matrena Kotchoubey, which colored the last and tragic incidents of his existence—is so well known that I will not narrate it here, even in the concisest form. Little Russia was then passing through a painful crisis—the consequence of Shmielnicki's efforts at emancipation, which had been warped and perverted by Russian intervention. The Polish lords, who formerly oppressed the country, had been replaced by the Cossacks, who not only ground down the native population, but railed at and quarrelled with their own chief. The hetmans and the irregular troops were at open war, the first striving to increase their authority and make their power hereditary, the others defending their ancient democratic constitution.

The Swedish war increased Mazeppa's difficulties. He found himself taken at a disadvantage between the claims of the Czar, who would fain have his Cossacks on every battle-field in Poland, Russia, and Livonia, and the resistance of the Cossacks themselves, who desired to remain in their own country. Being himself of noble Polish birth, brought up by the Jesuits, having served King John Casimir of Poland, and sworn allegiance to the Sultan, he saw no reason for sacrificing his interests, much less his life, for Peter's benefit. The approach of Charles XII made him fear he might, like his predecessor Nalevaiko, be deserted by his own followers, and given up to the Poles.

The appearance of Charles on the Russian frontier forced him to a definite resolution, and, in the spring of 1708, his emissaries appeared at Radoshkovitse, southeast of Grodno, where Charles had established his head-quarters. The King of Sweden's idea, at that decisive moment, would seem to have been to take advantage of the hetman's friendly inclination, to find his way into the heart of Russia, using the rich Southern Provinces as his base, to stir up, with Mazeppa's help, the Don Cossacks, the Astrakhan Tartars, and, it may have been, the Turks themselves, and thus attack the Muscovite power in the rear. Then Peter would have been forced back upon his last intrenchments, at Moscow or elsewhere, while General Luebecker, who was in Finland with fourteen thousand men, fell on Ingria and on St. Petersburg, and Leszcynski's Polish partisans, with General Krassow's Swedes, held Poland.

It was a mighty plan, indeed, but at the very outset it was sharply checked. Mazeppa insisted on certain conditions, and these conditions Charles thought too heavy. The hetman agreed that Poland should take the Ukraine and White Russia, and that the Swedes should have the fortresses of Mglin, Starodoub, and Novgorod-Sievierski, but he himself insisted on being apportioned Polotsk, Vitebsk, and the whole of Courland, to be held in fief. Thus the negotiations were delayed. Meanwhile Charles, perceiving that he was not strong enough to make a forward movement, made up his mind to send for Loewenhaupt, who was in Livonia, and who was to bring him sixteen thousand men and various stores. But the Swedish hero had not reckoned fairly with distance and with time. Many precious days, the best of the season, fled by before his orders could be obeyed. And, for the first time, he showed signs of uncertainty and irresolution which were all too quickly communicated to those under his command. Loewenhaupt grew slower than usual. Luebecker slackened his activity, and Mazeppa began to play his double game again: prudently preparing his Cossacks to revolt, in the name of the ancient customs, national privileges, and church laws, which Peter's reforms had infringed; fortifying his own residence at Batourin, and accumulating immense stores there, but still continuing to pay court to the Czar, wearing the German dress, flattering the sovereign's despotic taste by suggesting plans which would have annihilated the last vestiges of local independence, and accepting gifts sent him by Menshikoff.

And so the summer passed away. A winter campaign became inevitable, and the abyss which Peter's unerring eye had scanned began to gape.

It was not till June that Charles XII left Radoshkovitse, and marched eastward to Borisov, where he crossed the Berezina. Menshikoff and Sheremetief made an attempt to stop him, on July 3d, as he was crossing a small river called the Bibitch, near Holovtchin. A night manœuvre, and a wild bayonet charge, led by the King himself, carried him once more to victory. The town of Mohilef opened its gates to the Swedes, but there Charles was forced to stay, and lose more time yet waiting for Loewenhaupt. He marched again, early in August, in a southerly direction, and his soldiers soon found themselves in the grip of one of Peter's allies. They were driven to support themselves by gathering ears of corn, which they ground between two stones. Sickness began to thin their ranks. Their three doctors, so the fierce troopers said, were "brandy, garlic, and death"! Loewenhaupt had reached Shklof, and was separated from the invading army by two streams, the Soja and the Dnieper, between which Peter had taken up his position. The Swedish general, after having successfully passed the Dnieper, was met at Liesna, on October 9th, by a force three times as large as his own, and Peter was able, on the following day, to report a complete victory to his friends: "8500 men dead on the field, without mentioning those the Kalmucks have hunted into the forest, and 700 prisoners!" According to this reckoning, Loewenhaupt, who could not have brought more than 11,000 troops into action, should have been left without a man; as a matter of fact, he reached Charles with 6700, after a flank march which all military experts consider a marvel. But, not being able to find a bridge across the Soja, he was forced to abandon his artillery and all his baggage, and he led his starving troops into a famine-stricken camp.

There was bad news, too, from Ingria, where Luebecker had also been defeated, losing all his baggage and three thousand first-class troops. Charles grew so disconcerted that he is reported to have confessed to Gyllenkrook, his quartermaster-general, that he was all at sea, and no longer had any definite plan. On October 22d he reached Mokoshin on the Desna, on the borders of the Ukraine, where he had expected to meet Mazeppa. But the old leader broke his appointment. He still desired to temporize and was loath to take any decisive resolution. He was driven to take one at last, by the Cossacks about him, who were alarmed at the idea of the Russians following the Swedes into the Ukraine. It would be far better, so they thought, to join the latter against the former. One of these Cossacks, Voinarovski, who had been sent by the hetman to Menshikoff, had returned with most terrifying news. He had overheard the German officers on the favorite's staff, speaking of Mazeppa and his followers, say: "God pity those poor wretches; to-morrow they will all be in chains!" Mazeppa, when he heard this report, "raged like a whirlwind," hurried to Batourin to give the alarm, and then crossed the Desna and joined the Swedish army.

It was too late. The popular sentiment, on which both he and Charles had reckoned to promote an insurrectionary movement, confused by the tergiversations and the ambiguous actions of the hetman, had quite gone astray and lost all consistency. All Mazeppa could reckon upon was a body of two thousand faithful troops; not enough even to defend Batourin, which Menshikoff snatched from him a few days later—thus depriving the Swedish army of its last chance of revictualling. When the fortresses of Starodoub and Novgorod-Sievierski closed their gates against him, the whole of the Ukraine slipped from the grasp of the turncoat chief and his new allies. His effigy was first hung and then dragged through the streets of Glouhof in Peter's presence; another hetman, Skoropadski, was appointed in his place, and then came winter—a cruel winter, during which the very birds died of cold.

By the beginning of 1709 Charles' effective strength had dwindled to nearly twenty thousand men. The Russians did not dare to attack him as yet, but they gathered round him in an ever-narrowing circle. They carried his advanced posts, they cut his lines of communication. The King of Sweden, to get himself mere elbow-room, was driven to begin his campaign in the month of January. He lost one thousand men and forty-eight officers in taking the paltry town of Wespjik (January 6th). By this time the game, in Mazeppa's view, was already lost, and he made an attempt to turn his coat again; offering to betray Charles into Peter's hands if Peter would restore him his office. The bargain was struck, but a letter from the old traitor, addressed to Leszcynski, chanced to fall into the Czar's hands, and made him draw back, in the conviction that Mazeppa was utterly unreliable.

In March, the near approach of the Swedish army, then advancing on Poltava, induced the Zaporoje Cossacks to join it. But the movement was a very partial one, and Peter soon put it down, by means of a series of military executions, mercilessly carried out by Menshikoff, and of various manifestoes against the foreign heretics, "who deny the doctrines of the true religion, and spit on the picture of the Blessed Virgin." The capture of Poltava thus became the last hope of Charles and his army. If they could not seize the town, they must all die of hunger.

The fortifications of the place were weak, but the besieging army was sorely changed from that which had fought under the walls of Narva. It had spent too long a time in fat quarters, in Saxony and Poland, to be fit to endure this terrible campaign. Like the Russian army at Narva, it was sapped by demoralization before it was called on to do any serious fighting. Even among the Swedish staff, and in the King's intimate circle, all confidence in his genius and his lucky star had disappeared.

His best generals, Rehnskold and Gyllenkrook, his chancellor Piper, and Mazeppa himself were against any prolongation of the siege, which promised to be a long one. "If God were to send down one of his angels," he said, "to induce me to follow your advice, I would not listen to him!" An ineradicable illusion, the fruit of the too easy victories of his early career, prompted him to undervalue the forces opposed to him. He knew, and would acknowledge, nothing of that new Russia, the mighty upstanding colossus, which Peter had at last succeeded in raising up in his path. According to some authorities, Mazeppa, in his desire to replace Batourin by Poltava, as his own personal appanage, encouraged him in this fatal resolution. But it may well have been that retreat had already become impossible.

It was long before Peter made up his mind to intervene; he was still distrustful of himself, desperately eager to increase his own resources, and with them his chances of victory. On his enemy's side, everything contributed to this result. By the end of June all the Swedish ammunition was exhausted, the invaders could use none of their artillery and hardly any of their fire-arms, and were reduced to fighting with cold steel. On the very eve of the decisive struggle, they were left without a leader. During a reconnaissance on the banks of the Vorskla, which ran between the hostile armies, Charles, always rash and apt to expose himself unnecessarily, was struck by a bullet. "It is only in the foot," he said, smiling, and continued his examination of the ground. But, when he returned to camp he fainted, and Peter, reckoning on the moral effect of the accident, at once resolved to cross the river. A report, as a matter of fact, ran through the Swedish camp that the King, convinced of the hopelessness of the situation, had deliberately sought death.

Yet ten more days passed by, in the expectation of an attack which the Russians did not dare to make. It was Charles who took action at last, informing his generals, on June 26th (July 7th) that he would give battle on the following morning. He himself was still in a very suffering condition, and made over the command to Rehnskold, a valiant soldier but a doubtful leader, for he did not possess the army's confidence, and, according to Lundblad, "hid his lack of knowledge and strategical powers under gloomy looks and a fierce expression." After the event, as was so commonly the case with vanquished generals, he was accused of treachery.

The truth would seem to be that Charles' obstinate reserve, and habit of never confiding his plans and military arrangements to any third person, had ended by gradually depriving his lieutenants of all power of independent action. In his presence they were bereft of speech and almost of ideas. All Rehnskold did was to rage and swear at everyone. Peter, meanwhile, neglected nothing likely to insure success. He even went so far as to dress the Novgorod regiment—one of his best—in the coarse cloth (*siermiaga*) generally reserved for newly joined recruits, in the hope of thus deceiving the enemy. This stratagem, however, completely failed. In the very beginning of the battle, Rehnskold fell on the regiment, and cut it to pieces.

The Russian centre was confided to Sheremetief, the right wing to General Ronne, the left to Menshikoff. Bruce commanded the artillery, and the Czar, as usual, retired modestly to the head of a single regiment. But this was a mere disguise; in real fact, he was everywhere, going hither and thither, in the forefront of the battle, and lavishing effort in every direction. A bullet passed through his hat, another is said to have struck him full on the breast. It was miraculously stopped by a golden cross, set with precious stones, given by the monks on Mount

Athos to the Czar Feodor, and which his successor habitually wore. This cross, which certainly bears the mark of some projectile, is still preserved in the Ouspienski monastery, at Moscow.

The heroism and sovereign contempt of death betrayed by Charles were worthy of himself. Unable to sit a horse, he caused himself to be carried on a litter, which, when it was shattered by bullets, was replaced by another made of crossed lances. But he was nothing but a living standard, useless, though sublime. The once mighty military leader had utterly disappeared. The battle was but a wild conflict, in which the glorious remnants of one of the most splendid armies that had ever been brought together; unable to use its arms, leaderless, hopeless of victory, and soon overwhelmed and crushed by superior numbers, struggled for a space, with the sole object of remaining faithful to its king. At the end of two hours Charles himself left the field of battle. He had been lifted onto the back of an old horse which his father had formerly ridden, and which was called *Brandklepper* ("Run to the Fire"), because he was always saddled when a fire broke out in the city.

This charger followed the vanquished hero into Turkey, was taken by the Turks at Bender, sent back to the King, taken again at Stralsund in 1715, returned to its owner once more, and died in 1718—the same year as his master—at the age of forty-two. Poniatowski, the father of the future King of Poland, who was following the campaign as a volunteer—Charles had refused to take any Polish troops with him on account of their want of discipline—rallied one of Colonel Horn's squadrons to escort the King, and received seventeen bullets through his leather kaftan while covering the royal retreat. Field Marshal Rehnskold, Piper the chancellor, with all his subordinates, over one hundred fifty officers, and two thousand soldiers fell into the victor's hands.

The Russians' joy was so extreme that they forgot to pursue the retreating enemy. Their first impulse was to sit down and banquet. Peter invited the more important prisoners to his own table, and toasted the health of his "masters in the art of war." The Swedes, who still numbered thirteen thousand men, had time to pause for a moment in their own camp, where Charles summoned Loewenhaupt, and, for the first time in his life, was heard to ask for advice—"What was to be done?" The general counselled him to burn all wagons, mount his infantry soldiers on the draught-horses and beat a retreat toward the Dnieper. On June 30th the Russians came up with the Swedish army at Perevolotchna, on the banks of the river, and, the soldiers refusing to fight again, Loewenhaupt capitulated; but the King had time to cross to the other side. Two boats lashed together carried his carriage, a few officers, and the war-chests which he had filled in Saxony. Mazeppa contrived to find a boat for himself, and loaded it with two barrels of gold.

At Kiev, whither Peter proceeded from Poltava, a solemn thanksgiving was offered up in the church of St. Sophia, and a Little Russia monk, Feofan Prokopovitch, celebrated the recent victory in a fine flight of eloquence: "When our neighbors hear of what has happened, they will say it was not into a foreign country that the Swedish army and the Swedish power ventured, but rather into some mighty sea! They have fallen in and disappeared, even as lead is swallowed up in water!"

The Sweden of Gustavus Adolphus had indeed disappeared. Charles XII was ere long to be a mere knight-errant at Bender. The Cossack independence, too, was a thing of the past. Its last and all too untrustworthy representative was to die in Turkey before many months were out—of despair, according to Russian testimony—of poison voluntarily swallowed, according to Swedish historians. The poison story has a touch of likelihood about it, for Peter certainly proposed to exchange Mazeppa's person for that of the chancellor Piper. The cause of the Leszcynski, too, was dead. It was to be put forward again by France, but for the benefit of France alone; and with the Leszcynski cause, Poland itself had passed away and lay a lifeless corpse on which the vultures were soon to settle.

Out of all these ruins rose the Russian power, its northern hegemony, and its new European position, which henceforth were daily to increase and reach immense, immoderate proportions. Europe played a special part in the festivities which graced the return of the victors to Moscow, a few months later. European ideas, traditions, and forms appeared in the triumphal procession, and served as trappings for the trophies of victory.

Peter, playing the part of Hercules, and conquering a Swedish Juno, in a *cortège* in which Mars figured, attended by furies and by fauns, was a fit symbol of the alliance of Russia with the Græco-Latin civilization of the West. Old Muscovy—Eastern and Asiatic—was numbered with the dead.

CAPTURE OF PORT ROYAL[1]

FRANCE SURRENDERS NOVA SCOTIA TO ENGLAND

A.D. 1710

DUNCAN CAMPBELL

Each time that England and France quarrelled in Europe their colonies became engaged in strife. In 1690, when William III fought Louis XIV the able Governor of Canada, Frontenac, despatched his Indian allies to ravage New England, while with rare military skill he defended himself and his province. He could not, however, prevent the capture of Port Royal (now Annapolis) in Nova Scotia. This great fortress, the pride of Louis XIV, was attacked by the New England colonists under Sir William Phips, the Governor of Massachusetts, and was captured by a most dashing attack. When England and France made peace, Port Royal was restored to the French, much to the dissatisfaction of the English colonists, who saw clearly that as soon as another war arose they would have to make the assault again.

During the era of Queen Anne's War (1702–1713) French and Indian forays and incursions were frequent on the borders of Acadia and New England. Britain, meanwhile, was desirous of limiting the growth of France in the New World, and, with the provocation that had been given the New England colonies by the murderous raids of the French and Abenaquis Indians on her towns and border settlements, the English colonists retaliated by attempting, in 1704 and 1707, to recapture Acadia. They finally succeeded in 1710 under General Nicholson. The story of this expedition will be found appended in Campbell's narrative, as well as the account given of the disastrous failure of Admiral Sir Hovenden Walker's formidable expedition in 1711 up the St. Lawrence with the design of assaulting Quebec. On the capture by the New England colonies of Port Royal, and the expulsion of its French garrison, the place became an English fortress and was renamed Annapolis Royal, in honor of Queen Anne.

IN perusing the history of Nova Scotia, the reader is struck with the frequency with which the country, or, in other words, the forts, passed from the French to the English, and *vice versa.* As a rule, permanent retention was not contemplated. Hence

[1] From Duncan Campbell's *History of Canada.*

we find that when Port Royal was taken by Phips, he departed without leaving a solitary man to defend it. A few days after the expedition had left, the Chevalier de Villebon, the newly appointed French Governor, arrived, and if accompanied by the means, had a favorable opportunity of putting it once more in a state of defence and retaining it as a French stronghold. But Phips was not far off, and he therefore deemed it prudent, considering the small force at his disposal, to retire to the river St. John, where he remained for some years, destroying New England vessels and organizing schemes for the consolidation of French authority in the province.

In the mean time Villebon showed his temper toward the New Englanders by building a chapel on the disputed territory, and driving their fishermen from the coast of Nova Scotia. Villebon was succeeded by Brouillan, in 1700, and not only was an enemy to the fishermen, but actually afforded protection to pirates who preyed on the trade of Massachusetts, which inspired a degree of hostility in New England that, on the accession of Queen Anne, in 1702, the declaration of war which followed was hailed in that colony with demonstrations of joy.

The New Englanders had a long catalogue of grievances unredressed, hostile attacks unrevenged, and were more determined than ever to put forth their strength for the expulsion of the French from the province. In 1704 a preliminary expedition was despatched by them to the coast of Nova Scotia, consisting of a ship of forty-two and another of thirty-two guns, a number of transports and whale-boats, on board of which were upward of five hundred men, under the command of Colonel Church, whose instructions were to destroy settlements, and where dams existed to deluge the cultivated ground and make as many prisoners as possible. One detachment visited Minas, and spread desolation and ruin in that fertile region, through which Brouillan passed on his way to Annapolis, representing the people as living like true republicans, not acknowledging royal or judicial authority, and able to spare eight hundred hogsheads of wheat yearly for exportation, and as being supplied with abundance of cattle.

Another detachment went to Port Royal, which they deemed it prudent not to attack. Brouillan having died in 1706, M.

Subercase was appointed governor. In the spring of 1707 another expedition was sent from New England to attack Port Royal. It consisted of twenty-three transports and the province galley, convoyed by a man-of-war of fifty guns, on which were embarked two regiments of militia, under Colonels Wainwright and Hilton. The expedition arrived at the entrance to Port Royal on June 6th. A landing was soon effected; but Subercase's dispositions for resistance were so able that the English found it impossible to make any impression on the defences, and, after losing eighty men, the troops were reëmbarked and proceeded to Casco Bay, from which place the commanders communicated with the Governor of New England and waited orders. The failure of the expedition caused great indignation in New England, and the Governor immediately resolved to strengthen the army with a hundred recruits and to order a second attack. Accordingly the expedition again sailed for Port Royal, when Subercase was in a far more formidable position than formerly. After a siege of fifteen days, in which the English officers displayed unaccountable cowardice, the ships retired, having lost sixteen men, while the French had only three men killed and wounded.

Subercase immediately proceeded to strengthen his position in anticipation of a third attack. A bomb-proof powder magazine was accordingly constructed, capable of containing sixty thousand pounds of powder, and the fort was otherwise improved. This Governor, who had formed a high estimate of the climate, soil, and general resources of the province, was one of the ablest appointed under French rule. He made urgent appeals to the French government to colonize the country on a large scale, pointing out the advantages that would follow; but all his suggestions were disregarded, and he had the mortification, notwithstanding his zeal and personal sacrifices in the service of his country, to receive less encouragement and support from the home government than any of his predecessors.

In the year 1710 great preparations were made for the conquest of Canada and Nova Scotia. The New York House of Assembly sent a petition to Queen Anne, praying for such assistance as would expel the French entirely from the country. Colonel Vetch is said to have inspired this application, and to have submitted to the British government a plan of attack. Promises of liberal support are said to have been made, which, however, the government was tardy in affording.

The command of the New England forces was intrusted to Francis Nicholson, who was appointed Governor of New England, under Sir Edmund Andros, in 1688, being Governor of New York in 1689, and in the following year Lieutenant-Governor of Virginia. In 1692 he was transferred to the government of Maryland, and in 1698 sent back to Virginia as Governor-in-Chief, at which time he held the rank of colonel in the army. Nicholson was an earnest advocate of a confederation of the British North American provinces for purposes of defence, to which the people of Virginia were popularly opposed.

Nicholson sailed from Boston on September 18, 1710, with a fleet of about thirty-six vessels, including five transports from England, conveying a considerable force, composed of troops supplied by Massachusetts, Connecticut, New Hampshire, and Rhode Island, which arrived at Port Royal on September 24th. Subercase was not in a condition to resist so formidable a force; hence we find him writing to the French minister that the garrison is dispirited, and praying for assistance in men and money. The strait to which he was reduced is indicated by the following passage: "I have had means," he says, "by my industry to borrow wherewith to subsist the garrison for these two years. I have paid what I could by selling all my movables. I will give even to my last shirt, but I fear that all my pains will prove useless if we are not succored during the month of March or early in April, supposing the enemy should let us rest this winter."

But it was far from the intention of the enemy to let them rest; for three days after the despatch of the communication in which the passage quoted occurred, Nicholson sent a summons to the Governor requiring the immediate delivery of the fort, and in the event of non-compliance, expressing his resolution to reduce it by force of her majesty's arms. No reply having been sent to the summons, Nicholson prepared to land his troops, to which Subercase offered no resistance, as he could not trust the garrison beyond the walls of the fort on account of the discontent induced by the universal conviction of their inability to oppose the English, who mustered to the number of upward of three thousand, exclusive of seamen, to which force the Governor could not oppose more than three hundred fighting men. In the mean time the garrison became disorganized and many desertions took place, when the Governor, yielding to necessity, opened a communication with Nicholson with the view to capitulation.

The articles were, in the circumstances, highly favorable to the garrison. They provided that the soldiers should march out with their arms and baggage, drums beating and colors flying; that they should be conveyed to Rochelle, and that the inhabitants within three miles of Port Royal should be permitted to remain on their lands, with their corn, cattle, and furniture, for two years, if so disposed, on their taking the oath of allegiance to the Queen of Great Britain. The destitute condition of the garrison was manifested by their tattered garments and absence of provisions necessary to sustain them even for a few days. In conformity with the terms of the capitulation four hundred eighty men in all were transported to Rochelle, in France. A garrison, consisting of two hundred marines and two hundred fifty New England volunteers, was left in Port Royal, under Colonel Vetch, as governor—General Nicholson returning to Boston with the fleet.

The English, sensible of the disastrous consequences resulting from the policy hitherto adopted of abandoning Port Royal after having taken repeated possession of it, had now resolved to retain it permanently. The Acadians were alarmed at the indications of permanent occupancy which they witnessed, and evinced a degree of hostility which caused the Governor to adopt such measures as were calculated to convince them that they must act in virtue of their temporary allegiance to the British crown, as became faithful subjects. The restraints imposed were galling to the French, and they despatched a messenger with a letter to the Governor of Canada, referring to their general misery under British rule, and praying to be furnished with the means of leaving a country where they could not enjoy absolute freedom, but the letter contained no specific charges.

In the hope of regaining the fort, and impressed with the importance in the mean time of intensifying Indian hostility to English rule, the Canadian Governor sent messengers to the French missionaries to exert their influence in that direction. The consequence was that parties sent out to cut wood were attacked, and that travelling beyond the fort was rendered dangerous. Eighty men sent from the garrison on that service were attacked by the Indians, who killed about thirty of the party, taking the rest prisoners. Vaudreuil, the Governor of Canada, had made preparations to assist in the recapture of the fort, but intelligence of a strong force being in preparation to attack Canada prevented the accomplishment of his purpose.

General Nicholson, on leaving Port Royal, went to England, for the purpose of inducing the Government to adopt measures for the thorough conquest of Canada, preparations for that end being in progress in New England. His appeal was cordially responded to, and a fleet of twelve line-of-battle ships, with store-ships and transports, and having eight regiments and a train of artillery on board, the whole commanded by Admiral Walker, left England on April 28, 1711, arriving in Boston, June 25th. This formidable force, which consisted of sixty-eight vessels in all, having about six thousand fighting-men on board, left Boston on July 30th, arriving at Gaspé, August 18th, where wood and water were taken in. They sailed thence on the 20th.

The pilots seem to have been incompetent, for on August 23d the ships got into difficulties in a fog, losing in the Gulf of St. Lawrence, near Egg Island, eight transports and eight hundred eighty-four men. At a council of war it was determined to abandon the enterprise, and intelligence of the resolution was sent to General Nicholson, who had left Albany with an army for the purpose of attacking Montreal, and who consequently had the mortification of being obliged to return immediately. On September 4th the fleet arrived at Spanish Bay and anchored in front of Lloyd's Cove. It is questionable if the noble harbor of Sydney has ever since presented so lively a spectacle as on this occasion.

Admiral Walker was instructed if he succeeded in taking Quebec, to attack Placentia, in Newfoundland, but at a council of war it was declared impracticable to make any attempt against that place, while from the condition of the stronghold it could have been easily taken. On his return Walker was the laughing-stock of the nation. Literary squibs and pamphlets were showered upon him, and his attempts at a vindication of his conduct only rendered him the more ridiculous. He stood in the estimation of the nation in precisely the same position as Sir John Cope, the commander of the force sent to attack Prince Charles Edward Stuart on his march from the north of Scotland, in 1745, to Edinburgh, who, after having held a council of war, resolved to march in the opposite direction from that in which the enemy was to be found, and whose consummate folly or cowardice in doing so is a standing national joke.

The severe contests in which France and Britain were almost continually engaged required occasional breathing-time. Hence, notwithstanding the series of brilliant victories gained by Marlborough, the war had become unpopular, and the governmental policy had to be assimilated to the national will. France was equally desirous of peace, and no great difficulty was experienced in coming to terms. In the preparation of previous treaties, France had succeeded in making the cession to her of any portion of North American territory wrested from her a fundamental condition of agreement. Great Britain had hitherto shown a degree of pliability, in yielding to the desire of her great opponent, in this matter, which seems unaccountable, and certainly incompatible with British interests; but the representations of the New Englanders as to the impolicy of such procedure were so urgent and unanswerable that the Government had resolved that the period of vacillation was past, and that the exercise of firmness in the permanent retention of Nova Scotia was necessary. Hence, in the celebrated Treaty of Utrecht, in 1713, it was provided that all Nova Scotia or Acadia should be yielded and made over to the Queen of Great Britain and to her crown forever, together with Newfoundland, France retaining possession of Cape Breton.

General Nicholson, having been appointed governor of Nova Scotia in 1714, as well as commander-in-chief, Queen Anne addressed a graceful letter to him, dated June 23, 1713, in which, after alluding to her "good brother," the French King, having released from imprisonment on board his galleys such of his subjects as were detained there professing the Protestant religion, she desired to show her appreciation of his majesty's compliance with her wishes by ordering that all Frenchmen in Nova Scotia and Newfoundland who should desire to remain should be permitted to retain their property and enjoy all the privileges of

British subjects; and if they chose to remove elsewhere, they were at liberty to dispose of their property by sale ere they departed.

Meanwhile the Acadians, as well as the inhabitants of Newfoundland, were pressed by the French Governor of Louisburg, M. de Costabelle, to remove to Cape Breton, which the great body of the latter did. The Acadians, however, could not appreciate the advantages to be gained in removing from the fertile meadows of the Annapolis Valley to a soil which, however excellent, required much labor to render it fit for cultivation. It appears that they sent a deputation to examine the island and report as to its adaptability for agricultural purposes, for one of their missionaries, addressing M. de Costabelle, the Governor, says that from the visits made they were satisfied there were no lands in Cape Breton suitable for the immediate maintenance of their families, since there were not meadows sufficient to nourish their cattle, from which they derived their principal support. He at the same time represents the Indians—who had been also desired to remove—as being of opinion that living as they did by the chase, the island was quite insufficient for that purpose, as well as from its narrow limits, equally unfitted for the exercise of their natural freedom.

But while declining to leave Nova Scotia, the Acadians expressed a firm determination to continue loyal to the King of France, affirming that they would never take the oath of allegiance to the crown of England, to the prejudice of what they owed to their King, their country, and their religion, and intimating their resolution, in the event of any attempt to make them swerve from their fidelity to France, or to interfere with the exercise of their religion, to leave the country and betake themselves to Cape Breton, then called the Ile Royale. And they there remained until 1755, at which time the English and New England colonists finally drove forth and dispersed them with hateful cruelty.

CHRONOLOGY OF UNIVERSAL HISTORY

EMBRACING THE PERIOD COVERED IN THIS VOLUME

A.D. 1661–1715

JOHN RUDD, LL.D.

CHRONOLOGY OF UNIVERSAL HISTORY

EMBRACING THE PERIOD COVERED IN THIS VOLUME

A.D. 1661–1715

JOHN RUDD, LL.D.

Events treated at length are here indicated in large type; the numerals following give volume and page.

Separate chronologies of the various nations, and of the careers of famous persons, will be found in the INDEX VOLUME, with volume and page references showing where the several events are fully treated.

A.D.

1661. Execution of the Marquis of Argyle. Burning of the *League and Covenant* by the hangman, in all parts of England.

Episcopacy restored in Scotland.

In France Louis XIV assumes personal rule; Colbert begins his ministry. See "LOUIS XIV ESTABLISHES ABSOLUTE MONARCHY," xii, 1.

1662. Sale of Dunkirk to the French by Charles II. Passage of a new Act of Uniformity; ejectment of nonconformist ministers from their livings, in England.

A charter given the Connecticut and New Haven colonies.

1663. Hungary overrun by the Turks under Koprili.

Foundation of the French Academy of Inscriptions.

The Carolinas granted by charter to Clarendon and others.

1664. Passage of the Conventicle Act in England, directed against nonconformists or dissenters.

Victory of the united forces of Germany, France, and Italy, under Montecucoli, general of Leopold I, at St. Gotthard, Hungary.

Charles II grants the territory between the Connecticut and James rivers to his brother, James, Duke of York; New Amsterdam occupied and New Netherland taken by the English; New York is the name given to both province and city. James sells a portion of his domain, to which the title of "New Cæsarea" was first given, afterward changed to New Jersey. See "NEW YORK TAKEN BY THE ENGLISH," xii, 19.

East and West India companies formed in France; colonies planted in Cayenne, Martinique, Guadelupe, Ste. Lucia, and Canada.

1665. Continued persecution of dissenters in England by the passage of the Five-mile Act.

War between England and Holland.

Newton invents his methods of fluxions.

Completion of the union of the Connecticut and New Haven colonies.

Death of Philip IV; his son, Charles II, ascends the throne of Spain.

"GREAT PLAGUE IN LONDON." See xii, 29.

1666. Great naval victory of the English over the Dutch, in the Downs.

Resort to arms by the Scotch Covenanters; they are defeated.

"DISCOVERY OF GRAVITATION." See xii, 51.

War against England declared by France.

Foundation of the Académie des Sciences, Paris.

Burning of London. See "GREAT FIRE IN LONDON," xii, 45.

William Penn joins the Society of Friends.

1667. Opening of the first fire-insurance office in London.

Ravages up the Medway and Thames, England, by the Dutch, during negotiations for peace.

Treaty of Breda; peace between England, Holland, France, Denmark.

Publication of Milton's *Paradise Lost*.

1668. Triple alliance against France formed by England, Holland, and Sweden.

Recognition by Spain of the independence of Portugal.

Foundation of the mission of Sault Ste. Marie, by Father Marquette.

Introduction of the art of dyeing into England by Brewer, who fled from Flanders before the French invaders.

1669. John Locke draws up a constitution for the government of the Carolinas.

Candia surrenders to the Turks.

Expedition of La Salle from the St. Lawrence to the West.

Discovery of phosphorus by Brandt.

1670. A secret treaty (Dover) between Charles II of England and Louis XIV of France; Charles basely sells his allies, the Dutch, and engages himself to become a Catholic.

Incorporation of the Hudson Bay Company.

1671. Leopold attempts the subjugation of the liberties of Hungary; his drastic methods include the execution of Frangepan, Nadasdy, and Zrinyi.

Attempt of Colonel Blood to steal the English crown and regalia from the Tower; the King pardons and pensions him.

"MORGAN, THE BUCCANEER, SACKS PANAMA." See xii, 66.

Building of Greenwich Observatory.

1672. William III, Prince of Orange, has supreme power conferred on him by the Dutch. The De Witts massacred. See "STRUGGLE OF THE DUTCH AGAINST FRANCE AND ENGLAND," xii, 86.

1673. Passage in England of the Test Act, excluding dissenters and papists from all offices of government.

Battle of Khotin; defeat of the Turks by John Sobieski.

"DISCOVERY OF THE MISSISSIPPI." See xii, 108.

Occupation of New York and New Jersey by the Dutch.

Joliet and Marquette make discoveries on the upper Mississippi.

1674. Peace between England and Holland; the former regains New Netherland.

Occupation of Pondicherry by the French.

John Sobieski elected to the Polish throne.

1675. "KING PHILIP'S WAR." See xii, 125.

Battle of Fehrbellin; the Swedes, having invaded Brandenburg, are defeated by Frederick William. See "GROWTH OF PRUSSIA UNDER THE GREAT ELECTOR," xii, 138.

Beginning of the building of St. Paul's, London, by Sir Christopher Wren.

Leeuwenhoek discovers animalculæ in various waters.

1676. Rebellion of Bacon in Virginia.

Defeat of the Dutch admiral, De Ruyter, by the French, under Duquesne, off the Sicilian coast.

Building of Versailles.

1677. William of Orange defeated by the French at Casel. Freiburg captured by the French.

Mary, daughter of the Duke of York (James II), marries William of Orange.

1678. Invention of the Popish Plot by Titus Oates.

Peace of Nimeguen between France, Spain, and Holland.

First war between Russia and Turkey.

Struggle of the Hungarians, under Tokolyi, against Austria.

1679. Persecution of the Covenanters in Scotland; they take up arms but are defeated by Monmouth, at Bothwell Bridge. Murder of the primate, Sharp.

Passage in England of the Habeas Corpus Act.

La Salle builds the Griffon on Niagara River.

Peace of Nimeguen between France and the German Emperor.

1680. Beginning of the captivity of the Man with the Iron Mask. (Date uncertain.)

Execution of Viscount Strafford for alleged participation in the Popish Plot.

Alsace incorporated with French territory.

The Whig and Tory parties first so named in England.

1681. Strasburg seized by Louis XIV.

A patent by the crown granted to William Penn. See "WILLIAM PENN RECEIVES THE GRANT OF PENNSYLVANIA," xii, 153.

Renewed persecution of Protestants in France.

First museum of natural history in London.

1682. Attempt of Louis XIV to seize the Duchy of Luxemburg.

Bossuet, in behalf of the French clergy, draws up a declaration which sets forth the liberties of the Gallican Church.

Colonizing of Pennsylvania by William Penn; he founds Philadelphia; also, with other Friends, purchases East Jersey.

Expedition of La Salle to the mouth of the Mississippi. See "DISCOVERY OF THE MISSISSIPPI," xii, 108.

Death of Czar Feodor III; his sister, Sophia, regent in the name of her brothers Ivan V, of weak intellect, and Peter I (Peter the Great).

1683. A penny-post first established in London, by a private individual. Execution in England of Lord Russell and Algernon Sidney, for participation in the Rye House Plot.

Siege of Vienna by the Turks. See "LAST TURKISH INVASION OF EUROPE," xii, 164.

Attack on the Spanish Netherlands by Louis XIV.

1684. Forfeiture of the charter of the Massachusetts Bay Company.

Formation of the Holy League by Venice, Poland, Emperor Leopold I, and Pope Innocent XI against the Turks.

Genoa bombarded by the French. Louis XIV forcibly occupies Luxemburg.

An embassy sent from the King of Siam to France.

Publication by Leibnitz of his invention of the differential calculus. (See Newton, 1665.)

1685. Death of Charles II; his brother, James II, ascends the English throne. Insurrection of Argyle and Monmouth; they are both executed. Jeffries' Bloody Assizes. See "MONMOUTH'S REBELLION," xii, 172.

Pillage of the coast of Peru by the buccaneers.

"REVOCATION OF THE EDICT OF NANTES." See xii, 180.

A demand made for the surrender of Connecticut's charter; it is hidden in Charter Oak.

Bradford's printing-press arrives in Pennsylvania. See "ORIGIN AND PROGRESS OF PRINTING," viii, 1.

1686. Attempt of James II to restore Romanism in the British domains; a camp established by him at Hounslow Heath. Revival of the Court of High Commission.

League of Augsburg formed by William of Orange, by which the principal continental states unite to resist French encroachments.

A bloody crusade waged by Louis XIV, and Victor Amadeus II of Savoy, against the Waldenses of Piedmont.

Recovery of Buda by the Austrians from the Turks.

Appointment of Sir Edmund Andros as Governor over the consolidated New England colonies.

1687. Refusal of the University of Cambridge to admit Francis, a Benedictine monk, recommended by James II.

Leopold I compels the Hungarian Diet to make the kingdom hereditary in the Hapsburg family.

Battle of Mohacs; defeat of the Turks by the Duke of Lorraine.

Capture of Athens by the Venetians.

Appointment of Tyrconnel, a Roman Catholic, as Lord Deputy of Ireland.

Publication of Newton's *Principia*.

Assumption of power by Peter the Great, in Russia.

1688. Louis XIV declares war against Holland: he makes war on Germany.

Capture of Philippsburg by the French.

Battle of Enniskillen in Ireland.

Landing in England of William of Orange, on invitation of the malcontents in that country. See "THE ENGLISH REVOLUTION," xii, 200.

New York and New Jersey united with New England under Governor-General Sir Edmund Andros.

1689. William and Mary, she being daughter of the ex-king, are proclaimed King and Queen of England. Passage of the Bill of Rights.

James II lands in Ireland; he unsuccessfully besieges Londonderry; battle of Newtown Butler, defeat of the Irish Catholics.

Great Britain joins the League of Augsburg.

Overthrow of Andros in New England. See "TYRANNY OF ANDROS IN NEW ENGLAND," xii, 241.

At the instance of Louvois, his war minister, Louis XIV lays waste the Palatinate.

Battle of Killiecrankie, Scotland; defeat of the government forces by the Highlanders; Claverhouse, their leader, slain.

"MASSACRE OF LACHINE, CANADA." See xii, 248.

"PETER THE GREAT MODERNIZES RUSSIA." See xii, 223.

1690. Battle of the Boyne. See "SIEGE OF LONDONDERRY," xii, 258.

Presbyterianism reëstablished in Scotland.

Defence of Canada by Frontenac.

James II leaves Ireland and returns to France.

Destruction of Schenectady by the French and Indians.

Conquest of Acadia and unsuccessful attempt on Quebec by the English.

John Locke publishes his *Essay Concerning the Human Understanding*.

1691. Overthrow of the Jacobites in Scotland.

Battle of Salankeman; victory of Louis of Baden over the Turks.

Execution in New York of Jacob Leisler.

1692. Union of the colonies of Plymouth and Massachusetts.

Beginning of the witchcraft mania in New England. See "SALEM WITCHCRAFT TRIALS," xii, 268.

The duchies of Hanover and Brunswick become an electorate; Ernest Augustus elector.

Battle of La Hogue; the attempted French invasion of England defeated by the victory of the English and Dutch fleets.

Massacre, at Glencoe, of the MacDonalds.

1693. Defeat of the English fleet, off Cape St. Vincent, by Tourville, admiral of the French fleet.

Distress in France from famine and the expense of the war with England.

Founding of the College of William and Mary, Virginia.

Bradford's printing-press removed from Pennsylvania to New York. See "ORIGIN AND PROGRESS OF PRINTING," viii, 1.

1694. Attacks on the coast of France by the English.

Death of Queen Mary, consort of William. Cessation of the censorship of the press in England.

"ESTABLISHMENT OF THE BANK OF ENGLAND." See xii, 286.

Peter the Great of Russia employs Brant, a Dutch shipwright, to build a vessel at Archangel.

1695. Peace arranged between France and Savoy.

Azov captured from the Turks by Peter the Great.

1696. On the death of John Sobieski the Polish crown is purchased by Frederick Augustus, Elector of Saxony.

1697. Barcelona captured by the French.

Peace of Ryswick between France, Holland, England, and Spain.

Election of Francis I as King of Poland.

Battle of Zenta; crushing defeat of the Turks by Leopold I.

1698. Foundation of Calcutta by the English.

A Scotch colony established on the Isthmus of Darien: abandoned in 1700.

Peter the Great recalled from England by a revolt of the Strelitz guards; he subdues and disbands them.

Society for Propagating Christianity formed in London.

Partition of Spain arranged between England, France, and the Netherlands.

1699. Iberville settles a French colony in Louisiana. See "COLONIZATION OF LOUISIANA," xii, 297.

Reduction of the Turkish territories in Europe, by nearly one-half, arranged by the Peace of Carlowitz, between Turkey, Austria, Venice, and Poland.

Peter the Great introduces the computation of time in Russia by the Christian era, but adheres to the old style, which still obtains in that country.

1700. Russia, Poland, and Denmark make joint war against Sweden. The army of Peter the Great overwhelmed at Narva, by Charles XII of Sweden.

Foundation of the future Yale College, Connecticut.

1701. Frederick III of Brandenburg crowns himself King of Prussia. See "PRUSSIA PROCLAIMED A KINGDOM," xii, 310.

Passage of the Act of Settlement in England; the Hanoverian succession founded.

Beginning of the War of the Spanish Succession.

Charles XII defeats the Poles and Saxons.

1702. Death of William III; Queen Anne succeeds to the throne of England.

Command of the army of the States-General given to Marlborough, the English general.

Battle of Vigo; naval victory of the English and Dutch over the Spaniards and French.

Beginning of Queen Anne's War in America.

Foundation of a French settlement on the Mobile River, Alabama.

Charles XII occupies Warsaw; he defeats Augustus II at Klissow; Cracow entered by him.

1703. Methuen Treaty between England and Portugal, for facilitating commerce between those countries.

Peter the Great lays the foundation of St. Petersburg. See "FOUNDING OF ST. PETERSBURG," xii, 319.

Defeat of Augustus II by Charles XII at Pultusk.

1704. English conquest of Gibraltar from Spain.

"BATTLE OF BLENHEIM." See xii, 327.

At Boston is published the first newspaper in the American colonies of England. See "ORIGIN AND PROGRESS OF PRINTING," viii, 1.

Sack, burning, and massacre of the inhabitants of Deerfield, Massachusetts, by French and Indians.

Charles XII completes the subjugation of Poland.

1705. Failure of the French and Spaniards in an attempt to recapture Gibraltar.

Invasion of Spain by the English under the Earl of Peterborough; capture of Barcelona.

1706. Battle of Ramillies; Marlborough defeats the French under Villeroi.

Unsuccessful attempt of the French and Spaniards on Barcelona.

Birth of Benjamin Franklin.

1707. Sanction of the Union of England and Scotland by the Scotch Parliament. See "UNION OF ENGLAND AND SCOTLAND," xii, 341.

Charles XII subjugates Saxony; he dictates the Peace of Altranstaedt.

1708. Russia invaded by Charles XII.

Battle of Oudenarde; victory of Marlborough and Prince Eugene over the Dukes of Burgundy and Vendôme.

1709. Annihilation of the army of Charles XII at Poltava See "DOWNFALL OF CHARLES XII," xii, 352.

Invasion of Sweden by the Danes.

Recovery of Poland by Augustus II.

1710. Expulsion of the Danes from Sweden by Stenbock.

Request of the Irish Parliament for union with that of Great Britain.

"CAPTURE OF PORT ROYAL, CANADA." See xii, 373.

1711. After further successes in Flanders, Marlborough is removed from command; the Whig ministry falls in England.

Under Walker, the English and New England forces make an unsuccessful attempt on Canada.

Having taken up arms for Charles XII, the Turks nearly achieve the ruin of Peter the Great, whose army is hemmed in near the Pruth River; peace arranged, the Turks recovering Azov and other towns.

1712. Peace conference at Utrecht.

Newspapers come under the operation of the Stamp Act, in England; so many discontinue publication that it is called the "Fall of the Leaf."

Second Toggenburg War between the Reformed and Catholic cantons of Switzerland.

1713. Peace of Utrecht ending the War of the Spanish Succession. Great Britain acquires Newfoundland, Nova Scotia, Gibraltar, Minorca, Hudson Bay, and the Isle of St. Kitts; with the title of king the Duke of Savoy is ceded Sicily by Spain, and by France, Savoy and Nice with certain fortified places; the King of Prussia exchanges the principality of Orange and Châlons for Spanish Gelderland, Neuchâtel, and Valengin; Spain cedes to Austria, Naples, Milan, Spanish Tuscany, and sovereignty over the Spanish Netherlands; the harbor and fortifications of Dunkirk to be destroyed.

Charles I issues the Pragmatic Sanction securing succession to the female line in default of male issue.

1714. Establishment of the Clarendon Press at Oxford, from the profits of Clarendon's *History of the Rebellion*.

Death of Anne and accession in England of George (I), Elector of Hanover.

Capture of Barcelona by the French and Spanish forces; the citizens deprived of their liberties.

Fahrenheit invents his thermometer.

1715. Jacobite rebellion in Britain in behalf of the Pretender.

Death of Louis XIV; he is succeeded by his great-grandson, Louis XV; the Duke of Orléans regent.

A Barrier Treaty made between Austria, England, and Holland; it gave the Dutch a right to garrison certain places in the Austrian Netherlands.

END OF VOLUME XII